PRAISE FOR GIDEON HAIGH'S
MYSTERY SPINNER: THE STORY OF JACK IVERSON

'A classic.'
Sunday Times

'A superb book.'
Guardian

'Haigh's research, his writing, his subject all combine to make a
wonderful book.'
Observer

'The best cricket biography I have ever read.'
Matthew Engel,
Wisden Cricket Monthly

'Gideon Haigh pursues his extraordinary subject with a breadth
of awareness rare in the sports–biog trade.'
New Statesman

'Australia's finest cricket writer.'
Frank Keating

'A stunning and most moving book...a gripping read.'
Judges' citation in announcing *Mystery Spinner*
PriceWaterhouseCoopers Cricket Book of the Year 2001

THE BIG SHIP

WARWICK ARMSTRONG
AND THE MAKING OF MODERN CRICKET

GIDEON HAIGH

AURUM PRESS

First published in Great Britain
2002 by Aurum Press Ltd
25 Bedford Avenue, London WC1B 3AT
First published in Australia in 2001 by The Text Publishing Company

A catalogue record for this book is available from the British Library.

ISBN 1 85410 824 7

9 8 7 6 5 4 3 2 1
2006 2005 2004 2003 2002

Design by Chong
Printed by Griffin Press, Australia

Contents

Introduction

Towards the end of Warwick Armstrong's life, he occasionally went walking near his Sydney home with erstwhile teammate Hunter Hendry and the Australian opening batsman Jack Fingleton. The latter, a journalist with Sydney's *Sun*, could recognise a story when he saw it, and wondered if he might coax the legendary captain into reminiscing about his earlier life and times.

Given a reporter eager for their thoughts, few sportsmen today would be capable of containing themselves. But, while Fingleton found him 'the soul of affability', Armstrong 'preferred to talk of other things'. Only once, removing from his mouth a favourite crooked-stemmed pipe, did he venture a self-assessment. 'Many people in cricket hated me,' he remarked. 'And I guess—I certainly hope—many people liked me.' Then he shrank from further reflection. 'But what does it matter now? It's all over and forgotten.'

It was a typical musing. Armstrong was a stranger to superfluous comment. An English journalist who met him in July 1921 was struck not by his utterances, but by their punctuating silences:

Warwick Armstrong is portentous. He reminds one as he approaches of a character out of Conrad; there is an air of suppressed force about him. When I saw him coming out the coffee room at his hotel to meet me, I knew that at last I had met the strong silent man.

Armstrong bore a vivid contusion round his left eye, legacy of a bouncer from Middlesex's Jack Durston, but sported it as matter-of-factly as the handkerchief in his breast pocket.

> Mr Armstrong does not, I gather, lie awake o' nights wondering about the chances of his team. He knows what he wants from them and just how to get it. Even the immense bruise left on his face by Durston is not a disfigurement. It seems rather to complete the whole picture. His conversation reminded me of Mary Ellen, the character in George Birmingham's *General John Regan*. No-one who saw that superb play can have forgotten Mary Ellen. All she says in answer to every question is 'oi moight'.

This 'interview' in *Town Topics*, incidentally, contains barely any reported quotation, reflecting customs of the period's sporting journalism, but also attesting to Armstrong's verbal economy. Even the instructional book he published the following year, *The Art of Cricket*, is virtually barren of personal detail; there is little of his career, and nothing of his life. The copy he gave his father, in fact, contains the perfunctory handwritten dedication: 'To Dad, with the author's comps.' It is not even signed.

Armstrong's dismissal of the past to Fingleton was likewise characteristic. If he pondered deeds done, he never let on. If he harboured regrets, he did not part with them. His famous contemporary Dame Nellie Melba—an admirer, incidentally, who entreated Warwick not to be too soft on the English—once wrote in a friend's autograph book: 'They say. What say they? Let them say.' It could have been Armstrong's motto. He did not so much stray into trouble as amble straight up to it, sometimes twisting its nose for good measure. When the Victorian Cricket Association demanded that their twenty-eight-year-old star all-rounder apologise for withdrawing from a match minutes before the start in a dispute over money, for instance, he risked a life ban by refusing to express more than a token regret:

> Donald Mackinnon (VCA president): 'Have you received money on any other basis?'
> Armstrong: 'I am not here to discuss these questions. All I am here for is to explain why I did not play against New South Wales.'
> Mackinnon: 'I understand you have been paid a fee of £5 for a match on several occasions. We want this matter cleared up.'
> Armstrong: 'I don't know anything about that. The statement given by the

executive to the *Argus* was wrong, and I thank them for it. I want the whole thing cleared up and I have nothing more to say.'

With that, he left the room. The VCA did not carry out its threat.

Warwick Armstrong's belief that his deeds were 'over now and forgotten' has since grown truer by the day. In the eight decades since his career ended, the all-rounder routinely designated 'the W. G. Grace of Australia' has inspired only one brief monograph. When Steve Waugh's Australians won their ninth consecutive Test victory in February 2000, overhauling the record of Armstrong's 1921 combination, there were no encomia for the dispossessed record-holder, merely the few factoids that everyone remembers: that Armstrong was one of the 'Big Six' whose 1912 mutiny rocked the Australian game (true), that he weighed twenty stone (true, though only in the twentieth year of his career), that he once expressed contempt for English cricket by reading a newspaper while fielding during a Test (false). It was once the case that present-day heroes never quite measured up to the masters of the past. Today, it is confidently assumed that those of olden times would pale in modern company. When an expert panel last year selected an Australian Team of the Century, there was not one cricketer from its first quarter.

The passage of years has been hostile to Warwick Armstrong in an even more tangible sense. Precious little archival footage survives. So few action photographs remain that the most popular, which shows him essaying a drive during his final Test innings, actually illustrates him missing the ball: generations of sub-editors have cropped the crouching keeper from the frame. Historical records that might have filled the absences Armstrong left in his own story have also in many cases been erased. Both the schools he attended are long closed. The annals of his first club, Caulfield, and his second club, South Melbourne, were consumed in pavilion fires. The publisher for whom he wrote his book lost its records in the Blitz. The newspaper for which he became a correspondent ceased publication twenty-one years ago. Most of the records of the company he worked for and later ran, the Australian arm of distiller James Buchanan & Company, were destroyed when its office closed in 1970. Worst of all, Armstrong's own mementoes from almost forty years of cricket were incinerated while in storage for his 1935 relocation to Sydney. Of his personal life, there is still less to say. Scarcely a word remains of his wife, who died in June 1940. The last of Armstrong's siblings died more than twenty-one years ago, his son seven years ago, while the latest to bear the name, Warwick Windridge Armstrong, never met his grandfather.

To recapture the life and times of Warwick Armstrong is not, however, so fruitless a task. It is the essence of sport that it impresses on minds more firmly than other cultural activities. 'There is nothing so momentary as a sporting achievement,' historian Greg Dening reminds us, 'and nothing so lasting as the memory of it.' The press of Warwick Armstrong's period covered cricket exhaustively. When prudery compelled the suppression of information, writers sometimes scattered beguiling clues. And if Armstrong recoiled from recording his own part in the times he lived through, friends, enemies and eyewitnesses were not so reticent.

In another sense, too, Armstrong is immanent. The influence of the attitudes he exuded, campaigns he waged and fights he fought pervade Australian cricket so completely that we scarcely understand him as their progenitor. He appears strange to us. In a period when to be 'fit' implies almost a superior morality, a cricketer of his dimensions seems quaint, archaic, indolent. Portliness being so often equated with jolliness, he might even be thought a figure of fun. Yet there was nothing jolly about Warwick Armstrong. On a cricket field, he was uncompromising and unsentimental: not only a batsman and bowler of great attainments, but a maker of Australian cricket's traditions, some of which we are proud of, others we might prefer not to acknowledge.

In what cricket historians now refer to as the Golden Age, the twenty years from 1894, usually depicted as the high summer of amateurism and sporting chivalry, Armstrong was the ultimate pragmatist. He cheerfully played as a professional when it suited and was not averse to overt gamesmanship, verbal aggression, intimidation of umpires, disputation over playing conditions, even cheating the odd batsman out. He thought 'walking'—the custom of batsmen giving themselves out—foolhardy. He considered 'leg-theory'—the technique of bowling outside leg stump to deny batsmen runs—not only fair but effective. In some instances, he went further than any modern cricketer would dare. On one occasion, he kept a nervous young batsman on his Test debut waiting eighteen minutes to face his first ball, by bowling practice deliveries that were allowed to run to the boundary. On another, he proposed to the Australian Board of Control that his team deliberately win matches more slowly in order to increase gate takings, the idea being that the players and the board would split surplus profits.

He was, by nature, a *refusenik*. At twenty-three, he refused to play for Victoria unless his captain was sacked. At twenty-eight, he refused to play for Victoria unless properly paid. At thirty, he declined to sign a contract for a tour of England because it would have involved recognising an administration to which he felt no loyalty. At thirty-two, he turned down a tour of England because he felt that players were being cheated of their right to elect a manager. Twice in his career, sixteen years apart, he would not bowl in Test matches because of heckling spectators; on the latter occasion, he simply sat down and waited until they were quiet.

In other ways, Armstrong was a harbinger of cricket to come. On his last tour of England, he deployed two great fast bowlers, Jack Gregory and Ted McDonald, as no captain had before, though many since. He infuriated the English by insisting that his team's schedule was too onerous, that local professionals were dull dogs who played for themselves, and that gambling on cricket would bring corruption in its train: complaints without precedent in their time, today rather more familiar. Finally, in what proved the last two hours of his Test career, he stood idly in the outfield at the Oval, unmoved, unmoving, bored to blazes by a game going nowhere, allowing his bowlers to rotate themselves. For many years afterwards, almost every cricketing act that smacked of obstinacy, negation, even brutality, seemed to ape an equivalent deed of Armstrong's—even 'Bodyline', which some English apologists excused as merely their own version of the Armstrong way.

There was also something compelling about him, as there often is about dictators, autocrats, those who act on their own impulses, and above all *do not care*. He looked a life ban from cricket in the face, and did not blink. He was thrice dumped as Victoria's captain, and each time returned unrepentant. On the last occasion, he was sacked while still serving as Australia's captain, precipitating perhaps the most extraordinary public protests in our cricket history. Ten thousand met in the shadow of the Melbourne Cricket Ground to demand his reinstatement, and his appearance in the subsequent Test touched off the greatest ovation that Bob Crockett heard in thirty years as an umpire:

As his ponderous frame emerged from the exit of the Grey Smith Stand there was a tremendous roar, the crowd standing and cheering him. He was the crowd's hero…As he settled down and was evidencing that the

English bowlers were not going to get rid of him without a fight, a shrill voice came from the outer: 'You'll do me Warwick!'

There was, from Armstrong, no reaction. 'It would have unnerved most people,' noted England's wicketkeeper Herbert Strudwick, 'but Armstrong seemed outwardly unmoved.' He procured a chanceless hundred.

To appreciate Warwick Armstrong fully, we must understand his era. This seems obvious, yet most writing about him is quite ahistorical. He shaped, and was shaped by, a crucial climacteric in the Australian game's development. When he played his first Test in January 1902, the basis of international cricket in this country was an *entente cordiale* between the Melbourne Cricket Club and the period's leading players. As he undertook a record-breaking tour of England three years later, the first moves were afoot to establish a centralised national management body, which would eclipse first Melbourne then the players. A favourite son himself of the Melbourne club, and for a decade its employee, Armstrong often found himself manning barricades against this new regime. Yet he would be the only Australian cricketer to prosper under each mode of governance, accomplished enough as a player and steadfast enough as a man to withstand every effort at his usurpation. This book takes a wide brief: Armstrong's life is noteworthy not only in its own terms but as a representative of his age. His capacities, both as cricketer and controversialist, positioned him in the van of change, from the end of cricket as he understood it, to the beginnings of cricket as we understand it.

1

'Little Armstrong
Caught the Eye'

Hutton Street in the Victorian country town of Kyneton, eighty
kilometres north-west of Melbourne, is a footnote in several
notable Australian lives. In May 1870, fifteen-year-old Ned
Kelly appeared on three consecutive Fridays at the bluestone courthouse
on the corner, finally being 'set at liberty' from a highway robbery
charge. It is also the street on which Rupert Greene, Rupert Murdoch's
mercurial maternal grandfather, was born three years later. It seems
accordingly a most suitable origin for Warwick Armstrong, incurably
rebellious and commercially hard-headed, averse always to authority
unless it was his to wield.

Warwick Windridge Armstrong was born at 6.30 p.m. on 22 May
1879, with doctors Smith and Pestall and midwife Bevans in attendance:
the time was entered in an unknown hand in a family Bible. The house,
occupying allotments 5, 6 and 7, was a modest affair, and is long gone;
it was the most recent in a string of dwellings the family had occupied
and, rented from local stablekeeper William Hughes, reflected something
of the Armstrongs' downward social trajectory since arriving twenty-
four years earlier. Warwick's parents, John Andrewartha and Amelia Mary
Armstrong, shared the residence with the former's parents, an expedient
born of necessity. Armstrong, who went to war with authorities during

his cricket career over an unpaid shilling, and later accumulated a substantial fortune, would have found in his family's experiences a primer on the nature of money, in terms of both its power and its evanescence.

Warwick Armstrong's paternal grandfather Oliver Goldsmith Armstrong arrived in Hobart as a cabin passenger aboard the *Charles Eaton* on 22 June 1834. He was eighteen. His name was a token of family pride in its blood tie with the distinguished poet; Oliver's mother Catherine Armstrong *nee* Goldsmith was great-niece to the author of 'The Deserted Village'. Oliver's father William had been a whaler, apparently lost at sea, but his mother was very much alive, and arrived in Hobart herself aboard the *Hector* just over a year later: accused of stealing a bed tick and blanket worth 10 shillings, she was sentenced to seven years' transportation.

Ironically, Oliver had himself joined the colony's Convict Department. In August 1841, he became comptroller-general. At least his mother had finished her sentence in time to attend her son's wedding, to Agnes Frances Carpenter, an architect's daughter from Putney, on 11 November 1843 at St David's Cathedral. By the time the couple's first child arrived, Oliver was doing well, drawing £200 as superintendent of Port Esperance convict probation station. Their brood swelled over the next nine years to five boys, including John Andrewartha. Had Oliver imagined that changing hemispheres would free him from family obligations, however, he was mistaken. In due course, both his brother and a sister arrived, the former something of a waster, sacked from the Convict Department for horsewhipping an assistant superintendent, then drowned in circumstances suggestive of suicide. It may have been with relief that, after the cessation of transportation to Tasmania in December 1853, Oliver removed to the mainland with his family.

By December 1855, the Armstrongs and their four boys were in Kyneton, initially at a hay and corn store in High Street. The town was not quite two decades old, having first been traversed in September 1836 by Major Thomas Mitchell, who had named its Campaspe River for a lover of Alexander the Great. The settlement had about 300 inhabitants, and Oliver Armstrong quickly fell in with one of the most respected: Samuel Windridge, late of the 28th Regiment, and until recently the town's chief constable. The firmness of their families' friendship was later perpetuated in Warwick Armstrong's alliterative middle name.

Seeing his future in flour milling, Oliver undertook the management of the Degraves Mill: an imposing bluestone structure today serving as a residence. He and his sons also involved themselves extensively in the town's social life. Kyneton was renowned for horse-racing: there was great pride in November 1863 when local colt Banker won the Melbourne Cup. There was also an established local cricket club, playing in an open paddock later occupied by cattle yards known as Greasy Pole Corner. Oliver's sons Henry and John and Samuel Windridge's boys Samuel and John became members.

Cricket was then in Australia a game of ambiguous status, manifesting both the colony's received Englishness, with the social stratification that this implied, and the yen for more abiding equality. Henry Armstrong recorded in his journal a quaint example of these contradictory impulses in conflict. From April 1856, it became customary to hold an annual club ball at Wedge Street's Robert Burns Hotel. One year, however, club secretary Chas Kingk, a German from the District Road Board, decided that patrician and plebeian elements should not intermingle.

> On the occasion of the cricket club ball he produced a piece of chalk and drew a line across the centre of the room with a view to keeping the two classes separate. The immediate result of this was that the subscribers and guests that Kingk desired to keep apart from the aristocracy left the room in a body. This silly exhibition broke up the ball and put an end to the annual function forever.

More memorably and demonstratively, Warwick Armstrong would himself challenge such arbitrary sporting social distinction.

As the family prospered, Agnes bore three more children: a son, Warwick Goldsmith, and twin daughters, Olivia Catherine and Olivia Jane. Oliver also commissioned a handsome two-storey mansion, though it is unclear whether the Armstrongs ever resided there; their fortunes shortly suffered a devastating, double-edged blow.

Milling could be hazardous. In February 1862, hail smashed all sixty windows at Degraves Mill; two months later an exploding boiler at Blyth's Mill killed two. Nonetheless, in March 1863, Oliver and partner Isaiah Compton Jones leased the ten-year-old steam-powered Argyle Mill. The *Kyneton Guardian* reported that Armstrong and Jones were 'prepared to receive wheat for which highest cash prices will be given'. Within days, however, it bore grimmer news:

> On Friday afternoon a rather serious accident occurred at the mills owned by Mr E. Argyle which have recently been let to Messrs Armstrong and Jones. The store to the north of the mill, which is of but recent construction, gave way, the north wall falling outwards. About 12,000 bushels of wheat were on the premises, a portion of which was injured by the stones and debris falling upon the bags, bursting them and scattering their contents on the ground. The delay and the damage by the rainy weather which followed the accident makes it an altogether untoward circumstance for Messrs Armstrong and Jones who have so lately started business on their own account.

Oliver Armstrong bore the brunt of the £1000 losses—Jones was, Henry Armstrong felt, 'slightly inclined to be a bounder'. Yet the setback might have been endured had it not been for a chilling discovery. Soon after the mill's collapse, the patriarch explained without elaboration to his two oldest boys, Oliver Jnr and Henry, that the family was ruined. 'He didn't say much but even then I was old enough to see how he was shaken,' recalled Henry. 'I don't think he ever recovered from this blow. It seemed to take all the heart and energy out of him and he gave up the fight against the world.' His sons, Oliver confided, would have to assist in redeeming the family finances. Oliver Jnr was already a bank clerk, and Henry had been articled to Kyneton solicitor Fred Boulton. Now John would have to accept work as an office boy with solicitor George Booker, while Colville trained as a surveyor and Albert as an auditor. The mystery behind the family's destitution? Henry related:

> Mother was a waster and nothing could be done to check her extravagance. At the time of the collapse of the mill, Dad went round and got in accounts of all he owed. The principal one was at the Blue Stone Store Grocery and, while Dad thought he was paying a monthly bill and keeping clear of debt, Mother had managed a private account of her own which at this time had run up to over £200. It was the same at other places of business...and Dad found that he was at least £500 in debt...He never in my hearing breathed a word of reproach against Mother for what she had done, but he was a changed man afterwards. His whole future seemed to be black and hopeless to him...Even in our darkest time Mother's extravagance and wastefulness kept us at our wit's end.

The straitened Armstrongs rented a crowded cottage in Mitchell Street, then Piper Street's disused Great Western Hotel. Oliver tried starting afresh as a hardwood dealer. His American Saw Mill Company rented facilities near Mount Macedon from a William Brooks Hoffman at £125 per annum. But he soon fell behind in his rent, and a *Kyneton Observer* report of 14 February 1865 is intriguing:

> It appears that Mr Armstrong was going to his mill…to pay his men as usual and when within about half a mile he suddenly received a blow in the back from some heavy weapon which knocked him down. His assailant fell upon him, while another man came forward and lent his assistance. Mr Armstrong seized the man (who fell on top of him) by the throat, and the fellow at once drew the pistol and presented it at his head. Mr Armstrong raised his arm at the moment the pistol was fired and the charge passed through his coat sleeve and through his hat. Before he had any time to take any other steps in his defence he was rendered senseless by several blows on the head.

Oliver lost £197, and appears again to have been fortune's butt. Yet all may not have been as it seemed. Henry Armstrong's narrative neglects this incident. It also seems convenient that a bullet discharged from a revolver at one's head should pass through both a coat sleeve and a hat, that the brigands should prove unidentifiable and the funds irrecoverable. Oliver declared bankruptcy sixteen days later, ascribing his losses to the flour mill mishap and the robbery and 'not from any extravagance or improvident habits of my own'—nowhere was his wife's role in the family's ruin noted. Was the robbery a gallant sham? Desperate predicaments sometimes entail desperate remedies.*

At the time, it probably helped to be friends with upstanding Samuel Windridge. Certainly there does not seem to have been any softening of the families' mutual regard: Oliver and Samuel served on organising committees for the races and the church bazaar; Henry joined the Prince

---

* Oliver Armstrong was not technically insolvent, reckoning his debts at £2040 9s 9d and his assets at £2334 5s 10d, although the official assignee commented that the latter were 'altogether overvalued'. How long Oliver's financial affairs took to resolve is unclear; the last document in his bankruptcy file shows that the estate was still officially assigned in October 1878.

of Wales Light Horse, a local militia which Samuel captained. Henry even persuaded his father to join a new theatrical troupe; their act was somewhat undermined when, demonstrating a sailor's hornpipe, Oliver split his son's cricket trousers.

Hasty stitching would have been necessary—the cricket club was an integral part of family life. John Armstrong became a stalwart, bearing at various times all its offices, and occasionally their inevitable trials. His clubmates' varying humours are suggested by the *Kyneton Guardian*'s report of a meeting with Chewton in which John led his team:

> we would suggest that nothing detracts so much from the interest of a game as disobedience by a team to the commands of their chosen captain. This was noticeable in one instance particularly, one of the Kyneton men having apparently been disappointed in not obtaining the position he aspired to, palpably sulked on it and made no attempt to field at all, standing throughout the game with his coat on and a pipe in his mouth.

Others were more serious. Another club patriot whom Henry noted in his journal was 'Flynn of Boggy Creek'. This was Thomas Flynn, a convict made good. A farmer's son from Cork, he had been transported to Hobart for pig stealing in January 1842 on the *Prince Regent*—the same ship, coincidentally, freighting Ned Kelly's father to the colony. Time served, Flynn profited during the gold rush, providing bullocks hauling hopefuls' belongings to the goldfields for up to £100 a ton. Marrying a farmer's daughter, Honora Barry, he had established himself at a farm known as Riverview. His son Tom was an outstanding cricketer who later represented East Melbourne and Fitzroy, becoming caretaker at the latter's ground and a respected umpire.

The Armstrongs and Flynns also mingled at Kyneton District Football Club, which played the fledgling indigenous game destined to become Australian Rules. John was its secretary when Tom—described in the *Footballer* as 'grand anywhere, splendid runner and dodger'—was captain. At least in this setting, sport seems to have played the 'melting pot' role often ascribed it. The Armstrongs and Flynns were a contrast in social mobility: the convict supervisor's family descending the scale, the convict's family ascending, the Armstrongs Anglicans, the Flynns devoutly Catholic. Sport represented one of their few common pursuits.

Oliver Armstrong continued relying on his sons for financial support. Henry, in Melbourne with what had become Hurry and Briggs, remitted funds. John, his replacement in the firm's Kyneton office, also provided £1 a week. For the next few years, the Armstrongs would continue to be dogged by misfortune. Their twin girls having died in infancy, thirteen-year-old Warwick Goldsmith succumbed to typhoid in April 1872. An undertaker's invoice survives charging £10 for 'covered coffin, mounted, lining, ruffling and pillow': no small expense for a family with their travails. Oliver's burden was perhaps slightly relieved when Henry returned to Kyneton three years later to practise opposite the Junction Hotel, and would have lightened considerably when John married Tom Flynn's sister Amelia on 1 May 1878.

Twenty-six-year-old John Armstrong's marriage to twenty-five-year-old Amelia Flynn, while evidently convenient for both families, was as unusual as their original friendship. As Edmund Campion comments, 'Catholics were Australia's first ethnics.' Outnumbered yet never inconspicuous, and often distrusted because of the Irishness of Australian Catholicism, they found many social circles impermeable. Even Catholics from abroad could regard the antipodean laity as second-rate; an Irish Christian Brother writing home in December 1868 thought them 'far behind others in business and intelligence', being predominantly 'hewers of wood and drawers of water'.

Victorian Catholics had fared reasonably well by comparison with those in New South Wales; two—John O'Shanassy and Charles Gavan Duffy—had become premier. Yet the colony had followed South Australia willingly into voluntarism—the withdrawal of state aid from churches—and its 1872 Education Act was the most explicitly secular in Australia. Mistrust, moreover, was mutual: the Catholic Plenary Council discouraged intermarriage with Protestants, believing it 'a terrible blot upon the character of our Catholic community'.

The Armstrong nuptials were conducted in Kyneton's St Mary's Church by Reverend Horatio Geoghegan, the town's Catholic priest for twenty-two years and 'a constant manifestation of priestly virtue and zeal for the spiritual welfare of his flock'. Held on a Wednesday and occasioning no newspaper coverage, it does not appear to have been a large wedding. Nor did the couple honeymoon; John Armstrong had scheduled the football club's annual meeting for the following evening at Temperance Hall. But nor does it seem to have raised too great a flutter: the groom was a popular young man, the bride from one of Kyneton's best families, and the best man was another local cricketer and footballer, Samuel Windridge's twenty-three-year-old son John. While John Armstrong would not himself convert to Catholicism for another twenty years, first son Warwick was baptised by Geoghegan at St Mary's on 24 August 1879 when he was three months old—an anticipation of the 1885 Plenary Council *diktat* permitting intermarriage where the non-Catholic pledged to raise offspring in the partner's faith.

As his birthplace, Kyneton retained a civic pride in Warwick Armstrong's later achievements. Samuel Windridge's grandson Bill named three of his nine children for prominent cricketers, the first in honour of the family's chief source of reflected glory: Warwick Armstrong Windridge was born in 1923, followed by James Sutcliffe Windridge in 1929, and even Donald Bradman Windridge in 1938. But the time Armstrong himself spent in Kyneton was brief. When two bypass bridges opened in Kyneton bearing his name on 22 May 2001, the 122nd anniversary of his birth, they were an apt memorial: the town was his bridge to the world.

The bridges cross land once occupied by Riverview, his maternal grandfather's estate, and the birthplace on 29 August 1880 of Warwick Armstrong's brother Jack. This arrangement for the family's second child suggests that father John was absent, perhaps securing lodgings ahead of leaving Kyneton. He had by this time accepted a job in the Melbourne office of what was now Hurry, Briggs and O'Hea, and the family must have followed him to the city soon afterwards—John was there for the commencement of the cricket season.

The Armstrongs and their infant sons were established in Emerald Hill, between the port of Melbourne and the Yarra, by year's end. It was a patchwork of different classes, in pockets heavily industrialised, the north-west between the river and City Road being especially grimy and disreputable. The Armstrongs were more commodiously situated in Stead Street, a narrow avenue of look-alike cottages, named for and owned by brothers Joseph and Thomas Stead—Joseph, then mayor, owned the east side; Thomas, his partner in a timber merchants, the west. The family rented a four-room brick house at number three. Rate books reveal their neighbourhood as a representative cross-section of middle-class Melbourne—clerk, photographer, bootmaker, civil servant, cordial-maker—although with aspirations: for their first few years, the Armstrongs lived next door to William Lewis, a wool merchant later in state politics.

Melbourne was in the throes of the fastest growth in its history, the so-called Land Boom: the number of dwellings in Emerald Hill would double over the decade. As yet, however, it remained relatively spacious. A short walk from Stead Street, at the western end of the lagoon known as Albert Park Lake, was also a picturesque oval, home to the South Melbourne cricket and football clubs. John Armstrong would probably have gravitated there anyway—as Richard Twopeny's *Town Life in Australia* counselled, 'in Australia not to be interested in cricket amounts almost to a social crime'—but he happened to have an *entrée*.

John had known Hurry, Briggs and O'Hea's George Major some years already: a surviving file of the firm shows them handling a probate case together in February 1878. Now they were workmates, twenty-nine-year-old Major welcomed the new arrival. He had been a serviceable player of the indigenous football code: 'As a footballer, Mr Major was "some punkins" at the game,' said *Melbourne Punch*, 'and old fossils will tell you he was a rum 'un to tackle'. He remained a vigorous cricketer, with one slight qualification; he had been no-balled for throwing early in his career and suspicions lingered, *Boyle and Conway's Annual* for 1877–78 describing him as a quick bowler 'inclining to shy'. Not that this had diminished Major's standing; regarded as 'South Melbourne always to the backbone and spinal marrow' and admired as one who would 'rather give up the game than do anything unfair', he would act as Victoria's sole selector from 1883 to 1887. He was in his legal career, moreover, fast rising: by 1884, he made partner in his firm, which became Hurry and Major at 91 Chancery Lane.

John Armstrong was himself a modest cricketer. A medium-pacer handy in junior XIs, his career described the well-worn course of invariable selection at the outset growing less frequent as personal and professional responsibilities impinged. In his first summer, he obtained 101 runs at 14.4 and 13 wickets at 9.9 for South Melbourne's third XI— in an era of rough technique and rougher pitches the former secured him the prize for the highest batting average. He enjoyed his best performances the following season, gathering 130 runs at 11.8 and 48 wickets at 8, and joined the six-member match committee, though his performances trailed off thereafter, until in 1884–85 he could steal time for only a final handful of games. Nonetheless, paternal precedent had been established. Warwick Armstrong's first exposure to cricket was probably watching his father and George Major representing South Melbourne by Albert Park Lake. Seventeen years later, with fretful pride, they watched John's son make his Test debut at the Melbourne Cricket Ground.

As securely as Saturdays were John's, Sundays were Amelia's. St Peter's and St Paul's Catholic Church was ten minutes' walk from Stead Street. Its parish was the largest outside the city. After a decade's work, interrupted at times by want of money, a handsome bluestone chapel regarded as 'one of Melbourne's finest pieces of architectural beauty' had recently been completed, seating 600 who listened on Sundays to the strains of a £300 organ. The small chapel this replaced, meanwhile, became a denominational school; although no rolls survive, it is probably where Warwick and Jack Armstrong began their educations.

Sport and religion: the majority of Australian households at the time would have imbibed of both influences. Yet the Armstrongs were unusual. When Amelia Armstrong bore a daughter in September 1882, Olivia Amy was baptised at St Peter's and St Paul's, a church her Anglican father could not enter. While John Armstrong doubtless savoured the status of being the male breadwinner, Amelia would have enjoyed at home at least a spiritual dominion. Two further daughters, Muriel Goldsmith, born in November 1884, and Amelia Goldsmith, born in March 1887, were received into the faith at St Peter's and St Paul's. That her children understood hieratic rituals also appears to have been important to Amelia: Warwick, aged six, was a sponsor of Muriel's baptism.

Thomas Flynn's daughter was by all accounts a strong-willed woman. While photographs of her husband suggest a benevolent figure, his smile visible even through a luxuriant beard, Amelia in the presence of a camera was staid to the point of severity. This self-awareness perhaps owed something to her family's circumstances. Amelia had entered marriage with money, and acquired a reputation for shrewdness with it. Her attitudes to wealth may have been reflected in her favourite fictional character, Amelia Sedley of Thackeray's *Vanity Fair*, the dim though kind-hearted girl who befriends Becky Sharp at Miss Pinkerton's school, but whose marriage is imperilled by the dissipation of her family's fortune.

When the Armstrongs moved from Emerald Hill, it was Amelia who acquired their new residence. With Thomas Flynn's death in March 1888, Amelia came into her inheritance, and contracted to purchase 'Arra Glen' in North Caulfield's Hawthorn Road two months later. This was a substantial undertaking, requiring a £200 deposit and the assumption of a £600 mortgage, payable in half-yearly instalments at 6 per cent interest. Nor, at the Land Boom's peak, could anyone be sure of a bargain; grand houses were then mushrooming almost overnight in North Caulfield, and entire estates being hammered together in weeks. Settlement, however, proceeded unhindered on 8 June. John's only contribution appears to have been conveyancing: Hurry and Major were Amelia's lawyers.

Interestingly, rates inquiries were addressed to husband rather than wife, as was a surviving December 1888 letter from a neighbour asking to lay a pipe across the property; it was probably assumed that such a residence could only belong to the male provider. John and Amelia would have known better.

The Armstrongs had made steady material progress in Emerald Hill. They had built an additional wooden room at 3 Stead Street after Olivia's birth, perhaps a nursery, moved to a more spacious west side home, then finally to William Lewis's former residence. North Caulfield, newer but wealthier, represented further advancement: Arra Glen was a splendid investment, constructed of handmade bricks, and containing four bedrooms, spacious dining and living areas. There was a deep cellar and stables for the family phaeton. Abutting the property was a vacant lot, known simply as 'the paddock', on which the family grazed its horse; it became the venue for Warwick Armstrong's childhood cricket games.*

After a tide of Irish Land Boom labour, North Caulfield was also a burgeoning Catholic community. In September 1888, St Kilda's parish priest inaugurated a mass at the new Town Hall in neighbouring Malvern: the Armstrongs' next child, Thomas Goldsmith, born in

---

* Arra Glen, long since demolished, was on the site now occupied by 84, a brick house, and 86 Hawthorn Road, a block of units. The 'paddock' was at what is now 82. The whole site backed onto a cobblestone laneway running from Derby Place to Salisbury Street, down which the 'night man' called to tend the outside lavatory.

October 1889, was baptised there. Soon after, foundations were laid in nearby Stanhope Street for what would be the Armstrongs' house of worship for more than thirty years, St Joseph's. A small brick building, it opened six months later, with weatherboard schoolrooms: though again no records exist, it seems likely that Warwick and Jack Armstrong, then ten and eight, enrolled there for a period. The original St Joseph's was superseded after three years by a more imposing structure, centre of its own parish; Lucia Goldsmith, seventh and last of the Armstrong brood, born in September 1892, was the fourth infant baptised there. It was there, too, in December 1894, during one of Archbishop Carr's triennial visits, that Warwick and Jack Armstrong were among thirteen boys and thirty-seven girls to receive the sacrament of confirmation.

For the boys, there were additional benefits to relocation. Directly across Hawthorn Road was verdant Caulfield Park. When the initial land sales had been made in Caulfield in 1854, large tracts of the area were swamp. Unsuitable for housing and inimical to sanitation, these pockets were transformed into parkland: Black Swamp became East Caulfield Park, Crosbie's Swamp became Donald Mackinnon Reserve, Leman Swamp became Koornang Park. Vast Paddy's Swamp, meanwhile, was reborn as Caulfield Park, since September 1888 home to Caulfield Cricket Club.

The *Australasian*'s long-time cricket correspondent 'Felix'—former Australian Test captain Tom Horan—referred to this setting in the only known reference to Warwick Armstrong's early cricketing potential. 'Felix' described him as playing for a 'junior club out Caulfield way' and 'often being barred from matches' because he played too well. Horan would have known: he was a St Joseph's parishioner whose sons later played school and state cricket with Armstrong. Yet if it is so—no scores survive to verify it— it was quite a feat: Armstrong was a tiny boy. And the cricketer so famous for his size and strength never forgot it.

A feature of Armstrong's advice to youngsters in *The Art of Cricket* is appreciation of the plight of the undersized. He enjoins them to observe orthodox methods, to be patient, not to be intimidated. 'Boys who are really keen on the game don't take any notice of the ordinary smacks on the leg,' he counsels, 'and those who fume and fuss about them are sheer funkers.' He is specifically solicitous of 'the small and undeveloped boy', who 'finds it difficult to realise that he will eventually be strong himself', and who is reassured that 'strength will bring in its train the ability to dispose of overtossed balls'. To adults, Warwick addresses a 'plea for attention to the weak', urging their constant encouragement. 'I know what a pat on the back will do for cricketers far past their boyhood, and in the cases of small boys who are weak it is a pleasure to encourage them and to see their eyes sparkle when told that all they require is time in which to grow stronger.' He even deplores coaches who pick 'the stronger boy, whose mere strength makes him a run-getter' to the exclusion of 'a weaker boy with more natural ability, but whose lack of strength prevents him from making runs'. Armstrong does not invoke his own experiences, but the affinity appears based on more than observation.

Little is known of Armstrong's early upbringing. What exists suggests an average child, keen enough on sport to play in the 'paddock' until light petered out. Criticism of sports-mad colonial youth was then not uncommon. In *Our Countrymen,* Henry Lawson reviled the 'average Australian boy' as 'a cheeky brat with a leaning towards larrikinism, a craving for cigarettes and no ambition beyond the cricket and football field'. Edward Kinglake in *The Australian at Home* contended: 'Above all things, an Australian schoolboy dreads making himself ridiculous. He shows this in his games. The only ones he really cares for are those men play. As for any which exercise the imagination, he thinks them effeminate and despises them.' How closely Armstrong fitted this stereotype is unknown; he was probably unexceptional.

The nature of Armstrong's original cricketing tuition is also unclear. An interview he gave the *Cape Times* nearly thirty years later suggests that it came at his father's hands: 'When asked what really makes a great cricketer, Mr Armstrong summed up his analysis with one word: heredity.' As youngsters, he and Jack probably developed along similar lines. 'Brothers frequently bat very much alike,' Armstrong asserted in *The Art of Cricket*, again with authority seemingly based on more than observation.

Personally, however, the brothers seem to have been rather different. Warwick had grey eyes and a boyish reserve; his brother's cobalt blue eyes came with a sunnier nature. Family lore has it that, rather than spend his first few pennies of pocket money, Armstrong saved it for a week until another distribution was due; only then was it spent. Father John, victim of improvidence, and mother Amelia, beneficiary of thrift, would have looked on approvingly. But brother Jack spent freely—

perhaps he'd inherited his paternal grandmother's habits. It became a watchword that, given sixpence, the older boy would salt half away, while the younger spent the lot.

Such small differences later grew more marked, and all the Armstrong children grew up with distinct attitudes to money: some were parsimonious, some prodigal. Warwick Armstrong never outgrew his youthful predisposition, to the extent that a later teammate, Hunter Hendry, remembered him as 'a very mean man'. Perhaps the virtues of prudence were underscored by the Land Boom's collapse in 1891, which devastated North Caulfield as surely as everywhere else. On the streets round Arra Glen, the Armstrongs would have encountered work gangs of the unemployed breaking bluestone spalls and laying footpaths for subsistence wages. Yet while other families suffered theirs did not. John commuted daily from Caulfield railway station. His daughters would greet his return with their pet cockatoo, which sat on his walking cane for the short walk home. The evening meal would be consumed with silver cutlery bearing a family crest. And Warwick Armstrong began attending Cumloden, a new fee-paying boys' school.

Cumloden's Cambridge-educated principal W. Martin Burn had come from running Wadhurst, the boarding house at pucka Melbourne Church of England Grammar School, which he had made more pucka still by introducing a house system along English public school lines. He founded Cumloden on a two-hectare rise dotted with pines in Caulfield's Alma Road. Designed 'to prepare boys for home and colonial universities, the course of study containing all branches of an English education', it featured five sizeable schoolrooms, a carpenter's shop, sanatorium and gymnasium.

Choosing secondary education for their boys would not have been straightforward for the Armstrongs. Responding to the secularisation of state education, the Catholic Plenary Council had decreed that children at state schools were to be denied absolution at confessional. That edict was interpreted more pragmatically at a local level, for Catholic secondary schools were still rare. Malvern had Sacre Coeur College for girls, but De La Salle College for boys was not established until February 1912. Christian Brothers College operated near Cumloden, but its relations with Archbishop Carr were strained; the Brothers denied his inspectors permission to examine their students in secular subjects. Cumloden had qualities, meanwhile, which would have appealed to

John Armstrong. It had quickly become a respected sporting member of the Schools Association—a group of smaller private schools including Caulfield Grammar, Geelong College, Haileybury College and South Melbourne College—and took cricket seriously. Burn employed an English coach, one H. S. Crowther of Kent, and secured for practices nearby St Kilda Cricket Ground. 'Felix' visited the oval on one of his habitual weekly rambles in November 1893 and bailed up the groundsman. 'I saw some fine young lads playing on a capital pitch and asked whether a match was going on. "Oh no," replied Mac, "those are the Cumloden boys practising. They practice double-wicket regularly on this ground."'

One of these lads was almost certainly Warwick Armstrong. He quickly found a place in the school's XI, and as a favourite of another *Australasian* columnist: 'College Sports' correspondent Reginald Wilmot, who signed himself 'Old Boy'. When Cumloden met King's College on 27 October 1893, for instance, 'Old Boy' commended Armstrong's third-highest score of 13 and his 'virtually infallible' fielding as long stop. When Cumloden next met St Francis Xavier, 'Old Boy' commented: 'Little Armstrong, who caught the eye of "Felix" in an off match against East Melbourne, played clean and correct cricket for 21 not out.'

No records survive of the East Melbourne 'off match' other than Armstrong's score of 63. But the youngster had now been identified by two writers who would be influential patrons throughout his career. Wilmot was then twenty-four, a Melbourne University cricket blue and erstwhile Essendon footballer embarking on a journalistic career spanning six decades in the *Australasian* and the *Argus*. A proselytising champion of 'clean sport', he would be a councillor of the Victorian Amateur Athletics Federation for thirty years. Horan was forty, past playing, but mining a rich seam of intercolonial and international experience encompassing the inaugural Test in Melbourne. His playful but oracular writings, punctuated with snatches of verse, were the most authoritative and popular of their day.

On 18 November, Armstrong contributed 50 to 5–316 against Carlton College, who themselves crumbled for 10 and 40; this victory secured for Cumloden the Schools Association premiership. He appeared in a newspaper for the first time, a tiny figure reclining at front left in a half-page photograph of Cumloden's XI in the *Australasian* of 6 January 1894. But it was the 1894–95 season that would essentially 'make' young

Warwick Armstrong. In the summer of what is widely regarded as the first great Test series—England narrowly beat Australia in a five-match feast of entertainment—Armstrong commenced playing among men.

While young cricketers today usually advance incrementally—under-12, under-14, under-16 and so forth—Australia has traditionally blooded youngsters among men, sometimes with celebrated results. Both Donald Bradman and Neil Harvey, for instance, played first in adult company at thirteen, Bradman remaining unbeaten in his first five innings for Bowral Town, Harvey scoring a bonny hundred in a district final for Fitzroy. In Armstrong's case, he crossed Hawthorn Road and joined Caulfield Cricket Club which was six seasons old and still too small to erect a pavilion. Its first XI competed for a trophy staked by prominent locals, the Knox–Kelly Shield. In 1893–94, it had finished second. In 1894–95, it won. To participate at fifteen in a senior premiership must have been a heady experience. The third name on the shield—spared by a 1955 fire which incinerated Caulfield's rooms—is 'W. W. Armstrong'.

The same blaze consumed the club's records of that season, and Caulfield's games attracted only desultory interest in the local *Caulfield and Elsternwick Leader*. We do know that Armstrong finished ninth in the batting averages at a modest 11. Yet John Armstrong appears to have recognised that his son was undergoing a sporting rite of passage; he became a volunteer helper at the club, then joined the committee. And the impact on Armstrong's cricket once he returned to Cumloden was obvious. On 1 March 1895, Cumloden made only 63 against Kew High School at Richmond; Armstrong contributed 35. Three weeks later, the team barely exceeded 100 in either innings against King's College at South Melbourne. 'Cumloden should beware of becoming a one-man team,' warned 'Old Boy', 'for Armstrong with 56 and 60 not out did far more than his share.'

In the wake of the Tests of 1894–95, cricket at Cumloden expanded, two XIs growing to five. Warwick Armstrong also bloomed, suddenly experiencing an adolescent growth spurt that turned him from a small boy into a tall and gangling youth, who experimented with bowling fast. On 5 April 1895 against Brighton Grammar, he seized three wickets in an over, one with 'an express ball which, for pace, break and pitch, might have come from the armoury of the Surrey Express'—the 'Surrey

Express' being Tom Richardson, England's leonine fast bowler of 1894–95. Of Armstrong's undefeated 67, 'Old Boy' commented, 'He is undoubtedly one of the best bats in schools cricket at present.'

'Old Boy's' attention mattered to Armstrong. Forty years later, he contributed a laudatory introduction to Wilmot's only book. He recalled the length of their relationship—actually misremembering it: 'I was a small boy at University College when he first wrote of me and my cricket, and I have known him ever since. He is favourably known to all first-class cricketers in Australia.' Armstrong was now going from strength to strength. In Christmas week of 1895, Cumloden received a vice-regal invitational side, Captain Wallington's XI, whose matches doubled as society functions; Armstrong's forthright 90 in a 52-run victory spoiled their party. Beginning 1896 in similar form with his first school hundred against University High, he attained another landmark: at sixteen, he was trialled in Melbourne's pennant competition.

Grade cricket does not today sound a great achievement, but in an age where intercolonials were few and internationals fewer, competition featured many first-class and Test cricketers. Forty-year-old St Kilda was also one of the competition's leading clubs. Its Junction Oval, reclaimed marsh on which Melbourne Zoo had grazed alpacas, was graced by an attractive stand and girdled by a cycling track. But on the eve of St Kilda's meeting with Richmond on 11 April, it rained. On Arra Glen's roof, it must have beaten a forbidding tattoo. At Richmond, it turned turf to mud. 'A fast and true wicket at Richmond is excelled by none in the colony,' averred 'Felix', 'but when they get a bad wicket then you can be quite sure that it is bad.' Richmond floundered for 44, St Kilda for 54—Armstrong was stumped for 2. The teenager looked on the following Saturday as Richmond batted his team into a corner, his only contribution a brave outfield catch. On the final Saturday St Kilda crumbled for 116.

Armstrong, however, did not fail; for a time, he was St Kilda's best hope. Batting at number six, he saw four quick wickets fall, but with 36 made Richmond wait a further hour and a half to finish the game. 'A young player named Armstrong from Cumloden,' commented 'Felix' approvingly, 'showed form sufficient to justify the inference that he is likely to be a batsman of value to the club should he throw in his lot with them next season…He kept his end up and played like a cricketer from start to finish.'

2

'A Long Thin Young Streak'

By 1896, Warwick Armstrong was a fine cricketer in the making. The *Australasian*'s 'Old Boy' referred to him routinely as 'the young Cumloden crack' and 'the inevitable Armstrong'. He was also broadening his bowling abilities, abandoning speed in favour of spin in imitation of Australia's captain on its tour of England that year, Harry Trott. As the only role model Armstrong ever cited, Trott merits some study.

A local postman and son of South Melbourne's long-serving scorer, Trott first played there in 1884–85, John Armstrong's last season with the club. He blossomed into a sound opening batsman, but was distinguished more by the cunning evident in his subtle slows. He became noted for giving youngsters a leg-side full toss, chuckling as the ball was disposed of: 'I see you know what to do with that rubbish.' The next ball would appear identical but, some slight reconfiguration of the field having occurred, often induce a catch and a lecture: 'That first ball was to give you confidence, son. The second to teach you a lesson.'

Trott, a genial man inseparable from the hat which he wore everywhere but the bath, also had a gift for leadership; the Anglo-Indian batting guru Prince Ranjitsinhji thought him 'probably the best captain Australia ever had'. Previous skippers had tended to rigid field settings and predetermined bowling changes. Trott moved fieldsmen and shuffled bowlers ceaselessly, his plots often involving himself as change bowler. Leg breaks were a novelty, and Trott kept them so, using himself sparingly, sometimes replacing himself shortly after a wicket. This impressed the adolescent Armstrong: 'Trott had an almost uncanny knowledge of batsmen who were likely to succumb to his wiles and, after he had met with a success, he would at once take himself off and put on some other bowler of a different type.' Armstrong reminisced of two Tests, one he probably witnessed at the Melbourne Cricket Ground in March 1895, one he must have read about at Old Trafford in July 1896:

> At Melbourne, we have not forgotten how Trott got [England's captain] A. E. Stoddart out lbw on the last morning of that final Test match which was to decide the rubber, nor are we Australians likely to forget how at Manchester he added W. G. Grace to his victims and again dismissed Stoddart. Having achieved these successes he threw the ball to Giffen and himself never bowled another ball in the innings. It was chiefly due to his careful judgment that we won that Test match by three wickets. It has been a constant source of surprise to me that so few bowlers have adopted the leg-break style. It was this lack of leg-break bowlers that was one of the reasons why I took Harry Trott as my model and I consider myself indebted to him for whatever successes have come my way as a bowler.

Armstrong's recollection was astray; in the former game, Trott actually continued bowling, and Australia lost both Test and series. But he saw very early that the paucity of leg-break bowlers worked to any practitioner's advantage. Aged seventeen, however, he faced a challenge of a different sort, not from his school but from within his own family.

As the 1896–97 season commenced, Armstrong's cricket took an unexpected backward step. Representing St Kilda against North Melbourne, he unaccountably arrived on the second day too late to bat. St Kilda was 8–40 chasing the hosts' 175 and, in Armstrong's absence, the innings lasted only two more deliveries. Captain Charles Wilson demoted him to number eleven during St Kilda's follow-on when he made a competent 24 out of 151. But he was dropped to the second XI for the following week, and this became his last match for the club.

Nowhere was this unaccountable lapse explained, though a surprising explanation was later ventured for Armstrong's severance of links with St Kilda. Chronicling Armstrong's career in July 1914, the *Herald* recalled:

He was a loose jointed lad in knicker-bockers at the time and he became shy when the onlookers laughed at him. The fact is that the crowd was greatly tickled at such a raw and somewhat quaint and overgrown looking boy knocking the bowling of more or less famous players about. Armstrong's shyness caused a check in his career.

The idea that Armstrong, so often in later years impervious to barrackers' barbs, might have shrunk from the teasing of a pennant cricket crowd seems laughable. Yet it is hardly something a writer would have confected. Perhaps his rugged exterior was more cultivated than appeared; perhaps, too, his growing bulk was an armour of sorts. Whatever the case, on returning to Caulfield, Armstrong found himself in an unusual position. His committeeman father John had emerged from retirement to captain a team in the new Lewis–Chandler Trophy, and rolled back the years by beginning the season with 4–14 against St George and 82 against East Caulfield. Caulfield, indeed, would win the competition; the club president presented a modest John with a superb specimen of this short-lived cup at the annual meeting.

There was also another rival in the household. Now at a new school, University College, Jack Armstrong was making strides, bowling medium-pace like his father and often good for runs. For his brother, perhaps, this was more vexing: Jack seems to have been one of those characters who did everything with ease. Warwick had apprehended Jack's gifts as a bowler early and often harnessed him for practice on 'the paddock' adjacent to Arra Glen, but Jack had gradually grown less willing. Various deals were struck: Warwick offering his brother a penny for his services; Warwick consenting to retrieve everything he hit. When even these inducements failed after a time, their compliant sister Olivia filled in.

An improving younger brother often stimulates an elder and Jack may have stirred Warwick to the uniform excellence of his performances at Cumloden for the balance of the year. He had the advantage that his school was a full member of the Schools Association, while University College was not, and led it to that season's premiership with 5–8 against Brighton Grammar and 6–17 against Kew High School in play-offs during the first fortnight of December. But Jack was also prospering, as sportsman and scholar, winning his school's history prize that year. And the brothers would soon find themselves in direct competition: in January 1897, both enrolled at University College.

Founded in February 1895 in a two-storey building called 'Clydeford' in Sutherland Road near Armadale railway station, University College may have been recommended to the Armstrongs by fellow St Joseph's parishioner Tom Horan—his sons James and Thomas were students. Indeed, it was generally a good location for a boy aspiring to newspaper attention—the *Australasian*'s football correspondent 'Markwell', John Healy, had his boys there as well. And despite being far smaller than Cumloden, with about thirty boys under the supervision of headmaster Michael Linehan, it had a bevy of good cricketers; to the Horans, Healys and Armstrongs could be added Bert Tuckwell, a stylish batsman who later represented Victoria.

The sporting season started badly for all concerned. An inquorate Schools Association meeting in February 1897 was unable to vote on including University College in its competition. 'Old Boy' reported Linehan's frustration, and added, 'His boys, too, are most anxious to enter the lists and they have suffered a great disappointment by their exclusion.' Warwick made the best of his opportunities in invitational matches, proving endlessly damaging with the ball; against Caulfield Grammar, he spun out 10–29. But in the second half of the year, Jack caught him up. When University College routed South Melbourne College for 29, Warwick claimed 3–11, his brother 6–13. Aroused, the older boy smashed 115 with eighteen fours, but then failed against Caulfield Grammar while Jack claimed 5–28 and scored an unbeaten 71. To be stimulated to play in a competition his team could not win, Warwick Armstrong had merely to look across the breakfast table.

As schools cricket went into hiatus at the end of 1897, there was Caulfield to play for. In the summer of another English visit—a series Australia would win comfortably under his idol Trott—the eighteen-year-old Armstrong could evidently not play enough. Having begun at the club as a callow junior, he was promoted to lead its first XI, posting his first recorded century in adult competition—a landmark for any aspiring cricketer. On 12 February 1898, Caulfield faced Collingwood's Capulets, beginning the day at 3–15 chasing 134. They were soon 7–45, then 9–86. 'Batsman' in the *Sportsman* approved his coolness: 'When the wickets were falling like ninepins he stood up to 'em and, taking all the risks, banged the bowling in free and attractive style all round the wicket.' Armstrong's 104 included a 79-run last-wicket stand.

While Armstrong's cricket education was now almost complete, his personal education strangely dragged on: now in his nineteenth year, he returned to University College for the first half of 1898. It's possible the school invited him back as a so-called 'honours student'; it was not uncommon for private schools to ask a notable athlete to return for an additional year, to strengthen their sporting efforts and act as a model for younger boys. University College had at last been incorporated in the Schools Association competition, and was probably keen for a positive start; indeed, as though to redeem their meaningless year, they administered some overwhelming defeats. One, by an innings and 67 runs in a day, was over his old school Cumloden at Richmond on 18 March; Armstrong bowled unchanged through both innings to take 14–44. And, a fortnight later, there was a match that perhaps impressed itself on Armstrong's imagination.

Armstrong made 59 out of 138 as University College lost by a run to Haileybury, though the dramas were predominantly off-field. Haileybury began the day by failing to give their opponents a teamsheet: technically sufficient to cost them the game. Haileybury's umpire then gave several debatable decisions, including the lbw which won his team the match, while that official's brother was as scorer suspected of inaccuracies. Most egregiously, Haileybury's principal intruded on the ground several times in the game's closing stages to direct bowling and field changes. Though he declined to press the issue of the teamsheet and his rival principal's trespasses—'I may attribute his action to excitement'—Linehan demanded that the Schools Association audit the scores. The association's secretary did indeed detect 'clerical errors' in Haileybury's adding, but decided that the result should stand. It was Armstrong's last school game and perhaps he remembered it: he seldom hesitated in later years to dispute fine points of cricket law and conduct.

In his elongated education, Armstrong had been fortunate. Unlike his father—shortly to become George Major's partner in Major and Armstrong—and his brother Jack—who would again receive a history prize at year's end—his academic attainments appear to have been modest. Yet he had found institutions congenial to his sporting talents: gender historian Martin Crotty has identified the 1880s and 1890s as the period in which Australian public schools adopted athleticism as an important mechanism of character formation. Armstrong had also received a secular secondary education, a contingency born of circumstance, but of value nonetheless, however unquantifiable. Though a Catholic—and one who would later marry a Catholic—he seems always to have moved in Protestant circles without friction. This could not always be taken for granted in Australia at the turn of the century, where modes of sectarian discrimination remained subtle and insidious. Of the 111 members in both Houses of the first federal parliament, for instance, only five are known to have been Catholic. When Armstrong became Australian captain in September 1920, he was the first Catholic to occupy the position for thirty-four years and the last for another thirty. The Victorian and Australian teams of which he would be a part would often contain men of strong religious conviction, including several freemasons.* Yet Armstrong, like most of his fellows, seems to have regarded religion as something one did on Sundays, diverging in this sense from his family's path. John Armstrong was finally baptised at St Joseph's on 2 November 1897—rolls show him as *conversus ad fidem*, or convert to the faith—and Armstrong's sisters in time would receive denominational educations. Strength of belief, indeed, would come to cast something of a shadow over their lives.

On 22 May 1898, Armstrong turned nineteen. Although University College had links with Hawksburn, he decided to return to pennant cricket with his father's old team, South Melbourne. It was probably George Major—for the past three years a South Melbourne councillor representing the Beaconsfield ward—who brought Armstrong into the fold. But there was also another attraction: in addition to commanding Victoria and Australia, Harry Trott was the club's captain. Armstrong would have savoured the prospect of his leadership.

---

* The majority of Australian players during Armstrong's career were Anglicans, some from staunch families: Monty Noble's brother was a clergyman. Freemasons were solidly represented, including Bert Oldfield, a sidesman at his church for four decades, Charlie Macartney and Arthur Mailey, not to mention Syd Smith, long-time secretary of the Australian Board of Control. Known Methodists include Hanson Carter, Jack Ryder, Roy Park and Carl Willis, a clergyman's son; known Catholics Jack Saunders and the Carroll brothers of Victoria. Coincidentally, the prewar period's two leading cricket writers, Tom Horan of the *Australasian* and John Corbett Davis of the *Referee*, were also Catholic, as was its leading administrator, Billy McElhone of the New South Wales Cricket Association.

It wasn't, however, to work out. On 8 August, Harry Trott collapsed at his mother's Doncaster home, suffering convulsions. 'He recovered sufficiently to bear removal to his house in Albert Park,' 'Felix' reported, 'but on the way into town on the train had another attack and still another on reaching his house.' Trott was semi-conscious for some time, and five weeks elapsed before more hopeful news, 'Felix' commenting that 'at no distant date all danger will have passed', although it was 'an absolute necessity that he should have a trip into the country where he will have the benefit of…a much-needed rest.'

When a subscription was struck to fund Trott's convalescence he went to stay with Australian teammate Harry Graham in Woodend. But he remained 'troubled by insomnia', and a doctor pronounced himself 'disappointed' with Trott's condition. In coming months, Trott's condition worsened considerably, and he was committed to Kew Asylum. 'Felix' commented: 'Harry Trott will be missed by his southern comrades who had been looking forward to having a good season under his command as it seems almost impossible that he will don the flannels for some time this season, if at all.' Armstrong would have been among those most disappointed. He put his best foot forward anyway, scoring an eye-catching 101 against University in only his second match.

The next game must then have been especially satisfying: Armstrong relieved his former club St Kilda of 173, laced with twenty-one fours. A twenty-second stroke destined for the boundary struck St Kilda's skipper Charles Wilson on the knee and laid him out for the day. 'Felix' felt quietly vindicated:

> He is only nineteen years of age, stands over six feet in height, and has nothing of the lath order of build, his frame being very strong and well-proportioned for his stature […] His cutting was powerful, clean and correct, and his driving made manifest that he has strength, as well as timing skill. He pulls in capital style, and glances well, too.

Armstrong had jostled his way to the front rank, and the call of the colony's selectors Jack Blackham, Frank Laver and Jack Worrall duly came a fortnight after Christmas: on 10 January 1899, he was named to represent Victoria against Tasmania, the team leaving with its manager a fortnight later aboard the 1100-tonne *Pateena*. This selection wasn't all it seemed: Tasmania was not a Sheffield Shield contestant, and Victoria flattered it with only a second-string XII, seven of whom were playing their maiden first-class matches. This would have seemed sufficient. The

Tasmanians had six weeks earlier succumbed to New South Wales in Sydney by an innings and 487 runs. But as hosts, augmented by former Test men Charles Eady and Kenny Burn, they proved unexpectedly formidable, overpowering visitors still queasy from a rough Bass Strait crossing. Bowled by Eady for 6 in the first innings, Armstrong gave a better account of himself in the second with 33, and claimed 4–78 from twenty-seven overs.

For Armstrong, it was a first taste of the pleasures of the touring cricketer. Lodgings were at Hobart's exclusive Carlton Club. Sunday entertainments included excursions to Mount Wellington and Port Arthur, where guests were fortified by strawberries and cream, while a four-in-hand was available for a journey to Launceston. 'The sea was a millpond on the way back,' reported the *Australasian*, 'and nobody missed the herring and potato supper or breakfast.' It was a life one could get used to. Spontaneous presentations then being a popular custom, Burn was presented with a bat by Tasmania's chief justice for making a century, teammate William Ward with a silver-mounted walking stick for his 97. The match's outstanding accomplishment was Eady's; his 92, 31 and 12–129 made him only the second Australian to aggregate 100 runs and ten wickets in a match. No-one suspected he had just played against the third Australian who would achieve that feat.

Armstrong's pennant season ended firmly, inflating his final aggregate to 471 runs at 47.1, which obtained for him a prize endowed by South Melbourne's vice-president for 'outstanding batting performances in the First XI'. But his sporting business by Albert Park Lake was incomplete. Shortly, he would don the red and white tunic of its football club.

Australian Rules bears passing resemblance to other codes of football round the world but, as defined by its principal progenitor Tom Wills, it is indisputably 'a game of our own'. Its initial ten rules covered only a page and, though now far more intricate, the game still carries hints of its *laissez-faire* origins in the parklands of inner Melbourne in the early 1850s: the oval ball is kicked, punched, bounced, carried and otherwise harried toward a team's goals with few interruptions and no off-side inhibitions. The strenuousness is intentional: it drew its first players from the ranks of cricketers, exhorted to play by a letter from Wills in *Bell's Life* of July 1858 recommending its efficacy in maintaining winter fitness. Warwick Armstrong followed in an established tradition.

Armstrong had first played competitive football at Cumloden five years earlier. For an undersized boy, it must have been intimidating. The public schools game, for instance, contained no scope for reports. 'It is no uncommon occurrence,' an umpire lamented in the *Australasian*, 'to see one player in a team whose mission is to lay out the best player in the opposing team.' And the native code remained something of a free-for-all at every level, as Armstrong found on joining Caulfield Football Club, a member of the new Metropolitan Junior Football Association playing at Caulfield Park. Accounts of its matches are often spicy. 'One or two players who were annoyed at the decisions deliberately threw the ball in the umpire's face,' complained the *Caulfield and Elsternwick Leader* of a game against Brighton in June 1895. An away game at Oakleigh, which the *Malvern and Armadale Express* visited in July 1898, involved hardships familiar to any suburban footballer:

> The local cricket club had refused to allow the footballers use of their building. Under the circumstances they had to make the best of a bad job, the local boys using the pavilion steps as a 'dressing room', while the visitors availed themselves of a shed in the state school grounds which, while a bit drafty, proved a godsend when rain descended.

By this time, however, with some extra inches and pounds, Armstrong had become a senior player at Caulfield, a ruckman handy round the goalmouth, while his father had again joined the committee. And in, one suspects, stepped again the ubiquitous George Major who had just become president of South Melbourne Football Club. Armstrong was trialled in the last round of the 1898 season, doing enough to be asked back.

South was a proud club. It had won five premierships in ten seasons as part of the Victorian Football Association, and recently joined the new Victorian Football League composed of the city's premier clubs. Thus the first sizeable sporting crowds before which Armstrong performed were not for cricket but for football; it would have been a toughening experience.

Armstrong's appearance in the first round on 13 May 1899 was auspicious. Against Carlton before his home crowd, he bagged three of his team's ten goals—a harvest at a time when low scores were the norm. But he disappointed in the next two rounds, earning a reproof from

'Follower' in the *Leader*: 'I am beginning to think that Armstrong's efforts against Carlton were a flash in the pan. He has certainly done nothing since to justify the good opinion I, in common with those who saw his play, formed.' Selectors apparently agreed: he missed the ensuing seven rounds. Yet it is also possible that he was injured: if anything, the VFL was even more violent than football at lower grades. 'You were allowed to push a man from behind without penalty,' reminisced South Melbourne's legendary Peter Burns. 'Think of the golden opportunities presented! There was the opposition high mark just settling under the dropping ball when you gave him all you carried right plumb in the small of the back. The busters were indescribable.' Armstrong's club was probably as vicious as any in its methods. 'Markwell' of the *Australasian* was especially critical of South's encounter with Geelong, whose sharpshooter Ed James 'had his jumper torn off his back by an opponent, the umpire appearing all the while blind to what was going on'. At least they refrained from language as extreme as Collingwood's Dick Condon, banned for life the following year after telling an umpire: 'Your girl's a bloody whore.'

In a sense, indigenous football was still outgrowing its sprawling and unregulated origins, when games had spilled over consecutive Saturdays and were sometimes played without umpires altogether. Though rule changes by the new VFL had opened the game up somewhat, handball was still infrequent and the place kick remained the preferred form of assault on goal: on 22 June, Essendon's virtuoso Albert Thurgood sent one spiralling more than 107 yards. Play moved slowly, often in a lumpen mass, as players were not distinguished by numbered guernseys. This left time for defences to fortify and for personal scores to be settled without distraction.

Whatever the reason for Armstrong's absence, he returned to the team on 22 July against Collingwood, and became a conspicuous con-tributor. When South Melbourne visited Geelong on 5 August, Armstrong 'opened the eyes of the residents with sixty and seventy-yard [place] kicks'. The following week's bounty of five goals against St Kilda also earned commendation from 'Dropkick' in the *Sportsman*, though this was qualified by reference to the wretched opposition: 'When a team meets St Kilda these days, the only interesting point is as to how many goals will be put up against them'.

Despite a spasmodic season, South Melbourne's flag fantasies remained intact. Though sixth in the minor premiership, beaten at least once by every team bar St Kilda, the streaming of the season's last stretch into two sections still offered an avenue to honours. It transpired that on 9 September, to book a place in the grand final against all-conquering Fitzroy, Geelong needed to beat St Kilda by a huge margin, and South Melbourne needed to lose to Essendon. St Kilda was duly crushed—23.24.162 to 0.1.1—but South Melbourne won a hard-fought victory despite playing a man short. Armstrong, as the *Argus* saw it, 'marked and kicked well' and was also 'using his weight'. In all sorts of ways, this would become an Armstrong characteristic.

The VFL grand final a century ago was a far cry from the watch-stopping, nation-diverting mass entertainment it has become. The game was not even at the Melbourne Cricket Ground—where cricket-pitch preparation took precedence—but at St Kilda. A flavour of the event can be adduced from the *Argus* advertisement of 15 September:

GREAT FINAL MATCH FOR PREMIERSHIP
FITZROY V SOUTH MELBOURNE
ST KILDA CRICKET GROUND
TOMORROW 3PM
Ground 6d, Stand 1/- extra
Come early
Bring exact change

The 4823 crowd was not a patch on crowds of today. The same was true of the spectacle. It had been a consistently wet season, but conditions this Saturday were so poor that South proposed postponing the game. In the end, the wind was so strong that all six of the game's goals were scored at the city end. Advantaged in the first quarter, South Melbourne opened a fourteen-point lead, but trailed by a point at the half. Though Armstrong's team led at the last change, a Fitzroy goal after fifteen minutes of the final quarter ultimately guaranteed them the narrowest of victories, and it proved Armstrong's only chance for winter distinction. The following season he would play only thrice, for four goals. Signs are that he was turning into a first-rate player. Of his last appearance against Melbourne, on 4 August 1900, 'Markwell' said: 'I doubt that Armstrong has ever shown better form than in this match.' But by then cricket beckoned. Though his retirement from football was never formally announced, its cause is not hard to guess. Even as late as the 1970s exceptional individuals remained capable of excellence in both football and cricket, but the ranks of sporting all-rounders were already thinning: of Armstrong's football comrades, only wingman Herb Howson also played interstate cricket, and that but once against Tasmania in January 1903. While football had been invented for cricketers, Armstrong's decision to renounce one in favour of the other manifested the flowering of both games, and their increased specialisation and divergence.

Football nonetheless probably left its mark on Armstrong, through the experience of big crowds, and big men, at close quarters. He never again remotely resembled a 'loose jointed lad in knicker bockers' who 'became shy when the onlookers laughed at him'; in the South Melbourne line-up before the 1899 Grand Final, his comportment is confident, his smile laconic. Likewise in a photograph of the first Sheffield Shield team of which he was part two months later, he stands at the back smoking, the image of insouciance even among Test men like Hugh Trumble, Harry Graham and Billy Bruce. He had endured, even excelled, in one of the world's most gruelling games; broaching big cricket on 24 January 1900, when he represented Victoria against New South Wales for the first time, was perhaps less challenging as a result.

Few cricket rivalries were as intense as that between Victoria and New South Wales. Sixty-three prior encounters over forty-four years had generated an unending sequence of incidents, including run-outs of batsmen at the bowler's end, bowlers accused of and no-balled for throwing, and even a riot. Seldom had the rivals fielded teams so swollen with talent as on this occasion: seventeen past and future internationals featured in this Sydney game, in which Australia's premier all-rounder Monty Noble made a chanceless 155 and took 9–157. Yet twenty-year-old Armstrong, whom umpire Bob Crockett recalled as a 'long thin young streak', did not appear misplaced. He bowled the hosts' captain Syd Gregory with his second delivery, and the *Sydney Morning Herald* judged him a tricky customer: 'Armstrong gave the batsmen a lot of trouble. He breaks from both sides, and now and then gets in a fast ball.' His second-innings 45 in an hour and a half impressed Australian opening batsman Frank Iredale, who in the *Australasian* judged him 'a welcome addition to the ranks of first-class batsmen in Australia'. And the match most influential in Armstrong's destiny was shortly to come.

Days after returning home, Armstrong represented South Melbourne against Melbourne, grandest club in the land. Most of its best, including Trumble, had just embarked on a tour of New Zealand, but Melbourne's captain Bruce had drafted a serviceable XI. Armstrong destroyed them almost on his own. In his first thirty deliveries, he took two wickets without grudging a run; in an hour and a half, he smothered his opponents for 141 with 6–19. The *Sportsman*'s 'Batsman' found Melbourne's men demoralised—'The feeling amongst them seemed to be that after their feeble display they had nothing to look forward to'—and they weren't mistaken. In the remaining three hours, Armstrong clattered an undefeated 133 with fifteen boundaries. After a further sixteen fours the following week, his 270 had underwritten a 468-run victory.

Armstrong's pennant record for the season assumed proportions impossible to ignore—665 runs at 95 plus a dozen cheap wickets—and he had in fact brought his South Melbourne career to a close. On the receiving end once, Melbourne had no wish to suffer again. No official record exists of his recruitment, although Bruce, who also sat on the club's committee seems its likeliest instrument. Occupant of the nation's foremost sporting arena, the Melbourne Cricket Ground, the club always wanted the best. Armstrong it perceived among them.

3

'I Do Hope My Boy
Makes a Hundred'

'It is a great pity that so many good players should leave the leading suburban clubs,' wrote 'Mid On' of the *Leader*, Harry Hedley, of Warwick Armstrong's defection from South Melbourne, 'but who can blame them?' Who indeed? By joining the sixty-year-old Melbourne Cricket Club Armstrong became part of the country's most prosperous and prestigious sporting institution, described by Australia's captain Joe Darling as 'the Marylebone of Australia'. Its influence now stretched far beyond cricket; it had lain the colony's first asphalt tennis court in 1878, absorbed the Melbourne Football Club in 1889 and the Richmond Bowling Club in 1894, and established its own lacrosse team in 1896. The year Armstrong arrived, it added a rifle club, which proved so popular that it subsequently opened its own miniature range.

At the turn of the century, indeed, the club was full to bursting at its constituted limit of 2500 members, but Armstrong entered under an eighteen-month-old dispensation permitting the committee to open the ballot 'to players of established repute in all sports affiliated with the club'. He was admitted on 18 June 1900 along with two lacrosse players. Having paid his £3 3s entrance fee and £2 2s annual subscription, Armstrong would have grown more conscious of his good fortune. Membership was a *passe-partout* to Melbourne's social, political, judicial and mercantile elite, encompassing in the next fifteen years three consecutive state premiers and successive prime ministers; it was, as *Melbourne Punch* put it, 'accepted as a certificate of good citizenship more even than of good fellowship'. But then, as a cricketer, Armstrong enjoyed within the club a status himself. Cricket had brought it into being and remained its chief source of pride. By sheer affluence and energy, Melbourne had established itself as Australia's paramount cricket authority, funding the visits of English teams to the colonies, and underwriting the journeys of Australian teams to England. The *Australasian Star* described its plenipotent secretary Major Ben Wardill as 'an international institution'. Stocky, upright, he had the air of a riverboat gambler and a neatly trimmed Mark Twain moustache. Although his smart new Ludstone Chambers secretariat at 352 Collins Street had a telephone line—number 278—he ran the club's affairs by post, reaming off about twenty letters a day, all briskly handwritten. Not until January 1906 would the club rent its first typewriter.

For the cricketer this was an *entrepôt* of skill and know-how. Nets were in operation at the Melbourne Cricket Ground all day for members' convenience, with a staff of professional bowlers in attendance. Among those who enjoyed an afternoon hit was impresario J. C. Williamson, who would 'don immaculate flannels' and drag his secretary Ashton along. On their first visit, apparently, Ashton had the temerity to bowl his boss first ball.

> Mr Williamson surveyed the wreck furiously indignant and, turning to the perpetrator of it, said, 'Ashton, did you finish the letters before you left?' 'No sir,' was the response. 'Well,' returned the irate manager, 'you will be good enough to return to the office immediately, sir.' So Ashton had to go; and not until he had pasted a more diplomatic ground bowler all over the shop was the great man's good humour restored. After that Ashton used to send them down well wide of off stump.

Around 5 p.m., more serious stuff commenced. 'In the Melbourne nets alone,' reported 'Felix', 'there are on a brilliant summer evening sometimes 100 players hard at it.' Wardill actually dispensed with the club's coach Charlie Lawrence in October 1900—the famous Surrey émigré was approaching his seventy-second birthday—but that had no measurable impact on the quality of its practices. Who could not learn of the game from playing with such eminences as Billy Bruce, Hugh Trumble, Harry Graham, Alfred Johns, Charlie McLeod, and even a rising star like Warwick Armstrong? Daniel Reese, a young batsman from New Zealand, recalled their companionship as 'a feast to my cricketing mind'.

> The evening practices on the Melbourne Ground were something of a revelation to me, as also were the long nets extending to the bowling crease with netting over head at the batsman's end…There were six nets altogether, with a professional bowler at each; the ground staff, except for the head groundsman, were all cricketers, and part of their work was to bowl at the nets in the evenings. Ten minutes batting, with two bowlers, sometimes three, and no lost time chasing balls, gave the best practice possible. One sometimes hears of Australians and New Zealanders referred to as 'Saturday afternoon cricketers' with little big cricket; but energetic practice, such as was available at Melbourne three or four nights a week, often gave players more batting than some county cricketers would get in matches in England.

At any time, while the light on a summer's eve remained, one might see half an Australian XI at play. There'd be the little left-hander Bruce, with his feather-light bat, rehearsing his repertoire of dabs, glides and glances. There'd be the light-hearted but long-headed Trumble, purveying his off breaks or practising his slip fielding by bouncing a tennis ball off a wall; he maintained that, as a pressurised ball bounced from hard hands, this overcame the instinct to snatch. There'd be keeper Johns confiding some aspect of cricket lore to eager ears, like that he gave his understudy Elliott Monfries: 'We're very pleased, Monfries, with your wicketkeeping, but you've got one bad fault you can easily remedy. You're too gentle on umpires. When you appeal, shout like crimson hell.' And there'd be Warwick Armstrong, who spent most sessions in testudinal defence before, as Reese recalled, concluding with a flourish:

> At the end of practice at the nets, Armstrong always finished by opening out and having a few hits, when it was positively dangerous to bowl to him, for the power of his straight drive was tremendous. A half volley would come back like a cannon ball, and I have seen bowlers deliver the ball from a few yards behind the crease in order to have time to get out of the way!

Armstrong's Melbourne career began with consecutive fixtures against his two old clubs, South Melbourne and St Kilda; he amply demonstrated what they had lost with 45 and 109. In the season's opening

Sheffield Shield fixture against South Australia, his fifth first-class match, he pocketed his maiden first-class hundred, and a noteworthy one at that. With Victoria an insecure 5–155 chasing 267, Armstrong turned back the formidable Ernie Jones and George Giffen with calculated aggression:

> Jones on the South Australian side was a terror to many players, and at the beginning of their innings Victoria would invariably lose one or two wickets quickly. I remember one match where several wickets had fallen, the tall Warwick went to the wicket and changed the whole position. Against fast bowling, he had the necessary knack of holding a firm grip and not taking the bat too far back. He would, at times, play forward firmly to Jones, and the ball seemed to fly to the boundary with the speed of a swinging off-drive.

Daniel Reese's recollection is notable for the detail it offers on Armstrong's method, in particular his brevity of backlift. Though genuinely fast bowlers were relatively few at the turn of the century, Armstrong had already surmised that shortening his downswing was prudent. Jones, a burly Broken Hill miner, knew no variety but flat out; Armstrong, with 118 in 165 minutes, harnessed that aggression to his own ends. Further solid scores followed. He still resembled a big, awkward boy—long legs, capacious boots, adolescent cowlick contained by the tight-fitting Victorian cap. Harry Graham nicknamed him 'Razor', doubtless for his sharpness, though perhaps also for his downy upper lip. Nonetheless, he never failed to impress. Much later, G. C. Dixon of the *Herald* would recall the words of 'an old international' while watching 'a young giant at the wickets':

> The batsman was not stylish. He had a rather ungainly stance, as so many big men have; he was heavy-footed and awkward, and he frequently appeared to be in difficulties. But he never made a serious mistake, he watched the ball so carefully that his defence was almost impregnable, and when he did hit, which was seldom, the ball struck the pickets with a rattle that told of the tremendous power in those wide shoulders. 'Say what you like,' said the old international, 'but that young fellow is going to be a champion.'...That young fellow's name, as you may already have guessed, was Warwick W. Armstrong.

Victoria's highest scorer in a season of Sheffield Shield triumph, Armstrong was by season's end an indispensable member of the side. 'Young Armstrong, who is modest and gentlemanly, never puffed up by success, should have a great cricket career before him,' forecast 'Mid On'. 'At the present moment, I know of no "coming" player with a better prospect of having to get his portmanteau labelled "passenger to England".'

Like all other aspects of life at this zenith of empire, the cricket season was interrupted by the death of Queen Victoria on 22 January 1901. Though her interest in the game had been minimal, cricket joined the communal mourning. The Saturday of Armstrong's Sheffield Shield match against New South Wales in Sydney was cancelled as a mark of respect; players everywhere wore black armbands.

Melbourne, however, was still buoyed by imperial and federal spirit. On 9 May, the new federal parliament convened there for the first time. A huge illuminated crown crested Spencer Street railway station where the Duke and Duchess of Cornwall and York detrained, and temporary grandstands were erected along their processional route. Newcomer Reese was taken with the signs of salutation, 'Welcome to George and Mary': typical, he decided, of 'the colonials' affectionate familiarity'.

In opening proceedings, the Duke inspired cheers of support in describing the 'splendid bravery' of the 16,000 Australian servicemen under arms in South Africa. The Boer War had been a timely reassertion of Anglo-Australian kinship, strained during the 1890s by post-Land Boom disinvestment, and Australians basked in the golden opinions of their fighting men. The times called for an English cricket tour, on which Ben Wardill was at work. Though the Marylebone Cricket Club informed him on 13 May that it would be 'impossible' to raise a team, Melbourne's secretary successfully enjoined the leading English amateur Archie MacLaren to assemble a touring party.

Though Australia held the Ashes by dint of a single victory in the 1899 series in England, success or failure could easily be influenced by sudden retirements and unavailabilities. Indeed, there was doubt for a time over the future of Australia's captain, South Australian Joe Darling. He had foreshadowed retirement after his last visit to England 'in fairness to my wife and children' and was now farming in Tasmania. He advised Wardill that he would be involved in shearing until 30 November 1901, and accordingly be unable to play cricket before the First Test in Sydney a fortnight later. In the event, he was accommodated.

Nonetheless, Australia was unexpectedly mauled by an innings and 124 runs.

Luck interposes in the making of every sporting career, and when Armstrong represented Victoria against New South Wales at the MCG soon after, he enjoyed a lavish ration. Leslie Poidevin, Australia's twelfth man during the First Test and the junior next in line for promotion, had broken his right index finger at a fielding practice and been scratched from the game. Then, just before lunch on the first day, Victoria's captain Jack Worrall tossed Armstrong the ball. Having to this time taken only five Sheffield Shield wickets, he suddenly claimed two choice ones: Victor Trumper and Charles Gregory.

When Armstrong took block not quite a day later, Victoria was ailing at 3–39 in pursuit of 221. At 8, he was offered a full toss by the apprentice leg-spinner Gother Clarke which he hit straight back. It was dropped. It was neither the last full toss from Clarke, who had a frightful day, nor the last missed chance; Armstrong disposed unfailingly of the former, and coolly shrugged off the latter. His 137 in four and a half hours was a Victorian record against New South Wales, and critics applauded the whole rather than contemplating the parts. When Noble and Trumble met Darling afterwards to select the XI for the Second Test, 'Observer' of the *Argus* was convinced that Armstrong's name should be uppermost:

> He has stepped from junior ranks into the first flight of club cricketers. He had a trial in a big match, he succeeded at once, and has gone on— always upward. He seems to be one of those cricketers rather born in the game than trained to it. He will go on the next Australian tour of England and come back a great cricketer, both in form and physique.

When it did come, Armstrong's Test selection was overshadowed by an altogether unexpected choice: twenty-three-year-old New South Welshman Reg Duff, with a solitary century in thirteen prior first-class matches. 'Felix' painted an enchanting picture of his call-up:

> On the night of Monday, Bob McLeod, Syd Gregory and Reg Duff were walking down Collins Street near the Town Hall. 'I wonder,' said Syd, 'am I in the team?' 'I'll go up to the *Argus* office and see,' said Bob. Up he went, got the information, and was himself staggered that Duff was in. Turning to Syd, he said: 'You're in, Syd.' Then turning to Duff: 'And so are you

Duff.' Duff looked fixedly at Bob and replied with the most forceful contradiction he could frame. But he was in.

Duff's 'forceful contradiction' is not surprising. Its Sydney defeat notwithstanding, this was a first-rate Australian side: Armstrong would class it the best in which he played. Thirty-one-year-old Darling, a punitive left-hander with a boxer's physique and a rolling gait, ran the team with brusque confidence: in the last home series, he had scored a record three centuries, including what remains the fastest by an Australian in Tests against England. His deputy Trumble, veteran already of four tours of England, bowled brisk off-breaks with a fly fisherman's patience: only Dennis Lillee among Australians has taken more English wickets. Noble, a painstaking batsman and bowler of waspish medium pace, provided all-round stiffening: no Australian has overtaken so quickly the Test 'double' 1000 runs and 100 wickets. In Clem Hill and Victor Trumper, both in their early twenties, the team coupled the two defining Australian batsmen of their generation. South Australian Hill, according to Englishman Bobby Abel, was 'the fastest man on his feet I have ever seen'. New South Welshman Trumper, wrote another English contemporary Charles Fry, had 'two strokes for every ball', and gave always 'the impression of generous abandon'. Into this company, Armstrong had now made an intrepid stride.

His initiation would be stern. On New Year's Eve 1901, it rained plenteously over Melbourne. Storm clouds that had banked up all day finally burst at about 5 p.m. 'I have never seen hail like it in my life,' recalled Reese. 'Hailstones the size of bantams' eggs broke almost all the skylights in Melbourne, as well as the glass-roofed verandahs.' Nineteen hundred and two then dawned fine and sunny. In an era when pitches were unprotected from the elements, this concatenation of circumstances filled cricketers with foreboding.

Today, when covers are fetched at the first hint of mist, the nature of cricket on uncovered pitches is hard to comprehend. It is actually easy to exaggerate. Batsmen did not bat on trails of mud every day of the week. On the contrary, as we shall see, conditions at the turn of the century generally favoured batsmen—it is merely that weather sometimes permitted bowlers to exact a retaliatory toll. Nonetheless, the Australian 'sticky dog' was especially treacherous, the sun tending to bake the top while leaving the sub-soil damp beneath, causing some balls to stop, some to soar. And, for batsmen, such conditions were held to be the supreme challenge. 'Such words as "dangerous", when applied to wickets, imply a normal man not of unique eyesight or acrobatic celerity,' wrote the English batsman Albert Knight in his *The Complete Cricketer.* 'They have no meaning to the genius who cuts from his eyebrows.' For skippers, too, they involved a complex set of simultaneous equations, with an eye on the pitch, the sky, the clock and the rival captain, the object being to maximise one's bowling time against the opposition's best batsmen, and to shelter one's own important wickets. This might involve reversing an order, or even instructing batsmen to get out, declarations not being permitted on the first two days of a first-class match. Armstrong's first Test would be a classic of the genre.

When Darling called incorrectly, Australia commenced its innings at noon, and by 2.52 p.m. had been bustled out for 112; Armstrong, preserved until the fall of the seventh wicket, scavenged 4 not out. England's reply began at 3.10 p.m., shortly sagging to 5–36. Spectators dared not avert their eyes. 'Felix' captured their rapt attention: 'An invalid colonel from India is in the Ladies' Reserve and, in the full height of that brilliant scene on New Year's Day, he glanced around and exclaimed: "Thank God there's such a game as cricket." And so say all of us.' MacLaren instructed his remaining batsmen to slog, hoping to expedite Australia's second innings, which he did by 4.16 p.m. Although they led by 51, Darling's team faced an anxious vigil before stumps, the captain being especially perturbed:

> The crowd was jubilant but I well remember saying to Trumble that unless we could kill time and have some good batsmen left for the next day we were beaten, as England was certain to have a good wicket to bat on…Knowing what a determined batsman Trumble was—he was a far better batsman than most people thought—I took him in first with me to try and kill time and not trouble making runs.

Australia's *ersatz* openers were not separated until 5.40 p.m. and, though four further casualties were sustained that evening, honours were essentially shared on a day twenty-five wickets had tumbled for 221 runs. Darling had rightly foreseen easier batting conditions ahead—after cutting and rolling on the second morning, the *Age* reported, 'the conditions were as opposite as possible to those of the opening day'—but his reconfiguring of Australia's order meant that Armstrong in his second Test innings batted last. There remained much to do—Australia's 284-run advantage still appeared slight on a surface improving by the over.

Chance paired the team's two colts, both playing their second Test innings; Duff was already 29. Curiously, chance also paired their fathers, as 'Felix's' all-seeing eye detected:

> The veteran South Melbourne player George Major is seated under the elm and tells me that Warwick Armstrong's father was in the MCC reserve. Sitting next to him was a stoutish man, who said: 'I do hope my boy makes a hundred.'
> Mr Armstrong said: 'Who's your boy?'
> And the friend replied: 'Duff.'

For the next hour and a quarter, England stood a delivery away from the commencement of its fourth-innings chase. MacLaren had three fine bowlers at his disposal: leg-spinner Len Braund from Somerset, left-armer Charlie Blythe from Kent, and Sydney Barnes, a maven of medium-pace already responsible for nineteen wickets in the series. They toiled in vain. Often a vivid strokemaker, Duff was discretion itself, Armstrong even more discriminating. 'Felix' imagined him thinking: 'Now then Warwick, you are battling for a place in the Australian team for England. Don't take any risks, play the game and beware of Braund's leg-trap. Never mind if the runs come slowly, your business is to stay there.' Every run met with applause, the 300th with a unanimous roar, and time was called with their partnership worth 67, the New South Welshman on 71, the Victorian 25. Not until 1.15 p.m. on the third day were the pair parted, by which time Duff had gathered 104 in almost three and a half hours, Armstrong an unconquered 48 in almost two and a half, and their partnership had swollen to 120.

Further overnight rain delayed play on the fourth day until after lunch, with England 5–147, but only thirty-four minutes were needed thereafter to prosecute Australia's 299-run victory. In the unlikely guise of a last man, during one of the greatest of Test matches, Armstrong had secured an Australian place he would lose only once in the next two decades. It may be, too, that the occasion rubbed off on him as much as he on it. Of the players involved, only Armstrong would survive into the era of wicket protection. He deplored it—'the last thing management thinks of is cricket, the first thing is the gate'—and despised the doped wickets on which pampered batsmen piled huge scores in the 1920s and 1930s. One suspects he was harking back to his Test baptism: ideas he would hold to for a lifetime were already then being formed.

After victory in the Third Test, Darling returned to his sheep property. The three selectors—now Trumble, Noble and Hill—rotated a number of players, mindful of Australia's impending tour of England: Jack Saunders, Albert Hopkins, Charles Eady, Joe Travers. When he left Melbourne for Sydney on 10 February, umpire Bob Crockett recalled, there was some doubt of Armstrong's position in the starting XI for the Fourth Test:

> An umpire is often an unofficial adviser off the field and one day a selector came and asked my opinion of the inclusion of Saunders and Armstrong. I had a high opinion of both men and strongly advised that they be played…Both were put in and Australia had reason to be glad of the selectors' decision.

Saunders took 9–122, Armstrong batted two hours for a crucial 55, coming in at 5–119 with Australia pursuing 317, and sharing vital partnerships with Noble and Hopkins. English amateur Arthur Jones described this new cricketer for his countrymen in the *Pall Mall Gazette*: 'Armstrong again showed that he is a player with a head. When he was in with Noble, he followed the lead set by his partner, and was content to stay there with a view to wearing the edge off the bowling, but with the advent of Hopkins he forced the game.'

Armstrong finished his first four Tests as a minor-key triumph—narrowly at the head of Australia's averages, with 159 runs at 53—and was rewarded with the English trip 'Mid On' had foretold. He was among the first ten names released on 18 February; the squad was completed with the announcement of another four on 4 March.

Inevitably, the eve of an Australian trip to England was the pretext for outpourings of imperial sentiment. Tours were routinely referred to as 'going home', a pilgrimage to the centre of the race and culture of which Australia was indivisibly a part. Even Victoria's English governor, Sir George Clarke, admitted to feelings of dual nationhood, commenting at the Melbourne Cricket Club's farewell dinner for MacLaren's men: 'If our team wins we say: "Hurrah we win." If it loses we say: "Bravo our brothers under the Southern Cross (loud cheers)." Whether fighting Boers in South Africa, or playing cricket in Australia, the mother country is proud of Australia.'

England in 1902 held an unusual lustre, too, by virtue of the forthcoming coronation of Edward VII; the Australian entourage would include a number of imperial pilgrims, including Sir Edwin Smith of the

South Australian Cricket Association, Sydney Cricket Ground trustee Syd Fairland and Melbourne Cricket Club committeeman Thomas Morkham, also Victoria's Secretary of Lands. Manager Wardill, Darling, Gregory and keeper Jim Kelly were taking their wives and Trumble was making the trip his honeymoon, while unlucky Leslie Poidevin was venturing to Manchester's Victoria University to pursue his medical studies. The second time Warwick Armstrong put to sea, he was rather more comfortable than the first; the 5400-tonne Orient liner *Omrah* was four times the size of the little *Pateena* that had freighted him across Bass Strait three years earlier.

The Australians were accompanied on the *Omrah* by MacLaren's team, completing their round trip. A spirit of cricketing brotherhood prevailed. On-field rivalries were forgotten, shared Britishness celebrated, in rounds of bull board and deck billiards. MacLaren, whose wife was from Melbourne, told the Australians about the yearlings he had just acquired at the Newmarket sales. Darling, whose ancestry was Scottish, was teased by colleagues about his old pair of tweed trousers. Two teams of cricketers were, in differing senses, on their way 'home'.

4

'Strictly on Business Lines'

The cricket era in which Warwick Armstrong rose to prominence has been described as the Golden Age, usually dated as dawning with the 1894–95 Ashes series and concluding at the outbreak of the Great War. Seldom in its history has the game ridden so high in public opinion, and in its own. As Archdeacon William Sinclair—'an enthusiast for robust sport'—wrote in 1900:

> Its influence is not merely in correct eye, sinewy muscle, vigorous nerve, activity of motion, or the encouragement of outdoor life. All that is important, and has very materially helped for a hundred years to improve the race, and produce generations of men of whom any country might well be proud. But cricket has a wholesome effect on character as well. Coolness of judgment, good temper, patience, reserve and courage are not only qualities which are of use to the really able and successful cricketers, but they are qualities also which long training in this greatest of games tends to produce.

The age's goldenness has historically tended to radiate from England, or to be more precise, in retrospective contemplation of what Neville Cardus called 'hot days in an England of forgotten peace and plenty'. Even at the time, historian Brian Dobbs contends, the era had nostalgic qualities, an 'artificial enjoyment by proxy of a long lost rural England populated by kindly squires and humble swains with rough exteriors but hearts of gold'. In Australia, the period had a different burnish.

Cricket's resonances as 'the English game' need little elaboration. Australians believed in Henry Parkes's 'crimson thread of kinship', still used British currency and postage, and venerated British institutions. They worried at times about their lack of sophistication and polish, and fretted to hear Englishmen speak as Willoughby in Joseph Furphy's *Such Is Life:* 'Even in your cities I observe a feverish excitement, and a damnable race for what the Scriptures aptly call "filthy lucre". Your colonies are too young…Cultivated leisure is a thing practically unknown.' Playing cricket soothed such anxieties. Yet cricket was capable of serving national as well as imperial ends. Long before federation Australians had fielded XIs beneath a united banner. On their pathfinding trip to England in 1878, at a time when 'Australia' was a geographic rather than a political expression, Dave Gregory's team had promoted themselves as 'a representative Australian side' and borne canvas bags bearing the legend 'Australian Eleven'. It would become a common claim that cricket success had expedited the push for nation-hood: the *Bulletin* toasted the triumph of Harry Trott's men in 1897–98 as doing 'more to enhance the cause of Australian nationality than could be achieved by miles of erudite essays and impassioned appeal', While Trott himself was a member of the Albert Park branch of the Australian Natives Association. 'Felix' proclaimed in the *Australasian* that cricket had 'done much, very much, for Federation', Monty Noble in *Cricket* that it had 'done much to draw the colonies very much closer together'.

It is certainly no coincidence that many of those who had fostered the nation's birth had strong cricket connections. The first prime minister, Edmund Barton, was a former vice-president of the New South Wales Cricket Association, future prime minister George Reid its current president, South Australian premier Charles Kingston a vice-president of his state's association. In Melbourne, the links were especially robust: Australia's first treasurer Sir George Turner was president of St Kilda Cricket Club, Melbourne's federal member Sir Malcolm McEacharn president of East Melbourne Cricket Club, and three consecutive state premiers Alexander Peacock, William Irvine and Thomas Bent members of the Melbourne Cricket Club. Alfred Deakin might have had no interest in the game but in February 1904 it gave him a famous metaphor for the absurdity of factional politics: 'What a game of cricket you would have if there were three elevens sometimes playing on one side, sometimes on the other, and sometimes for itself.'

Cricket, too, was white, in a region of the world which beyond Australia's shores was not. Sporting success allowed the country to parade both its purity and the necessity of its protection from racial contaminants. Mat Ellis, a Victorian teammate of Warwick's, related to Sydney's *Sun* how he explained the tenets of the White Australia policy to a couple of curious English cricketers:

> Thinking to divert their thoughts into other channels, he [Ellis] dragged them into the waxworks, and pushed them along to the chamber of horrors, where he gave details of each gruesome murder. But white Australia would obtrude itself, for they came to a group in which a Chinese was shown in the act of murdering two white children. 'There,' said Mat, 'that shows you the need for a white Australia.'
>
> 'Too awful,' exclaimed one Englishman, 'too awful'. Then he lost control of himself and grabbing hold of the wax figure he shook it vigorously until its head fell off. 'That's even too good for you!' he screamed. 'What you need is this!' And he kicked the Chinaman and broke him. That one kick cost £25.

Such attitudes now seem antediluvian and, if we were to take a snapshot of Australian cricket in 1902, we might think the same of its manners and mores. Games were both fewer, the Sheffield Shield involving only six matches, and longer, Test and first-class fixtures being played to a finish; no captain had declared, draws were unknown. The five-ball over had disappeared only recently: Armstrong's inaugural first-class match in January 1899 was actually the last in which they were used. Five was still awarded for a hit over the ropes on the full: Armstrong would play in the first Australian match in which six was awarded for such a blow, at Adelaide in November 1905. Scoring was faster, and innings were shorter: on only three occasions in a twenty-year Test career would Armstrong see a batsman bat longer than six hours.

Even the equipment Armstrong and his contemporaries used seems antique. Pads were of open-slatted cane, batting gloves usually open-palmed, and sometimes scorned altogether. Balls were larger than today, their 24 centimetres in circumference being reduced to 22.9 in 1927. Bats were generally lighter, stumps slightly smaller and sightboards still not in general use. Some customs appear especially quaint. Where today the application of any 'substance' to the cricket ball is taboo, Australian cricketers openly applied powdered resin to their fingers to make grip-ping the ball easier. When Englishmen complained, Noble sniffed: 'If they don't use it, they are very foolish. The objection is a very trivial one.' Not until October 1931 would the use of resin be forbidden.

In other respects, however, Australian cricket was close to fully formed. After decades in which the cross bat had been viewed as an offence against nature, the full repertoire of strokes was in use. Noble recalled his career's beginnings in 1894–95 as a time when cricket was 'languishing under the spell of orthodoxy and passive resistance which were fast throttling the people's appreciation of the game', and con-trasted it with the glories that then unfolded:

> When I first wielded a bat it was considered distinctly bad cricket to pull to the on-side, where there were no fieldsmen, a ball pitched outside the off-stump or on the wicket. It had, forsooth, to be played in the regular and approved manner either straight or to the off-side where there were nine and often ten obliging fielders waiting to gather it in. The batsman was supposed to wait until the bowler lost his accuracy and direction and at length pitched one outside the leg stump before it was polite to dispatch it for four to where no fieldman lurked.
>
>   I can remember how a few bold spirits in Australia defied convention and, caring little whether it was considered good or bad play, provided the score was increased, developed the stroke which proved so prolific from a run-getting point of view. Soon their methods were adopted by others and in a few years the stroke outgrew all prejudice.

The popularisation of the pull and hook, strokes that became Australian trademarks, he ascribed to Trumper and Hill. Trumper's first coach had implored him constantly: 'Leave it alone, Vic; that wasn't a ball to go at.' Hill had been threatened with omission from his school XI if he ever essayed a pull. But their huge scores—Trumper an unbeaten 300 in England, Hill a towering 365 in Australia—had demonstrated that enterprise need not entail unsoundness.

A precondition of venturesome strokeplay, of course, is reliable turf underfoot, and here perhaps was the greatest advance. Hard, grassy and true Merri Creek soil had been in use at the Melbourne Cricket Ground since about April 1880, while the subsequent employment of Bulli soil at the Sydney Cricket Ground and Atherstone soil at Adelaide Oval led to surfaces of such adamantine hardness that timeless matches could easily span a week. Bulli especially, introduced to Sydney's wicket table in February 1895, was a marvel of the age. It was fast, bounced evenly, and made batting a joy. Archie MacLaren observed: 'You've only got to stick your tongue out and it's a four.' Taking guard, observed his English contemporary Reginald Foster, was an art in itself: 'It is impossible to make a block hole. You either scratch the ground with your boot sprigs or ruffle it.' It had the added benefit of minimal porosity—a critical quality when pitches were exposed to the elements. 'You can't pluck blades of grass from an Australian pitch,' commented South African Ernie Vogler, 'but you can scratch it.'

For bowlers consequently, except where weather interposed, the game could be gruelling. Exasperated by another pitch of polished perfection, Hugh Trumble once exclaimed: 'Cricket in this country is a black man's game.' Yet Trumble was perhaps the foremost example of a bowler who made a virtue of necessity, cogitating endlessly on batsmen's weaknesses, and experimenting with a widening variety of deliveries. This, Arthur Jones observed in the *Pall Mall Gazette,* was an Australian characteristic as evolved as pulling and hooking:

> The Australian is far ahead of us in bowling. Why is it? Because on the perfect wickets out here it would be impossible for him to get any batsman out unless he made the ball do something. Watch an Australian bowler: he is always doing something to the ball with his fingers, and never bowls a ball down unless he has some object in view.

Fielding was also improving. Throwing had long been an Australian strength; as England's *Cricket of Today* put it: 'We are constantly having quoted to us the case of the earlier Australian XIs to this country, with their machine-like quality of fielding the ball and returning it to the wicket in one movement.' With the rise of baseball as the preferred winter sport of cricketers, including Trumper, Noble, Duff, Jim Kelly and Frank Laver, it had improved further still: at Sydney's Federation Carnival on 4 January 1901, Trumper had won a competition with a throw of 110.2 metres. Catching, too, was increasingly reliable, sometimes scaling heights of unprecedented brilliance. Hill could boast at the end of his career of having dropped only three catches; enjoying *Jack and the Beanstalk* one evening at the Adelaide Royal, he even caught a shoe that flew from the foot of leading lady Sybil Arundell (Hill returned it to the stage where it was 'neatly taken by one of the company'). Stopping, intercepting and retrieving were being recognised as skills in themselves. In Syd Gregory, Australia had a cover-point considered the best of all time: small, mobile and fearless. Once, when Gregory was on patrol against Yorkshire, a batsman who had played a string of fruitless cover drives remarked admiringly: 'Yon booy could feald a cannon baal.'

Above all, while the tug of empire remained strong, there was emerging a sense of playing cricket as 'Australians' rather than as transplanted Englishmen. Almost four in five Australians were now native-born, and Armstrong would play Tests with only one man not—the 1902 team's deputy keeper Hanson Carter, born in Halifax, Yorkshire. Although tours of England would be described as 'going home' for many years, the sense was purely figurative: the fluidity of national allegiances in Test cricket's first two decades, when several players had represented both countries, was at an end.*

This nativism was reflected in the national cricketing uniform. The 1899 team was the first to adopt the motley of 'sage green and gold', hoisting a flag in these colours above their London headquarters at Holborn's Inns of Court Hotel. The Australian cap and blazer were becoming ornaments of value, the likes of Victor Trumper clinging to theirs proudly. 'Trumper always wore an old Australian XI cap,' reminisced Clem Hill. 'It was bottle green, but nevertheless he stuck to it to the end, and there was no end of bother if Duff or some of the other humourists of the side got hold of the cap and hid it.' The caparison, moreover, was for Australian players alone, as a letter of Ben Wardill reminded Frank Laver:

> A man I don't know called on me just now and wanted to know where he could get the Australian XI uniform and colours for a friend of his in Montevideo (South America). I told him he couldn't get them, he was not entitled to wear them. He has been in South America for 8 years, is not even a member of any Australasian club, and his friend thought he could wear them to show off his loyalty to Australia!!!

Australians already had a reputation for competitiveness, even dourness. A visitor from the *Strand* on Darling's 1899 team had found

---

* In the absence of strict rules of qualification, five Australians also represented England between 1877 and 1899: Billy Midwinter, Billy Murdoch, Jack Ferris, Sammy Woods and Albert Trott. Trott, recruited by Middlesex after failing to make brother Harry's 1896 Australian team, was the last, appearing twice for England against South Africa in February and April 1899.

them welcoming but earnest: he could 'conscientiously recommend a breakfast with the Australians as a first-rate recipe to anyone afflicted with an attack of the blues', but perceived the 'serious spirit' of their quest for victory where 'anything likely to interfere with their attaining that result is to be rigidly eschewed'. Even a batsman of such *brio* as Trumper believed unstintingly in the superiority of timeless cricket: 'Limit the time and you would have too many snatch victories...That would mean risks and that is not Test cricket, not as we understand it in Australia.' Encountered for the first time, this ethic could be bracing. After the Australians' first visit to South Africa at the end of 1902, local player Louis Tancred described them in words that would not ill-fit Steve Waugh's modern XI:

> They demonstrated to the casual South Africans that nothing counted so much for success as strenuousness and intensity. In no instance did they relax their keenness; never did they permit themselves to lose sight of the principles of playing as hard as they could and giving no chance.

A question arises of whether this competitiveness ever stepped over the line into what we now regard as gamesmanship—something at odds with perception of the Golden Age as a prelapsarian period of fair play, as expressed in Noble's homiletic *The Game's the Thing*: 'Cricket teaches you to be clean...It discountenances boastfulness, shady tricks, and unhealthy practices, and sets high value on quiet demeanour, gentlemanly conduct and modesty.' Yet even during this *belle epoque,* it seems, Australian cricketers adhered to a homespun etiquette. During his record stand of 231 against England at Lord's in June 1896, for example, many were of the opinion that Trott had been caught low at slip by Tom Hayward on 61, and his refusal to budge caused J. A. H. Catton to investigate:

> During luncheon I ventured to ask Hayward if the catch was above suspicion and for my pains I got this reply: 'Do you think I should have tossed the ball up if I had any doubt about it?'...Another cricketer, whose name I shall suppress, went to far as to say that 'no-one but a —— Australian would have stood still.'

As captain in 1899, too, Darling had disputed fine points of law without compunction; at Old Trafford, for instance, he objected to England's use of nimble Johnny Tyldesley as substitute for the ageing Hayward. Nor were peers reluctant to assert their rights. Furious that umpire Dick Barlow reprieved Ranjitsinhji when that batsman was obviously thrown out at Trent Bridge, Frank Laver roared: 'Barlow, you are a cheat!' Lord Harris, chairman of England's Board of Control for Test Matches, actually agreed: 'It is quite evident this man is incompetent and shall not umpire any more of your matches.'

Sledging? It is hard to be categorical, but it seems unlikely. South African Dave Nourse, who opposed the Australians later in 1902, found them talkative but generous: 'Australians are always the same both on and off the field...They talk. If you do anything out of the ordinary on the field, they praise you. If you are unlucky, they pass along a cheery remark or two.' Dissenting a decision, too, if not taboo, required prompt atonement.[*] On occasion, players themselves would intercede to ensure justice. England's 'Tiger' Smith recalled a match where teammate Jack Hearne was recalled by Trumper after being caught at mid on 'because someone in the crowd had shouted "no ball" when Jack was about to play his shot'. On the other hand, even for Trumper, the custom of 'walking' was discretionary. His protege Charlie Macartney recalled the mortification on one occasion of being reprieved by an umpire when clearly caught at the wicket. He elected to throw his wicket away, but succeeded only in hitting the next ball out of the ground, and at the end of the over was timelessly admonished by his mentor: 'Don't throw it away; you will be given out many more times when you are not out than you will not out when you are out.'

It is important to grasp that Australian cricketers at the turn of the century were at the centre of the game's management. Though associations were constituted in each state from the various clubs, their roles were

---

[*] Two incidents, noted by 'Felix' in reports of Sheffield Shield matches between New South Wales and Victoria during 1901–2, are exemplary. The first involved an attempted stumping by Jim Kelly: 'Kelly showed his disappointment at a decision of Crockett's and the crowd took the cue and jeered the umpire. Kelly at once apologised to Crockett, not because he did not think the batsman was out when he appealed, but because his reaction allowed the crowd to see what he thought.' Of the second, a square cut apparently taken cleanly by Duff at gully, 'Felix' wrote: 'The instant he took the ball and before the appeal was made, Noble the bowler called out: "Don't throw it up" while Kelly called "no catch".' Kelly also intervened after crowd protests during the Fourth Test when Hopkins was adjudged caught at the wicket by Arthur Lilley, who wrote of the spectators in *24 Years of Cricket*: 'They at once altered their demeanour and commenced shouting: "Good old Lilley!"'

circumscribed: they ran the local pennant competition, from which they drew an XI to compete in the Sheffield Shield, and appointed a selector each for the Australian team, but little more. The Victorian Cricket Association in particular was a starveling body, which had never paid its associated clubs a dividend, and met at the handsome Young & Jackson's Hotel on Princes Bridge only because it was granted a room free. There was no centralised bureaucracy, and as the national selectors were also usually leading players, the Test side essentially picked itself. Not surprisingly, arrangements so potentially corruptible were open to criticism. In the context of the forthcoming tour of England, Victoria's captain Jack Worrall penned a swingeing critique in London's *Sportsman*, the more heartfelt because he had not been picked:

> The selectors for the Test matches in Australia have been Messrs Noble, Hill and Trumble, who were appointed by their respective associations to act in the above capacity…But no recognised body or institution in the whole of Australia appointed or asked the above trio to pick the members of the Australian team to visit England. It is an extraordinary position and not one that could take place out of Australia.

There is, however, little evidence to suggest nepotism and self-promotion. On the contrary, players took pride in their strong sense of mutual responsibility. One reason Trumper was so admired, for instance, was for his willingness to place the team first. Hill told a typical tale from the 1899 Lord's Test, recalling the trouble he had been given by Essex's Walter Mead. 'You stick up the other end,' Trumper confided, 'and I will have a go and try to knock him off.' Hill recalled: 'He did so for, in the next two overs, he treated Mead in such a manner that the English captain could not get him off quickly enough.' Noble gave this ethic its most articulate exposition:

> It is not how many runs a man makes but how he makes them that counts. Averages, like statistics, are sometimes capable of lying; merit cannot deceive; it takes into account the effort made under difficult conditions, such as bad or fiery wickets, runs made in the last innings when the game is apparently lost, readiness to sacrifice oneself in the interests of the side by going in, for instance, when the light is bad half an hour or so before the drawing of stumps, ability to hold the fort on a bad wicket until it recovers, in order that those who come after may benefit.

This spirit, significantly, transcended parochialism, a serious issue in the 1870s and 1880s. Asked why he had chosen New South Welshman Duff for his maiden Test, Victorian Trumble replied simply: 'Because Alf Noble says he is a champion.' Hill revealed that during debate over the last place in the 1902 team, Trumble pressed for New South Welshman Hopkins and New South Welshman Noble for Victorian Laver, while he himself vetoed several South Australians. 'No personal feeling was introduced into the picking of the men,' he told the *Age*. 'The Australian public can rely on the fact that each man chosen was deserving of his place.'

Touring cricketers, moreover, imposed on themselves strict codes of conduct. The 1902 tour contract included provision for a team committee to expel any member who, by 'wilfully and repeatedly making himself objectionable', was 'in any way jeopardising the success of the team on the field'. Another clause—altogether unimaginable today—restrained players from writing about the tour for the press 'with the culprit liable to a fine of £100'. This seems coy in an age where most newspaper copy was either unsigned or pseudonymous: Alfred Deakin had, for instance, just begun a thirteen-year career as the anonymous Australian political columnist of London's *Morning Post*. Yet the players' sense of the common weal was such that sources of potential disharmony had to be neutralised.

Why was this? Undoubtedly national pride and desire for success played a part. Historians Bill Mandle and Ken Inglis have written persuasively on the cultural foundations of Australian cricket as an expression of colonial self-affirmation. Yet financial self-betterment was an influence ranking not far behind. Australian cricketers visiting England were not merely pilgrims to the hub of empire, but apostles of free enterprise in search of profit. The precedent had been established by Dave Gregory's pioneering 1878 Australians—where each player had stumped up £50 as a provision against costs and taken a share of the profits—and remained ever thus. The only difference in 1902 was the underwriting of the Melbourne Cricket Club, which had begun advancing teams the means to cover their initial expenses, becoming essentially their chief creditor, to be repaid when the tour went into the black: on Armstrong's first tour, in fact, this 'patronage' was granted free of interest.

Such arrangements posed difficulties of definition. At home, most

Australian first-class cricketers operated as amateurs; that is without fee, although when so moved they could invoice their state associations for expenses incurred on a *per diem* basis. A few—probably less than a quarter—played as professionals and received a flat fee for their services (in Victoria £5 a match). The division broadly followed socio-economic contours: Armstrong's family was wealthy enough for him to play as an amateur; state teammates Jack Saunders, a stevedore's son and a clerk with Victorian Railways, and Tommy Warne, the Carlton club's curator, were professionals.

For home Tests, all played as what we might call semi-professionals: the association of the state in which a Test was held paid each player £25 plus daily expenses of 12s 6d from which individuals covered accommodation and incidentals. But when Australian teams toured England distinctions between amateur and professional blurred completely. Australian cricketers were designated amateurs, entitling them in English scorecards to the courtesy titles of 'Mr' or 'Esq', and lending them a social status. Yet they were also clearly keen to make a profit. Of Billy Murdoch's 1880 team, *Lillywhite's Cricketers' Companion* had complained: 'If the Australians did not make cricket their profession in their native land, they most decidedly did when they came to this country, for all who had anything to with them soon found out how keen they were about "pounds, shillings and pence".' The *World* lamented: 'The Australians make their own terms, insist on them, not always very gracefully, and play too obviously for the money's sake. They arrogate to themselves the rank of gentlemen.'

Nor was it merely English toffs who disparaged their visitors as 'gate money cricketers'; chief among grumblers were local professionals. The English game was then, and would many years remain, unambiguously split between amateur 'gentlemen' and professional 'players', inhabiting different hotels, occupying separate dressing-rooms, even entering the field by discrete gates. They regarded Australians, with amateur privileges but professional rewards, as the ultimate cynics. Philip Trevor vented complaints in his *The Lighter Side of Cricket*:

As a celebrated cricketer observed, 'I was paid £20 for the Test Match as a professional, but I could have afforded to be an Australian amateur at £100.' I fancy he rated the Australian's share of the gate money very much too high in this instance, but the overestimate in no way marred the strength of the argument implied…All that is contemptible and petty in that most contemptible and petty controversy, the social status question, has been dragged out of hiding in connection with the visits of the Australian cricketers.

Not every Englishman was scandalised by the Australians' mingling of pleasure and profit. Regarding it as correlative to Australia's youth as a nation, Leicestershire's Albert Knight even saw virtues in the attitude—albeit ones he could not quite endorse:

> Australia…save in a narrow circle that gathers round the vice-regal representative knows nothing of [England's] system of petty caste. Not in abstract theory is the toiling craftsman an equal of a baronet's son upon the cricket field out yonder, he is so in practice and is fully aware of the fact…It may be their infirmity—it is, I believe, their limitation. Personally one may not care for the easy laxity or good-natured indulgence which is born of cynicism as to the worth of men which deems everyone 'on the make'. But in practice its issue is wholly admirable. All players out there take the field as cricketers simply, and no official labels bar a human familiarity. The oneness of Australian cricket teams, the absolute impartial nature of their association and their outlook is in my judgment an admirable object lesson for Englishmen.

For their part, the Australians blinked uncomprehendingly at English mores. That it was *infra dignitatem* for amateurs to share facilities with professionals, Darling felt, ceded his men a tremendous advantage:

> In my time when playing against All-England at Lord's, it was a very common thing for an amateur and a professional to open the innings. The professional had to be waiting at his gate, but dare not go onto the playing ground before the supposed 'amateur' came out of the members' pavilion and entered the playing ground first. The amateur and professional then walked to the wickets from different gates about fifty yards apart and did not actually meet until they got near the wickets. Australia has never made any difference between the amateur and the professional, and that is one of the main reasons why Australian teams pull so well together whilst playing the game…

Darling's construction 'supposed "amateur"' hints at the Australians' other reservation; his men were worldly enough to appreciate the inauthenticity of many English 'gentlemen'. Far from being men of independent means free to play for love, they were frequently short of cash, and maintained the pretence of rank by other means. Some secured sinecures with their counties, like Archie MacLaren, 'coach' of

Lancashire, and Charles McGahey, 'assistant secretary' of Surrey. Many wrote cricket for newspapers and magazines, like Gilbert Jessop, Charles Fry, Arthur Jones, Pelham Warner and Ranjitsinhji. When teammate F. S. Jackson criticised this practice, Jessop put their case succinctly in the *Daily Mail*:

> The limited-income amateur, my dear Jacker, is just as enthusiastic on the game as he who is more fortunately placed. In order to still continue his favourite pastime, he has three courses open to him. Firstly, if he is good enough, he may induce the authorities to appoint him to an assistant secretaryship; secondly, if he has any ability whatever in the direction of putting his thoughts on paper he can accept the opportunity of doing so; and lastly he may become a professional.

It was not that the Australians disliked English amateurs. On the contrary, they viewed them with utmost admiration. MacLaren in particular was esteemed as the era's outstanding English batsman. 'Archie was the greatest,' said Trumper. 'All of us Australians think that.' Armstrong would be typical of his generation insofar as the opposition cricketers with whom he became friendliest were exclusively 'gentlemen': MacLaren and his Lancashire teammate Walter Brearley, later Surrey's Percy Fender and English captain Lionel Tennyson. To an extent, too, the Australians' sense of social equality with English amateurs justified their own money-mindedness. 'The cricketers meet all the best people of England and are received and entertained by the highest in the land, from royalty downwards,' claimed Frank Laver. 'And to move in such society costs a lot of money.' He was nonetheless confused by other manifestations of English cricket's caste system: 'What is more ridiculous than seeing two batsman on the same side enter the field from gates a hundred yards apart? I don't think the true amateur is so vain as to desire this distinction.'

Into the petty dodges of certain amateurs, meanwhile, Ben Wardill had particular insight, having brought so many to Australia as part of English teams. At the end of the 1901–2 visit, for example, there had been an unseemly private squabble between three English gentlemen and their hosts, McGahey, Jessop and Jones making a last-minute claim on the Melbourne Cricket Club for a £50 supplement to already ample expenses. Wardill scorned it but, once he had left as the Australian team's manager, his committee offered a placatory £50 to *all* the English amateurs: the disputatious trio, plus MacLaren, Charles Robson and Harold

Garnett. 'What an ass Jessop must be to talk about letting the public of England know how the amateurs of MacLaren's team have been treated,' vice-president James McLaughlin griped to Wardill. 'From what I saw and heard, Jessop himself would have a fine time explaining his position to the MCC authorities.'* This may explain the candour with which Wardill responded to the traditional question concerning Australians' amateur status from London's *Evening News*:

> We have no great leisure class in the colonies as you have here, and in order that the best men might come to England, it is necessary to conduct each tour strictly on business lines. The players take all the risk and, if the tour should break down from any cause, the loss is theirs. Should profits accrue after defraying all expenses they are divided equally among the members of the tour to recoup them for loss of time and salary during their eight months absence.
>
> If you call the Australians professionals, then the English amateurs who come to the colonies are even more so. Take the last team, for instance. The Melbourne Cricket Club paid everything: steamer passages, rail and hotel expenses, tips etc. In addition each man received a sum running into three figures of pin money and, indeed, in the case of one of the amateurs, the Melbourne Cricket Club were debited with the cost of the outfit he bought before embarking.

'Strictly on business lines' seems incongruous in a Golden Age context, yet it was the Australians' guiding principle. Wardill's words also explain his team's ambiguous status: they were neither true amateurs, playing without expectation of reward, nor true professionals, receiving a fixed salary. They were commercial cricketers, investors, entrepreneurs—as such, perhaps the ideal representatives of a young, restless, materialistic society, united by legislators, but still a bastion of individuality.

How much could a cricketer like Armstrong expect from touring England? Wardill correctly cited the risks involved: the 1893 tour led by John Blackham lost money, players returning out of pocket for their

---

* Melbourne's committee also covered an unpaid wine bill at Scott's Hotel of £41 9s 8d, 'the feeling being that though the club is clearly not liable, it would be better in the interests of all concerned if no unpaid accounts of the kind should be left unsettled.'

eight-month sojourn. But the 1896 tour generated almost £13,000 in revenue which meant a share of almost £680 for each player after expenses; the 1899 tour made almost £16,500 amounting to more than £800 per man after expenses. No wonder Trumble once remarked: 'We have some good days in England but the best of all is when we finish up.'

It was good money—an unskilled labourer a century ago earned around £100 a year—though it was still only roughly equivalent to the earnings of comfortable solicitor or doctor. Such bounty could also only be expected every three to four years; between times, a cricketer needed to perform consistently in the Sheffield Shield for minimal reward. And the profit shares are somewhat misleading: expenses not directly related to the tour's conduct, like suitable wardrobe, luggage and equipment were individual responsibilities. Players on tour actually funded themselves by drawing from the manager against their projected share.

There were further costs, too, involving the loss of professional advancement. Those in the public service like Trumper lost preferment: in 1902, he was earning £90 a year as a junior clerk in the Probate and Intestate Estates Office. Those in the private sector like Trumble missed promotions: having joined the National Bank in 1887, he was fifteen years later still an accountant at the Richmond branch. His son Robert says:

> He was lucky to get time off to play cricket for Victoria, and that was only because the head of the bank was Sir Frank Grey Smith, who was a very great cricket lover and looked after father a bit: he went to England five times and each time his job was held open for him to return. He told me many times over the years that he would have been much better off financially had he not played cricket, and stuck with the bank.

Money earned, furthermore, was easily gone. 'Some of the champions have benefited by their trips to the old world but not many,' commented *Melbourne Punch*. 'Easy come, easy go has been the rule. There are blue riband men who have lived on champagne and chicken who would be glad of a ticket to a fourpenny restaurant today.' One such was Syd Gregory. During the 1902 tour, his sports depot and hairdresser Gregory & Noonan in Sydney's Pitt Street collapsed; the Bankrupcy Registrar awaited his return. This misfortune yielded a valuable *tranche de vie*: court files afford priceless detail of the financial affairs of a leading Australian cricketer of his period.

Gregory began big cricket while a clerk in the Checking Branch of the Post Office on £100 a year. He resigned in order to tour England in 1893 but, losing money, had to seek his old job back. A public collection after his 201 against England at Sydney in January 1895 yielded him £123 which, after gifts to his parents, he invested in a sports depot, drawing from it a weekly £2 10s. Having married in January 1896, profit from that year's tour enabled him to buy a small East Woollahra cottage.

An unscrupulous partner who left the depot while Gregory was returning from the 1899 tour left him in financial difficulties. He kept the business afloat with his tour profit, cut his own wage, and at the beginning of 1902 took a new partner. David Noonan, a self-described 'keen follower of cricket' from Katoomba, was attracted by the glamour of partnering 'one of the leading cricketers in the world', and was bankrolled by his father to the tune of £550.

If the file reveals anything, it is Gregory's naivety. He hardly knew Noonan, and gave power of attorney over his share in the business to its hairdresser Oliver Richards. The business kept neither ledger, nor cash book, nor stock book, while Richards was too obsessed with a hair tonic called 'Capilla' to bother with mundane sporting goods.* Not surprisingly, Gregory testified, he began receiving confusing letters in England:

> About five months after I left I would receive a letter one week saying that the business was going wrong and the next they would say it was all right…On arrival here I was very surprised to find the shop was closed and that Noonan had assigned his estate…Richards simply accounted for the wreck of the business by saying that the customers had left. I never had any explanation from Noonan.

Gregory's principal assets after five tours of England were a silver watch, gold chain, silver cup and presentation clock valued at £13. After a sequestration order, he spent almost three years a bankrupt, working at the Sydney Water Board. Cricket had assuredly not made Syd Gregory rich. By the same token, without cricket, he would have remained a postal clerk on £100 a year.

---

* 'Capilla' was an unusual reflection of Gregory's cricketing fame. The formula was given to Gregory by a state teammate, who told the Supreme Court: 'My idea was to do Syd Gregory a good turn…I did not receive any interest in it for myself. Gregory and Richards often said "We'll remember you", and I replied I didn't want anything.' It was a good turn; the formula and trademark were sold to Richards for more than £400, relieving Gregory's debt burden greatly.

5

'The Whole Thing Is a Deliberate Effort to Ruin Me'

Running their own affairs, the Australians *en route* to England in 1902 were free to go their own sweet way. When the *Omrah* reached Marseilles, the team broke into three detachments: Armstrong joined Darling, Trumper, Duff, Hopkins and Carter in Paris; Hill, Noble and Jones detoured to Monte Carlo; Kelly, Howell, Gregory, Saunders and manager Wardill continued with the ship to Plymouth. Trumble, having remained in Melbourne another fortnight in order to marry, was bringing his new bride Florence on the *Oceana*. So vague were plans, indeed, that the first Australian players traipsed into London a week earlier than expected, throwing the Inns of Court Hotel's manager into confusion and catching the press unawares. They then had almost a fortnight before their first fixture; Armstrong's first game on English soil was actually as a guest of the Esher club against Thames Ditton on 3 May.

It is easy to imagine the young Warwick Armstrong in those early weeks of the tour, encountering London for the first time, assimilating its terrain, stupefied by its scale. For Australians of his generation, their school syllabuses crammed with English fact and lore, it was a place richly imagined, 'the great beating heart in the thick of things', a city containing more people than all Australia. 'London!' as an Australian journalist put it. 'I see it every night. I have been there hundreds of times already.' Nellie Melba, shortly to triumph in *La Traviata*, recalled the London of the time as 'an immense weekend party in which everybody was intent on getting the most out of life'.

Not all Australians found the city hospitable. Henry Lawson, soon to leave after two unavailing years seeking his literary fortune, invested his moans about London in a short story, 'Barney, Take Me Home Again', whose narrator is 'heart-sick…for the sunny South—for grassy plains, blue mountains, sweeps of mountain bush and sunny ocean beaches'. Darling's cricketers likewise encountered a bitterly cold spring. Photographs of their practices at Lord's show them cocooned in layers of sweaters; they would rarely be out of them during one of the bleakest summers in memory. Darling recalled that his players occasionally wore blazers beneath their shirts as insulation, Noble that Duff became so dejected that he pasted a picture of the sun inside his cap. Duff was wont to describe the English summer as having 'set in with its usual severity'.

There was, nonetheless, great prestige attached to being a visiting Australian cricketer. The tourists' first match was against London County led by fifty-three-year-old W. G. Grace, no longer a Test player but still the *emeritus* professor of English batsmanship, at Crystal Palace, that flourish of imperial showmanship. Their third game at the Oval was watched by the Prince of Wales himself, with Prince Charles of Denmark. Britons that year looked forward to their cricket more than usual. Three years of fighting in South Africa had fatigued them; as foreign secretary Sir Edward Gray put it: 'This generation has had enough excitement.' They wanted to see the stupendous *Ben Hur* at Drury Lane's Theatre Royal, to laugh at George Robey and Dan Leno at the London Pavilion, to read Edward Kennard's *The Golf Lunatic and His Cycling Wife*. The pomp of the first coronation for sixty-five years and the prospect of a Test series against Australia were complementary indulgences: Edward VII would be known as 'the sporting King', one of his many offices being patron of Surrey County Cricket Club.

However impressed by the splendour surrounding them, the Australians went about their tour 'strictly on business lines'. On the door of their Inns of Court common room was blazoned 'Private. Reserved for the Australian XI.' A waiter guarded the threshold to ensure they were undisturbed. Though invitations rolled in to banquets across England—from cricket clubs, lord mayors, chambers of commerce, stock exchanges and private individuals—Wardill declined all bar those held at Lord's and the Oval; this was an 'unwritten law' of the team, on the grounds that a cycle of grand occasions interfered with match preparations. Each day started instead with a communal breakfast, beginning with porridge, and accompanied by lots of fresh fruit—though not coffee, eschewed as 'being bad for eye and nerves'. The team even had its own medical officer, Rowley Pope, an eccentric ophthalmic surgeon from Sydney who accompanied the tour at his own expense as factotum, doling out cures, keeping records, filling in as a fielder, and generally advising ungraced antipodeans about English customs, like knotting a bow tie or recognising a fish knife: a service he would fulfil for another thirty years.*

The press had eagerly built the Australians up before the tour, including Armstrong, subject of a glowing testimonial in the weekly *Cricket*:

> Of the five new members of the Australian team now nearing England, it will be no disparagement to the rest to speak of Warwick Armstrong as the player of greatest interest to English cricket at the moment. 'Victoria's young batsman with a future': this is how he has been described by one of the most capable of Australian critics. Not that he is a batsman and nothing else, be it added. On the contrary, on his cricket during the last Australian season he is an all-round cricketer of undoubtedly great possibilities.

He did not disappoint. In only his second bowl on English soil, he routed Nottinghamshire: for the next twenty years, he could not improve on his figures of 8–47. 'Mr Armstrong, who had the advantage of being unknown to the batsman, is a right hand slow-medium bowler,' *The Times* related. 'He has a deceptive flight, varies his pace and appears to break either way.' And, despite the inclement weather, the Australians romped home with an innings to spare in three of their first seven matches. But they faced two significant problems in their early weeks. The first would heal in time: Trumble, the key to Darling's attack, broke his right thumb at practice. The second would rumble more than a year:

---

* In Australia's game against Cambridge University on 9–10 June, Pope played both for and against his countrymen. He made 2 not out, then substituting for the opposition caught Hopkins at short leg. 'You beggar,' said Hopkins. 'And I did feel like making runs today.'

there were doubts over the legality of two of the team's bowlers—cast worse still by an Australian.

On 15 April, shortly before the team's arrival, an article had appeared in London's *Sportsman* claiming: 'Every member of the 1899 team knew that Noble repeatedly transgressed Law 48. I will let the English experts find out whether any other member of the team has a doubtful delivery.' The identity of the second was resolved by a letter to umpire Jim Phillips, which he showed the visitors, to the effect that he should no-ball both Noble and Saunders if he wished to make a name for himself.

The accuser was Jack Worrall, not only Victoria's captain but Saunders' captain at Carlton. The article was bad, the letter worse. Phillips, the recipient, was one of his day's more enterprising cricket per-sonalities. A native of Dimboola, once a Melbourne Cricket Club net bowler, he now commuted between the hemispheres as a cricketing jack-of-all-trades—umpire, scorer, journalist, player, and agent for Worrall's Melbourne sports depot. Pertinently, he was Law 48's most vig-ilant policeman: having no-balled Ernie Jones for throwing during a Melbourne Test in January 1898, he had subsequently set out to pro-scribe all the bowlers with impure actions in English county cricket. This had earned plaudits from, among others, Ranji: 'I, for one, think that cricket communities in all countries owe a debt of gratitude to Phillips for having partly smoothed the way for other umpires to treat such unfair actions, be they in England or Australia, in the way that they deserve.' Trouble was he sometimes impressed as enjoying this celebrity.

Learning of the *Sportsman* article, Darling led a disgruntled deputation to its Fleet Street office. The editor agreed to publish no further contri-butions from Worrall—to modern eyes a surprising concession, but cricket's good name was at stake. In the event, Phillips made no move against either Saunders or Noble in the two Tests he umpired, but the Australians had long memories—Worrall's words would, ultimately, pitch Armstrong into his first significant public controversy.

For Australians, Test cricket in England at the turn of the century took getting used to. England had constituted a Board of Control for Test Matches four years earlier, but international engagements still followed the county season's contours. Tests consequently lasted three days; indeed, they would do so for the duration of Armstrong's career, antithetical to the timeless cricket he played at home. Somehow, though, this did not hinder their capacity for incident—at least not yet. The 1902 series, despite rain that reduced the Second Test to 105 minutes, would prove a benchmark.

Rain had the final say in the First Test at Edgbaston, though not before Yorkshire's George Hirst and Wilfred Rhodes had routed the visitors for a paltry 36. Australia then won the Third Test at Bramall Lane by 143 runs, thanks principally to Noble's 11–103, a bonny century from Hill, and a starburst of strokes from Trumper. Trumper adorned the Fourth Test at Old Trafford with an unprecedented hundred before lunch on the first day, his opening stand with Duff worth 135 in seventy-eight minutes; this on a pitch and outfield exposed to two days' solid rain. The game ended in the closest Test result to that time: from 3–92, England lost its remaining batsmen for 28, succumbing by three runs. The tension was so acute that Wardill's wife, crocheting as she watched, involuntarily ran a needle through the palm of her hand. Packing afterwards, keeper Kelly complained that he could not find his gauntlets—he was still wearing them. Then Gilbert Jessop's breakneck 104 in eighty-five minutes wrested the Fifth Test for the hosts, the final fifteen runs eked out by last pair Hirst and Rhodes.

The tour's highest achiever was Trumper. By the time of Edward VII's coronation on 9 August—Darling's team watched the procession to Westminster Abbey—the twenty-four-year-old Australian was also securely enthroned as the batting wonder of the age. On a succession of surfaces as remote from his native Bulli as could be imagined, in a year when it seemed about to rain whenever it was not, he raised a record 2570 runs with eleven centuries, all at headlong pace—in the entirety of the tour, he negotiated only three complete maidens. 'Trumper was a marvel,' Englishman Len Braund told Leslie Poidevin, in an article by the young doctor in the *Referee*. 'I bowl up a ball, he comes out to it, I know that I have beaten him in the flight, and then, at the last moment, he will lay back and cut me for four. The very same ball next time he hits to square leg. Now what is a fellow to do?' Darling's only inquiry of the team's coachman every morning when he embarked for a day's play was: 'Is Vic aboard?' If so, the brake could set off.

Though Armstrong had nothing so spectacular to show for his five Tests, he enjoyed consistent success in the tour's thirty other first-class matches; having played only sixteen first-class games before the trip, he thrived on the heavy workload, collecting 1075 runs at 28, 72 wickets at 19 and thirty catches. His most important innings was against Lancashire on 5 June. The visitors at the time appeared rattled—after their ignominious First Test display, they had been routed at Headingley by Yorkshire for a humiliating 23. 'With the exception of Trumper,' reported *Cricket of Today*, 'all played a more or less nervous and faulty game, as if…shattered by the successive failures at Birmingham and Leeds.' Armstrong stayed two and half hours for an unbeaten 87, before a deluge. In six hours over two days at Hove against Sussex, he and Noble also added 428: his proportion of what remains the Australian sixth-wicket record was an unconquered 172. Then there were those heady Tests, their deathless feats and breathless finishes. As the *Herald* recalled of the Oval, 'the fate of nations' seemed to depend on each ball. 'A stout police constable' on duty at the ground was seen to weep when England won.

Wardill remitted £900 to Australia on 4 July 1902 covering the team's advance from the Melbourne Cricket Club; henceforward, all was profit. And, as a private enterprise, the Australian XI was free to exploit investment opportunities. South African mining magnate Abe Bailey—a disciple of the late Sir Cecil Rhodes and president of Johannesburg's pucka Wanderers Club—wrote to Wardill inviting the Australians to tour his country; grim Boers had finally lowered their colours at Vereeniging on 31 May. When Bailey guaranteed a minimum £2000, the Australians accepted with alacrity, leaving London on 20 September.

The tour began amid shibboleths about sport's capacity to mend political differences. 'Who shall say,' asked the *Cape Times*, 'that the spectacle of Dutch and English youths "together joined in cricket's manly toil" against a common rival will not have its own wholesome effect in allaying racial difference?' The recency of war in which 20,000 had died in concentration camps alone, too, doesn't seem to have bothered the Australians. Hill recalled the journey south for its luxury: 'At the time, South Africa was booming and there were a number of millionaires on the boat who made our journey as pleasant as possible. And how they threw the money about!'

There was ample evidence of war once they arrived. Entering Table Bay, their steamer *Dunvegan Castle* narrowly avoided colliding with the homebound troopship *Syria*. They would be accompanied throughout their tour by the Wanderers' cavalryman club secretary George Allsop, so attached to his mount that he stabled it at the ground. They read of bodies being found at Maritzburg from the battle of Belmont, fought three years earlier, and were chaperoned round Ladysmith, scene of the famous 118-day siege raised by General Sir Redvers Buller in February 1900. But they were more taken by Johannesburg, the 'Golden City', in which they arrived on 10 October. The streets were wide and well-kept. Mine chimneys stretched into the distance. The Wanderers Club had recently issued £30,000 in debentures to underwrite its expansion, and scattered its largesse freely. Although the Australians saw little of Bailey—busy campaigning for Rhodes' old House of Assembly seat Barkly West under the slogan 'Vote for Bailey and British Institutions'—they quickly felt at home amid their hosts' customised Britishness. During their smoke night at Wanderers Hall, with high commissioner Lord Milner in the chair, 'God Save the King' was roared with gusto. Hill reciprocated with 'My Gal's a Lady', Noble with 'The Longshoreman' and 'The Mighty Deep'.

The excitement that attended the Australians' arrival was genuine. 'Already Johannesburg seems to consist of half Australians,' reported the *Rand Daily Mail*, 'and the number of people who went to school with Trumble, lived next to Darling or dandled "young Trumper" on their knee is extraordinary.' The hosts thought little of their chances in the three-match rubber. Of legend, the Boer leader Paul Kruger was told by his lieutenant Joubert that eleven Australians were coming who had beaten all England; Kruger replied that the Transvaal stood no chance against such invaders. South Africa's leading cricketer Charles Llewellyn commented dolefully: 'We have little chance of defeating what I consider to be the most powerful combination Australia has yet sent to the old country. Trumper I consider a marvel and, with Hill, can do wonders as a batsman.' Yet during the First Test at Wanderers, the inaugural cricket meeting between the countries, the South Africans enjoyed the better of a draw, the Australians struggling to acclimatise to the altitude of 1800 metres and the peculiarities of the coir matting pitch. It was Armstrong who then came into his own during the Second Test, opening Australia's second innings with his team 65 runs in arrears. Louis Tancred, who dropped him at point when 25, wrote of his chagrin:

> Never did the sound of ball against a bat sound so discordant to the writer
> as in that game when the spirits of the South African side might have been

raised had the chance been accepted. The crisp shots went like hammer strokes, and each run that showed itself on the board looked emblazoned and ineradicable.

Armstrong forbore the other trials of concentration. With Australia 2–117 shortly before tea, a dust storm blew up from the bare and grassless field, reducing vision to only a few yards, and delaying play half an hour. South Africa grabbed four quick wickets on resumption, but Armstrong neither panicked nor even hastened. Resuming next morning at 94, he was an undefeated 159 when Llewellyn bowled his last partner. His 210-minute innings, only the second time an Australian had carried his bat through a Test innings, had been inscribed with sixteen boundaries. Armstrong was presented with the ball, along with a cigarette case by 'CBL', Llewellyn himself. The ball—still in the Armstrong family's possession—feels large in the hand; doubtless it looked large to Armstrong. It is also bald of lacquer, attesting the abrasiveness of the Wanderers outfield a hundred years ago.

The Australians could feel satisfied. They won that Second Test by 159 runs and, after travelling to Cape Town aboard the *Scot*, the Third by ten wickets. Their resolve had not slackened, and jolted callow opponents like Dave Nourse, for whom Darling's captaincy was an education:

> The way he handled his bowling, and how he worked his men in the field, was a revelation to us. He only had to say 'So and so, go on at the bottom end', and every fieldman knew where he was to go, and took his place without another word. But they all understood the game so thoroughly that it was second nature to them.

Good crowds, furthermore, had followed the tour: £2849 was banked, more than enough to meet Bailey's guarantee. In all, each Australian player would gross more than £800 for the tour entire. On 14 November 1902, they boarded the *Sophocles* bound for Australia, encountering Harry Trott's brother Albert. He had played with Middlesex for the last three years, and would shortly take up an appointment with Hawke's Bay in New Zealand. They afforded a piquant contrast: Trott, now a landless 'professional', his countrymen 'amateurs' far better rewarded.

The Australians reached Melbourne on 4 December after nine months abroad with many happy memories, and one unpleasant one: Jack Worrall's insinuations concerning Noble and Saunders. Their indignation shortly found an outlet. Four months earlier, Wardill had cabled the New South Wales Cricket Association suggesting, as a tour epilogue, a Sydney fixture between Darling's men and a Rest of Australia XI. Discovering that their opponents would include Worrall, they privately communicated their unwillingness to participate. 'Felix', always well informed, commented: 'There is…the suggestion that the match was abandoned because the Rest includes a player whose contributions to a certain London paper were strongly objected to by members of the Australian XI.' A replacement fixture was organised between the Australians and a New South Wales XIII, eventually ruined by rain.

A few days later, with Victoria due to meet New South Wales at the MCG in their annual Boxing Day derby, a telegram from Darling reached the Victorian Cricket Assocation's secretary Edward Heather: 'Trumble not available interstate matches, Saunders and Armstrong refuse to play if Worrall chosen. Other Australian XI players unanimous prefer not play against him.' A letter the following day outlined Worrall's indiscretions and restated the threat.

This bold intrusion on the sovereignty of a state's selections reflected how seriously the Australians regarded Worrall's insinuations. It was also an act of amazing audacity on the part of Armstrong and Saunders: Worrall was a sporting institution, not only the state's captain at cricket, but also a champion Australian Rules footballer. Seventh child of an Irish miner, he had been spotted by Fitzroy talent scouts while playing in Ballarat, and was Champion of the Colony in 1887 and 1890. Having recently commenced a coaching appointment at Carlton, he would lead them to three consecutive Victorian Football League premierships, while his sports store opposite the General Post Office was 'a favourite resort of sporting men'.

Withal Armstrong and Saunders were dictating from a position of strength. They rode high in public opinion. If the VCA supported Worrall, moreover, the implication was that the Shield match would proceed without the leading New South Welshmen, including the renowned Trumper. When VCA delegates convened to discuss the threat on 22 December at their usual meeting place—the upstairs room at Young & Jackson's Hotel—their position was invidious. The three Melbourne Cricket Club delegates—vice-president James McLaughlin and Armstrong's pennant teammates Billy Bruce and Alf Johns—launched into bitter denunciations. McLaughlin said that Worrall's remarks about Saunders amounted to 'the most serious statement' ever made about a cricketer. Bruce and Johns moved 'that the selection committee be instructed to omit Mr Worrall's name from the members of the team and all other teams until further notice'.

Worrall's initial response was mild. He emphasised his friendliness with Phillips and divulged that he had written at the umpire's solicitation—'for that reason, both men might have been taken unawares and said too much'. He would happily recant if his remarks were considered derogatory. Steadily, however, his response hardened. Forces were at work intent on his exile and impoverishment: 'I have done more for Victorian cricket than either Armstrong or Saunders and as much as Trumble. The whole thing is a deliberate attempt to ruin me. Although it has not succeeded a lot of harm has been done to me.' East Melbourne's Sam McMichael stated succinctly: 'The question was whether they would sacrifice Worrall or sacrifice Saunders and Armstrong and thereby knock interstate cricket on the head particularly with reference to NSW.' University delegate Lawrence Adamson crafted a more emollient expression of the predicament: 'That while admitting Mr Worrall's great service to Victorian cricket, this association recognises that, as matters stand between him and the members of the Australian team, it would be better for the interests of the game if Mr Worrall voluntarily retired from the Victorian team.' Worrall acquiesced, the match proceeded; but the antagonists weren't finished yet.

When the VCA reconvened on 13 January 1903, the Melbourne delegates unexpectedly broadened their front. Johns stated that he could no longer work with Worrall as selector. Bruce demanded Worrall's resignation. 'Mr Worrall said he again found himself in a funny position,' reported the *Argus*, 'but he would leave the matter to the association and stand down if they wished it.' Again, however, Worrall would have his say:

> The plain fact was that the action was simply taken against him by some members of the committee of the Melbourne Cricket Club in a spirit of pure vindictiveness. They had even been round the executive of the Carlton Cricket Club threatening all sorts of things in the event of his not being removed from his position in the club. He thought this was just all a question of personal spite on the part of certain members of the Melbourne Cricket Club, although he did not like to have to say it.

'Oh, by all means say it if you think it,' McLaughlin retorted. 'I shall have something to say on that point. You are making very serious accusations against the Melbourne club.' Worrall pressed on, contending that in a 'vindictive spirit', certain Melbourne committeemen 'wanted him out of the team first and then off the committee and they would do their best to get him out of the association'.

> McLaughlin: Can you give any solid reasons for saying that? Let us hear the whole of them.
> Worrall: A very high officer of the Melbourne Cricket Club is inimical, because he has tried to use me for his own purposes to the detriment of the association but found I was not to be so used. That gentleman had asked me to call a meeting of delegates of the clubs, to preside at that meeting, and make a speech pointing out how detrimental the association was to the true interests of cricket.
> McLaughlin: You should mention names.
> Worrall: It was Mr Wardill.
> Bruce: Who are the other members of the Melbourne committee who wished to get you out of the Carlton club?
> Worrall: If you must have the names, it was Mr Johns and Mr McLaughlin.
> McLaughlin: I don't like to use hard words, but that is absolutely not true.
> Worrall: My authority is Mr Gleeson, treasurer of the Carlton club.
> McLaughlin: Since you name an authority I have no hesitation in saying, in the coarsest terms, that it is a lie.

The spark the two cricketers had lit had now been fanned into a blazing row, fuelled by an abiding distrust between the VCA and its most powerful constituent. Ostensibly the presiding authority in the state's cricket, the association was a penurious body, and looked on Melbourne with a mixture of respect, envy and irritation. The approach that Worrall alleged Wardill to have made probably related to a VCA financial crisis in April 1901 when it appeared that Melbourne might actually usurp the association altogether. More sober counsel had prevailed. 'Felix' among others commented that 'it will be a sad and sorry day for cricket in Victoria if any one club, no matter how rich it is, is entrusted with control of Victorian interstate cricket'. Melbourne had settled on a more constructive role, coming in July 1902 to the aid of many more straitened pennant teams by distributing among them £1000 from the proceeds of the English team's tour. But suspicion of Melbourne's motives died hard, and Worrall enlarged his allegations: 'I am told that the Melbourne Cricket Club intend to go further and, if possible, bust

up this association…if they do not get their way. But if I am the difficulty in the way, I am perfectly willing in the interests of peace to resign
my position.' When the tumult died, Worrall's resignation was accepted.
Nine months later he also quit as Carlton delegate, commencing a
lengthy exile from the game.[*]

The dispute would have two important consequences. Five months
later, Marylebone commenced negotiations for what would be the first
team it had sent to Australia. Phillips had written unguardedly to the
VCA that, in his view, Saunders threw every ball he bowled of a particular type, probably his quicker one. At a meeting on 23 June 1903, Bruce
described the letter as 'a most impertinent interference' and advocated 'a
very strong protest indeed in justice to Mr Saunders'. It happened that
ready means were available for such a protest; Marylebone wanted to
bring Phillips as its umpire for the tour, a common practice hitherto.
Wardill informed Marylebone's secretary Francis Lacey that Phillips was
persona non grata in Australia. 'It would be a very unpopular thing to
bring him, as the public are well aware through the press of what has
taken place.' Phillips never umpired in his own country again: three years
later, he renounced cricket altogether to become a mining engineer in
Canada. By boycotting Worrall, then, Armstrong and Saunders effectively
ended the practice of visiting umpires; not for more than ninety years
would an imported umpire stand again in an Australian Test match.

The dispute also revealed the extent of the *animus* between
Armstrong's club and the smaller members of the association. When this
flared again the following year, cricketers would find the consequences
less palatable.

While his elders fought their feuds, Armstrong paraded his new cricket
credentials. When Victoria met New South Wales at the MCG on

---

[*] Victorian cricket was slow to forgive Worrall, and it was sometimes wondered
why his spell in purdah should be so long. 'Short Slip' of the *Sydney Mail*
commented on 15 January 1908: 'Surely it is about time that Worrall's weakness
was forgotten.' Finally, two years later, Worrall was appointed coach of Victoria's
colts, although Wardill remained a sworn enemy. When E. C. Beale of the Auckland
Cricket Association wrote to Wardill inquiring after possible Australian coaches,
Melbourne's secretary replied: 'We have no-one here worth having.

Boxing Day 1902, having elected as Worrall's successor East Melbourne's popular Frank Laver, Armstrong claimed a first-innings hat-trick: Alick Mackenzie, Test teammate Albert Hopkins and Charles Gregory. 'Why, the shouts that rent the air must have been heard on the far South Yarra heights and beyond, and reached the elm trees in Fawkner Park,' 'Felix' wrote excitedly. 'Again and again, the cheers rang out and Armstrong was the hero of the hour.' The VCA presented their young titan with a silver inkstand. Better was to come: in the match against South Australia, Armstrong bowled his state to victory with 5–20; in the rematch with New South Wales at the SCG, Armstrong's 118 in 175 minutes included a straight-driven five that lodged on the red-tiled roof of a booth at the end of the Smokers' Stand. The Victorians then undertook their state's first cricket visit to Queensland. 'The XI from Victoria is probably the strongest to be seen in Brisbane since the departure of Stoddart's English XI,' prophesied 'Cover Point' of the *Brisbane Courier*, 'and a fine game of cricket seems assured.' Fine perhaps, brief certainly. On the first day, greeted by a 'rousing cheer', Armstrong struck 145 in 195 minutes including thirteen fours and two fives, one caught inches from the face of a woman in the pavilion by a vigilant comrade. On the second day, he and Laver took only 11.1 overs to rout the locals for 40 in their second innings.

Armstrong's season ratified his all-round prowess: 580 runs at 58, 23 wickets at 19. He'd even kept wicket twice in emergencies. News came from England that *Wisden Cricketers' Almanack* had garlanded him as one of its Five Cricketers of the Year, bracketing him with Trumper, Kelly, and Englishmen Charlie Burnup and John Iremonger. Armstrong, twenty-four, not five years since he had played his first pennant game, was a cricketer of global renown. Perhaps this explains his next move: he turned professional.

Worrall…might take an offer for a season but I doubt it. I don't like the man.' Whether Saunders did have a faulty action is a moot point, though he did not tour England again when form suggests he should have. After the next Australian team for England was selected three years later without his name, it was inferred that there were concerns about his delivery, and that English umpires were prepared to call him. 'In paying deference to these threats,' wrote 'Mid On' in the *Age*, 'the Australians are showing a lack of backbone which is humiliating to themselves and extremely unfair to Saunders.'

6

'Where Is This Association Going to Find £500?'

Amateur sportsmen at the turn of the century belonged to a blessed species, even, perhaps especially, in a country like Australia where the pursuit of material wealth was so naked. As *Sydney Mail* rowing correspondent John Blackman put it:

> The ideal amateur is a person of education, refinement, leisure and means. He does not count the cost, nor does he question the gain. As a winner, he is fully satisfied with the acknowledgment of his relative merit and seeks neither money nor goods with which his victory may be magnified in the eyes of others and his fame sustained in after years.

In certain pursuits, this purity of breed was policed with sweeping interdicts, like the Victorian Amateur Athletics Federation definition of 'amateur':

> One who has never competed for a money prize, staked bet, or declared wager, or who has knowingly and without protest competed with or against a professional for a prize of any description or for public exhibition, or who has never taught, pursued or assisted in the practice of any athletic exercise as a means of livelihood or for pecuniary gain.

Cricketers, as explained, were in a somewhat different category. The amateur was entitled to claim expenses—a concept borrowed from a practice enshrined by the Marylebone Cricket Club more than twenty years earlier—but state associations remained coy about the question. Some administrators prided themselves on their resistance to what they regarded as extravagant levies: no less than Victor Trumper was knocked back in December 1899 by the New South Wales Cricket Association after invoicing them 10s a day. Officials also affixed the tag of professional to cricketers with little provocation; as the example of Bill Howell illustrates:

> Mr Howell had a farm about forty miles out of Sydney…and when he goes to Sydney or Melbourne to play interstate matches, though he is away about three weeks, he never asked for any remuneration. It was generally his harvest time at that time, and he had to leave his lands—about five men—with no-one to look after them. When he came to Adelaide, he put in a claim of £15, and he had told them that he was out of pocket even after getting that. When he put in the claim the New South Wales Cricket Association had told him that they had no clause in their constitution under which they could pay the amount asked unless they called him a 'professional'. He told them that he did not care what they called him, but he expected to receive the money, so they paid him the £15 and called him a 'professional'.

Joe Darling related this story to the South Australian Cricket Association, and asked whether it was 'fair' that Howell should have had his amateur status revoked. Yet clearly Howell cared not. Some cricketers, it would seem, felt more keenly about nomenclature than others. The inference of events at the Victorian Cricket Association in 1903 is that Warwick Armstrong was one of these others.

As a result of his past season's exertions, Armstrong wrote to the VCA on 24 June 1903 claiming £18 10s. It appears to have been his first claim on the association, but it was a large one; its finance committee 'carefully considered same', but it was agreed on 6 July that Armstrong should be paid only £12 10s. Armstrong subsequently notified that he wished in future to be treated as a professional: for three matches for Victoria in 1903–4, he would earn £15; for four in 1904–5, £20.

What was vexing from the association's perspective is that young men from respectable families who had been to good schools did not, as a rule, play as professionals. And it seems that attempts were made to dissuade Armstrong from his course by at least three association representatives, later very significant figures in Armstrong's career: Peter McAlister, one of the state's leading batsmen and the delegate of East Melbourne, and Mat Ellis and Ernie Bean, both peripheral members of the Victorian team but more prominent as the delegates of Fitzroy and North Melbourne respectively. As state selectors over more than a decade, they would later squabble bitterly with Armstrong, and one such fight caused Ellis to recall the events of 1903 in Sydney's *Referee:* 'As a young cricketer and against the advice of those who are maligned, Warwick Armstrong demanded the fee of a professional cricketer from the VCA, and he was paid as such for several years.'

There was some logic to their argument. In turning professional, Armstrong effectively disbarred himself from holding any association office; the VCA's statutes set forth that 'no professional cricketer or paid official of any associated club shall be permitted to be an office bearer or representative of the association, or of any subcommittee thereof'. And, although captains were still elected by teammates, it was informally understood that a professional would not be an acceptable candidate. There does, indeed, seem to have been an immediate consequence of Armstrong's new classification. On 10 November, the VCA met to discuss its appointment to the national selection panel. Three nominations were received: Frank Laver, Alf Johns and Armstrong. Laver declined to stand, and Johns was reluctant to do so. It appeared that Armstrong, all of twenty-four, and a professional to boot, would be elected unopposed. *Sotto voce* discussions took place; Johns 'after pressure' consented to stand, and was elected when Armstrong's nomination was mysteriously withdrawn.

Ultimately, however, this was a disagreement concerned less with logic than sentiment. McAlister, Bean and Ellis felt it inappropriate for a leading cricketer to draw what amounted to a wage from the game; Armstrong demurred. One wonders why—an intriguing question underlying Armstrong's mutable cricketing status is what exactly was his living at the time. As explained, the jobs of Australian cricketers at the turn of the century were usually of secondary importance to them. Buttressed by the occasional tour windfall, a Trumper or a Trumble could subsist on a low-level clerical wage and still live in reasonable circumstances. At the time of his pay dispute with the VCA, though, Armstrong appears to have taken this state of affairs to its logical extreme by having no job at all.

Armstrong's education at University College had prepared him for a clerical career—it offered tuition in skills like typewriting, book-keeping and shorthand—while electoral rolls describe him as an 'accountant'. But in reiterating its payment terms for amateur and professional cricketers on 15 September 1903, limiting amateur *per diems* to 10s, the VCA introduced for the first time the understanding that this applied also to those 'out of employment'. And during a later discussion of the policy, Bean stated that the amendment was crafted with Armstrong in mind: 'This resolution was passed in 1903 to meet Mr Armstrong's case as he was out of employment.'

This is revealing. Unlike most colleagues, of course, Armstrong had no pressing need for a job. He had made a tidy sum touring England. He was unmarried, without dependants and still lived at home. The only pressure on him to seek employment would have been the expectations of well-bred members of the Melbourne *bourgeoisie*, and of leading cricketers. Yet, even so young, Armstrong was already the realist. He excelled at cricket; why could he not choose it as his living? Perhaps, unconsciously, he echoed the famous opening line of Joseph Furphy's *Such Is Life*, published that year: 'Unemployed at last!'

Over the next few months, Armstrong did find a job, albeit a token one, as a temporary clerk in the Central Office of the Postmaster General's Department, based at Treasury Place. The PMG had a history of employing Australian cricket notables, including George Giffen and Harry Trott, and Armstrong might have been attracted by its famously indulgent attitude towards them. When Armstrong's boyhood idol Trott was a postman, colleagues complaining of his frequent absences were told, 'Harry Trott is a national institution.'

Trott, in fact, had recently returned to the postal service as a sorter, and made a low-key return to pennant ranks. Armstrong worked alongside keen cricketers in Central Office, including his Melbourne teammate Elliott Monfries and the East Melbourne pair Mal Shepherd and Reggie Reeves, who doubtless ensured that work obligations did not impinge on Armstrong's sport.* But that Armstrong had found a

* Armstrong's period with the PMG is not noted by Public Services Rolls, but in the 1903 *Commonwealth Government Gazette*, with the notation 'the provisions of

bolthole was perhaps just as well: he would shortly learn how precarious a pursuit cricket could be.

The English team led by Middlesex's Pelham Warner that arrived aboard the *Orontes* on 2 November 1903 was the first to bear Marylebone's colours, and one of the best to visit Australian shores. The bowling—with Wilf Rhodes and George Hirst to complement Len Braund and the enigmatic variations of Bernard Bosanquet—was out-standing. The Australians, meanwhile, were anxious. Darling was unavailable, leading to the election of Noble as captain. Trumper again stood out like a good deed in a naughty world, but Hill, Gregory and Hopkins were only modest contributors, and Armstrong was perhaps the chief disappointment; after a fighting 48 in the First Test at Sydney he passed 40 but once in his remaining ten innings of the first-class season. For the only time in his career Armstrong was dropped from the Australian XI.

The most dramatic contributor to England's 3–2 victory was Bosanquet, progenitor of the googly. The Australians had first been awakened to this innovation in August 1902, when Bosanquet opened the bowling against them for Middlesex and promptly trapped Jim Kelly lbw with what appeared a leg break but turned wickedly the other way. 'There was a josser out there bowling leg breaks from the off,' Kelly told disbelieving comrades, and the delivery's novelty value was still acute; Bosanquet's devastating 6–51 in the Fourth Test at Adelaide helped England recapture the Ashes.

The bowler who most tormented Armstrong, however, was Rhodes: a shrewd and inexhaustible left-arm spinner, and an assassin on surfaces aroused by rain, as he demonstrated with 15–124 during the Second Test. Quite why Armstrong should have been his victim eight times in ten meetings that summer is unclear, although a column by 'Observer' in the *Argus* may contain a clue. 'Observer' was Donald Macdonald, one of the period's most distinctive and protean journalists, not only an accomplished sportswriter, but a war correspondent who had been

---

the Commonwealth Public Service Act 1902 shall not apply': from this it can be deduced that his clerical position was temporary. Monfries, Shepherd and Reeves, by contrast, all went on to senior public service positions. Monfries became head of the GPO in South Australia, New South Welshman Shepherd secretary of the High Commissioner's Office in London and Reeves chief clerk in the Commonwealth Audit Department.

besieged at Ladysmith and the newspaper's country life columnist in his weekly 'Nature Notes and Queries'. He would watch Armstrong closely throughout his career, often with considerable insight, and at season's end related what appears to have been the fruit of conversations with the young Victorian:

> In the early part of this season when he lost his place in the Australian XI, Armstrong was undoubtedly out of sorts. He admitted himself on many occasions as being hampered by a listless feeling that made exertion difficult without quite realising what was wrong with him. For the time, he had undoubtedly lost tone.

This suggests that Armstrong was playing that season under the handicap of some illness which, though enervating, went untreated. Joyce Taylor, an orphan raised in the Armstrongs' guardianship, says it was a characteristic of the family that illnesses were seldom admitted, or even discussed: one was expected to soldier on. Later in his career, indeed, Armstrong would demonstrate a remarkable capacity for playing either in the grip of or immediately after serious debilities. On this occasion, however, it is possible he either did not or would not recognise his infirmity. The end of Armstrong's season, certainly, is consistent with a gradual recovery of strength and stamina. An authoritative 107 against North Melbourne on 19 March was followed by an extraordinary orgy of scoring at University's expense.

By stumps on the first day, Armstrong had accumulated 222 out of 4–320. Afterwards, he confessed to his partner and workmate Monfries still greater ambitions: the record score for Melbourne senior grade cricket. Perhaps it was the record-holder that spurred him on. The benchmark for eight years had been a score of 417 against the same club by Jack Worrall. Monfries recalled:

> '417?' I said; 'who do you think is going to stay with you?'
> 'I'll risk someone, at the other end,' drawled Armstrong.
> 'Well,' I said, 'I'll darned well see if you can do it. You know what cricket is, but by Jove, I'll shut my teeth.'

The match did not resume for a fortnight, the clubs taking an Easter break; Melbourne sent a team to western Victoria, where Armstrong continued his convalescence with 88 against Hamilton and 7–19 against XVI of Portland. But Monfries did shut his teeth when they recommenced, so successfully that he was still there with a century of his own in a partnership of 433 when Armstrong completed his objective. Giving only two difficult chances at 250 and 411, Armstrong compiled 438 in 445 minutes, containing forty-six fours and a five, out of Melbourne's 8–699. Armstrong later 'remarked upon the calibre of the bowling and the splendid manner in which our opponents stuck to their work in the field', though neither had prevented him securing strike for five or six balls of every over. Melbourne's committee voted that the scorecard be 'printed on satin' and presented him with a heavy silver tea and coffee set worth £10.* He concluded the season in the same monopolistic vein against his former club South Melbourne, with 72 and 12–48. 'Armstrong,' decreed 'Felix' in the *Australasian*, 'is himself again.'

With Australia scheduled to 'go home' again in 1905, the preceding Australian summer was vital for Armstrong. He had only to the end of 1904 to lay claim to a position; as the team intended visiting New Zealand *en route* to England, Darling, Noble and Victoria's Bob McLeod were naming their first tranche of players early. Perhaps with this in mind, Armstrong quit his post-office position on 30 November. When Queensland came to Melbourne, he took out on their hapless bowlers a year of frustration. After scoring a chanceless hundred in 115 minutes, he doubled it in even time, hitting twenty-nine fours so forcefully that his bat finally split in two. As he shared stands of 197 in 110 minutes with Frank Laver, and 206 in 100 minutes with Vernon Ransford, 'Felix' reported that 'the ball travelled to the fence with such frequency as to become monotonous.'

---

* Wardill's actual letter to Armstrong on 21 April 1904 reads: 'The MCC committee have voted the sum of £10 for a trophy for yourself for the record Australian score against University. Will you please make a selection of something suitable and let me have it so that I may have an inscription placed upon it?' They did not recognise Monfries' part in the partnership, though this may have been because they had recently voted him a £3 3s gratuity for 'the very great ability' with which he had kept wickets for Victoria: Monfries chose an electroplated cheese dish. Armstrong's tea set survives, almost as good as new. It consists of a teapot, coffee pot, sugar bowl, milk jug and tray on which is inscribed: 'Presented by the Melbourne Cricket Club to Mr W. W. Armstrong for the highest individual score in a single innings in Australia 438 MCC v University CC April 1904.' In fact, Armstrong's was no such record: for whatever reason, Wardill had overlooked Tasmanian Charles Eady's mountainous unbeaten 566 for Break-o'Day against Wellington in March 1902.

Darling remained ambivalent about Armstrong, confessing later that he was 'tenth man picked' when the first ten names were published on 1 January 1905. He may have been more impressed by Armstrong's 85 against South Australia a couple of days afterwards, and Sydney critics set further store by an impressive half-century against New South Wales a month later. The *Referee*'s hard-to-please 'Not Out', John Corbett Davis, thought he discerned a new, improved Armstrong: 'Hitherto, the big Victorian had failed to take advantage of his gifts from nature. If he bats in England as freely and hits the ball as hard as he did on Monday, English bowlers will find him a higher class and more dangerous batsman on all counts than he was in 1902.' Another good omen was Armstrong's sixty overs on a benign surface to take six wickets, all Australian caps. There was, however, a bigger story breaking than Armstrong's rehabilitation.

As we have seen, power in Australian cricket at the time rested principally with the players and the Melbourne Cricket Club. Ambitions for a more formal structure were stilled by the ignominious example of the Australasian Cricket Council, a national governing body for the game established in March 1892 by the associations of Victoria, New South Wales and South Australia. The ACC's one notable act had been to invest a £1000 donation from the English *grandee* Lord Sheffield in an eponymous Shield, but even then the eleven-member committee had made its decision on the odd vote. Other interventions like the foisting of an unpopular manager on Australia's 1893 team had poisoned relations with the players who were already unhappy not to be separately represented, and who, by carrying on essentially without reference to the organisation, gradually turned it into a laughing stock. 'How men can be found in the colonies to keep the farce going is a mystery,' commented 'Mid On' of the *Leader* in March 1899. 'It can only be explained by crediting those who do so with possessing a keen appreciation of that which is comical.' At its last meeting ten months later, chairman George Moir had discussed the lessons learned from the council's dismal dissolution:

> Mr Moir…felt sure that ere long a body would be found capable of thoroughly managing Australian cricket. In all the doings of the council, he had been satisfied, with Mr Darling, that playing members should have a voice in the control of affairs. The men who were playing the game were in touch with what was going on, and he was satisfied that they should be represented on the governing body.

Such was the spirit in which the next attempt to initiate a national administrative body began. When J. C. Davis, infected with federation zeal, proposed a new council at an NSWCA meeting on 18 November 1901, he envisioned a nine-man committee with two delegates and a player from each of New South Wales, Victoria and South Australia. But the idea went nowhere. The players and the Melbourne Cricket Club carried on as before; as Wardill told an audience in Adelaide *en route* with Darling's team to England on 18 March 1902, the players were really the bosses, Melbourne merely their benefactor:

> There was no-one else willing and able to undertake to manage the visits of English teams to Australia, and therefore he thought the club worthy of their best esteem. In taking teams overseas, all they had done was lend their name to the teams going home, and provided financial assistance to set them on their feet in England. It was simply a matter of grace, so that the teams would not go home in any other way than they should go. That was the only bond between Australian cricketers and the Melbourne Club.

As the Worrall affair in January 1903 intimated, however, not everyone regarded Melbourne as a benevolent influence. How, they remonstrated, could a private club be the *de facto* seat of administrative power in Australian cricket? 'What is urgently needed in Australia is a Board of Control comprised of representatives of three associations of Victoria, New South Wales and South Australia,' claimed Worrall himself. 'Something must be done to stop the encroachment of an oligarchic institution like the Melbourne Cricket Club.' The coming tour would, in effect, bring this about.

On 6 July 1904, Marylebone circularised parties interested in the formation of an Australian team, promising a 'warm welcome' should an XI visit the following year. Copies of its letter reached not only the Melbourne Cricket Club, but all the state associations, and the one sent to Melbourne's Ludstone Chambers secretariat was not answered immediately: Wardill was on two months' sick leave. The NSWCA's Billy McElhone sensed an opportunity. Estimating the advance that the Melbourne Cricket Club offered to the cricketers at around £1500, he asked the VCA and SACA to contribute a third each. The VCA responded affirmatively. The SACA was more reticent. But McElhone clearly believed that, if the advance could be raised, the associations could simply nominate a manager and take control of the Australian team.

It was an ill-conceived idea, and gives the appearance of 'policy on the run'. Having returned to work, Wardill perused Marylebone's letter, apologised for delay, and set about his task as normal, dealing with Darling and the players' nominee as manager, Frank Laver. When the matter came before the VCA on 8 November 1904, Melbourne's Billy Bruce commented witheringly:

> He had been informed that the probable players had never approached the NSWCA or any other association for financial assistance. The [Victorian] association had acted on the letter from NSW without any inquiry, and he did not know that they had any power to interfere in the appointment of a manager…Until some controlling body were formed, he thought the association going too far.

One can imagine Wardill's bemusement when he received a letter a fortnight later from the VCA's secretary Edward Heather requesting Melbourne's assistance in raising £500: a request, essentially, for the Melbourne Cricket Club to participate in its own marginalisation. Not surprisingly, Wardill retorted that 'so far as my committee's knowledge extends, they see no necessity for such action'.

It should not be assumed, however, that Melbourne and the players were a completely solid front. Some on the committee felt that the players were getting rather too good a deal from the club, while one at least was in favour of the associations having a greater say in the management of overseas tours: former Test player Bob McLeod, elected to Melbourne's committee in August 1903, had begun making some unusual waves after succeeding Alf Johns as VCA delegate and national selector in September 1904. When the association met again on 13 December, indeed, Melbourne was represented by a very odd couple: McLeod and Armstrong, the latter acting as proxy for James McLaughlin. Proceedings had an air of unreality, discussing the whys and wherefores of a guarantee fund that the cricketers themselves were bound to reject, and Armstrong became involved in some tart exchanges with his fellow Melbourne delegate and University's Lawrence Adamson:

> McLeod: Cricket should not be in the hand of two or three players. The money was required for the game not for the players. The trouble did not come from the players but from those wanting to make mischief. The association controlled cricket all the year round and now it was told it had nothing to do with it.

Adamson: The NSWCA have asked us to join in and we have agreed and we must go on.
Armstrong: Where is this association going to find £500?
McLeod: Never you mind. We'll find it.

Matters were threatening to get out of hand. 'Here's a pretty mess, here's howdy do, as they say in *The Mikado*,' wrote 'Old Cricketer' in the *Herald*. 'Three potent, grave and dignified tribunals set at nought by half a dozen wilful cricketers. What's to be done?' Joe Darling was militant:

It is a matter for the players and I don't see that it concerns the associations at all. The England trip is a financial speculation on the part of the players who entrust the manager with their business and hold him responsible for all accounts. If they lose money on the trip, the associations will not recoup them. The players have as much right to appoint their own manager as I have to appoint a manager of my business.

But the VCA and NSWCA persisted: clinging to the illusion that, if they could raise the money, the players would have to accept, they mooted a conference in Sydney in three weeks' time with the SACA. When Laver's appointment as manager was confirmed, the NSWCA even reprimanded Noble, a delegate for Paddington and the association's appointee as a selector: 'The association reminded their selector Mr M. A. Noble that the team was going to England under the auspices of three associations, Victoria, New South Wales and South Australia, and consequently the appointment of a manager must be adopted by these associations.' It wasn't and mustn't, as 'Mid On' of the *Leader* explained:

The actual facts thus misrepresented are that the Marylebone has not asked the associations or anyone else to send a team. It merely issued a printed circular not addressed to anyone in particular stating that if a team of Australians visited England next year, the club would give them a hearty welcome etc. That circular was also sent to the Melbourne Cricket Club, so why the associations should construe it as a special invitation to themselves is hard to understand. In fact, it was not an invitation to anybody, and to put it forward as an excuse for attempting to upset arrangements under which Australian cricket has become world famous during a period extending over twenty-six years is paltry and absurd.
   Furthermore, it is not true to state that the team is going to England 'under the auspices of the three associations', as the South Australian association has gone no further than to notify that, if a proposed conference of associations goes ahead next month, it will consider being represented.

What a ridiculous farce such a conference would be when the team is due to leave for New Zealand on 1 February to fulfil engagements already entered into and definitely arranged?...The two associations may continue to say that they will 'finance' the team, but they cannot force upon its members an advance of money which they have not asked for, which they do not require and which they decline to accept.

For its part, the Melbourne Cricket Club pulled Bob McLeod into line. At its 20 December meeting, the committee effectively let him off with a warning, 'the general feeling being that Mr McLeod's explanation of his attitude at the last meeting of the association was in the circumstances reasonable and that...no further action is necessary at present'. And it was too late for the associations, this time anyway. When it was confirmed that the tour would proceed as planned, Noble diplomatically smoothed matters over:

We have never suspected that there was any ulterior motive in the offer of financial assistance, and we are sure that when the NSWCA offered, in conjunction with the VCA and the SACA, to finance the team, it was not with the object of forcing the money on the players but merely to let us know that, if assistance was required in that direction, it would be forthcoming...Of course, we have privileges which must not be interfered with, but as for quarrelling with the associations, nothing has been further from our ideas.

When the conference of the associations proceeded in Sydney on 6 and 9 January 1905, however, its consequences would be far-reaching. From it emerged a draft constitution for a Board of Control for Australian cricket with powers to direct future Australian teams at home and abroad; next time, it was clear, the associations would be better prepared. As Ernie Bean told the VCA on returning, this would 'resolve once and for all who ran Australian cricket'.

By chance, Bean soon after represented North Melbourne against Melbourne. Armstrong, in his newly belligerent vein, blasted a chanceless 156 in two and a half hours before Bean had him caught. In their many future conflicts, Bean would usually have the final word, though not before Armstrong had delivered his views at length.

'Wee Armstrong': later synonymous with size and strength, Warwick Windridge Armstrong was an undersized boy. Dressed for a portrait by Vandyck of Collins Street, and at bottom left in a photograph of the 1893 Cumloden school XI, there is little hint of the height and heft to come. His alliterative second name was a tribute to family friend Colonel Samuel Windridge, former chief constable of Kyneton (right).

South Melbourne Football Team
Grand Final
South Melb. V Fitzroy
at the Junction Oval
16-9-1899

H. Latchford, J. Kyle. V.P., W. Myers, V.P., R. Gammie, C., I. Fisher, C., C. Dyson, C., H Godling, V.P., Cr T Craine, Pres., H. Elms, C., J. Monteith, V.P., J A. M'Arthur, Sec.

J. Marshall, Trainer, C. Colgan, F. James, J. Lowey, H. Lampe, W. Armstrong, J. Garbutt, W. Windley, J. Kinneburgh, Trainer

A. Triman, G. Davidson, F. O'Hara, T. Gilligan, D. Adamson, Capt., F. Arnold, G. Pleass, W. Fraser,

Henry Hewson, C. Godling, A. Henley, H. Purdy, J. O'Hara, Herbert Howson, H. Jeannerett.

'A welcome addition to the ranks': Armstrong's adolescence was as much about Australian football as cricket—a toughening experience. In the South Melbourne team before the Victorian Football League Grand Final of September 1899 (right), a lanky twenty-year-old Armstrong stands sixth from left in the third row. Fifth from left in the back row of the Victorian team for his Sheffield Shield debut against South Australia two months later (below), he already cut a cool and insouciant figure.

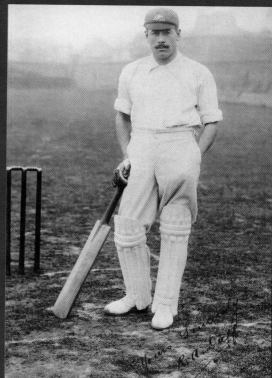

'In battle with the giants of the game': a fuzzy top lip at the time of his Test debut in January 1902 belied Armstrong's considerable maturity (top left). With the match in the balance, he shared a partnership of 120 for the last wicket with Reg Duff (top right), while their fathers sat together in the members' enclosure. Insatiable for achievement even in minor cricket, he shattered the Melbourne pennant cricket record score in April 1904 with a score of 438 against University (above).

'A bit of a trick': Jack Armstrong (top left) had been his brother's schoolboy rival, but by 1905 Warwick (top right) had left him far behind. En route to England that year, the Australians stopped in New Zealand for a short tour combining business and pleasure, their recreations including pigeon shooting on the Wanganui River (Armstrong takes aim). On the field, his eye was even more accurate: he averaged 127 with the bat, 6.9 with the ball.

7

'Temperament Temperament Temperament'

As the Australian team left Sydney for Christchurch aboard the *Navua* on 1 February 1905, Warwick Armstrong was on the brink of proving himself the equal of any all-rounder in the world. Before describing these feats, however, let us try to build an identikit of him as a player, and as a representative of his sporting caste. For he was not merely a great cricketer, but a subtly revolutionary one, one whose game was built on attitudes and emphases strikingly recognisable even a century later. There is next to no footage of Armstrong playing cricket, and few action photographs. Nor, at least at this stage of his career, did he inspire writers to flights of eloquence. Yet we may not have missed out on too much. He was, at all events, a business cricketer.

In the early years of the twentieth century, Armstrong was a strapping athlete, by any standards: 190 centimetres tall and displacing about 90 kilograms. A letter concerning uniform measurements from Ben Wardill to Monty Noble dated 2 December 1903 gives still more detailed and impressive dimensions:

Dear Alf,
Got Clem's cap just now.
Armstrong's got another measurement which substitutes for the one sent yesterday: length 31½", sleeve 34", chest 40" waist 37".

With such dimensions, Armstrong could look ungainly. His feet were famously huge. When Caulfield Council presented him with a travelling case on the eve of his first Ashes tour, jockey Percy Kennedy asked waggishly, 'Will he be able to get his boots into it?' The air of awkwardness was heightened by a habit of wearing his cap with peak tugged to one side, which E. H. D. Sewell of the *Evening Standard* noted lent 'no neatness to the general affect', while he seems in the Australian dressing-room to have been something of a messpot: his nickname was 'Clum', which the *Argus*'s Reginald Wilmot explained as originating from a 'tendency to untidiness'. Like many big men, too, Armstrong played on his size: where he appears in Frank Laver's classic account of the 1905 Australian team, *An Australian Cricketer on Tour*, it is usually in the role of the resident roughhouser, a sort of Unbearable Bassington. Describing the team's travels in New Zealand, for example, Laver includes an account of boating with South Australian Algy Gehrs on Lake Rotorua:

> In the first boat Armstrong and Gehrs undertook the responsibility of navigating the craft. Doubtless they did it to their own satisfaction if not to that of the other occupants. When remonstrated with for pulling the boat beneath the overhanging willow and dense green foliage on the banks, they merely replied: 'We are calling for passengers.' But the patience of their companions was soon exhausted, and a general melee ensued during which lumps of weeds and mud were used with such dexterity that it soon became impossible to distinguish one passenger from another so bespattered with mother earth were their faces and clothes.

Laver also includes a good-natured confession of his incompetence as skater on a rink in Christchurch:

> Sometimes good samaritans came to my assistance and, arm-in-arm with me, helped to keep my nether parts together. Some of these good people were ladies. Warwick Armstrong and Bill Howell were not so generous, they seemed determined to lay me out, and were frequently successful in stretching me out parallel with the floor when least I expected it.

Boys will be boys, of course, and at twenty-five, Armstrong was still the third-youngest member of this Australian side. Laver could be boisterous himself. In one of the few extant newsreels of the 1905 team, the players can be seen jostling for position in a team photo. As members busily swap places, Laver jabs a hearty reverse V-sign at one of his pals, who laughs gustily. Laver wrote:

Whilst the twenty-four photographers were at work on us a cinema-tograph photographer was busy with them as well as with us with a curious result. I was unaware of his presence and it was only later on at the Palace Theatre that I knew he had been there. We were highly amused at some of the antics we cut while being photographed.

The footage is silent, so we cannot hear the retort; but the laughing teammate, of course, is Warwick Armstrong.

When Armstrong walked onto a cricket field, traces of playfulness van-ished. Despite his physique, he was known as an accumulator of runs rather than a fast scorer. He could hit the ball immense distances, once clean out of Trent Bridge over the stand at the Radcliffe Road end: a feat only two other batsmen have accomplished. But more often he trod the path of patience. This disappointed, among others, Clem Hill: 'I have often wondered why the big Victorian has not persisted in hitting the ball harder in all his games. He plays ever so much better when he is forcing the pace, because then he is seen as a batsman of the most pol-ished character.' Yet 'polish' was never Armstrong's objective. He studied the bold and brazen batsmen round him and did not see himself in sim-ilar light. A contemporary like Trumper often gave the appearance of testing the limits of abilities, essaying strokes of escalating daring. Armstrong, by contrast, confided sardonically in *The Art of Cricket*: 'A good batsman will wait for his opportunities and then make no mistake in the ball selected for punishment. It is only the greatest players who can make these opportunities for themselves. The majority of us have to receive assistance from the bowler!'

What was he like to watch? The Edwardians being a generation smitten with style and 'stylist' being the highest praise they could bestow on a cricketer, writers of the Golden Age often provided wonderfully nuanced descriptions of the period's players. Armstrong, though, gave them trouble. It was straightforward to rhapsodise of a Trumper or a Ranji, but accounts of Armstrong's innings are sometimes comically eco-nomical. When he scored his maiden hundred in England at Sussex, for example, *The Times* confined itself to two terse remarks. At the end of the first day, when Armstrong was 76 not out, it commented: 'Mr Armstrong's methods were not attractive.' At the end of the second, Armstrong having proceeded to an unbeaten 172, adding 428 for the sixth wicket with Noble, it remarked: 'Mr Armstrong's cricket was never so attractive as that of his partner.' Attempts to delineate his methods, even where laudatory, usually commenced with a commentary on what Armstrong was not, like one by Leslie Poidevin in the *Sydney Morning Herald*:

> Armstrong was never a stylist; his pose at the wickets gives an impression of awkwardness which is not dispelled when he shapes to play the ball, and his strokeplay is essentially laboured. In a word, his style may be described as artisan in type. His methods, however, are remarkably effective; they show a most admirable blend of aggression and caution, backed by the right temperament for their application. His defence is very sound, watchful and painstaking; his strokeplay is limited in its variety, but very sound in its execution. His scoring strokes are practically all made in front of the wicket, and they are made in such a way that he allows himself a very big margin for error every time; consequently, though he gives the impression of smothering the ball a good deal, his play is notoriously free of mistakes.

The same descriptive dilemma applies to the fullest illustration of Armstrong's methods: the eleven plates included in that 1905 pictorial tour de force *Great Batsmen: Their Methods at a Glance*, compiled by the George Beldam, a competent county cricketer cum popular photographer, and Charles Fry, the Golden Age's most technically accomplished batsman and belletrist. Armstrong's inclusion in their gallery of 'Individualities' was a great honour, bracketing him among the Australians with Trumper, Hill, Duff and Noble. Yet from Beldam's images of Armstrong, something seems wanting.

Great Batsmen was recognised at once as a classic—'the best book about England's game yet published' said the *Evening Standard*—and revolutionised the study of cricket *praxis*. Its harnessing of the young art of photography to analyse the old art of cricket appealed to the Edwardian affinity for novelty and delight in the ornate; more than a hundred cricketers consented to be photographed in specially erected nets at Lord's, the Oval and elsewhere, although the understanding of some was less than complete. When one county secretary heard that each exposure took 1/1000th of a second, he remarked: 'Oh well, then, you'll soon be through with our eleven—about 1/100th of a second for the whole team.'

Beldam's images were revolutionary because the cricketers were asked to play at a real ball—sometimes delivered by a bowler, sometimes by Beldam with an 'electric push' to open the shutter of his Adams Videx in his other hand—rather than mime a phantom stroke. Yet the pre-occupations of the collaborators make the book subtly contradictory: Beldam was fascinated by the mechanics of his art, Fry with those of his. The latter's commentary on Armstrong is typically acute, describing his reach, the power of his square cut, and a distinctive forcing stroke through cover-point 'which he plays without any movement of the feet, simply timing the good length ball on the off stump with a short arm swing and a full use of the wrist'—reminiscent of Daniel Reese's description of Armstrong's knack against fast bowling 'of holding a firm grip and not taking the bat too far back'. But exasperatingly, having described Armstrong's idiosyncrasies, Fry illustrated him demonstrating orthodox shots, all but one of them drives; in other words, he subjugated his subject's individuality to his own belief in the 'correct' way to play. The images themselves are disappointing for the same reason: one drive that looks absurdly stiff-legged and rigid is described as 'perfect form'; another, probably the most vibrant picture in the sequence, the bat blurring at the end of its arc with the force of the shot, is twitted as 'not quite so good, the weight being slightly drawn away from the stroke'. Yet Armstrong's cardinal virtues at the crease were not ones that Fry—the great maven of 'timing, footwork and mechanism'—was ever likely to detect.

Armstrong's chief batting attributes had little to do with, as *Great Batsmen* put it, providing models for the modern sculptor 'of athletic perfection in nowise inferior to those of Ancient Greece'; teammates admired him instead for an uncannily nerveless calm, founded in sedulous preparation. His kit may have been untidy; his mind was not. Frustratingly silent about many aspects of the writer, *The Art of Cricket* overflows with cricketing practicalities from equipment maintenance to practice methods. Armstrong even reflected on the little-considered matter of the cricket sock:

> There used to be a double-soled sock made which I happen to know some English players found a great protection for their feet. It is a good thing to change both one's boots and one's socks during the afternoon interval; because the change always appears to relieve tired feet. Another point worth knowing is the soaking of the sole of the sock with whisky,

which tends to take away that tired feeling at the tea interval when one has been bowling or running about all day on a hard ground.

Armstrong used a bat light by modern standards, in common with most contemporaries, in the region of 2lb 2oz to 2lb 4oz, with a partiality for those with eight or nine straight grains across the face, slightly underpressed, and a preference for the popular Wisden Crawford Exceller.* On arriving at the crease he would hammer a bail into the surface to mark his guard, then liked to break his duck with a single from a half-cock shot forward of point. Even when his weight increased, Armstrong believed strongly in turning over strike, and was run out only twice in eighty-four Test innings. In the middle, he radiated exceptional confidence and self-reliance. Charlie Macartney, later a teammate of many years, recalled:

> On occasions he had streaky periods, and in one match I was associated with him at the wickets, he was edging the ball to fine leg and through the slips, with extreme confidence. When I remarked to him that so-and-so was bowling specially well, he said: 'Oh I don't know—I can play him all right with the edge of the bat, just wait till I get the full face onto him!'

Australians were less minded about 'correct' technique than the English, and increasingly proud during the Golden Age of their preference for intuition over instruction. The great Fred Spofforth lectured the English: 'In Australia, boys learn by watching each other and any grown up cricketers who they see. The result is individuality, and their natural ability is not dwarfed by other people's ideas.' Leslie Poidevin saw cricket as bred in the Australian bone: 'There's something marvellous about a young Australian's devotion to and aptitude for the game. He gets no "coaching". He merely takes a bat and it seems to be "in him" to know what to do with it.' Armstrong went further. Cricket, he told the *New Zealand Herald*, involved winning a mental game: 'He [Armstrong] admits that physical attribute is necessary as the foundation of a champion, who must he says be "born so". For the rest he prescribes

---

* The only bat of Armstrong's surviving from prewar days is in the collection of the Melbourne Cricket Club; from the Wisden range, it has 'W. W. Armstrong' written in ink on the back of the shoulder. Armstrong provided testimonials for the firm to the effect that: 'Throughout the whole of my career in Interstate and International cricket, I have used nothing but the Wisden "Crawford Exceller" Bat,

"temperament temperament temperament".'

The idea is a commonplace now—consider the many panegyrics extolling Steve Waugh's 'mental toughness'—but not so in Armstrong's time. Armstrong's suspicion of coaching, too, was one he shared with many contemporaries. A quarter of a century later, he would be among a group of Australian Test players consulted when the New South Wales Cricket Association considered appointing a professional coach. All disagreed with the proposal, on grounds that 'that the natural Australian freedom of style might be sacrificed by the introduction of orthodox teachings'. 'Style' would not be the first word to occur to one about Armstrong; 'natural' suited him well.

Reviewing Australia's 1902 tour, *Wisden* editor Sydney Pardon expressed a higher opinion of Armstrong's bowling than his batting, 'there being something in his leg-breaks—probably a deceptive flight of the ball—that made him curiously difficult to hit'. It was a comment that writers would paraphrase again and again, without truly fathoming that 'something'. Leg spin is the most adventurous of cricket's arts: bold, speculative, dangerous. Yet Armstrong reshaped it to suit his roundhead disposition.

Where most leg-break bowlers experience bouts of prodigality, Armstrong's hallmark was accuracy. He approached bowling like a machine. He would tug the peak of his cap and roll up his right sleeve before each delivery, amble six steady paces, tilt his head to the left, and deliver with an irreproachably high arm onto a precise length. Like Hugh Trumble, whose father had encouraged his quest for accuracy by instructing him to bowl at a feather on the pitch, Armstrong's net practices at Melbourne included spells where he would bowl at a coin. Elliott Monfries recalled: 'I used to say that if I had to nominate a bowler who could shift a half-crown on the pitch more times than any other bowler, I would name Warwick Armstrong, and he, mind you, a bowler

_____

and therefore you will understand that I regard the "Crawford Exceller" as the highest grade bat produced, and have pleasure in recommending same.' Armstrong's name also appeared on the products of another London sporting goods manufacturer F. H. Ayres, which in 1912–13 marketed a bat called the 'Warwick Armstrong'—although, in the days when bats were not bedecked with colourful stickers and symbols, he would not necessarily have had to use it.

with a leg-break action.' His accuracy was so pronounced that he was known to grind patches away on his perfect length, as 'The Breaker' of the *Dominion* noticed after a game he played against Wellington: 'When the wicket was being rolled out on Saturday morning, Harry McGirr pointed out a patch that had been torn on the pitch on the first day by Armstrong's length balls. A good-sized plate would have covered the lot.'

Armstrong's action was, however, distinctive for two reasons. Firstly, he delivered from very wide on the return crease: highly unusual, as it had only recently been widened from three feet on either side of the stumps to four. The effect was unsettling, as Charles Fry explained:

> His peculiarity consists in the fact that, instead of delivering the ball close to his own wicket, he delivers it from nearly the full width of the crease, so that, as he brings his arm over quite high, his ball which pitches on the leg stump comes, not down the line of the wicket, but across it from the off; and the batsmen is never quite sure until the last moment whether the ball will pitch on the leg stump and continue so as to hit the wicket, or pitch just wide of the leg stump and continue so as to hit the legs or pass outside of them.

The reason for this uncertainty was a second, related, characteristic. Armstrong's homespun three-point grip of thumb, first and second fingers—the last bent under the ball and snapping up as the thumb came down to impart rotation—was based on a counter-intuition all his own. Most great slow bowlers have enjoyed renown for their 'sidespin': the rotation that makes the ball deviate from a straight line. They have, in other words, sought to break the ball *more* than batsmen expected. But Armstrong often imparted far heavier 'overspin' or 'topspin': forward rotation of the ball that makes it continue on its line, sometimes dropping in the last stages of flight. He strove, to put it simply, to break the ball *less* than batsmen anticipated. Noble felt that Armstrong 'used this particular ball more and with greater success than any other bowler in my time'.

This was almost a paltry trick; after all, cricket knows few more spell-binding sights than the hypnotic, floating leg-break fizzing past a groping bat. But here again was Armstrong, the business cricketer: the 'straight break', while unspectacular, worked. Again and again in reports of matches he played, one finds hints of its unsettling nature. It brought him his very first pennant wicket in October 1898, Melbourne's George Moysey, as 'Batsman' of the *Sportsman* related:

He caught Moysey napping with a ball on the off-stump which the batsman thought would break away but didn't. As the batsman did not play the leather, there was the usual rattle among the timbers that astonished Moysey and sent him pavilionwards disconsolate and no doubt displeased.

It brought him his second Sheffield Shield wicket, Syd Gregory, bowled for 66 in January 1900. Round this episode, umpire Bob Crockett wove a charming story; apparently, Gregory had just glanced at the scoreboard and confided: 'Seventy, Bob. I never think I've got a score till I get seventy.'

Syd lay back for a cut for four. The ball had all the appearance of a leg-break which Syd knew exactly how to treat. It wasn't a leg-break after all, however, but had a lot of overspin. Instead of breaking a foot as Syd expected, it whipped the bails off. 'I ought to be damn well shot,' said Gregory as he left.

Armstrong was still hoodwinking accomplished batsmen with this artifice decades later. When he took 12–77 against Surrey in May 1921, the *Herald* reported that stylish opener Donald Knight even fell for it twice:

To one ball of Armstrong's which pitched straight and went to the off he stepped in front and left the ball alone. When the next ball was delivered apparently with the same leg break action but really with overspin and no leg spin, Knight did the same and was very much lbw. The trap was so simple that one thought it would be a lesson to this brilliant batsman. Yet in the second innings, he fell into the same trap; and his countenance, as he slowly came back, wore the pale cast of thought. Presumably he had plumbed unsuspected depths of cricket guile.

As this suggests, Armstrong could turn the ball from leg when he chose. But this was a feint; the 'straight break' held the danger. By the end of Armstrong's career more than half his first-class wickets would have been either bowled or lbw, and he would be regarded by the eminent Australian coach Eric Barbour as having 'made the "straight break" famous all over the world'. In his poem 'Watching Benaud Bowl', Alan Ross likened leg-spin to love: 'Requiring commitment, the taking of a chance'. In Armstrong's hands it became more like attrition, requiring patience, the aversion of risk. And in England he would further refine this interpretation with a philosophy of field-placing that provoked outrage.

As the euphemism Douglas Jardine adopted for his strategy during the 'Bodyline' series of 1932–33, 'leg theory' is part of cricket's lexicon in disrepute. Yet it has not always sounded so sinister. Cricket has a propensity for attaching elaborate names to simple ideas, and the 'theory' is as straightforward as bowling at a batsman's legs with fieldsmen oriented to the on side, usually with the intention of inhibiting scoring. It has been, moreover, part of cricket for more than a century, an alternative to more conventional and equally self-explanatory 'off theory'.*

Armstrong probably first encountered a 'leg theory' bowler at the outset of his Test career, Somerset's Len Braund being an accomplished practitioner. Australians found him puzzlingly foreign to their own benchmark for wrist spin, Harry Trott. 'Trott bowled at the wicket with the ball breaking away,' Joe Darling told the *Register*. 'Braund's is a different theory. He bowls outside the legs and has nearly the whole of the team on that side of the wicket. It is difficult to compare them, they belong to different schools.' There was similar puzzlement when Armstrong first attempted something similar in Victoria's match with Lord Hawke's touring Englishmen in March 1903. The match notes of statistician R. H. Campbell include the bemused marginalia: 'Armstrong when bowling had five on the leg side.' Eight months later, when Pelham Warner was leading his Englishmen against Victoria, Campbell's notations include the astounded observation: 'Armstrong bowled with only a mid-off.'

Armstrong met little success in either outing, as might be expected; so much cricket precept being based on the idea that the correct line is off stump, it is no easy thing for a bowler to reorient to on or outside batsmen's legs. Furthermore—and this is of prime importance—bowling with such primarily negative intentions was not quite the done thing. Armstrong's comrade Noble put the case against as clearly as any:

---

* 'Off theory' seems to have been first explained by Billy Murdoch in *Longman's Magazine* of January 1883: 'At the present time, when bowlers place their men on the off side and bowl on what I might term the "off-theory", batsmen should be very careful what they hit at.' Perhaps the earliest written reference to 'leg theory' is also Australian. In his 1898 autobiography *With Bat and Ball*, South Australian George Giffen refers matter-of-factly to Victorian leg-spinner Bill Cooper (two Tests for Australia in 1881–82 and 1884–85, 9 wickets at 25 each): 'Cooper bowled the leg-theory almost as remarkably as the off-theory is practised nowadays'.

I deprecate most strongly the use of leg theory as a means of saving runs; it is a method usually introduced only to save your face. There is nothing clever about it, and it is not effective as a destructive element with class batsmen…Generally the feeling engendered by its use is not good for the game. I have never used this method myself and have discouraged its use by all bowlers under my leadership.

Noble was as good as his word when Armstrong first trialled his leg theory against England in the first two Tests of the 1903–4 Ashes series. By the Third Test, 'Observer' of the *Argus* noted, Armstrong had reverted to orthodox methods: 'Noble was successful in dissuading Armstrong— who seems a bit obstinate in his theories—to drop that hopeless plan of posting a lot of men out to leg and bowling wide of the batsmen's pads.' But Armstrong *was* obstinate. He flirted again with the idea the following season, this time with increasing success. In his conversion to leg theory, indeed, we glimpse his pragmatism once more. Elliott Monfries recalled a flavoursome exchange during a match between Victoria and New South Wales after Armstrong, with seven on the leg, had bowled consecutive maidens to Reg Duff:

> In changing ends after the second over, I said to him: 'My word, Armstrong, you've got a hide bowling stuff like that to Reg with only two men on the off.'
> 'Well,' said he, 'did he hit me?'
> I didn't pursue the subject!

There was a phrase a hundred years ago to describe someone tackling cricket like Warwick Armstrong: such men 'played at keeps'. It could be a term of disapprobation, as though the player was somehow breaching the game's spirit. Armstrong did not see it so. Great cricketers, and outstanding athletes in general, are often said to thrive on the 'big occasion'. Armstrong needed no such stimulus—quality of opponent and size of event were immaterial.

This is no small point. To do justice to all Armstrong's minor cricket feats would require a book twice these dimensions, but one example is actually upon us: Australia's brief visit to New Zealand in February 1905. New Zealand was still a cricketing backwater, and Australia encountered little resistance, but Armstrong played very much 'at keeps': in the two and a half weeks, his batting average was 127, his bowling average 6.9. When a national team was mustered to challenge the visitors at Lancaster Park, Armstrong defeated it virtually on his own with 126 and 10–52.

Such gluttony for achievement seems at times even to have annoyed his fellows. Addressing cricket's besetting issues in July 1906, the *Australasian Star* commented knowingly of the 'average monger': that is, 'the man who wishes to appear high in the average lists and takes no risks, and a couple of not outs assists him materially'. An incident was cited on Australia's 1902 Ashes tour when 'Armstrong so palpably played for a not out that Darling threatened to send him in first so that he would have to get out'. This may explain, in fact, why Darling *did* use Armstrong as an opener on the journey's homeward leg through South Africa. But Armstrong never lost this desire to dominate every match, whatever the circumstances, whatever the occasion. And in England during 1905, he would demonstrate the ability to do just that.

8

'Take Armstrong Off!'

The Australians began their usual indirect route to England on 23 March 1905, taking in Suva, Vancouver and New York. Awaiting the team's arrival at the Inns of Court Hotel was Joe Darling, who had travelled directly from Australia on the *Marmora*, and who was duly confirmed as captain by a team ballot, with Noble his deputy and Hill the third selector. One of their first decisions was to draft Armstrong as the team's regular number five, a considerable promotion from the positions at seven and eight he had occupied three years earlier. Quite possibly, the decision reflected Armstrong's own partiality, as his later teammate Charlie Macartney documented:

> Armstrong had what amounted almost to a superstition—he always wanted to go in No 5. When playing under other captains he invariably secured that position, and when he became captain himself, the first name he would put down on the batting list was himself in the No 5 place. Whether it was superstition or not, that position in the batting order was ideal for him.

So it proved. Coming in at 3–12 in the second match against Nottinghamshire at Trent Bridge on 8 May, Armstrong struck 112 in two hours, complemented in the second innings with an unbeaten 56.

Against Surrey, he cruised to 83 in 135 minutes, and helped Duff add 98 in 50 minutes in a second-innings run chase. The *Sportsman* saw him 'rising to the occasion with a resource and deadly earnest that wore down all opposition', and acclaimed his square cutting: 'His wrist might have been moulded in Vulcan's forge then tempered to the flexibility of the yielding foil in the most perfect modern workshop.' In the *Daily Mail,* W. G. Grace himself forecast great deeds: 'He will make a lot of runs during the tour, being a much improved bat.' There was no way of knowing how quickly the prophecy would be fulfilled.

On the evening of 17 May, the Australians accepted an invitation from Nellie Melba to *La Traviata* at Covent Garden, paying their respects with a signed bat and a bouquet in the shape of cricket stumps with the word 'Australia' written across them. Suitably uplifted, they relieved Marylebone of 6–555 at Lord's the next day. *The Times* ranked Armstrong's unbeaten 248 in only four and three-quarter hours, with thirty-eight fours and two fives, as 'the best thing he has done in cricket in England'. The best, and probably the least in character: belligerent, bold, almost reckless. When the Lancastrian fast bowler Walter Brearley bounced him, he pulled fiercely; when the Scottish leg-break bowler Harold McDonnell sought to confuse him with flight, he hit freely in the air, bisecting four men on the fence in front of the wicket. These innings would become the foundation for a tour of all-round accomplishment that no cricketer visiting England has since paralleled: not Miller, not Mankad, not Sobers. Yet Armstrong's feats are today largely unrecalled, for they were commingled with a controversy that soured their attainment. Even as he proved himself the equal of any cricketer in the world, Armstrong contrived to become the most unpopular cricketer in England.

Although the Australians had been favoured by fortune so far, scoring at rates faster even than in 1902, there were signs already that this was not one of the formidable teams of yore. Its reliance on older players had already been criticised at home; the team's average age at the time of the First Test was thirty years and nine months. The bowling appeared particularly thin: Bill Howell and Charlie McLeod were seldom threatening, and Noble, while batting with great consistency, had fallen away badly as a medium pacer. 'He seems to have lost interest in his bowling,' commented Leslie Poidevin in the *Referee,* 'or else the subtle touch has left his fingers.' Much responsibility had fallen on Laver, a wily medium pacer but in his thirty-sixth year, and Albert Cotter of New South Wales, very fast but only twenty years old, and Armstrong. Would it be enough?

On the opening day of the First Test, Australia fared well. Laver and Cotter sufficed to dismiss England for 196. But when England struck back on a sultry second day, confining Australia to a lead of 25, Armstrong was compelled to step in. MacLaren and Hayward had steered their side to 0–110 by 3 p.m. when Armstrong was delegated the ball at the pavilion end, with 19,000 spectators anticipating an afternoon of batting pleasure. He spoiled their reverie. With three short legs, a deep square leg, and only one man patrolling the off side, he bowled his leg theory for over after stultifying over. The crowd was stirred to anger, and aired their grievances so heatedly that Armstrong several times 'stopped in the middle of his run from delivering the ball in consequence of their behaviour'.

Whose idea it was to implement leg theory that day is unclear. Darling must have approved the measure, but it seems probable that Armstrong had considered it well ahead of time. A correspondent of *Penny Magazine* visiting the Australians' digs had found him locked in private thoughts: 'Armstrong is one of the silent ones. It is said he meditates on the weaknesses of batsmen. Once he was seen to be arranging various glasses and salt cellars in an odd way round his plate and it was thought he was evolving a new method of placing his men on the on side.' But this question is ultimately of lesser importance than the response: to critics, Armstrong's thirty-five overs for 50 runs and Hayward's wicket was a travesty. *Cricket* thought it sullied Australia's reputation as a nation of fighters:

> It has always been counted as one of the greatest points in favour of the Australians that they never despair, no matter how much the game may seem to be going against them. It would be a thousand pities if they were to lose the reputation which they have so deservedly gained as a team of fighters. But…when their bowling was mastered they seemed to give up all hope of victory, and their only object in life seemed to be to keep the runs down.

The Times bent over backwards to be fair, but could not condone the exercise:

No doubt it was of the most material importance, from the Australians' point of view, to check the run-getting, and Mr Armstrong succeeded with a vengeance; and Mr Darling cannot be blamed for keeping him on so long. But that such a policy should be the proper one is much to be regretted in the interests of the game.

The only commentary favourable to Armstrong was from Major Philip Trevor, just resuming his literary career after two years garrisoned in South Africa, and building a substantial following in the *Daily Mail*: 'Armstrong was the object of a contumelious attack which disgraced those people ill-mannered enough to participate in it and all because he bowled good length leg-breaks which the batsmen ludicrously failed to hit.' And Trevor, surely, was onto something: the Englishmen's lack of initiative, while in a position of strength, is perhaps the proceedings' strangest aspect. The Test is one of the few Armstrong mentioned directly in *The Art of Cricket,* where he commented that the batsmen 'solidly refused to be tempted by any of my baits, because however badly runs were needed the game was in too critical a state to take unwarranted risks in getting them'. Yet this seems charitable. By about halfway through Armstrong's spell, England were in little danger of defeat; having scored with freedom at the other end, they were 284 runs ahead by five wickets standing by the close. The following day, too, when England extended its score by 127, Armstrong was allowed to bowl a further 17 overs for 17 runs. In fact, dull as it may have been to watch, Armstrong's grotesque 52–24–67–1 was a spell of bowling that would resonate for many years after.

With Trumper unable to bat in the second innings, nursing an injured back, England prevailed by 213 runs, Bosanquet preying on anxiety about his googly in claiming 8–107. Though the hosts had been a little lucky, winning with five minutes left and shortly before a torrential storm, doubts about their visitors had been largely confirmed. Armstrong now strove manfully to fill the breach. Abetted by rain, he stood between England and victory in the next two Tests. In the Second at Lord's he top-scored with 33 in a miserable 181 on a rain-damaged pitch, and took 5–71 from 40 overs. In the Third at Leeds, he was the best batsman with 66 and 32, interspersed with 77.3 overs yielding 7–166.

Protests about Armstrong's recourse to leg theory did not die down;

as at Nottingham, the Headingley crowd objected strenuously. The English novelist A. A. Thomson, having attended the match as a boy with his uncle Walter, recalled many years later:

> To those who believe negative bowling is a modern invention, it must be said that it was practised in this game…perhaps it was when it started. Armstrong was bowling practically at the square leg umpire, uncle Walter said, while McLeod at the other end discharged the ball more or less in the direction of point. As did 20,000 Cornishmen of an earlier era, an even larger number of angry Leeds 'loiners' wanted to know the reason why. Sarcaastic. That's what uncle Walter said they were.

Wisden took the connoisseur's standpoint: 'The cricket was very flat and tedious. As a display of stamina and steady skill it was astonishing, but nothing more could be said for it'. *The Times* thought that the spectacle's austerity betrayed modern decadence:

> No-one can say that in these modern days that the Australians played anything but the correct game. They must know themselves that their bowling is not strong. They were in the worse position and, in these days of statistics and calculations, public opinion is on the side of any tactics to avert a defeat. The drawn game is so common that it is being canonised.

Criticism washed over Armstrong; he grew in stature daily. On a damp surface at Bristol against Gloucestershire, he collected 7–16. Opening the batting at Bath against Somerset, he piled an unbeaten 252 from 2–469 with thirty-one boundaries on the first day. Trumper held the record for an Australian in England with an undefeated 300 at Hove in July 1899, and Armstrong set to overtaking it as methodically as he had Worrall's pennant record fourteen months earlier: on the second day he spent ninety minutes inching to 303 not out. Despite his earlier strictures, Darling appears to have condoned the exercise; the *Bath Herald* heard his repeated shouts from the boundary: 'Steady Warrie.' Perhaps he had determined to keep his key all-rounder happy; certainly he needed Armstrong time and again. Surrey were 2–100 needing 56 to beat Australia at the Oval on 29 July when Armstrong came on. Ignoring cries of 'Take Armstrong off!' from the crowd at the sight of his leg-side formations, he claimed 6–25 to guide Australia home by 22 runs. A fortnight later, as if to demonstrate his versatility, Armstrong claimed 11–70 against Middlesex bowling to orthodox fields.

There seemed no challenge too great, no situation he could not redeem; sometimes, indeed, his confidence defied restraint. As a slip catcher, Armstrong actually had a poor time: *Cricket of Today* complained that he was 'wholly out of place'. Yet, Elliott Monfries learned, he resisted Darling's efforts to move him:

> Armstrong knew enough about Joe to keep away from the slips but, after two or three games, when a right and a left-handed batsman were in and things a bit mixed, he attempted a try on…'Tibby' Cotter was the bowler and, choosing the right moment, Armstrong sneaked into the slips.
>
> For a great wonder this move was unnoticed by Darling, and Cotter, running to the wicket, was just about to deliver the next ball when Hill at mid-off throwing both arms in the air yelled: 'Hey!' Wondering what on earth was the matter, Cotter stopped abruptly to find Hill pointing at Armstrong but looking straight at Darling and saying: 'He's there again Joe!'
>
> 'Come out of that,' said Joe, and before a big crowd of spectators away went poor Armstrong very sheepishly to another position. Knowing Armstrong as I did, I can imagine he later got even with Clem.

For the Australians, the 1905 tour was a bittersweet affair: although unbeaten against the counties, they left the Ashes behind. Trumper's back injury commenced a catalogue of misfortunes. Kelly broke a hand. Laver strained his leg by slipping in a footmark against Scotland and played in elastic bandages for the rest of the tour. Gregory, bowling in jest in the same game, repeated the mishap and played in only two of the remaining fifteen matches. At Derby, Hopkins required stitches when cut by a glass he was using to bathe himself in lieu of a dressing-room bath. Darling, meanwhile, was bitterly dissatisfied with English umpiring, especially when officials he had twice settled on as preferences were given other appointments:

> The result of the two umpires not being available was that two inferior umpires had to go into the hat to make up five. As luck would have it, both these umpires got a Test match. In the last Test where we had a chance to win, two very bad decisions by one of these umpires had the effect of making a draw of the match instead of a possible win for Australia.

There was, however, no disguising England's superiority. The summer is traditionally identified with their captain, the Hon. Francis Stanley Jackson. The son of Lord Allerton and an amateur of impeccable pedigree—Harrow, Cambridge, Yorkshire—he took little part in cricket thereafter, becoming a Unionist MP. But Australia encountered him at his absolute peak: winning all five tosses from Darling, he made 492 runs at 70 and took 13 wickets at 15. With Fry and MacLaren augmented by the dependable professionals Tyldesley and Hayward, Jackson had at his disposal perhaps the best batting unit England has sent into the field. They enjoyed it, too. 'We all admired and liked the Australians of those days,' wrote Fry. 'But, by Jove, we did like beating them!'

It is odd, therefore, that their initial response to Armstrong's leg theory was so inert. Commentaries were often quite savage. *Wisden*'s Sydney Pardon considered the whole Australian strategy misconceived: 'Darling's policy with regard to Armstrong's bowling in the Test matches was a mistaken one...To bowl as he did at Nottingham and Leeds was frankly a confession of weakness.' Others were even more scornful, as Leslie Poidevin summarised in the *Referee*:

> His [Armstrong's] leg-theory methods have aroused the ire and indignation of many crowds, have inspired the phlegmatic members of the press box to endless sarcastic sallies and condemnatory passages. The player-critics have branded them as uncricketlike. He has been called the 'run-restrainer', and to the partisan spectator, pressman or expert, the policy of keeping down the runs on the occasion where the other side wants runs and wants them quickly does not commend itself. Some of the official critics have even sent down from the press box the suggestion that the MCC should take steps to prohibit or prevent their recurrence.

Poidevin was anxious to defend his countrymen, but himself could think of no better riposte than that old stand-by: the other team did it first, citing the bowling of England's Len Braund in 1901–2. It becomes clear in hindsight, however, that the root of the English objection was principally cultural. The Golden Age in England was more truly, as Neville Cardus remarked in *English Cricket*, 'the Golden Age of batsmanship', in which 'the great batsman could absorb himself in the perfection of his own art in the face of an attack largely reduced to a static mechanism'. The measures of law-givers and the attention of innovators were geared towards batsmen's welfare, often transparently, in the interdict against throwers, the introduction of the six, and the adoption of marl in the preparation of pitches. The objective was carefree, adventurous, rousing batsmanship—of the type, it was held, that only amateurs could truly provide. The sole attempt to redress the favour bat enjoyed over ball was of a piece with the foregoing: the attempt in 1900–1 to liberalise the lbw law, in order to punish those batsmen, mostly professionals, who had become adept at using their pads as a defensive bulwark. The proposal failed anyway.

So amateur batsmen ruled the roost, and they knew it. Darling recalled a flavoursome episode from the end of the 1905 tour, when Jackson took yet another century from Australian bowling for C. I. Thornton's XI at Scarborough, having been reprieved after a run out appeal before he reached 50:

> Jackson was out by yards and had no possible chance of getting home. The umpire, who was a former player, gave Jackson not out. This was bad enough, but what disgusted all of us was the fact that Jackson turned to the umpire who was standing at square leg and told him it was a good decision.

The order of precedence was simple: the mostly professional bowling classes were meant to take wickets, of course, but their other purpose was to allow their mostly amateur batting contemporaries to shine. Measures bowlers took to counteract such inequities were unpopular. Nobody could quite bring themselves to ban Bosanquet's googly— perhaps because it had helped England win several Test matches—but obscurantists deplored the degree to which it might restrict batsmen's scoring opportunities. Armstrong's leg theory was still more an affront to purists. At Trent Bridge, Laver recalled, MacLaren responded by 'kicking at the balls and sitting on his bat when Hayward was receiving Armstrong at the other end. I think "Archie" must have done this without quite realising what his action really meant.' On the contrary, one suspects that MacLaren knew precisely what he wished to convey: that this bowling was beneath him, no more than low cunning. As Albert Knight decreed of Armstrong the following year in *The Complete Cricketer*:

> His perfect accuracy of length (no machine could have maintained a more consistent length) was a constant source of irritation to batsmen, and to punish such bowling—very clever in a way of its own—is supremely difficult. You can upset the equilibrium of men with a policy of pinpricks; the true bowler carries a flaming sword.

By pursuing his methods, in other words, Armstrong was not being a 'true bowler'—a rather quaint perspective, even insulting. And Armstrong did take umbrage, at least to Fry's comments in the *Daily*

Express that his 'plan of campaign amounted to defensive rather than aggressive tactics' which were 'bound to make cricket dull for the spectators'. Fry recalled in his autobiography that Armstrong became 'rather angry' with him as a result.

Fry's response to Armstrong's leg theory, in fact, takes us to the heart of the matter. His whole upbringing was at odds with such an approach. Of his school cricket at Repton, Fry recalled: 'If one hit the ball in an unexpected direction on the on side, intentionally or otherwise, one apologised to the bowler.' His belief in sport's punctilios was such that, a gifted footballer for Southampton, he decried the penalty kick: 'It is a standing insult to sportsmen to have to play under a rule which assumes that players intend to trip, hack and push their opponents, and to behave like cads of the most unscrupulous kidney.' Accordingly, he was deeply troubled by Armstrong at first, and may also have been concerned that leg theory would achieve wider application; as, indeed, there is evidence it did.*

At the same time, however, Fry essentially refuted his own contention with two brilliant counterattacking innings: a bold 70 in an hour for Sussex against the Australians, followed in the Fifth Test at the Oval by an imperious 144 with twenty-three fours. 'He was not content merely to make his ordinary strokes,' wrote *Cricket*. 'He invented new ones, and his off-play was forceful and masterful to a surprising degree.' Fry's colleague Arthur Lilley considered it 'extraordinary for a matured cricketer who had turned his thirty-third year to so completely alter his style as to quite nonplus the Australian attack'. Like every notable cricket innovation, Armstrong's had compelled a counter-innovation.

Perhaps the most perceptive remarks about Armstrong's bowling in that 1905 series were made twenty-one years later by a later opponent

---

* In his *C. B. Fry*, Iain Wilton writes of a match between Fry's Sussex and Kent: 'The apparent success of the Australian tactics meant that they were tried by county sides who were desperate to find a way of containing Fry. In the first innings of his next match, at Tonbridge, the strategy appeared to work once again: he was dismissed for just 9 after forty minutes at the crease.' In the second innings, however, Fry found the appropriate rejoinder: 175 in three hours. Against Kent five years later, Fry would also be involved in one of the period's more bizarre assertions of a batsman's rights, complaining that bowler Charlie Blythe was deliberately tossing the ball up so that the batsmen would be blinded by the sun. He was, it was reported, 'recipient of a somewhat hostile demonstration'.

and something of a blood brother: Percy Fender, the adroit amateur captain of Surrey, who represented England against the Australians whom Armstrong led in 1920–21. In a speech to the Junior Imperial League on the eve of Australia's 1926 visit to England, Fender sought to summarise the Australian way of cricket, its intensiveness, its lack of inhibition. He saw it embodied in Armstrong's leg theory and in his captaincy, by then also a byword for discipline and denial, which he contrasted with more staid English mores. 'We are going to see certain things in the Australian game which are not to their detriment but which are not in our game,' he forecast. 'We are up against a lot of things *which we don't do but which other people do* [author's italics].' Condensed and cabled to Australia, Fender's remarks provoked much wounded comment. But nobody better distilled the cultural differences between the Ashes rivals, differences which Armstrong epitomised.

Armstrong's efforts did not flag in the seven matches played after the Tests' completion. He relieved Northamptonshire of a hard-hit hundred, adding 140 in seventy minutes with Hopkins and 90 in thirty-five minutes with Trumper, bustled them out in a couple of hours, then routed Lancashire twice in a day with 12–92 in 30 overs. Pleased to have seen his prediction realised, W. G. Grace magnanimously declared during Australia's final match against South of England at Hastings so that Armstrong could attain 2000 runs in all matches: tributes came no greater than this from English cricket's patriarch.

Armstrong's record from thirty matches in 1905 remains unsurpassed by an Australian cricketer on tour. His 1902 first-class runs came at 50.05, the highest average by an Australian batsman touring England to that time. His 122 wickets at 18.2 entailed 6000 deliveries, a workload exceeded but once by an Australian bowler in England, and encompassed almost 300 maidens, a benchmark exceeded only twice. No wonder an Enderby vicar who sent Frank Laver a verse tribute to the Australian team saw Armstrong in heroic terms: 'Now here's the man with the well-worn name/Towering Armstrong of deathless fame/Strong of arm with bat or ball/When he curls them in how the wickets fall.' And there was another reason for Armstrong to feel gratified with his summer's exertions: the tour had been a colossal financial success, grossing more than £15,000, and in profit from 21 June when the Melbourne Cricket Club's advance was repaid. All the argy-bargy before the tour about control of its finances had been worthwhile: at home in flannels or frock-coat, Laver had proven a poised and popular manager.

Laver came from a remarkable band of brothers: Alfred was director of the Melbourne Benevolent Asylum; Charles a noted doctor and drover in Western Australia known to Aboriginal patients as 'Mr The Doctor', and after whom the town of Laverton would be named; William a virtuoso violinist destined to become the third Ormond Professor of Music at Melbourne University. Frank himself ran a fruit-preserving company in Collingwood with youngest brother Ralph, and within the team went by the moniker 'Vesoo', short for Vesuvius; *en route* to England aboard the *Ormuz* six years earlier, a female passenger with strangulated vowels had pronounced his name 'Mr Lava'.

A fastidious man, Laver had been a strict overseer. Not only did he specify the daily coach's departure time to the second, but he held to it; no-one was late more than twice. He had won wide praise for his dili-gence, a correspondent from *Fry's Magazine* describing his hotel room in terms of a statesman's study:

> As likely as not you will find him after dinner in his bedroom at the Inns of Court Hotel…seated in his shirt sleeves at a roll top desk. There he will tell you of his last great fight with twenty photographers who all wanted to take the group at the same time and who managed somehow to achieve their object, or of his tussle with a certain pressman who missed his appointment and spent a small fortune fruitlessly in telegrams and tele-phone messages, and so and so and so on, till he gazes at the pile of letters, and you suggest that his time is fully occupied and he does not deny it.

Laver's position and the principle of player autonomy it embodied were, however, even then under threat. And Armstrong would have a leading role in their defence.

9

'Pledged to Stand or Fall Together'

The struggle for the control of Australian cricket, between the country's leading players aligned with the Melbourne Cricket Club on one hand and the state associations of New South Wales and Victoria on the other, had been years in the making. A recurrent theme of anecdotes during the first few years of the century is, for instance, the Australian dressing-room. In England, Frank Laver recalled, players welcomed guests with considerable informality:

> Public men and celebrities often come to our dressing room to be introduced. Sometimes the situations are comical. Upon one occasion the present prime minister of England, when he was First Lord of the Treasury, came in, and while shaking hands with some of our team, the wearing apparel was very scanty. One gave his right hand to Mr Balfour whilst he held his trousers up with his left. Another had one leg in his trousers and the other out. Others were drying themselves after a bath without even that much covering.

In Australia, by contrast, unwelcome intrusions brought out a proprietorial streak among its occupants. The Test immediately before Armstrong's debut, at Sydney in December 1901, was almost derailed when players demanded that their precinct be off-limits to officials. Joe Darling recalled:

This was like a bombshell to the New South Wales Cricket Association 'deadheads' who were debarred from even entering our room let alone bringing their friends in and usurping our seats. At first, they tried to defy us, but when I told them that we players insisted on having control of our dressing room and players' reserve, and that, if our demands were not agreed to, the Test Match would not start, and I would not even toss with MacLaren until we got what every reasonable thinking man must admit was our rights, they grudgingly put a man on the door.

In England, of course, the players were their own bosses. In Australia, they were at least nominally at the direction of state associations. And the *cordon sanitaire* they demanded round their dressing-room was symbolic. Cricket was their domain. Others trespassed.

By 1905, however, the players were beginning to encounter stirrings of resistance. The management of sport was centralising. The Australian Federal Cycling Council had been formed in May 1901, the Australian Athletic Council in April 1902, the Australasian Lawn Tennis Association in September 1904. A new generation of administrators, meanwhile, saw the concentration of power in the hands of cricketers, and commercially minded 'amateur' cricketers at that, as barring the way to the future. Theirs would be a struggle between an old Australia and a new, if not in the way one might imagine. The players stood for an abiding frontier spirit, for fetterless free enterprise, the administrators for the counter-vailing forces of consolidation and bureaucracy. And even as Warwick Armstrong was excelling in England, events that would shape his career were unfolding at the opposite end of the earth.

Thwarted in their efforts to take financial control of the 1905 team, the founders of the new Australian Board of Control for International Cricket smarted. The relatively mild and inclusive constitution drafted by Ernie Bean of the VCA, Harry Blinman of the SACA and A. W. Green of the NSWCA at their initial Sydney meetings was over the next four months amended, growing steadily more authoritarian. Indeed, the strife into which Australian cricket dissolved over the next seven years origi-nated in a handful of deletions.

Object (b) of the board was originally relatively anodyne: 'to control, regulate and if necessary finance' Australian teams going abroad. This positioned it as a sort of central bank, a 'lender of last resort' should other measures fail. At the instigation of the NSWCA's Billy McElhone, however, the words 'if necessary' were struck out, on grounds that 'it should be obligatory upon the Board to finance the visits of teams to England and elsewhere'. Rules 1 (b) and (c), meanwhile, began as including provision for the appointment to the board of 'one representative of the Australian eleven' and 'one representative of the Inter-State players, playing in Sheffield Shield' to be elected annually. These, too, were excised. In fact, by the time the constitution was ready for ratification, one clause alone contained any mention of players: Rule 9, allowing that 'the appointment of Manager of any Australian Team visiting England or elsewhere shall be made by the players interested and submitted to the Board for confirmation'.

The tone of the amendments was too much for the SACA, which professed misgivings, and way too much for the Melbourne Cricket Club, which dropped out of negotiations and formed a 'Board of Control sub-committee' including Billy Bruce and James McLaughlin to keep watch on developments. The club wanted to bring an English team to Australia in 1905–6, or failing that 1906–7, and now faced what amounted to a rival promoter.*

For rivals they were. Recognising that the board would amount to what people believed it to be, McElhone had the NSWCA secretary Percy Bowden write to Marylebone Cricket Club secretary Francis Lacey as early as 21 February to announce that the board would be assuming the management of tours to Australia—a body that had still to agree a constitution. Concerned by such cheek, Melbourne's committee brooded. The Australian team, then in New Zealand, was asked for its views; not surprisingly, they were unimpressed by a board on which they were not to be represented. 'Australian players will stick to the Melbourne club if they bring out a team,' Clem Hill wired Ben Wardill from Auckland on 18 March. 'Each one said certainly they would. Have spoken to all the fellows and every one is very much against the associations.' At a committee meeting three days later, Bruce moved successfully, in the face of opposition from his pro-board colleague Bob McLeod,

---

* The possibility of a rival promoter would have worried Wardill: he had experience of what this could cost. In one of Australian cricket's stranger episodes, in 1887–88, two English cricket teams had accepted invitations to tour Australia, one led by Lord Hawke lured by the Melbourne Cricket Club, the other led by Arthur Shrewsbury enticed by the SCG trustees. Both tours had been financial disasters, Melbourne alone losing almost £3600.

that 'this club decides to secede from the Victorian Cricket Association, the date of the notice to be given thereof to be left to the judgment of the sub-committee of the Board of Control'. This was permission to declare war, should the need arise. McLeod, a lone dove among hawks, resigned from the committee soon after.

McElhone's gambit, however, worked: Lacey wasn't sure with whom he should be negotiating a tour. On 5 April, Marylebone's secretary sent Wardill a puzzled cable: 'Don't understand, please write fully.' Wardill dismissed McElhone's works as an 'attempt by two associations to establish Australian board of control'—an attempt his committee intended thwarting. Deciding that it needed a representative to advance its interests in England, it empowered committeeman Major Thomas Morkham, sailing 'home' aboard the *Omrah* on 11 April, to ensure that any team visiting Australia did so under the Melbourne Cricket Club's aegis. Wardill wrote to Lacey: 'My committee trusts that you will not take any steps with regard to the proposed Australian Board of Control until you have had the opportunity of an interview with Mr Morkham and your committee.' The northern summer of 1905 was to involve more than a showdown between Australia and England.

Almost a century later, one wonders why the associations of New South Wales and Victoria chose this moment to escalate their conflict with the players. Doubtless it had much to do with the personalities of the board's founders. The body's nominal chief was its forty-four-year-old chairman Lawrence Adamson, the principal of Wesley College, who had recently succeeded James Aitken as president of the VCA. A devout Anglican and lifelong bachelor, he was widely admired for having inculcated in his school some of the ethos of his English *alma mater* Rugby School. His interest in cricket's management was of a piece with other *pro bono* works, such as chairmanship of the Victorian branch of the Royal Life Saving Society and presidency of the Lost Dogs' Home, and in keeping with his abhorrence of professionalism in sport, for he was also a leading light in the Victorian Amateur Athletic Association and the Victorian Amateur Football League. Yet the board's chief power-brokers were New South Wales' Billy McElhone, a lawyer with the eponymous firm of W. P. McElhone & Co, and Victoria's Ernie Bean, a senior official in the Government Printing Office.

Their backgrounds were quite different. One of nine children, McElhone was from a wealthy Catholic political family. Father John had been a cheerfully corrupt and incurably litigious member of the Sydney Municipal Council; in February 1880, he had punched a frequent antagonist Daniel O'Connor in the left eye in retaliation for being called 'a servile lickspittle'. Though an altogether more sophisticated man, combining an advocate's flair for debate with a solicitor's zeal for procedure, Billy McElhone retained his father's comfort with conflict: he would be called 'as tenacious as a terrier after a rat', and his manner at NSWCA meetings likened to that of a 'warhorse prancing at the scent of battle'. Although his nephew later played several games for NSW, McElhone was no cricketer; his sports were string-pulling and head-counting.

Ernie Bean *was* a fair cricketer, good enough to play club cricket until he was forty-nine and to represent Victoria eight times, if over eighteen years. A career public servant, he was probably never so severe on others as on himself. An abstainer from alcohol and tobacco who married at thirty-four but died childless, he seldom worked fewer than twelve hours a day and concerned himself with every aspect of his association's affairs— he even compiled the statistics for the VCA's annual report. Though he was born in Miner's Rest, his deliberate pronouncements emerged from beneath a waxed moustache in an accent betraying his father's Yorkshire roots. With his familiar sidekick Harry Rush of Prahran, a strict Wesleyan who also died childless, Bean would form a formidable duo.

Unlike the aspiring politicians who had first filled administrative roles, and also the gerontocrats who later ruled Australian cricket, neither McElhone nor Bean was old: in 1905, McElhone was thirty-four, younger than Joe Darling, and Bean thirty-eight. They were representatives of a new class, white-collared urban professionals, able, ambitious and dedicated. Neither represented a big club, McElhone being delegate of East Sydney and Bean of North Melbourne, but both came to dominate cricket affairs in their state, partly because of their manifest capabilities, partly because they concentrated their associations' decision-making within executive committees over which they presided.

Perhaps the chief reason that McElhone and Bean moved at this point, however, was because they could. In November 1903, the Sydney Cricket Ground Trustees had let their arena for a cycle meeting, displacing a scheduled NSWCA trial match. The association initiated proceedings in the Equity Division of the Supreme Court in order to prove the precedence of local cricket's needs in the management of the ground, and obtained from Justice Simpson a favourable judgment. The Board now had a crucial bulwark against the Melbourne Cricket Club. Although Wardill had guaranteed access to the MCG and Adelaide Oval, McElhone told Bean that the NSWCA was stacking schedules at the SCG in order to preclude other attractions, advice Bean gleefully spread. Wardill told SCG trustee Philip Sheridan, an old friend, on 24 May 1905: 'They are trading on this with the other [Melbourne] clubs, telling them we have no show.'

The SACA's refusal to join a board on which players were unrepresented left the VCA and the NSWCA with a dilemma: technically, indeed, their new body was in breach of its own constitution. The players, meanwhile, though far away, were keenly conscious of their rights. They were not resistant to the principle of a board *per se*, but abhorred one on which they would be voiceless. After a meeting with Marylebone at Lord's on 9 June, attended by Darling, Laver and Morkham, Australia's captain cabled SACA secretary John Creswell with satisfaction: 'Marylebone Club will not recognise Board of Control unless South Australia is included…Australian XI players do not agree with constitution of the board as agreed to by New South Wales and Victoria.' Clarifying his *parti pris* further in a letter from Manchester, Darling wrote:

> We as players are still in favour of a Board of Control, provided it is properly constituted, and to do this it must thoroughly represent the interests of Australian cricket. Before the Australian players will recognise the Board of Control, the following clauses must be embodied in the constitution…as follows:
> 1 Players must have direct representation on the Board of Control;
> 2 Players to arrange and finance all future visits of Australian XIs to England, the same as they are now doing;
> 3 Australian players chosen for an England trip to appoint their own manager and to arrange and control everything in connection with it, same as they are now doing.*

---

* The Australian players also drew support from, among others, members of the English team they were playing; Archie MacLaren wrote in the *Daily Chronicle*: 'It is a pity that the NSWCA frequently opposed the Melbourne Cricket Club, which has always managed affairs satisfactorily. It is possible that a thoroughly representative board can be formed, but doubtful if its control would be any improvement on what players have aleady done, their mistakes being few and far between.'

This was quite a wish list, even for the Melbourne Cricket Club. Perusing the letter, its committee minuted 'unanimous disappointment at its terms, which except as regards the stipulation for membership of the board of control are either very debateable or unreasonable'. As it would need the players' co-operation in any dispute, however, the committee kept its own counsel. Others were not so restrained. Defeat in England had cost the players ground in their own country: the Sydney press was particularly sour. Chief among critics was the *Referee*'s influential editor J. C. Davis. This was odd, given that he had four years earlier mooted a board specifically inclusive of players, but his former St Aloysius school-mate McElhone must have convinced him otherwise. Davis responded tartly to Darling's remarks, contending that it was 'immaterial' whether the players agreed to the board's constitution. 'Several of the Australian players are recognised professionals even under the elastic rules out here,' he wrote, 'and it need not be reiterated that the Marylebone club itself would be the last body in the world to agree to any legislative rights being extended to its professionals.'

Had Australia won the 1905 series in England, history might have taken a different course. Indeed, it was one of the stranger outcomes of the dividing of Australian cricket against itself that, whatever the private patriotic hopes of administrators for on-field success, defeat better suited their purposes. An immediate outcome of England's victory was that the Melbourne Cricket Club abandoned plans to bring an English team in the Australian summer. Wardill wrote Morkham on 8 August 1905: 'The committee do not deem it advisable to bring out a team this year…although had our fellows done better in the Tests, there might have been a chance.' The result, 'Stumps' of the *Town & Country Journal* remarked, provided further grounds for the board's existence:

> Before the team left Sydney, many keen followers of cricket were of the opinion that it would stand no chance in the matches against England. Such proved to be the case and, while defeat was bitter, it was welcomed because of the formation of the Australian Board of Control. Had the 1905 team been successful, it was quite on the cards that future XIs would again be selected on the same 'mutual admiration society' lines.

This strange effect of the administrators' squabbling—where the Australian officials became like barrackers against their own team—emerges neatly in consecutive paragraphs of the VCA's 1904–5 annual report:

Mr W. Armstrong is to be congratulated on holding a 'double first', being the head of the averages in batting and bowling, while Mr F. Laver has done excellently with the ball besides filling the onerous position of the manager of the tour. Both these gentlemen are to be congratulated on their splendid performances.

The leading feature of the year's transactions was the establishment of a Board of Control for International Cricket, your association feeling strongly the necessity of absolute reform in this direction especially in regard to the irresponsible system which has hitherto obtained in the control, management and selection of Australian teams visiting England.

Armstrong and Laver, of course, were the embodiment of that 'irresponsible system', and inseparable allies in its defence.

The VCA had another rod with which to beat the Melbourne Cricket Club: the concept of district cricket. Playing strength in the city's pennant competition was acutely concentrated; almost all the state's Sheffield Shield representatives were drawn from the Melbourne, East Melbourne and South Melbourne clubs. Reconstituting the competition along district lines, where clubs would only be able to draw on players within defined residential areas, would both help smaller clubs, like Bean's North Melbourne, and further eclipse Melbourne's influence.

Debate about the concept had in August 1904 reached a Rubicon. The VCA tabled a report by its Electoral Cricket Sub-Committee presenting two possible schemes, one offering Melbourne a tiny district on which to draw, the other allowing it to compete on a partial basis against the odd team in each round in matches where no points would be awarded. The former was absurd: Melbourne had at the time, scattered all over the map, 3376 members, with a further 730 on the waiting list. The latter was almost as unattractive: Melbourne would be in a competition it could never win.

Melbourne's opposition to district cricket was not merely a matter of self-preservation. Teams defined by geography threatened the whole idea of a 'club': the cricket team as voluntary assembly would be transformed into the cricket team as local amenity. In his history of East Melbourne, threatened likewise by the VCA proposal, Alfred Clarke eloquently defended the old ways:

In our position, the district can never take the place of the club. The young player gravitates to the club where the chosen companions of his school-days are likely to be associated with him. The district system compels him to play wherever he should chance to reside, without regard to his predilections or associations. To my mind, this is utterly subversive to that *esprit de corps*, club pride and community of feeling which are such potent factors in producing the wholehearted player, playing the game for himself and furthering the interests of the club he voluntarily associates with, and when his active part in the game ceases passing on the splendid traditions of his club to the generations taking his place.

Like the board, however, district cricket was an idea whose time had come. Electoral systems had been operating in Sydney since 1893–94, and in Adelaide since 1897–98. Melbourne had successfully resisted implementation of the scheme in 1904–5, and did so again in 1905–6, but could not defer it indefinitely.

Adamson offered the chance of a rapprochement between the board and the Melbourne Cricket Club. A Melbourne member himself, he proposed at a board meeting on 10 August 1905 that the club be invited to join. When McElhone demurred, Adamson made the considerable concession that the VCA guarantee Melbourne one of its board seats. After Melbourne's James McLaughlin attended the next board meeting in Sydney on 22 September as an observer, the VCA agreed to the measure and the board drafted a revised constitution. Yet it was a phony peace, and both sides went about their business with daggers clumsily concealed. The board persuaded the Queensland Cricket Association to join its ranks, on what proved the false promise of a Brisbane Test. Melbourne stalled on its nomination of a delegate to the board, and continued planning an Ashes series in Australia in 1906–7. Wardill cabled Morkham—returning to Australia with Armstrong, Duff, Hill and Newland on the *Omrah*—asking him to visit a representative of the Western Australian Cricket Council with a view to its joining Melbourne and the SACA in luring an English team. The intent of the antagonists was clear: both board and Melbourne wished to present themselves to Lord's as a representative Australian cricket body suitable to host a Marylebone tour.

The players, meanwhile, were restive. Although it is now difficult to determine who exactly knew what, Joe Darling's remarks in an address to the SACA on 31 October 1905 suggest that they were not only well-informed but had canvassed the likely consequences of resistance:

He went on to say that the Australian team players…had pledged to stand or fall together. If New South Wales disqualified their players, the players in other states would stand by their colleagues. If an English team came out to the present Board of Control, the Australian players would not play against it. The Marylebone Cricket Club knew that.

Melbourne, too, clearly had expectations of being able to assemble its own team. On 3 November, the committee instructed Wardill to inquire of Syd Fairland whether the Sydney Cricket Ground was one 'under which no matches can be played without the consent of the Board of Control & c & c, and whether the ground will be available for the visit of an English team next season'. Fairland, equally, was ready, despite the Equity Court's decision, to stand firm with them: 'Neither the Board of Control nor the NSWCA has any control over the SCG, which will be available for any British team which may visit this state in a duly representative capacity'. Melbourne's committee considered this answer 'very satisfactory'.

To the casual observer, the 1905–6 season unfolded like any other, in the usual succession of grade and Sheffield Shield matches. Warwick Armstrong himself struck a rich vein of form at all levels, following 165 in four hours in a handsome Victorian win over South Australia with an undefeated 200 against Williamstown in 144 minutes complemented by 8–118. After two seasons as a professional, he also reverted to playing as an amateur, without explanation, yet most likely because he wished to be considered a candidate for Victoria's captaincy.

Larger issues, however, were now at stake. Melbourne and the board were a long way from agreement. The SACA, meanwhile, was holding aloof. Citing the failure of the Australasian Cricket Council, it thought a national body not involving the players unsustainable. 'It would be absolutely useless to form another board,' said committeeman Mostyn Evan, 'unless it had the cooperation of the men who provided the sport.' Again it is difficult to ascertain who knew what—Wardill's letter books from this period have apparently disappeared—but it is hard to imagine Armstrong, as a representative at Melbourne, being ignorant of events. He was certainly present at a meeting of players that Darling convened in Adelaide during the Sheffield Shield match there, at which Australia's captain discussed a plan under which the leading players of New South

Wales would join an Australian XI against an English team brought by Melbourne the following season. This plan would, almost assuredly, have been discussed between cricketers of Victoria and New South Wales when they met at the MCG over Christmas. When Darling led South Australia in Sydney in a match beginning on 6 January 1906, there was another of those apparently frivolous off-field skirmishes which, for the players, nonetheless held great figurative significance:

> The weather was extremely hot and, when we adjourned at four o'clock for afternoon tea for the usual fifteen minutes, the first thing we did on reaching our dressing room was to have a wash. We all then adjourned to the players' reserve portion in front of our dressing room where the afternoon tea was being served, but McElhone and some leading notoriety seekers were present with other 'dead head' friends who had rushed the afternoon tea provided for the players. The waiters were very busy with this crowd when we arrived, so much so that we could not get a look in even sideways. So pronounced was it that, as captain of the South Australian side, I got up and walked over to the large tea urn, called two mates whom I could rely on at a pinch, and we took possession of the tea urn and served the players with tea and kept the 'dead heads' waiting.

Armstrong also crossed swords with the VCA when, having been selected for the season's last Sheffield Shield match, he withdrew in order to captain Melbourne on a short tour of New Zealand apparently without informing the association secretary. On the motion of Fitzroy's Mat Ellis, seconded by East Melbourne's Charles Nodrum, he was censured; not that Armstrong would have cared.

It was amid these hostilities that Wardill made his most significant move towards an English tour in 1906–7, recruiting the cream of Sydney cricket: Noble, Trumper, Duff, Cotter, Hopkins, keeper Hanson Carter and cricketing clergyman Ernest Waddy, plus four talented Burwood teammates, batsmen Jim Mackay and Austin Diamond and bowlers George Garnsey and Jack O'Connor. The circumstances of this secret coup are mysterious: the Melbourne committee's minutes do not mention negotiations until 27 April 1906, when it was noted: 'Players' signatures submitted with form of agreement from Mr Noble regarding terms & c. Mr Noble to be written to stating that sub-committee agrees of terms similar to previous team's arrangement.' In fact, the business was probably transacted during a match between New South Wales and an Australian XI starting on 12 January where all the eventual signatories bar one were playing—the game, ironically, was being staged for the benefit of Australia's retiring keeper Jim Kelly, raising him £1400. It would appear that four players received letters, while the others signed a group invitation.

The reason for this vagueness is that Wardill was playing a dangerous game. Publicly, Melbourne was negotiating to join the board. Privately, it was organising an English tour of which it understood the board disapproved. As early as 20 November 1905, the NSWCA executive committee had advised Melbourne that 'in the event of its bringing out a team from England in opposition to the direction of the NSWCA, no matches could be played in New South Wales, nor would the representative players of the state be permitted to take part in such matches wherever played'. And the mystery remains because none of the players involved would surrender to the NSWCA any document they had signed, probably because it would have revealed some awkward truths. As Percy Bowden later put it:

> At the time of the players entering into this mysterious agreement, which as far as can be gathered is dated about the month of January last, they were aware that my association had…in part and parcel of the Board notified the Melbourne Cricket Club that it would refuse to recognise an English XI unless it came out under the invitation of the Board…There can be no question that the majority of players concerned entered into this agreement with their eyes open with the express intention of defying the government body in this state.

While the recruitment to Melbourne's cause of the eleven New South Welshmen was the keystone of Wardill's plan, it may be that his ambitions were still wider; one source, Darling's memoirs, suggests that he also recruited cricketers from Victoria. Although the timing of his recollection is at odds with events and there is no verifying administrative record, Darling mentions both Warwick Armstrong and Frank Laver in this connexion. The text of what the *Australasian Star* said was the full petition, which it printed on 30 June 1906, certainly suggests that it was designed to encompass players from all over Australia:

> We, the undersigned players of the Australian states, hereby declare that we will play against an English team in Australia if brought out by the Melbourne Cricket Club, and the South Australian Cricket Association, on any of the principal grounds in South Australia, Victoria, New South Wales or Queensland, or we will play against any team sent out under the auspices of the Marylebone Cricket Club to the Melbourne Cricket Club.

Publicly, the recruitment of Victorian players did not become an issue during the subsequent dispute. Privately, Darling suggests, it was a bone of contention: 'Some of the Board delegates, particularly Bean and McElhone, openly boasted that they would not be satisfied until they drove out of the game all the players who had signed that letter. Warwick Armstrong was the last.' It is difficult to be certain in the absence of other proof, but if we are to judge Bean and McElhone by their subsequent actions, Darling's assertion may well be accurate.

In the early months of 1906 rumours of an impending showdown abounded. Melbourne's tardiness in appointing a board delegate, to which its agreement with the VCA of the previous October entitled it, was considered deeply suspicious. 'Short Slip' of the *Sydney Mail* interpreted it, probably rightly, as a filibuster:

> The Board of Control will need to move expeditiously. A team is wanted in Australia in the spring. There are persistent rumours that the delay of the Melbourne Club is with an object…supposed to be an invitation to someone to bring a team to Australia…Should a team be brought out there will be a hard fight and the Board of Control will stand or fall by the result.

Again, Adamson sought to make peace, hosting a dinner with Melbourne's president Roderick Murchison and vice-president James McLaughlin. Adamson was accompanied by Mat Ellis, a renowned raconteur who appeared to thaw relations 'with a series of happily chosen anecdotes'. Yet the antagonists were fundamentally irreconcilable. The SACA petitioned the NSWCA and the VCA one last time on 19 April 1906 to reinclude the words 'if necessary' in the board's Object (b). The NSWCA and the VCA one last time declined. When the SACA stood its ground, Wardill showed his hand: on 1 May, he informed the VCA that Melbourne not only declined to nominate a delegate to the board but had withdrawn from the association. The South Melbourne and Richmond clubs followed suit. Wardill also wrote to the SCG Trustees requesting to reserve dates for Tests and tour matches at the ground in the coming season.

Francis Lacey, kept abreast of developments by Wardill and Creswell, announced three days later that Marylebone was declining the board's invitation to send a team, as the board could no longer be construed as a body representative of Australian cricket. Melbourne and the SACA were now at liberty to come to the rescue, announcing: 'That in view of the failure of the proposed Board of Control to induce the Marylebone Cricket Club to send a team to Australia for 1906–7, and in order to avoid the lapsing of the tri-yearly international visits, the SACA and the Melbourne Cricket Club invite the Marylebone Cricket Club to send a team to Australia this season.' As winter closed in on Australia in 1906, cricket had carved itself perfectly down the centre.

10

'The Issue Is Now One to Be Decided by Out-and-out Fighting'

Writings on Australian cricket history abound in strange omissions, and the strife of 1906 may be chief among them: it is rivalled in importance perhaps only by the World Series Cricket breakaway of 1977, which in a sense was merely an outcome of the board hegemony established seventy-one years earlier. It has produced not so much as a journal article, let alone a book, and omnibus histories of the game dispose of it perfunctorily: Jack Pollard's compendious five-volume chronology of Australian cricket grants it five sketchy paragraphs; Chris Harte's *History of Australian Cricket* and Keith Dunstan's story of the Melbourne Cricket Club ignore it altogether.

There are strong parallels between the events of 1906 and those of 1977. In both cases, the board was pitted against a private promoter of cricket attractions which had signed the choicest talent in the land. The salient distinction is that, when Kerry Packer's agents went recruiting, the board was the established authority. In 1906, it was the Melbourne Cricket Club with tradition behind it, the inchoate board the interloper. So little has been written about the events of ninety-five years ago, while their ramifications were so profound, that one must strive to understand them. This story takes us some distance from Warwick Armstrong—he was largely a spectator, albeit an interested one, in the evolving struggle—but it shaped his career as surely as that of every other Australian cricketer of the time, and in future.

Now that secession from the VCA had occurred, the full ambit of the Melbourne Cricket Club's plans emerged. Not only did it want to organise an English tour, it was planning a whole new local competition along district lines of its own demarcation: the club would subsidise the projected League of Victorian Cricketers, also to involve South Melbourne and Richmond alongside smaller clubs like Williamstown, Coburg, Malvern, Brighton and Port Melbourne. It appears, indeed, that word reached the board of Melbourne's recruiting drive through a leak from a meeting of the proposed league. The *Sydney Morning Herald* described a council of war, probably one held at Ludstone Chambers on 4 May 1906, between Wardill, McLaughlin, Trumble, Morkham, Melbourne treasurer Charles Forrester and potential members of the mooted competition:

> It was stated during the meeting that the Melbourne Cricket Club accepted the responsibility for financial arrangements of international and interstate cricket and the question was raised how far the club was justi-fied in making that statement. In reply the letters written by the New South Wales players agreeing to play on behalf of the club were produced and used as a lever against the VCA. Efforts were evidently made to keep the matter quiet but word leaked out and, the information coming to the VCA, the wire was soon put into use to inform the NSWCA.

Billy McElhone sought details himself, then wired Bean his plan for retaliation: 'Letters written by Melbourne to players January. Executive meet them tomorrow. Unless they withdraw will be disqualified imme-diately.' In fact, the dispute's first casualty was Adamson, mortified by the turn of events and acknowledging in his resignation from the VCA that a more procrustean approach was needed:

> The time for negotiations is over; the issue is now one to be decided by out-and-out fighting. I may or may not have been of some service while matters were still in the diplomatic stage, but I feel that my usefulness is now gone, nor have I the time to devote to the increased business which must now press upon the association.

'Out-and-out fighting' was exactly McElhone's intent. With the exception of Trumper, Cotter and Hopkins, involved in a private tour of northern Queensland, each of Melbourne's Sydney signatories was summonsed by the NSWCA: Noble, Duff, Carter, Waddy, Mackay, Diamond, Garnsey and O'Connor. Some refused to answer questions, but Noble and Duff stated calmly that yes, they were 'prepared to play for any cricket body, regardless of the direction of this association, even in New South Wales'. All were told that, failing withdrawal, they would be banned; as secretary Percy Bowden told the *Australasian Star*: 'What else are we to do? If such actions were permitted, it would strike right at the root of the sport. You see, it's either the association or eleven players who are going to run this show.'

To modern sensibilities, this seems an overreaction. After all, what had the players done? They had merely agreed to play against an English team, if such a tour could be organised by Melbourne, on the basis of the established *entente cordiale* between players and the club. They had received no money, no guarantee of money, nor any promise of selection. Yet the association's sense of betrayal is easy to understand. So far as its knowledge had extended, it had been negotiating the creation of a national board; now it learned that one of the intended members, Melbourne, had been courting its leading players throughout the process. To other observers, still more was at stake: the mutiny soon came to mean all things to all men. The *Sydney Morning Herald* viewed it as a wrangle between amateurism and professionalism:

> Players who so readily agreed to play anywhere should be admonished. Professionalism may kill cricket unless the public firmly impresses upon our players that the game is not played for their sake, and that, as important as the players of today may be, there are more important matters still in the future of our great national game.

'LBW' of the *Referee* saw a battle between Sydney and Melbourne:

> It is ridiculous that Australian cricket can be controlled by one club and that club the Melbourne club. This state is the home of Australian cricket. That has been proved by our cricketers on the field, by the spectators who keep the game flourishing, by the cricket association which has made so many improvements over the last dozen years, and by English visitors who candidly acknowledge the cricketing supremacy of this of all Australian communities.

To the *Worker* in Sydney, it was a struggle between old and new:

If bowls were not such a harmless, innocent sort of game, it would be easier to wish that Noble and Trumper, who are now as fat as they are faithless to good sportsmanship, would take to it passionately and permanently. With the ringleaders out of the way, some progress might be made toward fixing things up gradually and international cricket could be resumed in two or three years.

To Joe Darling, however, it was a matter of the players' rights to a voice in the game and to their free trade:

All the players would like to see the Board of Control properly constituted and thoroughly representative of all cricket interests in Australia: the associations of NSW, Victoria and South Australia, the Melbourne club and the players. We are quite willing to give way on the last point provided the Board does not interfere in the financing of Australian teams to England. The cricketers have initiated these trips and taken all the risks. They have done all the work in connection with them, and hard work it is, too. The day may come when there is a deficiency and that will have to be borne by the players…Many ruin their prospects of business advancement and when their days are done they have no situations to fall back on. Trips to England to a certain extent tend to unsettle a man, and no employer can put in a responsible position a man who is always wanting to get away to play cricket.

The players, moreover, promised a fight to the finish, one telling the *Australasian Star*:

It's a jolly good job…that the climax has come at last. It's unhappy, but trouble was wanted before the association will ever realise their position. They simply run us for all they are worth. It is the first-class men who put the association in the position they are today. Through the efficiency of the players, we hold a position in the front rank of the world's cricket, yet we find the association ready to turn and rend us limb from limb at the slightest provocation…As the best part of the association hardly know bat from ball, it does not seem likely that the public will flock to see them play if they take the places of the men they are trying to drive out.

Melbourne had fought an adept private campaign. McElhone now ran a masterful public one. He proved a skilled propagandist; one need not withhold admiration merely because many of his remarks were pure casuistry. One honeyed interview with the *Sydney Morning Herald*, in particular, is a masterpiece of disinformation.

What about the fact that Marylebone, the game's ultimate authority, was unprepared to deal with the board, and had long-standing ties with Melbourne? A simple misunderstanding, McElhone replied:

> There is no doubt that the Marylebone club has a very wrong idea about the method of government of cricket in Australia, probably brought about by their dealings with the Melbourne Cricket Club extending over many years. But this impression should be removed, as the club is now in full possession of all details relating to the government of the game in Australia.

No mention that the board had asserted to Marylebone the previous year an authority it had not possessed, and that it presently had neither a chairman, nor an agreed constitution, nor a revenue base to fund a tour.

The board had no desire to deprive Australian players of their profit share on tours of England, McElhone continued. It wished merely to be an honest broker ensuring that every player received an equal entitlement:

> The associations only require sufficient sums to properly manage the game, and, as the profits derived from interstate and international cricket in Australia are ample for the purpose, they have not the slightest intention of interfering with the profits of an Australian XI in England, but they insist on the whole of the monies going through the hands of the board and being divided by that body among all the players entitled to share in its distribution.

McElhone was here contradicting remarks at a smoke concert a year earlier by the VCA's Mat Fitzgerald, who had explicitly stated that 'it was intended the Board should take a share of the profits of cricketing tours', which 'they would hand to the associations' for distribution among clubs. His implication, too, that the players could not be trusted to distribute tour profits among themselves *pari passu* is unsupported by any solid evidence. Yet who could demur such sweet reason?

Likewise, McElhone went on, the board was exercised purely by the objective of optimising Australian on-field performance and selection:

> Far too many matches are played by the Australians on an English tour to the prejudice of the Test matches, and the board propose to so regulate the fixtures on future tours, so as to enable the team to enter the field against England at their best. Rightly or wrongly, there are many who hold the

opinion that, in the selection of Australian teams visiting England, matter other than the cricketing capabilities and the personal stability of players are taken into consideration and, if such other considerations do exist, the board, by seeing to the division of the profits among the players would put at end to such a state of affairs.

The first remark here actually contradicted McElhone's earlier undertaking that the board would not interfere with tour profits: by regulating fixtures, it would be doing exactly that. The second remark—prefaced by the telltale 'rightly or wrongly' which always licenses a speaker to say what he pleases—was also meretricious: there is little to suggest bias or nepotism in Australian selections at the time and, even if there had been, it was the associations of Victoria, South Australia and New South Wales themselves who appointed the selectors. Again, however, the comment would have struck many as entirely reasonable; who wanted other than that the best team should represent Australia at all times?

McElhone aimed to create a spectre of unregulated, irresponsible and self-interested players in need of a centralised control. And, in Sydney at least, he largely succeeded. 'The management of the finances by an officer appointed by the Board,' opined the *Sydney Morning Herald*, 'will go a long way to assuring the public that everything is square and above board.' Even those hitherto unconvinced of the board's *bona fides*, like 'Short Slip' of the *Sydney Mail,* began coming round:

> It could not be seen that the Board had any right to insist on financing teams to England. Object (b) of the constitution gave the Board power to do what it liked with the profits of the tours and it was everywhere thought that it was the intention of the Board so to do. Holding the view that the player is entitled to the full in whatever fee his services can command, that clause was strenuously opposed in these columns. Now the Board say that it is not intended to take away any of the profits of the Australian XIs but simply to handle the money and to see that all share alike. It was unfortunate that that statement was not made many months ago.

The most astringent criticism of the players, meanwhile, appeared in *The Times* in London. This was crucial: the hearts and minds of English cricket authorities were as much the prize as control of the Australian game. The unsigned article drew also on that abiding English gripe about the professionalism of Australia's *soi-disant* 'amateurs':

About the players, one can no longer mince matters; they play—Noble has openly averred it—for what they can make out of it. 'The Australian XI?' said one of its leading members when last it went home. 'Call us a joint stock company and hit it at once.' For, of late years, money has governed the arrangements of every trip. Men have been chosen on condition they accept half instead of full shares in the prospective profits. Last trip, one man went for little more than his steamer fare and there is strong suspicion that another purchased his place as a certainty by agreeing to forgo £200 of his prospective share. It is time that the extreme politeness of English sportsmen should come to an end, and that Australian professionalism should be taken for what it is.

The article could almost have been dictated by McElhone. Perhaps it was; much of the detail is pure invention.* But, unruly press influences restrained, McElhone now broadened his front. He wrote under the terms of the Equity Court judgment to the SCG Trustees on 10 May demanding use of the ground on every Saturday from the start of October 1906 to the end of April 1907 plus several midweek dates, throwing the trust into confusion. Four days later he convened a meeting of the NSWCA, where he recommended that players in league with Wardill be suspended unless they recanted within two days. Noble, showing considerable courage, attended the meeting as a Paddington delegate and spoke against the motion. The players had given Melbourne their word of honour, he insisted, and were not showing the association disloyalty; they merely declined to recognise a board on which they weren't represented.

Noble: In the past, the teams that went to England had an absolutely free hand in the making of their arrangements. Now the New South Wales Association came along with all its forces and said to the players: 'We no longer want you to manage your own affairs. You have to clear out. We are going to do it for you.'

---

* The only known cases where Australian cricketers had toured England on other than full shares were in 1896, when keepers Jim Kelly and Alf Johns split a share rather than have one go and the other stay, and in 1899, when Victor Trumper was a last-minute inclusion on a half share, then promoted to a full share after his undefeated 135 in the Second Test at Lord's. Darling responded angrily to *The Times* article: 'Not only is it wrong about the 1905 XI, but it is also wrong for previous tours I have made.' Likewise, in a letter to *The Times* of 14 August 1906, Laver insisted of the 1905 tour that 'all shared alike'.

A voice: Quite right.

Noble: The players were prepared to intimate to the Melbourne Cricket Club that this was the last occasion on which they would play for anyone until the Board was formed representing all the principal cricket interests (laughter).

McElhone denounced this 'herring drawn across the trail' and lectured: 'The players should realise that the game was not being played for their benefit (cheers). As soon as the public came to believe that monetary considerations swayed the game, cricket would go down (cheers).' The motion was carried and, failing to recant, Noble, Duff, Diamond, Garnsey, Mackay, Carter and O'Connor were disqualified. Waddy alone escaped sanction, having written Wardill rescinding his earlier agreement. The meeting closed with a 'vote of thanks' to the press for 'its unanimous support of the association': no less, perhaps, than the press deserved. When Trumper, Cotter and Hopkins returned to Sydney from the far north a fortnight later, they were also ousted; not only were the ten to be banned from interstate cricket, in fact, but from grade cricket as well.[*] 'Not Out', McElhone's old school chum in the *Referee*, found some bellicose imagery to describe events—of a sort, perhaps, one could only write in a nation that had never been to war:

> This is the saddest business one has ever known in Australian cricket. However, just as nations succeed only after war, bloodshed and trampling over their dead comrades, the leading cricket associations of Australia must now trample over some of those who are among the ablest exponents of the game…in their efforts to put Australian cricket on a sound basis.

In sporting terms, the dispute was now little short of war: structures built over decades were shivering into fragments. Melbourne was heading off in one direction, with its League of Victorian Cricketers, its

---

[*] One club refused to institute the ban: Paddington, home of Noble and Trumper. Among many speakers who attacked the association at a meeting on 6 July, John Pope, Noble's fellow delegate to the NSWCA, said that the trouble was caused by a 'personal hatred shown to Mr Noble'. When the association then threatened to expel the club if it did not toe the line by 16 July, Noble and Trumper resigned voluntarily. Pope wrote to the latter: 'Mr Noble and yourself have always had the club's interests at heart, and this opinion is now borne out by your perfectly spontaneous action.'

England tour and the cream of New South Wales cricket.* The board was heading in another, also striving to organise an England tour, but considering a visit from South Africa if that fell through. The intention of players aligned with neither, meanwhile, was unknown, although one told the *Australasian Star* to expect a strike:

> A prominent player not suspended by the association said: 'They must remember that, in the events of their services being called upon, many cricketers will take the same stand as those suspended...Do you think I would play to the detriment of those who have been suspended? I would be the worst sort of black leg.'

It is fascinating to imagine how a summer unfolding along such lines might have operated. Perhaps fortunately, it did not. The dispute was about to erupt on another front altogether, one threatening the Melbourne Cricket Club's very existence.

Although Melburnians looked on the Melbourne Cricket Ground as the property of the Melbourne Cricket Club, it was not. Under a deed of grant issued in June 1862, the ground was vested in four trustees. As traditional occupant, of course, the club was more or less in control, and had poured fortunes into the arena's development: Wardill's estimate was that the club had during its tenure spent more than £100,000 on the MCG, and more than £80,000 on associated expenses and salaries, only a third of which had been paid for by gate receipts, the rest by members. In October 1905, however, the last original trustee, Thomas Hamilton, had died. The three others were all Melbourne Cricket Club committeemen—president Roderick Murchison, James McLaughlin and Thomas Morkham. But, in a surprise move, premier Thomas Bent had taken the opportunity to appoint not one but six new trustees: ministers

---

* The situation was so fluid that Wardill considered a novel solution to staging a tour without access to the SCG, envisaging a series with two matches at the MCG, one in Adelaide, one in Perth and one in Christchurch. According to a *Sydney Morning Herald* report, he spoke informally with New Zealand's visiting premier Richard Seddon about a game coinciding with the planned New Zealand International Exhibition, which would have been the first Test staged on neutral territory. Unfortunately for Wardill, Seddon died at sea aboard the *Oswestry Grange* on 10 June, and subsequent events prevented the resumption of negotiations.

John Murray and James Mackey, Legislative Assembly members Alexander Peacock, William Watt and George Fairbairn, and Lands Department representative James Skene.*

The Melbourne committee was apprehensive. At a series of meetings, committeemen tried to ascertain the intentions of the new trustees, minuting on 21 June that 'the majority of the trustees stated they had no intention of injuring the Melbourne Cricket Club and that no steps would be taken of any importance without the club being heard'. Two days later, however, chairman Mackey granted a VCA request for matches on a series of dates in the forthcoming summer including two Test matches against England. Never mind that it was not clear any English team would be touring in 1906–7. Never mind that Mackey appears to have consulted only minimally with fellow trustees. The implication, the *Argus* explained, struck at the Melbourne Cricket Club's heart:

> It will be seen that, notwithstanding the fact that the Melbourne Cricket Club have, during their occupancy of more than sixty years, expended large sums of money on the ground and incurred heavy liabilities in connection with the fine grandstand being erected, the trustees assume complete control over the ground. They claim that the ground is vested in them and that the Melbourne Cricket Club has no better tenure than permissive occupancy. In other words, the club is in no better position than any mushroom club which may choose to ask to play on the ground.

The Melbourne committee hastily took legal advice; it appeared that Mackey had acted *ultra vires* in giving his consent to the fixtures without convening a trustees meeting. But Melbourne's resistance was crumbling on other fronts as well. The New South Wales players were growing edgy: Noble was a strong man, but no revolutionary. Perhaps if his players ended their agreement, he reasoned, the board would show similar goodwill; he wired Wardill on 23 June: 'Probably release would relieve situation pave way settlement.'

---

* Bent's intentions are unclear. He was then president of Melbourne's greatest club rival, East Melbourne, although it is also possible he sniffed political advantage. It may be significant that, in February 1907, Bent won to his side a conservative faction in the Legislative Assembly, led by Peacock and Donald Mackinnon MLA, the new VCA president, called the Opposition Corner Party. With their support at the next election, Bent won one of the greatest majorities in Victorian political history, and ruled until January 1909.

The man in whom the balance of power finally reposed, however, was John Creswell. Secretary of the South Australian Cricket Association since 1883, forty-eight-year-old Creswell had often brought a Solomonesque wisdom to battles of officialdom waged in other states, and now did so again. A friend of Wardill's, and close to neither McElhone nor Bean, he nonetheless believed in the principle of a Board of Control, if it could be constituted without trammelling the players' interests. The issue for him was those two words 'if necessary' with regard to the financing of Australian tours. The VCA and NSWCA would clearly not consent to their reinclusion in the board's constitution. But, in view of McElhone's published undertakings not to 'interfere' in English tour profits, could the board perhaps define 'finance' in such a way that the players were protected?

At a Melbourne meeting on 25 June, Bean's VCA executive agreed to Creswell's request. Creswell then visited Wardill to inform him that the SACA would now probably join the board. For Wardill, this must have been a crushing blow, and initially he pleaded with Creswell to maintain solidarity. Yet he was also sensible enough to understand that the current stand-off was unsustainable, and that it was now a matter of obtaining the best terms when a peace treaty was signed. In return for joining the board, the SACA received a clarification of 'finance' dictated by McElhone: 'The Board shall see that all profits of the tour be distributed equally between the members of the team. The Board has no intention of interfering in any way with the profits earned by the players on the tour.' In return for renouncing its role as the underwriter and enabling agent of tours to and from Australia, and also agreeing to disband its proposed League of Cricketers, Melbourne was granted *inter alia* a seat on the board, a promise that the suspensions on the players of New South Wales would be lifted, and most importantly an undertaking that the VCA's letter to the MCG's trustees would be withdrawn. After a meeting between the Melbourne committee and the VCA executive on 10 July lasting from 4.30 p.m. to midnight, Wardill wired the NSWCA: 'The committee of the Melbourne club has released the players from their obligations.'

The Board of Control had won. Indeed, it had won overwhelmingly; the extent of its victory was not yet clear. The 'Big Six' dispute of 1912, which historians have covered in some detail because of its colour and movement, is essentially no more than an aftershock of what we might call the 'Big Ten' dispute of 1906. It ended at a stroke forty years of cricket tours to Australia backed by private interests; henceforward and to this day, with the exception of the two years of World Series Cricket, the board has been a self-constituted monopoly. The position of the players was likewise never the same—the board, once it eclipsed the Melbourne Cricket Club, dictated from a position of strength.

Melbourne remained wealthy, and grew wealthier, but its involvement in the future of Australian cricket would be circumscribed. One wonders, indeed, whether Wardill ever quite overcame his disappointment at the SACA's compromise. The Melbourne committee solicitously voted him a £100 a year pay rise on 28 August 1906, but he never seems to have been quite the same man again. Although his letter book from 1906 is missing, those of 1905 and 1907 survive. The letters in the former are bright, full of energy and confidence, those in the latter notably duller, more procedural, less expansive. Maybe he sensed what was coming. In the event, neither Creswell nor Wardill saw the drama played out: Creswell died suddenly in March 1909, Wardill retired in June 1911. Which was, perhaps, just as well.

The SACA formally joined the board on 28 July 1906, electing as its three delegates Harry Blinman, Mostyn Evan and, a little cheekily, Joe Darling. Melbourne nominated committeeman Arthur Aitken. On the board side, however, there was little grace in victory. Rather than reinstate the New South Wales players immediately, the NSWCA let them twist in the wind a little longer. As an anonymous delegate told the *Australasian Star*:

> There is no reason why they should get concessions. It was neck or nothing, and if they'd won where would we have been?…We have been flouted, our authority has been ignored. Now when we look like coming out on top, why should we turn to them the other cheek? The players will have to pay the price of their actions.

When finally the suspensions were lifted the following month—'in view of their having admitted the authority of the NSWCA in cricket matches and the association's right to discipline any player disobeying its rules or directions'—the association did so with a parting shot: the recalcitrants were disbarred from holding any association office for a period of three years from 1 July 1906. McElhone's principal target was clearly Noble, who took it stoically: 'During the recent dispute, we made several important concessions. These were done in the interests of Australian cricket, and it is disappointing that the association did not see fit to meet us half way.' In the spirit of compromise, Noble even endorsed a wire that McElhone sent to Marylebone reissuing the board's invitation for an English touring team, although the reply from Lord's confirmed the worst: 'Committee consider it is too late to send a team.'

Nor did Ernie Bean wax generous at the VCA. When Melbourne, South Melbourne and Richmond were readmitted to the association at its meeting of 13 August, they were gratuitously stung for £5 per delegate.[*] Bean then pushed ahead with district cricket in the face of spirited opposition not only from Melbourne but also from South Melbourne and East Melbourne at a meeting on 10 September. 'It's quite time enough to say good day to the devil when you meet him!' exclaimed a South Melbourne delegate, although only Melbourne took the step of staying out: it agreed to compete as an 'extra team', meeting clubs with the bye in matches for which no points would be awarded.

Thus was peace restored. Or was it? When New South Wales named its first team to play Queensland from 7 December, Noble, Trumper, Cotter, Duff, Diamond and Carter were absent: all had withdrawn. Trumper, in fact, appeared distractedly in only two matches that season, and the cause of his waning interest was hardly elusive. The *Australasian Star* asked him directly if he would keep playing. 'Yes,' he replied. 'We think our duty to the game and to the public is greater than that to the association.' Would he then apply to have his disqualification lifted? 'Once bitten, twice shy,' he answered. 'For one, I won't crawl to them, especially as their object seems to be to heap every indignity on us.'

---

[*] Wardill offered to pay the £30 in rejoining fees levied on Richmond and South Melbourne. The VCA's letter to the Melbourne Cricket Ground trustees was, however, withdrawn as promised: a new pact between the trustees and the club was published in the *Argus* on 14 February 1907.

11

'Strongarm Warwick'

For most of the board's 1906 showdown with the Melbourne Cricket Club, Warwick Armstrong was merely an interested onlooker. In its early stages, he was actually captaining Melbourne on an eight-week New Zealand tour, where he characteristically gorged himself against puny opposition: with 868 runs at 124 and 83 wickets at 9.9, reckoned the *New Zealand Herald,* he was 'a team almost in himself'. Occasionally, his dominance bordered on absurdity. Against a Manawatu XVIII, he took 22–73, 'at times breaking nearly three feet across from leg'; against Wellington, he collected 10–143, as 'efforts to play him approached the ludicrous'. In the same game, he also scored 175 in 140 minutes and, when Melbourne was set 110 to win in three-quarters of an hour, an unbeaten 66 securing victory on the call of time. It was in part a social tour—Melbourne subsidised sight-seeing trips to Rotorua and Lake Wakitipu—but Armstrong permitted no levity. A game against Southland was marred by dreadful conditions: 'There was not a glimpse of the sun all afternoon,' reported the *Dominion.* 'The skies were leaden and a cold wind blew.' Most would have been content to idle in the pavilion: Armstrong barged to 335 in three hours, the first triple-century in New Zealand, and took 10–114.

An indicator of Armstrong's earnestness in even minor cricket emerges in a Melbourne committee minute, responding to a 26 March letter from team manager Arthur Aitken. The side was shortly to leave New Zealand aboard the *Monowai* for two two-day matches in Tasmania on the way home—hardly important fixtures, which three players had proposed skipping. This irked Armstrong. The committee noted: 'McLeod, Jennings and Irwin cannot stay in Tasmania, and Armstrong not willing to play if team not strengthened.' Though a few locals could easily have been drafted as reserves, Melbourne moved to placate its star all-rounder by sending four other players. Even with the club so admiring of him, Armstrong could be an awkward cove. And what went for Melbourne, went doubly for the Victorian Cricket Association. Armstrong was assuming in his state a problematical status: its premier cricketer, but one on whom the association would have preferred not to rely. His next interstate match explains why.

On 2 December 1906, Armstrong took his first job in two years, becoming a temporary clerk and shorthand writer in the Department of Home Affairs. The immediate effect was to jeopardise his availability for the season. He consulted his boss, a Colonel Miller, who granted leave for one Sheffield Shield game, but thought two would be asking too much. At a Victorian training session on 10 December, Armstrong told Melbourne's Arthur Aitken—also a state selector with Ernie Bean, Mat Fitzgerald, Harry Rush and Frank Laver—that he could play the MCG game commencing against New South Wales on Christmas Eve, but not the ensuing match against South Australia. There, momentarily, the matter rested. For the New South Wales fixture, in fact, teammates for the first time elected Armstrong captain.

As was increasingly typical of Victorian cricket, poor organisation and slack discipline reflecting off-field disharmonies, the game was a debacle. By the time the visitors had reached 2–129 at stumps chasing the hosts' modest 159, Victoria was in disarray. An injury to the keeper had left batsman Tommy Warne in custody of the gloves, while twelfth man Ted Goss was for some reason not at the ground—Noble obligingly offered his own substitute. Armstrong responded manfully, restricting the deficit to 154 with 6–66 from 28.3 overs, then grafting an unbeaten 168 in 230 minutes, including eighteen fours and a six onto the ground's raised asphalt bank at the pavilion end. In New South Wales' second innings, he cunningly deployed the rarely used Warne, whose looping leg-breaks obtained 6–50. It had been an impressive initiation as leader.

Off-field events, however, were more significant. When Victoria's team for the match against South Australia was published, Armstrong found that he had been included; he telephoned VCA secretary Edward Heather to reiterate his unavailability, deflecting Heather's suggestion that the association approach the Home Affairs Department on his behalf. He was consequently riled to learn later the same day that Rush had done exactly that: so far as Armstrong was concerned, he had said he would not play, didn't intend to, and didn't.

Without him, Victoria disintegrated. The manner of their 319-run defeat was as galling as the margin. Commencing the last day at 3–148, they squandered five wickets for 22, then discovered their last two batsmen missing: Fred Collins was attending to his clerical job with the AMP Society, Jack Saunders his duties as Carlton caretaker. The VCA promptly instituted an inquiry, summoning not only the truants, but also Armstrong and Warne (who had missed the game with a sprained wrist).

This seems gratuitous: why should Armstrong have been called at all? He evidently thought so, too; he did not attend the hearing on Friday, 4 January 1907, instead sending a letter outlining his leave situation and explaining that he did not 'consider any further explanation necessary'. In the event, the inquiry proved somewhat farcical, characterised by an exchange between South Melbourne's Henry Skinner and Fitzroy's Mat Ellis:

> Skinner: 'Do you think it was fair to the spectators? They paid their shilling and the balance of the players did not turn up. They would probably be in favour of imposing a fine of £10.'
> Ellis: 'I ask Mr Skinner: Would he pay 1s to see Collins and Saunders bat?'

Armstrong spent the weekend doing what he did best: his three-hour 251 at the MCG against Essendon included three sixes—one exiting the ground altogether and lodging amid unfinished brickwork in the Standing Gallery. 'I never knew of a hit clean out of the ground until Warwick's great feat on Saturday,' rhapsodised 'Felix'. 'The Essendon bowlers will be calling him Strongarm Warwick instead of Warwick Armstrong.' The VCA was about to learn the truth in this jest.

Armstrong was now annoyed. The *Argus*'s report of the hearing had concluded with a statement by Bean that Armstrong had advised of his withdrawal on 27 December. What of the three weeks' notice he'd given? What of Rush's meddling? As the VCA had scheduled a 'special meeting' at Young & Jackson's on Monday evening, he decided to appear. For once, this silent giant was in a talkative mood. 'I do not know by what right I am asked to come here,' he stated immediately. 'I do not admit that you have any right to call on me for an explanation, but out of loyalty to the association I have come.'

In the chair was the distinguished presence of Donald Mackinnon, the Legislative Assembly member for Prahran who had succeeded Lawrence Adamson as VCA president. Tall, lean, Oxford-educated, silver-haired and silver-tongued, he espoused with conviction the principles of amateur sport. He now read aloud the VCA's Rule 27, a liturgy empowering the association to proscribe players who did not make their best efforts to play once selected. Armstrong was unimpressed: 'I think that rule only applies to players who promise to play and then do not. In regard to the statement made by Mr Bean in the *Argus*…I will call Mr A. Aitken, one of the selection committee as a witness.' Aitken confirmed that he had informed his co-selectors in advance of Warwick's unavailability and, while the memories of Bean, Rush and Fitzgerald had conveniently lapsed, was supported by Laver.

This should have ended the matter, but Armstrong prolonged it. He wanted atonement: 'You have placed me in a very false position and I have been asked some very awkward questions. I think the committee should apologise to me, especially Mr Bean.' Bean hissed back: 'What I stated was correct. Mr Rush and Mr Fitzgerald told me they did not know until Thursday.' But what had really aroused Armstrong was Rush's visit to the Home Affairs Department, as he explained in describing his telephone conversation with Heather:

Mr Heather asked if some of the executive could go to the department and use a little influence to get leave for me. I said: 'The worst thing you can do to me is come near the office.' In the afternoon, the secretary of the department called me and said that two members of the association had been up asking for leave for me. In my opinion it was quite enough for me to say that I was unavailable…

Anyone with brains would have done the same…I take it as a piece of impertinence on your part to go to the head of my department after my telling the secretary not to come near the place. It is very hard that you should interfere with my living all for the sake of a game of cricket. Don't you think you should have asked me first?

Rush: We thought it was the best thing to do in the interests of the state and the association.

Mackinnon: Do you reserve to yourself the right to play when you like?

Armstrong: Yes, and the selection committee can leave me out when they like. It works both ways.

This was not the diplomatic Monty Noble before the NSWCA; this was a very strong-willed, angry cricketer determined not to be pushed around. Therein, one suspects, lies the subtext: radicalised by watching McElhone lord it over his comrades in Sydney, Armstrong had determined that Bean would never do the same in Melbourne. The closing exchanges imply that, while even his friend Laver was trying to smooth matters, 'Strongarm Warwick' wished to make a point:

Armstrong: The players nowadays seem to be treated like a bunch of schoolboys, and they are getting full up with it. If it goes on, there is no knowing what will happen.

Laver: I am very pleased that Mr Armstrong has been here to clear this matter up. I am glad he has given such a good explanation.

Fitzgerald: I endorse that. I think there has been a misunderstanding.

Mackinnon: I am glad to hear Mr Armstrong's declaration of loyalty to Victorian cricket. Not that we doubted it, but because the public both here and in New South Wales has been inclined to doubt the loyalty of the players.

Armstrong: That is absurd and unfounded.

Mackinnon: I am glad to hear you say so. It is a mistake to stir up trouble. I am delighted to hear the explanation, for the public were not unnaturally disappointed at your non-appearance and they are entitled to know the reason.

Armstrong: I do not want any more said about it.*

Armstrong might well have felt untouchable at the time. He followed his innings against Essendon with an undefeated 203 against University in 160 minutes, and in the Sydney rematch with New South Wales struck 111 in 158 minutes out of 194. Victoria, meanwhile, stumbled

---

* The affair's final outcome seems to reflect differing protocols for amateurs and professionals. Armstrong and Collins, amateurs, went unpunished, Warne and Saunders, professionals, were penalised—Warne was reprimanded for late withdrawal, Saunders docked 40 per cent of his £5 match fee.

from one disaster to another. In the second innings of the same game, they were routed for 31 on a rain-affected track. The VCA then named a team to visit Tasmania, specifying that players should expect 'no professional fees or remuneration for loss of time' and that the captain would double as manager. Armstrong absented himself: the team, led by Peter McAlister, was thrashed.

Bean would yet get his chance for revenge. And even before then, Armstrong would have to face another crisis, altogether closer to home.

Details of Armstrong's home life at this time are exceptionally scarce. We know only that he remained at Arra Glen with father John, mother Amelia, and younger siblings Jack, Olivia, Amelia, Muriel, Tom and Lucia, the last still at school. They were a solid middle-class unit: John a full partner at Major and Armstrong, now located at Leadenhall, 26 Market Street; Amelia a respected member of the St Joseph's parish. Their life seems to have been mostly unremarkable. The boys, doubtless encouraged by an enthusiastic father, enjoyed their cricket: Jack played for Caulfield, Tom at Xavier College then with his church. The boys also had jobs, with Jack an auctioneer's clerk, Tom at the Bank of New South Wales, and even Warwick momentarily settled. The girls' activities, meanwhile, were circumscribed. Muriel occasionally helped out at Major and Armstrong, the rest remained at home. Indeed, family lore has it that Warwick Armstrong's sisters doted on him, scrubbing his soiled creams, polishing his boots and starching his shirts. Olivia submitted lovingly to the task of knitting him an endless supply of cricket socks; the supply had to be endless as they invariably shrank on washing.

Jack Armstrong's reputation was as 'a bit of a trick': handsome, charming, averse to hard work. Having tried out unsuccessfully at Richmond three years earlier, he had not gone on as a cricketer, and now preferred holding court in the front bar of Collins Street's Federal Hotel. On 17 August 1906, however, twenty-six-year-old Jack suddenly married twenty-one-year-old Catherine Emily Rich. There was no explanation, no newspaper report of the wedding, and no evidence that Jack's elder brother attended; it was held at St Mary's Catholic Church in St Kilda, not the Armstrongs' usual place of worship.

Catherine Rich, from Grantville, New South Wales, was a mining engineer's daughter who shared a Hawthorn Road home called Aldinga, not far from Arra Glen, with her elder sister Annie. She was in the advanced stages of pregnancy. Marriage began a nightmarish ordeal for her. Shortly after the wedding, according to court documents, Catherine asked Jack to 'provide a home as I wished to live with him'. He replied that, if she found rooms, they would 'live together and do the best we could'. But a fortnight later, Catherine having paid a deposit on lodgings in South Yarra, Jack changed his mind. According to Catherine, he said 'he absolutely once and for all could not live with me and that I could do what I liked'. A month later Catherine travelled to Sydney, hoping to stay with a sister, who proved too ill to accommodate her, then journeyed on to Newcastle, where another sister took her in. A child, Mary Tait Armstrong, was born there on 27 October 1906.

In February 1907, Catherine tried unsuccessfully to renew contact with her husband. She returned to Melbourne and wrote again. When they met, however, Jack not only refused to provide her with accommodation but declined to contribute maintenance. John Armstrong interposed, arranging to pay Catherine 10 shillings a week in the form of a postal note, signed with his son's name to make it appear that Jack had sent it. Catherine fell back on her family again, returning to Sydney where her father afforded her lodgings while she waitressed in a tea room.

No record of events from the Armstrongs' perspective survives, and the only trace Jack Armstrong left of himself during this time was as a cricketer: newspapers show he played a full season for Caulfield in 1906–7, doing rather well. But one can imagine the impact of his indiscretion on a Catholic family. It is impossible to know Warwick Armstrong's degree of awareness, though again, living beneath the same roof as his father and brother, he probably knew the scandal in full detail; perhaps John took counsel of his oldest son, much as John's father Oliver had done with his oldest boys in 1863 after the family's ruin in Kyneton. Whatever the case, the postal notes ceased altogether in July, and Jack seems to have left Melbourne for an extended period. When Catherine wrote first to Jack then his father, this time threatening legal remedy, she received no reply.

Jack Armstrong's fecklessness under the circumstances is not difficult to understand: nothing in his languid charm equipped him to deal with its consequences. John's and Amelia's severity—for one can imagine the matriarch having strong views—is harder to comprehend. Perhaps John could not do other than continue indulging his sons. Perhaps Amelia saw Catherine's shame as vindicating the discipline she imposed on her own girls. It was a problem that would not go away, and would tax the Armstrongs for years to come.

Warwick Armstrong's fortunes would have comforted his parents. In December 1906, with that streak of inherited financial prudence, he acquired the vacant lot abutting Arra Glen, 'the paddock' on which he had twenty years before played cricket with Jack and Olivia. Purely an investment, and undeveloped in his lifetime, it probably explains his temporary public service job, which enabled him to sign the title 'Warwick Windridge Armstrong, Commonwealth Employee'. The Home Affairs Department had broad responsibilities, from census management to the activities of the government astronomer, although the terms of Armstrong's engagement suggest his duties were in a different jurisdiction: federal elections. Australians went to the polls on 14 December 1906, returning Alfred Deakin as prime minister, thanks to the support of twenty-seven Labor members. In any event, Armstrong was not long for the public payroll. He quit on 30 April 1907, this time for a business career.

Armstrong's new line—probably his first full-time job—was as a stock and station agent. Partner J. B. Wood had managed the stock department for A. A. Piggin & Co in Corowa, a rural centre on the Murray's northern bank. How they met is unknown, though there was then a Melbourne Cricket Club member of the same name, so it may have been under sporting auspices. Piggins was a successful firm: Arthur Piggin, Corowa's mayor, ran a representative office in Collins Street's handsome Olderfleet Building. That was where Wood Armstrong also raised its slate on 1 July 1907. The *Corowa Free Press* reported: 'Mr W. W. Armstrong, the noted cricketer, has gone into business as a stock and station agent in partnership with Mr J. B. Wood…On Mr Wood's account, many Corowa friends will wish the new firm a prosperous and successful career.' Wood Armstrong's main business was representing Corowa interests at fortnightly Melbourne auctions of livestock and hides, though shortly after opening it enjoyed a *coup* by acting for Messrs Matthew Lang of Collins Street in the sale of the huge Mount Poole Station (160,000 hectares, 25,000 sheep) in the Norparinka district to cattle baron Sidney Kidman.

At first, cricket's community was dismayed. Armstrong's retirement was bruited by the *Sydney Mail*'s 'Short Slip':

It is not clear that Warwick Armstrong will be playing this year, although it is intended to persuade him to do so if possible. Victoria and Australia cannot afford to lose the man who held pride of place in the batting and bowling on the 1905 tour of England...This news comes from Melbourne. I hear that he is now living in New South Wales, at Corowa, where he is in business.

'Felix' spread the word, but still hoped to 'see the renowned Warwick Armstrong at his best' in 1907–8:

I did hear that he would not play big cricket this season, through having gone into business, but the Melbourne executive will no doubt induce him to reconsider this determination...so that he can show us that he has not reached the zenith of his fame in the manly game. Sounds like a rhyme....

Wood himself intervened to scotch speculation, informing the *Sydney Mail*:

Your paragraph stating that Armstrong is in Corowa is not correct. I was in Corowa, and came on here to manage the Melbourne business of A. A. Piggin & Co of Corowa. Mr Armstrong entered into partnership with me here on 1 July, but he will play cricket right through this season and go home with the next Australian XI if selected. It would be a pity for him to give up cricket now that he is at the top of the tree.

It was clearly the ideal position, offering not only status but scope for sport, which Armstrong would need: Australia was again shortly to face an English team, the first invited by the Board of Control.

Ostensibly, Australian cricket had been at peace since the lifting of the disqualifications on the New South Wales stars in August 1906. In reality, it was merely a ceasefire. McElhone, now board treasurer, wielded power almost unilaterally. An example was this tour's arrangement. Having lost £1044 on its 1903–4 visit, Marylebone wanted a £10,000 guarantee for the forthcoming trip. The board was to discuss it in Melbourne on 19 and 20 April 1907, but delegates from South Australia and Queensland were shocked to learn on arrival that McElhone had already accepted the terms, committing them to contribute. Least of all was McElhone interested in those traitorous players. In May, led by Noble, a dozen leading Sydney cricketers petitioned again for representation on the board, the entreaty accompanied by similar petitions from Victoria and South Australia organised by Laver and Darling. But the proposal seeking two board representatives—'to be elected annually, one by the members of the last Australian XI, one by the remaining members of the interstate teams of New South Wales, Victoria and South Australia'—was summarily rejected on grounds that representation was 'restricted under the constitution to state associations'.

The NSWCA made a gesture on 16 June by lifting the suspensions from holding association office on the ten Melbourne mutineers. But residual ill-feeling about Noble's role in the affair was undisguised, and the association's 29 July meeting ranks as one of the most infamous affronts a great Australian cricketer has suffered. Four nominations were received for the three association positions on the board: Noble was the only one not elected. Four nominations were received for the three positions as state selectors: again Noble missed out, his nomination by Alick Mackenzie being mocked by vice-president C. F. W. Lloyd.

'Are you serious?' said Mr Lloyd.
'Certainly I am,' said Mackenzie.
It was simply a question of taste, said Mr Lloyd. Some men had no sense of the fitness of things. It was a menace to the good government of cricket.

'By what right has any member to make a speech such as he made?' wrote Laver in his column in the *Sporting and Dramatic News*. 'I should like to know who showed the bad taste. Why can't the past be buried?' He would shortly know how it felt, when the VCA met on 16 September to choose its board delegates: he, Bean and Rush were nominated, Bean and Rush elected. How different Australian cricket history might have been had the authorities yielded a little ground at this stage and supported either Noble or Laver as board delegates. It was this pertinacious continuance of past grudges as much as its future policies that underlay troubles ahead.

The English team was by now *en route* aboard the *Ophir*, led by Nottinghamshire amateur Arthur Jones and managed by Major Philip Trevor, without several senior players who had declined to tour, but augmented by that magnificent bowler Sydney Barnes, the debonair amateur all-rounder John Neville Crawford, and as apprentice opener Jack Hobbs. Armstrong's preparations for meeting them were interrupted. He began with 89 and 5–56 for Melbourne against Carlton, though thanks perhaps to his new job looked short of practice. He was named on 4 November to captain Victoria in a trial match, but suffered an eye infection and was 'ordered complete rest'. On his return, however, Armstrong's powers were overpoweringly evident. Against South Australia, he struck twenty-five fours and a six while batting five and a quarter hours for 231, complemented by 4–92 in 43 overs. In a narrow First Test victory in Sydney under his new captain Noble three weeks later, he scored 7 and 44, and claimed 4–96 from 53 overs of parsimonious leg theory. Trevor thought he had never 'seen a bowler stop good batsmen from getting runs on a good wicket as Armstrong stopped them', while 'Short Slip' noted that Noble 'frequently consulted with his first lieutenant Armstrong'.

His influence was increasing. The *Age* of 14 December reported that a note Trumper had pinned to the Australian dressing-room door restricting access had been removed by an NSWCA official: 'Trumper thereupon stated that he would not go into the field until it was restored…The spectators were kept waiting for a quarter of an hour after the game should have been resumed at 2.15pm, and then Noble and Armstrong induced Trumper to go into the field again.' When McElhone denounced the report, Trumper contradicted him:

> The players' room has always, so far as we can remember, been reserved for them and their immediate friends. Otherwise the position would be intolerable, because, if not, men could not even dress or speak with necessary privacy. The list in question was posted on the players' door by the decision of the team, and it was restored at the instigation of Mr McElhone only when he saw that the team was determined to insist upon it. Therefore, your report is correct.

'Mid On' of the *Leader* thought that both Noble and Trumper were 'distinctly feeling and being affected' by their skirmishings with the board: 'Trumper is not himself, and I was particularly struck by the unmistakeable change in Noble, who moved about like a man feeling keenly the effect of unmerited degradation.' The next outbreak of squabbling was in Melbourne. When Victoria met New South Wales at the MCG on Boxing Day, Warwick Armstrong was missing.

The crowd was a sirocco of whispers. Five days earlier, Armstrong had invoiced the VCA for expenses during the match against South Australia, seeking £4, or £1 a day. In fact, the VCA's maximum amateur *per diem* was 10 shillings—the result of Armstrong's brush with the association four and a half years earlier. Informed by association secretary Edward Heather that the finance committee had rejected his claim, Armstrong refused to play. Even 'Felix' was nonplussed:

> It is a great pity that this should have occurred because everyone would agree that Armstrong is absolutely our best man, in fact a genuine champion. But there is something beyond the mere monetary aspect of the matter. Many a Victorian cricketer has been out of pocket by playing for his colony or state, and has never put in a claim for a recoup. These Victorian cricketers considered it a privilege and an honour to be picked to play for their state. The idea uppermost in their minds was 'patriotism' not 'pay'. But we have moved into a different time, a time when pay comes first and patriotism last so far as cricket is concerned.

Armstrong's defiant oration a year before had not been forgotten; it was not long before his entire history of disobedience was being dragged up. The VCA published a *gravamen* in the *Argus* delineating its expenses policy, revealing that Armstrong had for two seasons played as a professional, and insinuating avarice: 'A number of players make no claim for loss of time or expenses incurred in taking part in interstate matches. No amateur player with the exception of Mr Armstrong has ever claimed more than the maximum fixed by the rules.' The wages of sin—or, at any rate, the sin of wages—were hinted: 'It was stated last night that the executive of the VCA was seeking an opinion from the Board of Control as to whether a player refusing to take part in interstate games under the rules of their state association was eligible to play Test matches for Australia.' The *Herald* urged harsh action:

> There is a strongly unpleasant flavour of cash in the latest cricket dispute which led Warwick Armstrong to refuse to take part in the interstate match commenced yesterday. Apart from that, however, the incident raises questions about the status of amateurs and professionals respectively in Australia. For two seasons at least Armstrong played as a professional in Australia. With the last Australian XI in England, he played as an amateur. Now he wishes to assume the title and status of amateur in his native land, and at the same time to receive certain payments. We are aware that in England, in certain notable cases, the distinction between amateur and

professional has been reduced to a mere shadow…That is a position that should not be permitted here.

Press supportive, public perplexed, Bean was poised to mete out exemplary punishment—not merely to Armstrong, but through him to the Melbourne Cricket Club. Armstrong, however, was obdurate, and in a letter to the *Argus*, written on 27 December, sketched the outline of his defence:

> In your issue of today I note that you published a resolution of the VCA passed on the 13th of September 1903 that amateur players taking part in interstate matches who are employees &c should be allowed expenses for the extent of 10s per day. I should like to say that I was unaware of such resolution until yesterday afternoon and, had I been, I would not have made a higher claim than there stated, although I was a loser by playing…In conclusion, I may say that on several occasions I have not made any claim on the association for playing in interstate matches in order to help the association.

It was no confession, and certainly no apology. Perhaps Armstrong was even enjoying the fight. 'Sometimes,' wrote Jack Fingleton, 'as if he didn't have enough to occupy his time, it almost seemed that he went looking for trouble.' This may have been such an occasion.

A year after Armstrong had walked into Young & Jackson's to excoriate the association for its impertinence, the tables were turned. But again, Armstrong would not be cowed. When Bean's North Melbourne colleague John Howlett began by questioning the presence of journalists, Armstrong interjected: 'You've put your case in the *Argus* and I want the public to hear what I've got to say.'

Heather recited the relevant VCA statute: 'Amateur players taking part in interstate matches…can at the discretion of the finance committee be allowed such expenses as are considered reasonable and do not exceed the sum of 10s per day per man'. He continued:

> I received an account from Mr Armstrong on Monday dated 21 December claiming £4, being £1 per day for four days including Saturday for services employed and loss of time in the match Victoria v South Australia last month. The account was before the executive on the same evening and it was not passed. I was instructed to inform Mr Armstrong that…the maximum amount that could be paid to amateurs in interstate

matches was 10s per day. I wrote a letter to Mr Armstrong and posted it on Tuesday night.

On Tuesday afternoon I saw Mr Armstrong at the South Melbourne Cricket Ground, and he asked me if the account had been passed. I said it had not, and after telling him that I had written to him, I explained the position. He said he would not play if it was not paid. I asked him to write me a letter giving me the notification officially. He said he could not be bothered. As soon as I left I told McAlister what had occurred and asked him to speak to Armstrong. I also told Mr [William] Ahern and telephoned to Mr Rush.

I saw Mr Armstrong again at 11.20 a.m. at the Melbourne Cricket Club Ground on Boxing Day. He asked if the association had come to a fresh arrangement. I said no. He said: 'Then I will not play.'

Once this chronology had been endorsed by McAlister, Rush and Ahern, Armstrong yielded some ground. Although relating a subtly different version of events, he introduced to it a tincture of regret:

I saw Mr Heather at the South Melbourne Cricket Ground on Tuesday afternoon and asked him whether the account was passed. He said that he would ring up Mr Rush and find out. I knew nothing of the resolution of the association until Thursday afternoon when I was told of it at the Melbourne Cricket Ground. Now I know of the resolution I admit I was wrong in refusing to play. Had I known of it, I would have come to some arrangement before the match and would not have acted as I did.

Armstrong budged no further. Regret he could feign, remorse he could not. Responding to a question from South Melbourne's Henry Skinner, Armstrong again disclaimed awareness of the VCA's expenses limit:

Mr Heather never mentioned the resolution to me. When I asked whether the account was passed, he said: 'No, it is not, but I will go and ring up.' The next time I saw him was Thursday.
Mackinnon: There has been a difficulty with you before about money matters, has there not?
Armstrong: Only once.
Mackinnon: Do you know there is a similar rule with the NSWCA?
Armstrong: No. I do not know the rules of the Victorian Association. I only know the rules of the game.

After Bean had enumerated Armstrong's past exactions as an amateur and professional, the secretary could contain himself no longer:

Heather: Do you mean to say I did not ask you to write a letter?
Armstrong: I do certainly.
Heather: Gentlemen, I leave it to you. I say that his answer is false.
McAlister: Look here, Warwick, do you think that what you have said is sufficient reason for you refusing to play?
Armstrong: I do.
McAlister: Well, that's all I have to ask.

At times, the hearing threatened to turn into an inquiry into the whole issue of cricket wages, as though Armstrong's two seasons as a professional had cursed him evermore. Armstrong was having none of this: 'I am not here to discuss these questions. All I am here for is to explain why I did not play against New South Wales.' And while one suspects a deliberate forgetfulness in his denying Heather's request for a letter—his reported reply, that he 'could not be bothered', has a tang of authenticity—two other admissions during the evening's proceedings cast doubts on the quality of VCA justice. Responding to a question by Richmond's William Kelly, Heather admitted that Victorian players had never been informed officially of the resolution about amateur payments; in other words, Armstrong was on trial for failing to observe a statute of which he had no knowledge. Later, too, Mat Fitzgerald asked Mackinnon if the executive had reached a decision.

Mackinnon: I understand so, but whether it has altered since hearing Mr Armstrong I do not know.
Skinner: I don't know how they could come to a conclusion without hearing him.
Mackinnon: Their conclusion was based on the facts at their disposal.

Amazingly, the VCA executive had taken its decision *before* hearing the defendant. That decision, of course, favoured the most stringent sanction. Bean moved that Armstrong 'be suspended from playing any matches under the auspices of the association and that a copy of this resolution be forwarded to the Board of Control and to each association on the Board'. He continued: 'The real question is: Did Armstrong have any justification in not playing in the match because he was not paid? Once upon a time, players put the game first and money afterwards. Now it is just the opposite…The real question at the bottom of this is money versus the game.'

Armstrong's teammate McAlister seconded the motion: 'I regret to have to do so but I cannot help it. He should have played. In any case, he should have done his best to play. We wanted to win this match badly.' But Armstrong was lucky. Heather's confirmation that the resolution was unknown to players, and Mackinnon's admission concerning his executive's prejudgment, had shaken convictions. Henry Skinner was not renowned for his charity. He was licensee of South Melbourne's Golden Gate Hotel, where staff had to empty their pockets before and after work, and his name was said to be 'descriptive of his methods'. But he now made an emotional plea for lenience:

> My view is that Mr Armstrong was not approached the right way, and he got his back up...The utmost we should do is bring him in here, give him a good strong censure, and warn that if it occurs again he will go out for life. In justice to one of our best players I ask this. You will be taking away a performer the public wants to see...I think he's wrong. We all do, but we should take a sportsman's view of the case. I am quite broken up over it.

When Skinner's motion was seconded, Fitzroy's Phillip Knuckey added that the 'apology' entitled Armstrong to consideration. Brighton's S. H. Hammond—clearly an Armstrong admirer—then commented that 'it would pay us to pay him £50 a match', provoking outraged interjections of 'this is a matter of principle!' But when Howlett also urged the executive to reconsider, Skinner volunteered to allow it by withdrawing his resolution.

Mackinnon, unconvinced, mounted his amateur soapbox:

> I feel very strongly about this matter, as the public do. Sport has reached a low ebb in this country when a leading cricketer in the state stands out of a game like this for such a paltry reason...I am inclined to think that, in the interests of cricket, we should come down with a heavy hand to keep the game clean...The great offence I see is that he is willing to play in other games where he is well paid, yet here he hangs out when the state is badly in need of his services. These are my strong feelings but, if the executive feel inclined to reconsider the matter, they can easily do so.

After a fifteen-minute intermission, they did. An apology was drafted which, with some additions of his own, Armstrong read aloud:

> I now see that my action in connection with the New South Wales match was utterly inexcusable and detrimental to the best interests of cricket and, as far as I am concerned, nothing of this sort will occur again. I still maintain that I was unaware of the existence of the rule for the payment of

amateurs' expenses, but I am very sorry for what has occurred and I hope that in future games some arrangements will be come to on the matter.

Parenthetically, Armstrong discussed his job at Wood Armstrong: 'I am differently situated to what I used to be. I am in business and my partner is frequently away in the country. When he is away and I am playing cricket, I have to leave the office with no-one in charge.' Mackinnon softened: 'I am glad you have made this statement. I am sure your position is the right one. No-one could defend the position you took up...Cricket would become intolerable if such things were allowed.' Once Armstrong had left, good humour was restored by an address from A. W. Green, one of McElhone's NSWCA henchmen: 'There were some players who felt that they should rule, and that men who gave up night after night should take a back seat...That was a wrong position to take up. They must have a clean environment if they wanted a clean game.' He was loudly applauded.

The controversy had still to blow itself out. The *Herald* chastised the VCA for lenience:

Apparently, if the association had been guided by its president, Armstrong would have been punished suitably for what he now admits was an inexcusable action. Australians are a great sporting people and it is important that our sport, in all its forms, should be kept beyond reproach. We cannot help feeling that if Mr Armstrong had been a less eminent player, his treatment would have been somewhat more drastic.

The *Argus,* suggesting facetiously that 'the doings of Mr Armstrong are more important at this moment than those of Mr Deakin or even of Mr Bent', considered the idea of pay for play:

It would seem from this dispute that Victorian cricketers, like Victorian footballers, are not quite sure whether they are professional purveyors of amusement, or sportsman who love athletic victory for its own sake. While the poet, the artist and the actor have long since abandoned the idea that they seek glory only, and are gathering fortunes by way of royalties, prices or salaries, cricketers keep up the fiction that they aspire merely to the laurel wreath, and 'expenses' cover a multitude of contradictions. Much money is paid by people who go to cricket matches, and beyond doubt the idea is growing that champion players, since they provide the amusement, are entitled to some share of the shekels which fall into the treasury.

The *Argus* was onto something. Sport was an 'amusement', its patrons aroused by big names. Why should practitioners not be entitled to a degree of financial security? In December 1907, in fact, professional sport was taking two tentative steps forward. In Australia, the New South Wales Rugby League was being ushered into existence—its first treasurer was none other than Victor Trumper, its first secretary James Giltinan, a former Sheffield Shield umpire. In England, the Football Players and Trainers Union was founded—the first union of its kind. Both initiatives would be decried, the latter quashed altogether by the Football Association after attempting affiliation with Britain's Federation of Trade Unions; 'Prepared to tolerate a toy poodle,' concluded historian Brian Dobbs, 'they [the FA] were not prepared to keep a bulldog in case it bit.' But the shift was under way. In a sense, it hinged on a single word in the *Argus* leader: 'or'. Amateurism held that it was impossible to be both 'professional purveyor of amusement' and 'sportsman who loved athletic victory'. Not perceiving the contradiction, Armstrong was bound to court conflict. Perhaps it satisfied him to do so.

12

'Better Than No Bread at All'

Three days after his brush with the VCA, Warwick Armstrong rejoined Australian colleagues for the Second Test, one of the Golden Age's forgotten masterpieces: a game of 1327 runs ending at 3.28 p.m. on the sixth day in a one-wicket English win. Armstrong's contribution could scarcely be faulted: 31, 77, a catch, a run-out, and 5–89 from 65 overs. 'As a master of the art of keeping down runs,' averred Philip Trevor, 'Armstrong has no equal among modern cricketers.' Yet the week of ceaseless equatorial heat probably told against the home side; though England needed 39 for victory when their ninth wicket fell, the Australians could not separate last pair Sydney Barnes and Arthur Fielder. 'Poor "Tibby" Cotter during the six days of extreme heat had been bowled to a standstill and could barely get his arm over,' recalled Clem Hill. 'Noble had been hurt and it was only under difficulties that he could take his place at the crease, while Armstrong like the rest of us was leg weary and sore.'

Close Test finishes being rare, the game's final scenes were tense beyond precedent. 'There were men round the ground so breathless with excitement they couldn't speak,' reported the *Sydney Mail*'s 'Short Slip'. 'There were occasions where every fielder seemed to be at short leg for Armstrong.' The game might have furnished Test cricket's first tie, Barnes related, had Armstrong's nineteen-year-old Melbourne colleague Gerry Hazlitt kept calm:

> It was like this. When we wanted two runs to win, Fielder was facing Armstrong and played one to Saunders at rather deep mid-off. Although it was quite a sharp run we made it easily through. The next ball I drew away to leg and played Armstrong with a gentle push on the off-side. He was bowling leg stuff with only two men on the off, Hazlitt at deep mid-off and cover nearly square with the wicket and I judged it to be a safe move.
>
> On playing the stroke I dashed off for the run, which was really a run and a half, but imagine my consternation to find when half-way down the pitch that Fielder was still leaning on his bat, dreaming no doubt of the run he had just made. I shouted: 'For God's sake, get off, Pip', and off he went like a hare, but in the meantime Hazlitt had dashed in and grabbed the ball and, had he kept his head and just lobbed it to the wicketkeeper, Fielder would have been out by yards.
>
> Instead, however, he had a wild shy at the sticks, missed and the match was over...Pip kept on running flat out and my last view was of him disappearing into the crowd around the pavilion. Had not the pavilion been in the way I think he would have finished up in England and been the first to bear the good news.

Hazlitt's impetuosity notwithstanding, one wonders that Armstrong persisted with leg theory until so late in proceedings, allowing priceless singles on an untenanted off: perhaps it was a case of his single-mindedness phasing into inflexibility. Nonetheless, Australians around this time would often have cause to bless Armstrong's stubbornness—during this period, in fact, one detects a shift in the emphasis of Australian batsmanship. With some of the glister worn from their Golden Age by consecutive Ashes defeats, critics began stressing different values.

Of particular interest is the dual meaning acquired by the words 'brilliance' and 'brilliancy'—now banal in their application to cricket, they were in this first decade of the twentieth century more ambiguous. One would not now read a series summary like Frank Laver's of the 1905 tour, for instance, complaining that his batsmen showed 'too much brilliancy'. In August 1905, Leslie Poidevin in the *Referee* took Australians to task explicitly:

> If the Australian batsmen were sounder in defence, the Ashes would not now be in an English urn. The tendency in Sydney to neglect this most essential factor of a batsmen's armour has surprised me beyond

expression…Critics and the populace unite in acclaiming the brilliance of the Australian batting, yet more often than not it is the brilliance of the fusee, whose flash dies away inevitably in the gloom, and so are the biggest matches lost or nearly so.

Poidevin, still pursuing medical studies in Manchester, had gleaned his impressions on a trip to Sydney the previous Christmas:

The one thing that impressed me most forcibly about cricket in Sydney as I recently saw it was the worshipful devotion at the shrine of so-called 'brilliance'. The batsman who makes his runs at anything less than a run a minute is to be despised, too slow to watch and not worthy of encouragement. Nothing satisfies the public taste more fully than a rapid succession of fours, even if risk is incurred in obtaining them. The admiration of the press goes out to the maker of 60 risky runs in half as many minutes, while the player with the sound and carefully-compiled 50 in twice the time rarely gets other than a disparaging mention.

Poidevin was not the only roundhead among the cavaliers; 'Short Slip' decried the effect of the mighty Trumper:

The Trumperian influence on batting is to be seen everywhere. We have not a stonewaller now, no, nor even a slow batsman; all are out for runs. This has been the case with us for the past few years, and to it may be attributed in a measure the fact that the Englishmen have beaten us during the last couple of tours.

In this way, Armstrong came into his own, as the game altered around him. As a batsman he was the apostle of adhesion, as a bowler the master of the maiden. A case in point was the Fourth Test in Melbourne. With Australia beset at 5–77 in its second innings on 10 February 1908, he played an innings of what Trevor described as 'masterly inactivity'.

Beginning with exceptional care alongside his young Melbourne teammate Vernon Ransford, Armstrong was 14 at lunch with Australia 5–111. Ransford proceeded to an attractive 54 before being caught at the wicket, but Armstrong was still there at tea, untroubled, and with his captain's full support. Umpire Bob Crockett recalled: 'Some onlookers, who always think they know more of the game than the captain, suggested to Noble that Armstrong, as he was well set, should open out. Noble simply said: "He'll do me."'

Not until the day's dying stages, accompanied by Hanson Carter, did Armstrong essay strokes with a whiff of risk: suddenly, he struck Braund for consecutive straight sixes, and tore into the tiring attack. 'Big Armstrong,' Hill recalled, 'rose to this occasion in the style characteristic of great Australian batsmen...Almost every hit from the big Victorian meant a threer or a fourer.' Armstrong's 112-run stand with Carter in eighty-two minutes broke the back of English resistance, and the local boy finished with an unbeaten 133 in almost five hours the following day. 'He had played a great innings for his side,' commented Trevor, 'and had completely altered the complexion of the game.' For good measure, Armstrong then bowled Fielder to complete the 308-run victory regaining the Ashes for Australia.

Trumper returned to form in the Fifth Test with 166 in four hours, but it was by recent standards an austere series. Australian critics had to interpret it by their new, more rationalist, standards: 'Armstrong and Barnes both bowled leg theory,' said 'Short Slip', 'and sometimes it was hard work for the spectators to keep awake and for the reporter to find something to write about. Taken by and large, the absence of brilliance on both sides was a disappointment, but to any extent the cloud had a silver lining because Australia won four out of five matches.'

The toast was Noble, an inspirational successor to the retired Darling, and so popular that a testimonial match at season's end raised £2000. Yet the season had also contained its share of intrigue. Victoria's first match after Armstrong's VCA hearing was against New South Wales beginning on 24 January 1908 at the SCG: Armstrong made a sterling 110 in 166 minutes and bowled 52 overs as his state at last recaptured the Sheffield Shield. Yet the team was captained by Peter McAlister. Victoria's outstanding cricketer, indeed, would not regain the leadership for three years.

Leadership ballots in Armstrong's time could be unruly. In the *Argus* in January 1914, Mat Ellis recalled a match before which McAlister had been compelled to stand aside for Frank Laver when passions became inflamed: 'The Victorian team was split into two sections and within five minutes of starting there was squabbling and quarrelling almost leading to blows over the captaincy. Mr McAlister withdrew from the position to make room for Mr Laver although on a vote Mr McAlister would have won.' No periodical of the time explained why Armstrong's teammates had ignored him in favour of McAlister, but a passage in Trevor's

With the MCC in Australia may. Deploring captaincy elections generally, he cited a 'recent instance' of the ill-feeling they generated which 'did not occur in a Test match':

> Two players who were good friends had a difference of opinion on a matter which had nothing to do with captaincy. The views of the player who was usually captain—he was, by the way, very obviously indeed the right man to be captain—prevailed, and to the other player was administered an official reproof. The majority of the players, however, seemed to think that even principle should have given way to private friendship. They wanted to express their sympathy with the reprimanded one, and they hunted about for a practical method of doing so. Fate put an instant weapon in their hands and they proceeded to use it. A match was played at the time when feeling ran somewhat high, and they elected the object of their sympathy captain.

Armstrong certainly fulfils the description 'very obviously indeed the right man to be captain', while 'official reproof' may describe the failure of the suspension motion against Armstrong that McAlister had seconded. And it would not surprise if there were Victorian players annoyed by Armstrong's abrupt withdrawal from the earlier match against New South Wales. They might not have liked the VCA, but they obeyed it; why should Armstrong have thought himself so special? Subsequent events also imply misgivings about Armstrong among state contemporaries. Trevor concluded: 'What happened was perhaps natural enough, and could easily happen again.' It proved a prophetic judgment.

Peter McAlister was an increasingly important figure in Victorian cricket. A thirty-nine-year-old officer of Melbourne's Metropolitan Board of Works, he was a staid but steady opening batsman with piercing eyes and an ecclesiastical air, who had on several occasions appeared close to a fruitful Test career but gathered only six caps with uniformly modest results. Indeed, he grew increasingly embittered by his omission from Darling's 1905 team—for which, for reasons unknown, he blamed his oldest cricket friend, Frank Laver.

McAlister's unhappiness with Armstrong during the dispute of December 1907 seems similarly to have poisoned a formerly friendly relationship. For some years an East Melbourne delegate to the VCA, he drifted steadily into Ernie Bean's orbit. On 22 June 1908, a VCA meeting approved the appointment for the coming season of a single selector. On 21 September, ahead of a widely respected rival candidate in Hugh Trumble, the VCA elected McAlister to the position, subsequently nominating him as the state's representative on the national selection panel for the following year's Ashes tour.

The press was incredulous. McAlister had never toured England: how could he pontificate on the best players for the conditions? The reasons for his choice, however, were not hard to guess at: relations between the VCA and its biggest club were again strained. Perceiving the VCA to have reneged on an undertaking for promotions and relegations between district cricket's grades, disadvantaging former allies in the abandoned League of Victorian Cricketers, Melbourne had almost quit the association again: committee minutes reveal that a vote to secede on 7 August 1908, moved by Ramsay Mailer, would have succeeded had two committeemen changed their views. In the long term, the dispute would impel the formation of the Sub-District Cricket Association. In the short term, it expressed itself merely as hatred. 'Anyone capable of seeing a hole through a ladder,' protested 'Mid On' of the *Leader*, 'can see that McAlister was not put forth as a more capable selector than Trumble, but because by securing the latter's rejection, another "snap at the MCC" would be delivered.'

Australia's forthcoming tour of England, the first since the board's creation, was also looming as a potential battleground. McElhone's decision to offer Marylebone such a huge guarantee in Australia had bitten him back: the £3400 deficiency was being made up by the three leading associations—none too cheerfully in the case of the VCA and SACA. All the more reason to again try prising open the players' profit strongbox, as the *Bulletin* urged:

> The players, those indefinite wraiths that have haunted Australian cricket like a nightmare for the past two years, are making this last effort to keep Australian cricket on a boodle basis…Cash hunting is obnoxious. The board was created to control international campaigns. The Board of Control must take charge of the coming expedition.

Although seemingly constrained from doing so by his understanding with the SACA's John Creswell, McElhone began making noises to exactly this effect. In an interview published by *Cricket* on 29 October 1908, he implied that his business with the unruly cricketers was unfinished:

After a keen struggle, and almost by force of arms, the Board have obtained the control of international cricket in Australia, and must now proceed to place all matters pertaining to the game in an international sense on a sound and lasting foundation…To adequately control the game, the Board must control the players, and unless it takes charge of the finances it cannot succeed in that direction. The claims made by the players for expenses etc are such that international cricket is, to all intents and purposes, practically run, not for the benefit of the game, but for the financial benefit of the players.

This puts McElhone's view well: in a sense, he was right. Australian cricketers touring England had at first taken the risks and earned the rewards. Yet their journeys were no longer mercantile adventures, precisely because players drew on a goodwill of their own manufacture. The cricketers of Warwick Armstrong's generation had become victims of their own success. To achieve his ends, McElhone now needed two tools: a lever to separate the Australian cricketers from their profits, and a fulcrum on which to place it. The first he invented: a clever scheme that cut the board a piece of the financial action. The second presented itself: Peter McAlister.

Here again is one of those strange omissions in Australian cricket history: the acrimonious prelude to Australia's 1909 Ashes tour features in none of the standard texts. Yet it was virtually a dress rehearsal for the 'Big Six' wrangle three years later, and very nearly precipitated the same outcome: the withdrawal from an English trip of Australia's leading players.

To present the players with a *fait accompli*, McElhone shrewdly hid his plan for as long as possible. Not until a week before Christmas did the board convene to discuss the tour's financial arrangements, and then with the secrecy of a consistory of cardinals—the press were excluded, and the SACA's motion that a shorthand stenographer be employed ignored. John Creswell recalled that, when the meeting reached the finance item on its agenda, there was a pregnant silence. Finally, Creswell moved and Melbourne's Arthur Aitken seconded that the tour occur on the usual profit-share basis. Only then did McElhone state that the board wanted a tenth of the gross profits for itself, in spite of his undertakings to the SACA eighteen months earlier.

This must have startled Creswell but, a practical man, he knew there was little point in outright resistance: with the VCA and QCA delegates behind him, McElhone had the numbers. He proposed a five per cent cut instead. The eventual compromise—not really a compromise at all—was that the board would take five per cent of the first £6000 earned and 12.5 per cent of any excess. After the board's cut, the balance would be divided among the players, although any player had the option of accepting a £400 fee plus tour expenses. Finances would be overseen by a board-appointed treasurer accompanying the team.

The meeting had touches of comedy. At one point, Creswell asked pertinently how the board planned using its money. No-one could answer. Finally, a Queenslander complained at the expense of rail fares from Brisbane. 'I pointed out that they need not come,' Creswell recalled, 'and could drop out when they liked.' He left wondering if the players could possibly accept the board's terms. The first interview with Noble and Hill by the *Argus* suggested they would not:

'If you are selected as members of the team, will you go on?'
An emphatic 'No' was the answer in each case.
'The terms are not good enough [said Noble]. The calculations are based altogether too high for the takings of a tour, and by the time all expenses and the Board's percentages are paid, there will be nothing like a fair rec-ompense to a man who has to take the risk of leaving his business for several months.'

Was this McElhone's intention: a boycott by leading players, permitting their replacement with more ductile loyalists? The board's rhetoric suggested so. 'We have them beaten,' a member told the *Australasian*. 'We would like very much to get the best men as players, but if we cannot get them we will get the best we can. The Board of Control is no longer going to exist in name only.'

On Boxing Day 1908, while Victoria and New South Wales met at the MCG, the famous fight between Jack Johnson and Tommy Burns was in progress in Sydney: so great was interest that a telegram service delivered round-by-round updates. The cricketers were preoccupied with a different contest. Noble invited both teams, plus Hill, visiting for a selection meeting, to meet at the Port Phillip Club Hotel on the fourth evening to appraise the board's ultimatum. Only Waddy—with a prior engagement—and McAlister—with a different loyalty—did not attend. Noble began:

I want you cricketers to understand that this meeting is not called in direct antagonism to the Board of Control. We all believe that a Board of Control is necessary in Australia. I have voiced this sentiment in Sydney many, many a time, and they didn't believe me when I said that the Melbourne Cricket Club should not control cricket in Australia. I say right here in Melbourne that I don't believe it should. We believe in the Board of Control because it is the elective principle we want to see established.

But—and it was a big but:

International cricket has been in progress for years and years. It has been made and fostered by cricketers themselves and I say that the Board of Control is going beyond its powers when it now interferes to such an unjustifiable extent in the earnings of the cricketers in England.

Allowing the board this cut of the tour's proceeds, Noble claimed, would be like taking three extra players to be paid for doing nothing: 'a ghost in the flesh'. Most hurtful, however, were innuendoes that the players were unfit to divide their own spoils:

It has come to my ears during the few days I have been in Melbourne that Mr McAlister—I wish he was here tonight to deny it—just before the last team went to England I asked him to come to dinner for the purposes of getting him to go to England on a half share or on terms unlike the rest of the team.
Voice: Absurd!
Mr Noble: Every cricketer knows, or should know, that I am strongly opposed to anything of the kind. So is Mr Hill. So is Mr Armstrong…The Board of Control has, I believe, the idea of appointing a treasurer for the tour. That seems very much like appointing a Grand Inquisitor, seeing that we are allowed to appoint a manager whose duties are to look after the finance.

Several cricketers spoke during the evening's proceedings. Hill commented tersely that the board were 'less concerned with cricket than with what they could make', Cotter drolly that 'if there is a wet season, we may have to work our passage back'. Finally, Armstrong weighed in. He repeated Creswell's question: 'What are they [the board] going to do with the money?' Nobody answered. 'The players are taking all the hard knocks and making all the money,' he continued. 'We should have a little idea where the money is going.' The VCA's Harry Rush had come to him 'not on one occasion but on several', promising that the board regarded tour profits as sacrosanct: Armstrong was 'not surprised' that this had proven false, but he was 'disgusted'.

The players appointed Laver to 'respectfully ask' for a meeting with McElhone. But time was against them. On 1 January 1909, Hill met McAlister and Iredale at Young & Jackson's to pick the first six 'certainties': Hill himself, Noble, Armstrong, Trumper, Ransford and, from nowhere, Queensland's Roger Hartigan. Twenty-nine-year-old Hartigan had made a hundred on debut against England the previous summer, but done little since; his selection smacked of a sweetheart deal with the QCA. 'There are wheels within wheels,' commented 'Mid On' of the *Leader*, 'and it must not be forgotten that Queensland representatives have been very consistent supporters of the board conclave which is bent on worrying the old players.' Nor for a week did McElhone reply to the players' request for a meeting—which he then rejected.

Though now only an observer, the Melbourne Cricket Club sought to mediate. At the VCA's 9 January meeting, Arthur Aitken proposed that the association recommend modification of the terms. He was ruled out of order, and a motion that the board be encouraged to meet the players was rejected.* If confirmation were needed that Australian cricket was now ruled by a small administrative cabal, exchanges at this meeting furnished it:

Mat Fitzgerald: The cricketers must be handled carefully. Their prime reason for going to England is to win the Ashes, and it is purely a private matter what the men make. Their profits depend upon their success as players.
Laver: I think there will be a meeting between the Board and the players, and that we might stop this discussion now.
Bean: You have gone so far now you had better go on.
Laver: I expect to hear from Mr McElhone in a few days.
Bean: You know your request for a conference has been refused.
Aitken: I am on the board and I don't know it. Why should Mr Bean know these things if I do not?

---

* Any Melbourne initiative was by now bound to be rejected by the VCA and the board. Its applications to join the district cricket competition as a full member would be rejected for another six years. At a smoke social on 12 March 1909 farewelling Armstrong and Vernon Ransford, club president Justice Leo Cussen complained: 'There is no body that I know of which is more loyal to the interests of Australian cricket than the Melbourne Cricket Club. It has had to suffer of late

Bean: I did not want to speak, but I received a telegram from Mr McElhone today, and the least said soonest mended.

By now, there was a threat that Australia's leading cricketers would not make the tour. What would the public think? 'Felix' thought he knew, speaking out in the *Australasian*:

> Australian players in the last thirty years have done immense service in advertising Australia…If the Board could advance any sound argument in favor of taking away from the Australian team a large share of the proceeds of the tour, the Board might get the support of reasonable men. So far not a solitary sound reason has been put forward for levying this extortionate, and therefore the sympathy of the public is entirely with the players…

Perhaps, McElhone thought, it *was* time for a gesture. He consented to meet Noble, Hill and Laver in Sydney on 14 January, for the purposes of 'clarification', though not conciliation. Asked about the treasurer's duties, for instance, McElhone described him as 'a check against the manager':

> The need is this: supposing the manager should make defalcations, which has happened before, as we know, then the Board are legally responsible to the men to account for their proportion, whatever it may be, that the manager may have got away with. The object is really for the treasurer to check the manager as far as possible by making the treasurer and the manager practically accountable to the Board.

Laver would have understood this: on his first experience of a sporting tour, the disastrous misadventure of the Australian baseball team's 1897 visit to the US and Great Britain, it is precisely what had happened. Yet he could hardly have missed the insinuation: the board did not trust him to do his job. McElhone did dangle a small olive branch: the board would schedule two pre-tour trial matches, their proceeds to be added to tour profits, and cover the honorarium paid its English representative

---

a great deal of criticism which is undeserved and it is hard to keep silent and to fall into line with other opinions when everything that our club may do in the best interests of the game is a matter for objection and suspicion…That the present form of government is a good one there can be no question. That a Victorian Cricket Association is a good thing, and a Board of Control a necessity is practically certain. no-one club could ever be able to control Australian cricket. But the personnel of the present cricket government is quite another matter.'

Leslie Poidevin for negotiating the itinerary. But the same day as these concessions were announced, the spirit in which they were made was revealed at a meeting of the NSWCA. Noble's involvement in the abortive Wardill adventure almost three years earlier remained a sore point and, when an argument began about the board's status, delegate John Clayton commented piously that the board was fighting not the players but their supporter, Melbourne.

> Noble: That is not correct.
> Clayton: Well I don't want to go into that, or else I might have to say something about an agreement which a certain person had up his sleeve.
> Noble: How long ago is that?
> Clayton: I don't care if it is twenty years ago. I shall never forget it.
> Noble: I thought you had forgotten that trouble.
> Clayton: No, I have reason always to remember it.

Finally, it seems, the strain told on Noble. 'Why have I been treated so in this association?' he exclaimed. 'I have not been treated fairly by this association.' At this, McElhone launched a tirade against Noble, culminating in the extraordinary statement that Australia's captain did not have the association's trust.

On 23 January 1909, Victoria began a Sheffield Shield match in Sydney. Armstrong was in the pinkest form, making 171 in four hours with a six and twenty-four boundaries. But a meeting of the players decided against further action: only Hill would decline to make the tour under the terms offered. A correspondent of London's *Sportsman* summarised: 'As far as I have been able to glean at the time of writing, the players have given way to the Board of Control, regarding a loaf with a small portion cut away as better than no bread at all.' Three days after the game's completion, Hill met Iredale and McAlister to select a further instalment of players: Cotter, Carter, the rising all-rounder Charlie Macartney, and Jack O'Connor, now representing South Australia. Selection of the balance was deferred until the trial matches' completion.

The day after the first of these games, the *Age*'s Sydney correspondent obtained an amazing scoop: the final members of the party. Three were uncontroversial: South Australia's Bill Whitty, and Syd Gregory and Warren Bardsley of New South Wales. Two were very strange: Victorian keeper William 'Barlow' Carkeek, not even playing the trial matches, and Peter McAlister. The scoop's most remarkable aspect was, however, that the selectors had not officially met. Hill fumed, McAlister fussed, describing the story as an 'unfounded rumour'. But the *Age* budged not, claiming that 'the announcement made by our Sydney correspondent was based upon good information', for the good reason it was correct. Details of the selectors' eventual meeting on 15 February, their source unknown, are contained in the papers of Arthur Gregory, aka 'Short Slip', at the Mitchell Library. After the selection of Bardsley and Whitty had been agreed with little discussion, it seems, Iredale suddenly proposed Gregory, Carkeek and McAlister. Hill was speechless.

Few cricket contemporaries seem to have had a kind word for thirty-year-old Carkeek, a blacksmith who played for Prahran, and later a loyal and deferential tool of his association. Hill was certainly not an admirer: 'Whatever his merits as a player, he [Hill] would offer the strongest possible objection to his [Carkeek's] being chosen.' The reasons are unclear. Perhaps there was some stain on Carkeek's past of which contemporaries were aware but chose not to commit to print. When Hill's opposition to his selection later became publicly known, one 'Old Hawksburnite' defended Carkeek in the *Argus*: 'Can any of us afford to throw mud at a fellow cricketer who has been not so fortunate perhaps as we in being able to cover up successfully perhaps the one indiscretion of his life?'

McAlister's proposed selection caused Hill even graver concern. Claiming that the Victorian was 'past his best' and 'not suited to English wickets', he advocated South Australia's Algy Gehrs and Tasmanian keeper Norman Dodds, but to no avail: 'In objection…he failed to move the other two selectors who stood to their choice and forming a majority carried their point.' Finally, accusing McAlister and Iredale of conspiracy, Hill said he'd 'decided to wash his hands of the entire affair' as he 'did not consider that the best men had been chosen'. Later that evening, a group of players including Gehrs and Whitty bumped into Laver on Princes Bridge. 'Bad luck chaps,' Laver said. 'Only one of you has made the team.'

For McAlister, however, this was a triumph worth savouring. That night, a function in his honour convened at the Queen's Arms Hotel, organised by East Melbourne's John Healy. Word arrived of the final Australian selections, at which all the fifty guests enthused, not least Barlow Carkeek who was 'heartily congratulated'. And when McAlister turned up, the hostelry rocked with cheers. 'We are glad to know that you have done what any man would have done and helped yourself into this team,' said Healy, adding quickly lest this be misconstrued, 'and on your merits.' McAlister's response exposed why he would shortly become one of Australian cricket's most controversial characters:

> I hardly know what to say after two hours of hard, bitter fighting. I have had something to fight out. I will try my utmost to show I can play the game. It has been a long, bitter struggle. It has been my ambition to get into the Australian team. I have been fighting for years to get this trip and no-one has had to fight harder than I have.

The lexicon is revealing: hard, bitter, fight, struggle, ambition. Few vignettes express better the passions of both McAlister and the moment. And the lengths to which the board would go to serve its purposes were revealed three days later at the Port Phillip Club Hotel.

Presided over by its new chairman, Queensland's Colonel Justin Foxton, this gathering was notable for procedural irregularities and transparent objectives. Four delegates present were proxies and, before McElhone could move the press's exclusion, their status was disputed. As the proxy of New South Wales' Colin Sinclair did not seem in order, McElhone wrote an authorising letter on the spot. Foxton then testified on behalf of East Melbourne's Charles Nodrum, standing in for the other Queensland delegate Joseph Allen. Surely this was not in order, ventured South Australia's Mostyn Evan: proxies were the business of associations, not individuals. The chairman airily 'deprecated technicalities' and began the meeting.

The effect of the proxies' eligibility was to balance the vote in favour of the board's hardliners by six votes to five: the NSWCA's McElhone, Sinclair and Iredale, the VCA's Bean and Harry Rush, and *ersatz* Queenslander Nodrum versus the SACA's Hill, Evan and Harry Blinman, and Melbourne's Arthur Aitken and Billy Bruce (representing Tasmania). And this was the way every vote played out. Evan's motion to admit the press was defeated. Evan's motion for a shorthand recorder was defeated. The meeting then turned to leadership positions. After Noble had been approved as captain, McAlister was appointed not only as vice-captain but as treasurer. Evan interjected: was the appointment of captains and vice-captains not the players' prerogative? Not at all, Foxton retorted: the board was empowered by virtue of Object (b), with its right 'to arrange, control, regulate and finance' touring teams. The board even appointed Noble's co-selectors, choosing Gregory and McAlister over the nominated Trumper.

More than thirty years of tradition had been overthrown in a trice. There were mixed feelings when the *Orontes* left Sydney on 17 March 1909, bound for Melbourne, Fremantle, Ceylon, Suez, Naples and Plymouth. 'Little bands of small-minded sycophants may prattle their nonsense in bar parlours and send-offs and spout sentimental drivel *ad nauseam*,' fumed 'Mid On', 'but for the first time an Australian team is about to leave for England with no public confidence.'

13

'I Still Bear This Incident in Mind against Armstrong'

arwick Armstrong embarked on his third English tour again as just a cricketer. For reasons unknown, his involvement with Wood Armstrong had ended in late 1908 or early 1909, and his only subsequent employment was another temporary public service position: a five-week clerkship in the Department of Home Affairs from 13 February up to his departure for England. Armstrong, of course, seems to have regarded 'a job' as something one did when not playing cricket. But he was pushing thirty, an age at which it usually dawns on cricketers that they will not play forever, and prudent enough to understand his sporting mortality. This trip was one in which he had to make an impact, and just as the Armstrong of 1905 had been an advance on the Armstrong of 1902, England would shortly see a new Armstrong again: 'the Big Man of Australian cricket'.

For Armstrong had grown. From photographs over the course of this decade, his weight first seems to have increased after the 1905 tour. He was certainly noticeably bigger during the 1907–8 series, nudging 110 kilograms, which made his sombre, obstinate batting seem all the more wilful. In a rather acidulous preview of the 1909 tour for the *Daily Mail,* Arthur Jones wrote:

Armstrong is no doubt a useful man in the side, but I would sooner see five minutes of Trumper than two hours of him. With his size (and when I last saw him he was getting immense), height and reach, there is no ground that (if he liked) he could not hit out of; but with very few exceptions he is content to play at keeps; which is very fine for one's average, but not very entertaining for fielders or spectators.

The reason for Armstrong's weight gain in these years is elusive. It does not seem as straightforward as his running to fat. It may, at least in part, be as simple as general family specifications: Jack and Tom were both strapping six-footers and, with the exception of Muriel, accordingly nicknamed 'Dot' by her family, all the Armstrong girls were on heavy lines. It is probably also related to Armstrong's consumption of alcohol which, if not compulsive, appears to have been habitual.

Sportsmen of Armstrong's day were coy about drink. In July 1906, inspired by an article in *C. B. Fry's Magazine* advertising alcohol's positive properties for athletes, the *Australasian Star* tested the thesis on a number of leading—if unnamed—sportsmen: a trainer, a footballer, a boxer, an 'aquatics enthusiast', a 'veteran bowler', and a cricketer. All swore alike: nobody ever drank. The cricketer was irked even to be asked:

> A prominent Australian batsman emphatically denied the allegations that cricket and drink were in any way associated. 'We have heard very frequently,' he said, 'that certain prominent cricketers are addicted to drink. It is unfortunate that some members of the public will persist in making these statements about men who get into prominence in any game or any walk of life.'
> 'But we have heard of cricketers who take a little too much.'
> 'Certainly. So we have had judges, members of parliament, doctors and others, but I contend that the men playing big cricket today are noted for their temperance.'

Perhaps he was thinking of Trumper, a teetotaller. But he was not thinking of Noble, never without a store of sugar lumps in case of a heavy session: Australia's captain believed that they 'absorbed' alcohol when dissolved in one's drink. Nor was he thinking of Duff, destined to die of alcoholic poisoning at thirty-three. And he was certainly not referring to Armstrong, whose reputation as an imbiber grew as his career progressed. Frank Laver remembered Armstrong's habit of carrying a bottle of whisky in his cricket bag. Arthur Sims recalled watching local supporters at Hamilton in New Zealand try to drink Armstrong under the table so that he would not make runs against them the following day, although his 'strong head' was up to the challenge. And the English writer Home Gordon recollected a social match Armstrong played for Marylebone where festivities concluded at 2.30 a.m. with the host inquiring after last orders:

> Armstrong replied that he would like a bottle of brandy, and finished it unassisted before catching the 7am boat, when he appeared fit as the proverbial fiddle. Subsequently, on my asking if this had really happened, he confirmed the tale adding: 'And it was one of the pleasantest innings I have played.'

One should be wary of exaggeration in folklore about sportsmen's alcoholic exploits, particularly in Australia, so fond of its reputation as a drinking nation. But alcohol is a great builder of bulk. One gram of ethanol produces seven calories of energy—fat produces nine, sugar and protein merely four. W. H. Auden's observation that 'not all fat men are heavy drinkers but all males who drink heavily become fat' has some foundation in fact. In any event, the reason for Armstrong's weight gain may not be so important as its effect.

Scholars of body image in the United States, such as Hillel Schwartz and Peter Stearns, regard the years of Armstrong's career, the first two decades of the twentieth century, as those in which Americans first became obsessed with size and weight. But that did not prevent 'big' people from carrying themselves with a certain swagger. The world was ruled by men whose proportions were part of their public personae. Britons had a king whose girth was mischievously described as 'wider still and wider'. Americans had just elected their heaviest president, William Taft. Any photograph of Australian political worthies from the first decade of the twentieth century demonstrates 'the dignity of an ample corporation': there's George Reid, who needed a long-handled buttonhook to do up his boots; Edmund Barton, christened 'Toby Tosspot' by the *Bulletin* in honour of his appetites; Sir John Forrest, always 'Big John'. Henceforward, too, his days of self-consciousness about being an 'overgrown looking boy' far behind him, Armstrong would often be 'Big Warwick'.

The *Orontes* left Port Melbourne on 23 March 1909 amid scenes of patriotic rapture, a police band playing 'Auld Lang Syne', and the sailors giving 'mighty hurrahs for Australia'. In transit, there were fewer pleasantries. Accustomed to the congenial Melbourne Cricket Club, manager Laver found the Board of Control a harsh taskmaster: he alleged later that they had failed to inform him where the steamer tickets were, sent tour contracts late, and allotted berths arbitrarily, causing 'friction and unpleasantness'. McElhone then tartly queried his request for the usual bridging loan to fund the team before gate receipts began: 'I cannot understand why in view of the advances already made an amount of £5–600 or anything like it should be required on arrival, and I am sure that unless strong reasons are given by you the Board will not agree to do so.' Even the team's notepaper caused irritation: McElhone insisted it bear the board's letterhead alongside the Australian XI symbol, which Laver griped would 'spoil the looks of the neat and pretty heading'.

The effect of this carping was predictable: the senior Australians decided, more or less, to ignore their board. After the final Lord's practice, a team meeting was called. Declining to accept the captaincy merely on the board's say-so, Noble wanted a player vote, and was duly elected. This appears to have had a profound impact on McAlister. Certainly he abstained from what he considered a 'very foolish' vote, as he believed the board's appointment of Noble sufficient. And having pined so long to tour England, he now found himself resented as a cat's paw of McElhone, almost a spy. His alienation was partly the function of an unbending personality: when Laver had sought a reconciliation with him at their East Melbourne farewell dinner, McAlister had refused to shake his hand. Yet one can sympathise. McElhone had placed him in an impossible position: in the team, but not of the team.

Three years later, the management of the 1909 tour would be the subject of a bitter pamphlet war between McAlister, Laver, the board, the VCA and the Melbourne Cricket Club, generating tens of thousands of confusing and contradictory words. Yet, in essence, the questions they wrangled over can be condensed to one, as simple as the issue of the letterhead on the team's notepaper: for whom were the players playing? McAlister would have said for the board: its secretary had negotiated the tour, its selectors had picked the party, its members had appointed him treasurer. Laver would have said for themselves: they were playing the cricket, they were sharing the profits, they had elected him manager.

These differences were manifested at the very outset of the tour in the disputed bridging loan. Although Laver claimed to have 'tried my utmost' to obtain it from the board, one suspects this was an exaggeration. In response to Laver's last letter from the *Orontes*, McElhone had wired: 'If required, contact Poidevin.' Laver ignored the advice, borrowing £300 from his own bank. It was the response of an irked man, and the member of an irked team, an attempt to defend its final fastness. It was also futile, which Laver may have come to realise: when Poidevin shortly arrived offering the required money, Laver accepted. The strangest aspect of this extremely strange transaction only emerged later. What the Australian team borrowed was not the board's money, but McElhone's. Grasping the symbolic importance of the loan as another means of placing the board's stamp on the team, and knowing it would take time to raise the funds from the state associations, he had hurriedly placed his own finances on the line as an interim measure.

The board's problem was that McAlister was not made of such stern stuff. Instead, as the tour unfolded, he became a martyr to his grievances, and made astonishingly little effort to fulfil his exchequer function. Although he claimed later that his efforts to do so were resisted at turns by Laver, and that he 'kept such records as were possible and checked the turnstiles regularly', he did not so much as buy a ledger. In fact, the tour's only financial record was kept by Laver, and on behalf of the team rather than the board: this would become significant in the final showdown between the players and McElhone.

What was Warwick Armstrong's attitude in this bitter stand-off? There are no words to judge him by, merely deeds. But the deeds in this case were eloquent. Armstrong was one of several players whose tour contracts were forwarded to Laver on the *Orontes* for signature. He refused to sign, as did Trumper—a striking disavowal of the board's jurisdiction. Once in England, he made his own silent protest against McAlister's presence: he insisted on playing only when Noble was captain, and would 'rest' from the five games in which the vice-captain took the helm. In this situation of extremes, in other words, Armstrong took the most extreme position of all. It was ever thus.

Armstrong was swiftly into stride in the tour's first game against Nottinghamshire at Trent Bridge with an unbeaten 106 and 8–82 from twenty-nine overs. His batting was characteristically cussed, his bowling uncharacteristically adventurous; in discussions aboard the *Orontes*, Noble had finally persuaded him to renounce leg theory, so vastly unpopular four years earlier.

Gathering 435 runs at 72.5 and capturing 32 wickets at 15.8 in the tour's first three weeks, Armstrong could scarcely be faulted. The Australians, however, suddenly stumbled, losing to Surrey at the Oval and to Marylebone at Lord's within a week. Perhaps off-field stresses were exacting a toll; certainly, there were some odd selections, especially in the cases of McAlister and Laver. Though officially vice-captain, McAlister did not appear until the fourth match, and then in embarrassing circumstances, scratching 5 and 19 against Surrey, and batting unaccountably at the end. According to *The Times*:

> Mr McAlister mistimed the first ball, a long hop, which he attempted to hook square and was nearly bowled. The second he played, but the third he made a very poor stroke. It was another short-pitched ball, and in endeavouring to cut it past point's right hand, he succeeded only in spooning it up to Hitch at third slip and Surrey had won a memorable game by five runs.

McAlister was excluded again after one more game, essentially ruling him out of the First Test. Perhaps this was Hill's prophecy fulfilled, that his 'style was not suited to English conditions'; probably it deepened McAlister's estrangement.

Laver's position was still more mysterious. After his appearance against Nottinghamshire, the *Daily Mail* published a cable from Australian selector Frank Iredale expressing 'great consternation' at the manager playing. It gained wide publicity. 'If the Australian selection committee is going to be criticised by a wire from home as well as running the gauntlet of the English critics,' commented E. H. D. Sewell of the *Evening Standard*, 'then it looks like getting it in the neck both ways.' The selectors responded by standing Laver down for the next six matches, although several players later confided that Iredale's intervention had caused great annoyance. Hanson Carter told the *Australasian*:

> The team strongly resented the action of Mr F. A. Iredale in cabling home and expressing surprise at Laver's inclusion in the first match. As a bowler, Laver in England was altogether different from Laver in Australia, and F. A. Iredale ought to know, for he had been in England on an Australian tour.

Ranks divided, selections muddled, the Australians were routed in the First Test, beginning at Edgbaston on 27 May. Armstrong battled an hour for 24 as his team was hustled out for 74, then limited England's lead to 47 with 5–27, but was otherwise powerless to prevent a ten-wicket defeat. Rain and bad light shrouding the game matched the visitors' mood. Defeated thrice in seven matches, Noble's team was freely written off. Even W. G. Grace felt they would need 'a lot of luck' to fight back.

Noble took stock. He asked Laver to play. This was a brave decision— the manager was pushing forty and far from fit—but proved inspired. Laver harvested 37 wickets at 9 in the next four matches. The Englishmen, led by the ageing Archie MacLaren, were in any case not so formidable. Only the impressive Hobbs was under thirty, and both Noble and Armstrong felt that England's immobile fielding and poor running between wickets ceded Australia an advantage. 'When the names of the English eleven [for the Second Test] were published,' Noble recalled, 'Armstrong and I agreed that if we could not beat the team we had better sell our kits.'

Ransford's spirited 143 not out at Lord's obtained Australia an 81-run lead but, with little more than a day remaining, prospects of a result were remote. *The Times* commented that 'all the symptoms are in favour of that most tiresome of all things—a drawn match'. Armstrong, however, produced what Noble called 'the finest piece of bowling on a good wicket I have seen': 6–35 from twenty-five overs, including five batsmen for eight runs in sixty-one deliveries. It was beyond even the *Daily Telegraph*'s perceptive Philip Trevor to explain:

> There must have been some reason for the failure one after the other of the finest batsmen in England in that time, but there certainly seemed to be absolutely nothing the matter with the wicket...Two things are quite certain: Armstrong bowled extraordinarily well, and the batting was unaccountably weak.

Armstrong, however, *does* seem to have bowled a new delivery that day or, tantamount, batsmen saw it so. Though bowling from the end suitable for his leg breaks, Armstrong defeated at least two batsmen, John King and George Hirst, with deliveries zipping the other way. In other words, it appears, Armstrong was the first Australian to bowl a wrong 'un in England, turning Bosanquet's weapon back on its creators. *The Times* reported that he 'at times got the off-spin with the leg-break action' which 'had all the batsman guessing and wondering what was coming next'. Recalling the spell in his *Sporting Pie*, the *Daily Mail*'s Frederic Wilson described Armstrong deploying 'the overspin ball that came off the pitch at an abnormal rate, that one which is a half-googlie, without apparently altering his action in the slightest degree'. Very cunning, he thought: 'It was not known in England then that he had that ball in his bag.'

As the visitors moved to a ten-wicket victory, Australian supporters cheered, laughed, coo-eed to one another across the ground, and flourished their team's colours. With Noble and Ransford, Armstrong took bows on their dressing-room balcony. The tide had turned. 'There can be no doubt of the fact that his great bowling gave us the victory,' Noble wrote, 'and was a powerful stimulant to our morale, the effect of which was apparent in the play of the team individually and collectively during the remainder of the series.' Noble now led the side with increasing authority, known as a martinet, but inspiring tremendous loyalty. Immediately after that Second Test, Australia played a friendly against Western Union at Glasgow. Armstrong batted last, after Bardsley, usually an opener. Like Hartigan and Macartney, Bardsley made a hundred, and was enjoying a fruitful last-wicket partnership with Armstrong when a note came from the dressing-room: Noble was telling him to get out. When Bardsley complied, Armstrong remonstrated: 'What the dickens did you do that for? Don't you think I'd like a bit of a hit, too?' Bardsley showed him the note. Armstrong understood. The captain's word was law.

Such attitudes might now seem quaint, but the tour also contained a handful of incidents that seem strikingly modern: two in particular involved Armstrong. The first occurred during the Third Test, which began at Headingley on 1 July, and where Australia secured a second decisive victory. Swinging Macartney through mid wicket, Hobbs slipped starting for a run, and dislodged a bail with his heel. The Australians appealed for hit-wicket, and Hobbs intended departing until partner John Tyldesley dissuaded him, whereupon umpire William West gave him not out. In *My Cricket Memories*, Hobbs described the sequel:

The Australians made a rare fuss. They gathered together in the field and confabulated. The chief offender was Warwick Armstrong, who got very nasty and unsportsmanlike, refusing to accept the umpire's decision. This upset me. I did not know whether I was standing on my head or my heels, with the consequence that two balls later I let one go, never even attempting to play it; and it bowled me. I still bear this incident in mind against Armstrong.

The incident was so unusual that the *Daily Mail* misconstrued Hobbs' dismissal as a chivalrous self-sacrifice: 'Hobbs in most sportsmanlike fashion made no attempt to play the next straight ball he received and so retired without adding to his total.' But there was clearly no chivalry involved; that Hobbs, a famously pacific soul, should have recalled this incident twenty years later suggests that Armstrong's language was 'nasty' indeed.

The other incident is still more noteworthy, given that it could not now occur. In 1909, bowlers were still entitled to bowl looseners, known as 'trial balls', down the side of the pitch—as many as they pleased, in fact, though a handful usually sufficed. During the Fifth Test at the Oval, Australia was in some difficulty: Laver had broken down, and England was 4–187 chasing 325 with ample time for a result. But the new batsman, a twenty-two-year-old all-rounder from Kent called Frank Woolley making his Test debut, had to wait to face his first international delivery: Armstrong chose the moment to stage history's longest 'trial ball' exhibition. The incident, as described by E. H. D. Sewell, had its funny side:

> Believe it or not, but before Woolley squared up to play his first ball nineteen minutes had elapsed...This unofficial interval was brought about almost entirely by Armstrong bowling several trial balls from the pavilion end, somewhat sketchy attempts being made to stop them at the other...the ball in consequence trickling down to the Vauxhall end screen, there to be fielded by urchins and handed over reverently to the bobby on duty, for him to risk his dignity and his helmet to fling back so that we might get on with the match which these 'Colonial chaps' had come so many thousands of miles to play and who did not...appear, after all, to be consumed with fervour to finish!

In his *King of Games,* Woolley corroborates the tale, without mentioning Armstrong by name:

> I remember that, owing chiefly to the bowling of trial balls, over a quarter hour elapsed between the fall of Rhodes' wicket...and the bowling of the

first ball to me. It was rather a trying time for me, especially as it was my first Test innings…After my long wait it is perhaps not surprising that 'Tibs' Cotter bowled me for 8.

What was Armstrong doing? Or Noble, Australia's foremost apostle of fair play? Sewell facetiously suggested that Armstrong wished to learn 'how slowly he could make a bowled ball reach the screen'. But surely he was taking the quest for psychological advantage over a newcomer to an unexampled extreme. It was forty years before Stephen Potter's classic essay in sporting whimsy, *The Theory and Practice of Gamesmanship,* found a name for 'the art of winning games without actually cheating'. Yet here was Armstrong experimenting with new techniques of intimidating opponents, just as four years before he had explored new techniques of inhibiting them. In his *The Log of a Sportsman* fourteen years later, indeed, Sewell implied that the 1909 tour marked a change in the Australian approach to tours of England:

> The Australian cricketer never gives away a chip of a bail, let alone a single wicket, from start to finish of a tour of England. For him…cricket is nothing but a hard business proposition, and he plays it mercilessly, with not an atom of give in his demeanour, but 'take all' as his motto. Which should be on the pocket of his blazer. Joe Darling's teams of 1902 and 1905 were the least saturated with this warlike spirit of playing cricket of any that I have seen, but with at least two of the others the marching orders were, quite simply: 'Win—at any price'.

Armstrong's abuse of the legislative scope for 'trial balls' had a consequence: the counties shortly tightened Law 18 to prevent a recurrence of Woolley's ordeal—a measure later adopted by Marylebone. Armstrong, though, appears to taken little notice; if never again at such length, he would continue the custom at intervals for the rest of his career, sometimes in defiance of officials. 'The Breaker' of Wellington's *Dominion* recorded such an episode almost five years later.

> Some Wellingtonian got out and Armstrong began to fill up the interval of waiting for the next man by bowling down the wicket, contrary to MCC rules. 'Mr Armstrong,' said the conscientious umpire, 'you can't do that. It's contrary to the laws of the game.'
> 'Aw,' replied the big fellow, 'what's the penalty?'
> The umpire correctly stated that it might be within his province to order the match replayed.

'Aw right,' retorted the Australian, 'ah'm going to bowl right on. What you going to do?'

Perhaps the most intriguing imponderable of both the Hobbs and Woolley episodes, meanwhile, is whether Armstrong would have shown an amateur such discourtesy; like most of the Australians of his generation, his opinion of the English amateur was high, of professionals poorer. Summarising the tour in *Country Life*, amateur MacLaren wrote of the Australians: 'No team could have played fairer. They proved themselves the best side and played like good sportsmen.' His professional comrades might not have agreed.

Armstrong's tour record was, as in 1905, exceptional. *Wisden* editor Sydney Pardon thought that his 1480 runs at 43.5 would have been better still had he given rein to his attacking instincts, but sensed that he was 'under orders'. Those who had ascribed his earlier bowling success to leg theory were disabused: he had taken his 113 wickets at 16.2, even more cheaply than in 1905. Bardsley, an unflappable left-hander, was the tour's outstanding newcomer with 2180 runs at 46.4. Valuable contributions were made by Trumper, Ransford and Laver, whose 70 wickets at 15 included 8–31 in the Fourth Test at Old Trafford. But Armstrong was again palpably the cricketer of the tour. 'Warwick Armstrong has been a veritable tower of strength to the side,' gushed 'Felix' in the *Australasian*. 'Batting and bowling he has rendered such excellent service that we may say quite naturally: "What would they have done without him?"' In an extensive tribute, *Cricket* wrote: 'Of him, it may truly be said that, whether he has been playing, in his native land, in England, New Zealand or South Africa, he has not failed to leave his mark—and a very large mark, too—on the scoresheet.'

The tour's only sourness was financial. Thanks to bad weather, the £13,228 gross was substantially short of McElhone's forecast of £18,000. After expenses and the board's contentious cut, only £473 was left for each player: paltry reward compared to the spoils of previous tours. Doubtless this widened the breach between the team and McAlister, the perceived board stooge. Having averaged less than 30 for the tour and failed in his two Tests, he had been even less productive as treasurer. He had kept no financial records and demanded Laver hand his documentation over. Laver recalled:

It was not till towards the end of the tour that he asked me, when by a chance remark he appeared to realise, for the first time, that he had been neglecting his duties. He mentioned something about the balance sheet, as if he took it for granted I was going to prepare it, but to his unconcealed astonishment, I informed him I wasn't going to prepare a balance sheet for the Board, as that was his duty.

Eventually, Laver lent McAlister the tour's cheque books and bank books, but the treasurer doesn't appear to have gotten far with them. The only activity in which they co-operated was shipping a slips cradle to their East Melbourne club. It arrived broken. So was their relationship.

Australia's cricketers now had some diversions planned. Most spent a fortnight touring the Scottish highlands; Armstrong so savoured the scenery that he acquired paint and brushes in order to render it on canvas. He and his comrades then headed for London in high spirits. Accosted by a persistent Indian journalist wishing to know if their homeward route would encompass his country, Armstrong replied dead-pan that he rather fancied settling in Calcutta or Bombay, and operating a sports depot from which he would also offer coaching lessons. A story duly appeared in Calcutta's *Asian* outlining this venture—it was, of course, pure invention.

With Noble, Cotter and Hopkins, Armstrong did intend an excursion on the way home, though there was no need for anything too venture-some: traversing the east at this apogee of empire, they would not set foot anywhere not controlled from Europe. Their trip is worth revisiting: as well as evoking a more leisured age, it expresses something of the cachet attached to Australian cricketers even a century ago. More so even than their English cricketing counterparts, they had become part of the imperial experience.

The quartet boarded the Marseilles boat train at Charing Cross on 13 October, and joined Laver at Naples on the *Mongolia* bound for Ceylon. Settled first by the Portuguese, then the Dutch, Ceylon had been under British control almost a century, with all that this entailed: discovery that a detachment of Australia's great cricketers was *en route* set Colombo cricket circles awhirl. The game was well-established there and, originally the colonists' preserve, had also grown permeable to the Sinhalese elite: it was, indeed, the pucka Sinhalese Sports Club that wired

Noble and Laver seeking a game. Six other European passengers were drafted to make up an XI.

Arriving in Colombo early on 30 October 1909, the *Mongolia* was greeted by welcoming dignitaries, anxious to commence play. The Australians were rather surprised at the elaborate preparations. While a brass band played martial airs, the picturesque ground on the seaside promenade of Galle Face burst with 5000 spectators 'on the tiptoe of expectation'. Tiffin was scheduled for an indulgent hour and a half, and governor Sir Henry McCallum arrived amid the strains of 'Rule Britannia' after judging the Mirigama Agricultural Show.

The match is more than a period curio: it provides another glimpse of the Australians' mercantile spirit. Although Armstrong made 69 runs without being dismissed and took 5–59 in the home team's 110, the visitors seemed most interested in their £10 appearance money each—a request that rather soured the occasion. After their guests had departed, the *Times of Ceylon* sniffed:

> We regret that we cannot rejoice in the conditions in which the match was played, and it is our opinion that we are better off without these matches altogether if they are to be regarded entirely as money making affairs. We are sorry that Messrs Noble, Armstrong, Hopkins, Cotter and Laver should have taken a £10 note apiece for a few hours cricket in Colombo...We do not see how the Australians justify their action in taking money for playing on Saturday. They all play as amateurs in England, and we take it they had no expenses...that amounted to £50.

Sinhalese Sports Club members, of course, were not the first to be so affronted by Australian mores, and word that Armstrong and his colleagues had sought reward for their Colombo engagement was noticed in England with distaste. 'As a discreditable piece of money grubbing this match would be hard to beat,' wrote London's *Truth*. 'I can assure my friends in Ceylon these Australians are no more amateurs than English professional cricketers. They are out to make as much money as they can.' The writer thought the action especially reprehensible in an outpost of empire: 'The match was against a native team and only tended to degrade the white man in the native's eyes.' At least, one might think, the Australians were uncontaminated by paternalism: black, white or brindle, everyone's money was the same.

Next stop along the Australians' route was Penang in the Federated

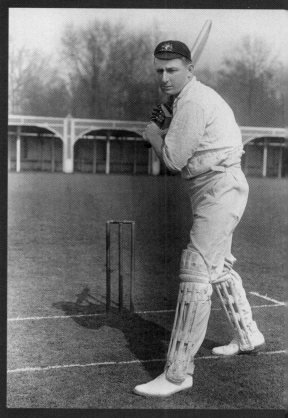

'Strong of arm with bat or ball': Warwick Armstrong's feats on the 1905 Ashes tour made him the stuff of postcards. Cap tugged characteristically over his left eye (left) and at the crease (right), he oozed the 'temperament temperament temperament' that he espoused.

'By Jove, we did like beating them': the Australian and English teams for the Fifth Test at the Oval were rich in talent. Seated in the second row are six ornaments of cricket's Golden Age: Charles Fry, Monty Noble, Stanley Jackson, Joe Darling, Archie MacLaren and Clem Hill. Yet it would be the last Australian tour of its kind; Armstrong, far right in the back row, stands behind manager Frank Laver, at the heart of a controversy that would engulf the game seven years later.

'I would sooner see five minutes of Trumper than two hours of Armstrong': by the 1909 Ashes series, Armstrong was becoming a byword for obstinacy and aggression, particularly when contrasted with the courtly Victor Trumper. Both, however, were taking a stubborn stand against the incursions of the new Board of Control.

'Strong sort of people': an Armstrong family grouping at their Arra Glen home at around the time Jack's hasty marriage brought unwelcome disruption to their lives. Tom, Warwick and father John stand slightly away from Jack, perhaps reflecting his diminished status. In the front row are Warwick's sisters Olivia, Lucia, Amelia and Muriel, with his mother Amelia second from right.

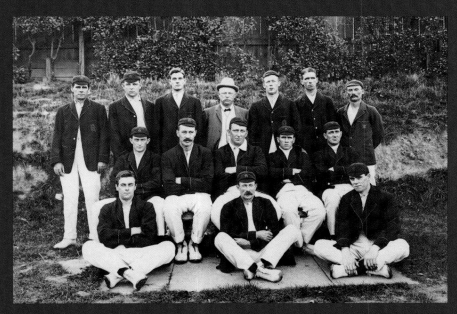

'The confirmed growler': the first Australian team that Warwick Armstrong led, to New Zealand in February 1910, was a surly crew. But he led them effectively, and even diplomatically, returning home with an offer to settle permanently in New Zealand. The Melbourne Cricket Club hastily interposed.

'A whole-hearted hatred': the falling out between former East Melbourne teammates Peter McAlister and Frank Laver, treasurer and manager of the 1909 Australians respectively, was the *casus belli* of the 'Big Six' dispute three years later. Equally significant was paceman Jim Kyle's revelation that the Victorian Cricket Association were machinating against Warwick Armstrong as state captain.

Malay States, where their P & O steamer *Assaye* arrived on 4 November. This was more to their taste, a charming city with an eighteenth-century air of serenity, and thoroughfares exalting its imperial connections: King Street, Carnarvon Street, Pitt Street, King Edward Place. There was no cricket for the Australians here—it had been too wet. Instead they joined crowds of white businessmen in pressed shorts and open-necked shirts at the Eastern and Orient Hotel, surveyed the stilted houses, fishing huts and bazaars, and partook of the local Malay Stengah. Then it was on to Singapore, this time for what the *Straits Times* was patriotically promoting as Singapore Cricket Week:

> We are all grateful to the Australians for helping so materially to join up the ties of brotherhood between all parts of the Empire. When they sent their first team to England it seemed a wild thing to do…We know better nowadays how splendidly the athletic qualities of the race have been developed in those young countries which have drawn to themselves some of the best blood of the Motherland.

Singapore was already one of the world's busiest ports, its harbour choked with steamers and sampans, its streets with rickshaws and their coolies. The architecture mingled exuberant pagodas among buildings along classic British lines. When the Australians participated in two semi-serious games against 'the Rest', they found the Singapore Cricket Club's ground surmounted by an ornate pavilion, recently extended in the style of an English country house, with decorative plasterwork and Elizabethan multi-paned windows; impressed, they presented an autographed team photograph to its designer, R. A. J. Bidwell. They might almost have been in England, but for the 95 per cent humidity that had reminded Kipling of an orchid house with its 'remorseless steam sweat that knows no variation between night and day'.

There is no evidence that the Australians charged appearance money here. Perhaps they felt otherwise recompensed, for they were lavishly entertained and comfortably billeted; with Cotter, Armstrong was guest of the Middlesex Regiment. 'Conspicuous as special guests' at Government House's Birthday Ball, where the band's selections began with the 'Eton Boating Song', they were also treated to a Tanglin Club smoking concert where Noble's 'really admirable bass voice' rendered 'I Fear No Foe'. When Singapore Cricket Club president Sir Arthur Young and local diplomat Ernest Birch whisked the Australians across the strait to Johore, its anglophile Sultan ran them swiftly round his rubber plantation in two handsome motor cars before an opulent luncheon. The *Straits Budget* reported:

> The hall was beautifully decorated and the tables fairly glistened with gold plate…The lunch included the curries for which Johore is famed. After the Sultan had proposed 'the King', Sir Arthur asked the company to join him in drinking the health of his highness, the Sultan of Johore, who is carrying on his father's reputation for having discovered the true secret of hospitality, which is to make every guest feel perfectly at home.

Finally there was a jaunt to Perak, a British protectorate, where Birch hosted a day's shooting. The Australians did not excel; beneath the headline 'Mr Birch's Guests Hunt the Nimble Porker', a *Malay Mail* correspondent commented that 'the prowess of the visitors, so far as shooting is concerned, is less noteworthy than in other directions'. Birch recalled that Cotter's efforts 'created more genuine fear in the minds of those shooting than he has ever succeeded in establishing by his fastest delivery on bumpy wickets', Laver that Hopkins climbed a tree, fearful of tigers. Armstrong, meanwhile, wasn't there at all; the *Times of Malaya's* reported that he was 'unfortunately laid up with fever'.

Malaria has shadowed mankind since antiquity, its twentieth-century overthrow one of medicine's chiefest triumphs. When Armstrong fell victim, it was known to result from a parasitic protozoa transmitted by the *Anopheles* mosquito, but remained deadly in tropical areas of poor sanitation—and Armstrong had lately passed through a few. Malaria conquers the body by stealth. The mosquito deposits its sporozoite, which invades then ruptures a red blood cell as it fissions into smaller merozoites which continue the process. This can take one week, or three, but the result is the same: four to ten hours of chills followed by severe headaches, fever and sweating. The parasites, too, reproduce synchronously, touching off paroxysms, bloating the spleen, and inducing anemia. Unless treated, attacks continue at intervals of forty-eight or seventy-two hours.

Armstrong was lucky. Lodging with Laver at the Perak home of R. B. Bannon, a cricketer against whom the Australians had just played in Singapore, he had immediate access to medical attention. Laver recalled that the attack had been 'coming on him for several days' and that 'a few days in bed under able treatment soon set him right'. Armstrong was well enough to rejoin teammates aboard the *Ipoh* at Port Sweetenham, then to leave Singapore on the Dutch mail steamer *Van Riemsdyk* on 19 November. But with malaria ninety years ago, 'setting right' was seldom complete.

Armstrong seems to have contracted a *vivax* malaria, which accounts for about 40 per cent of cases. It is more debilitating than deadly, having an acute phase of two to three weeks, but continues occupying the body, and can recur at intervals for many years. There was some irony to the fact that Armstrong and his teammates were bound for Tandjong Priok on the north-west tip of Java: the island was the world's biggest producer of quinine, an extrusion of bark from the cinchona tree that interferes with the parasite's reproduction and which for almost three centuries had been malaria's only effective remedy. Seventy years earlier, an Englishman in Peru called Charles Ledger had undertaken a minute study of the miraculous cinchona, identifying what would be named *cinchona ledgeriana* as containing the highest quinine concentrations. Snubbed in Britain, he had persuaded the Dutch to set aside vast tracts of Java as cinchona plantations, establishing it by the turn of the century as a virtual monopoly manufacturer. For much of the rest of his life, Armstrong would go nowhere without supplies of its wonder drug.

Java was a quirky final destination for Armstrong and his comrades. Part of the Dutch East Indies, it teemed with thirty-two million people, of whom only 65,000 were European, and a third of these soldiers. The capital Batavia boasted one famous hostelry, the Hotel des Indes, its five-hectare grounds lit by electric lamps. But there were no welcoming committees here, no English-language newspaper to record their visit, and Laver's recollections were of being observed as much as observing. Amid Batavia's bustling boulevards and bazaars, five hearty Australians were an incongruous sight, Armstrong's hulking figure queerest of all. Laver noted:

> Curiosity is a characteristic trait of the Javanese. They will immediately gather round anyone stopping to do anything. One day Armstrong wished to purchase fruit at a railway station where a crowd of food vendors was offering fruit for sale. Even when selecting the fruit a crowd began to gather, and by the time he had discovered the amount he had to pay—his knowledge of Malay is very limited, consisting of three words—a whole

army of food hawkers had formed a circle round him watching operations. They suspended their own business to do this.

Over their nine-day visit, the Australians visited the island's coffee, rice and sugar plantations, and were awed by the active volcanic craters of Tang Tagkoeban Prakoe: Armstrong decided to paint them, as he had the Scottish highlands and Malay peninsula. Again, though, Armstrong's stature and displacement left Laver laughing:

> Owing to Warwick Armstrong's enormous weight, he had a special carriage to himself on each occasion we visited the volcanoes, but when we first saw the exceedingly small horses they had saddled up for us to ride we refused on the grounds of cruelty to get on their backs…Armstrong was the first up but as he rose into stirrup, the poor horse's back bent like a bamboo cane and looked like it would break in two.

The reference is somewhat ironic. Although improved in health, malaria had taken a toll. When he and his teammates arrived in Sydney a week before Christmas aboard the *Baud*, *Cricket* cheerfully reported that his weight had dropped to 104 kilograms: 'May his shadow never grow smaller!' Such joviality was misplaced: malaria was a serious indisposition. At the time of Armstrong's return, there were two Australian outbreaks, one on the Umbrawarra tinfield in the Northern Territory, another at Kidston in Queensland—so grave that the government in January 1910 set up Townsville's Australian Institute of Tropical Medicine, Australia's first medical research centre. Cricketers in Armstrong's hometown, too, were even then mourning the loss of a popular player from Laver's East Melbourne: Harold Dawson had died of malaria while with the Niger Transport Company in Jebba, British West Africa.

If a sentence of indefinite recurrences disturbed Armstrong, he did not show it. Two days after Christmas, Victoria met New South Wales at the MCG. The mercury topped 100 degrees Fahrenheit on the first day and 103 on the second day, but Armstrong struck seven fours in 67, and claimed 6–112 from more than fifty overs in the game. There followed 124 in three and a half hours against South Australia with 5–131 from more than sixty overs. And there may have been more to these performances than physical resilience and native impatience: 1909–10 offered at least one prize worth coveting.

14

'An Attempt Is to Be Made
to Keep Warwick Armstrong'

Warwick Armstrong's appointment as captain of the Australian team touring New Zealand at the end of the 1909–10 season was partly recognition of accomplishments, partly luck. Four potential rivals, for various reasons, progressively ruled themselves out. The first was Trumper. He was full of forebodings about the board, and in England had confided them to the *Evening Standard*'s E. H. D. Sewell, who recalled:

> I had a long talk to Trumper, who made me aware of the storm which was about to break in Australia between the players and those who soon afterwards took up the reins of cricket in Australia, and some of whom, not being cricketers, drove the coach now and again into a ditch. I could then have published what is called a scoop, but I refrained, hoping the changeover would take place peacefully.

Trumper had returned from England early aboard the *Macedonia*, arriving well ahead of the rest of the team, intending a full grade and first-class season. In his absence, however, the New South Wales Cricket Association had quietly changed policies regarding the appointment of captains, vesting the responsibility in the selectors rather than the players. And when Austin Diamond was chosen, Trumper protested angrily that he was left 'only one course to adopt': he declared himself unavailable for selection even as player.

On 13 January 1910, Noble then notified the NSWCA of his retirement, citing 'the exigencies of my business' as a dentist—a gracious expression of his weariness at Billy McElhone's persecution. 'The pity of it is that such a splendid cricketer should be lost to big cricket solely through the lack of tact and judgment on the part of those who control the game in New South Wales,' 'Felix' mourned in the *Australasian*. 'When bitter prejudice gets the better of sound judgment, we can never have fair play.' Noble's treatment by the NSWCA, decided 'Mid On' of the *Leader*, had been 'a crime and a calamity', depriving Australian cricket of its 'brightest ornament'.

Clem Hill, having declined to tour England, also declined the New Zealand jaunt. Though still an Australian selector, he professed to being too busy at the Adelaide Stock Exchange. Again this was probably a pretext; Hill would, in fact, never tour under the board's jurisdiction. But it is the ineligibility of another candidate, whom the board might well have favoured, that is most intriguing. Peter McAlister began the season as Victoria's sole selector, and was elected captain by teammates for the state's meeting with New South Wales at the Melbourne Cricket Ground. He made 7 and 0 in a 272-run defeat. Then, having picked himself in the XIII for the ensuing match against South Australia beginning 1 January 1910, he without explanation 'stood out' on the morning of the game, and for the rest of the season.

McAlister would at the time have had other matters on his mind; his performance as treasurer on the 1909 tour had become a matter of administrative concern. The board met in Sydney a fortnight later, noted that it had placed its share of the tour proceeds on fixed deposit, but otherwise was in ignorance of the journey's conduct. At a Victorian Cricket Association meeting on 14 February 1910, Mat Ellis inquired ingenuously when a tour balance sheet would be available. President Donald Mackinnon, perhaps glancing at East Melbourne's delegates McAlister and Laver as he did so, replied that 'certain matters in connection with the tour had required adjusting by the Board of Control'. McAlister would eventually patch some financial figures together from further information Laver provided—perhaps the final indignity.

One suspects, though, that a key reason for McAlister's unease about playing that season was his relationship with Armstrong: the man who had refused to play under his leadership in England was hardly likely to have been an obedient subordinate in the Sheffield Shield, and the position of any captain without the confidence of his best player is more or less untenable. Certainly, it later became known that McAlister was in bad odour with his erstwhile colleague: one of the barbs Hill would fling at McAlister in their infamous selection table stoush three years later was that 'Warwick Armstrong had refused to play under him as captain in the old country'. An irony is that McAlister, with Hill and Iredale, chose Armstrong in the Australian team for its New Zealand sojourn. We don't know whether McAlister voted against him, of course, or complied with others. But he would have known that, once chosen, Armstrong's election as captain was a *fait accompli*.

Some wondered how Armstrong would acquit himself as Australian captain. Sydney's *Daily Telegraph* referred to his reputation for irascibility: 'Armstrong is the confirmed growler of the Victorian team. He growls at every conceivable thing. He growls mightily when a catch is dropped off his bowling. It will be interesting to know how he gets on as captain of a team mostly of colts in New Zealand.' But while 'growler' might have suited Armstrong, 'colts' scarcely suited his companions. The official photograph of the 1909–10 Australian team is unusually flavoursome. There is not the trace of a smile to be seen. In their ill-fitting blazers and rag-tag headgear, the team resembles a gang of Dodge City desperadoes, readier for a punch-up in a saloon than a game of cricket. In the centre, seated before their bewhiskered manager Alick Mackenzie, Armstrong looks meanest of all.

His team contained some irrepressible individuals. There was Richmond's Dave Smith, a fierce hitter and hearty drinker. His fondness for brawling would later result in a board reprimand. There was Glebe's Sid Emery, who bowled vicious googlies at medium pace from a run of random length, and was known as 'Mad Mick'. Noble once told Emery that control of his wrong 'un would make him a great bowler. 'If I could control myself,' retorted Emery, 'I'd be a great man.' And there was Tasmanian Norman Dodds, the talented keeper-batsman championed by Hill before the 1909 Ashes tour.

Son of Tasmania's chief justice, Dodds had excelled during the second trial match a year earlier, blasting an unbeaten 80 in little over an hour.

His omission from Australia's touring party had caused some soul-searching in Tasmania; Launceston's *Daily Telegraph* mentioned a 'peccadillo' during the state's game with Arthur Jones' Englishmen, when Dodds had 'incapacitated himself for a day through a little indiscretion in his choice of a boon companion from among the [English] team.' Whatever this implies, it is of a piece with a wayward soul. Prone to absent himself from club games to attend the races, and known to open a beer bottle by smashing off the top with his bat, 'Joker' Dodds was destined for a brief career and a brief life.

Dodds didn't get off on the right foot with Armstrong. In the very first match at Wellington, he and his skipper were involved in a messy run-out, which the *Dominion* reported in unusual detail:

> When he [Armstrong] had made four singles, his partner Dodds made a stroke past him and made a few steps. Armstrong also began to run, disregarding Dodds' belated instruction not to proceed, and passing Dodds just as he was getting back to his own crease. As the bails at the end which Armstrong has just left were lifted...Dodds was in the circumstances out. Armstrong was heard to say to Dodds: 'Well, I am not out'. But, as the latter did not evince any desire to leave the crease, Armstrong returned to the pavilion where he was again applauded.

The pair, however, would grow to like one another. Perhaps it was their shared obstinacy, perhaps the affinity of two natural outsiders to the cricket establishment. Whatever the case, Armstrong on this trip obtained from Dodds some of the best cricket of his career, and also the last; he never played again. With the death of his first wife, Dodds decamped to northern Tasmania with another woman, leaving his twin boy and girl in an orphanage. When he died in December 1916 aged forty, Armstrong was the only one of his cricket contemporaries to write to Dodds' children, expressing his affection and regard for their father.

In asserting authority, of course, Armstrong had the manifest advantage of being a great player. Those who might have loathed the character could take no exception to the cricketer. In the tour's third match against Canterbury Armstrong was at his best, coming in with his team 5–39 chasing 340 for victory, and reviving their innings to the extent of 8–307 by the close with an unbeaten four-hour 149. The Australians won every other first-class match, including the 'Tests' against New Zealand, at Christchurch by nine wickets and at Wellington by 162 runs. Armstrong's 393 runs at 56.1 and 16 wickets at 23 were a suitably man-sized contribution.

The Australians' irrefutable superiority set Armstrong one unusual challenge: diplomacy. No sooner had Armstrong's men arrived aboard the *Moeraki* on 9 February, for instance, than Wellington's mayor was cringing about his country's sporting standards:

> He declared that the New Zealanders did not blow about their skill at cricket, because they had no reason to (laughter). They could not play cricket for nuts. He reckoned that a New Zealand cricket team could…be got together which would beat portions of Australia—the Northern Territory (laughter), Western Australia and perhaps Tasmania—but it would not have a ghost of a chance against the other states.

Armstrong's reply was unusually gracious. Australia:

> had a very fine team he would admit, but he felt that the Mayor had been rather tough on New Zealand cricket. When he had visited the dominion on two previous occasions, he had come to the conclusion that they did know a little bit about the game. He would ask any player who was selected to play against his team not to think that he was 'out' before he was 'in'.

For one so tactless in his dealings with officialdom, Armstrong seems to have striven to do and say the right thing as captain. He settled on a policy of deprecating Australian strength, and reassuring New Zealanders about theirs. His opinion of the former he confided to the *New Zealand Herald*: 'Weak. Too weak in bowling. It's the same in batting. Cricket runs in cycles, and the current one is not the most promising.' His views on the latter he gave to the *Dominion* after Canterbury had run the Australians close:

> He is a man of few words, giving his opinion slowly and carefully, but emphatically when occasion demands it, just as emphatically as he hits a loose ball. 'It was a good match,' he said. 'A very good match. And it ended in just about the right way. Had it been played out, Canterbury might have won—I don't say they would have but they might have. We were considerably surprised by the fine form shown by Canterbury, they being onto us all the time with their batting and bowling…People have the idea that we are a wonderfully strong side but we are not. I am confident that New Zealand will be a good match for us and that the Test matches will be ding-dong goes.'

So often did Armstrong repeat this mantra that it had comical consequences. Reaching Christchurch on 10 March, Armstrong declared that

'New Zealand cricket has improved out of all recognition since my first visit to the dominion'. Which was fine, except that manager Mackenzie had the day before in Dunedin told a reporter it hadn't improved at all. 'The Breaker', a *Dominion* sports columnist, accused Armstrong of disingenuousness:

> If Warwick Armstrong wishes to settle in the dominion in the position of coach, well and good, but that is no reason why he should throw dust in people's eye by stating in direct contradiction to his manager that dominion cricket is improving…It is going back, very distinctly back, and the man who comes up with the politician's set string of platitudes 'to tickle the ears of the groundlings' is not a true friend of any strenuous human activity, sport or work.

And 'The Breaker' might have been onto something.

Armstrong's strenuous activity did not at this stage include work. He was again unemployed, having not held a job since his last temporary public service posting. This would not normally have concerned him, but chances were that his cricket income would soon be shrinking. After his disappointing profit share on the 1909 Ashes tour, the board's terms for the New Zealand trip were a miserly five shillings a day plus travel expenses—less than for a Sheffield Shield match. The VCA, meanwhile, had foreshadowed a crackdown on amateur expenses in interstate cricket. The *Argus* reported:

> Victorian teams have this season visited Adelaide, Sydney and Brisbane and the claims for loss of time in addition to professional fees amount to nearly £100…The association, rather than create any fresh trouble in the cricket world, has elected to pay most of the amounts claimed, but some of them are considered by members of the executive to be preposterous and special inquiries are being made about these.

Perhaps Armstrong, whilst endearing himself to New Zealanders, made it known he was a free agent. An offer came his way, from the Auckland Cricket Association's E. C. Beale, a prominent lawyer largely responsible for persuading Governor-General Lord Plunket to endow a shield for the country's first-class competition. New Zealand had recently been a fertile field for foreigners: Harry Trott's brother Albert had played for Hawke's Bay, Armstrong's erstwhile teammates Harry Graham and Charlie Macartney for Otago, while Beale had enjoyed great success in recruiting Sussex's Albert Relf. Yet no acquisition would have been as prestigious as Warwick Armstrong, Australian captain. The engagement's terms, and the seriousness with which Armstrong entertained it, are unknown. It is possible he pondered it long; he seems to have pondered it loud. Shortly after returning to Melbourne on 15 April, it became known that he was under offer, and he may all along have been fishing for a counterbid. If so, he succeeded.

Armstrong was beneficiary of another's misfortune, that of the Sydney's James Mackay—the luminous 'Sunny Jim', one of the Golden Age's most fabled talents. During his *annus mirabilis* of 1905–6, twenty-four-year-old Mackay had averaged 108 in grade cricket and 112.8 in the Sheffield Shield. Wounded in the crossfire between Melbourne and the NSWCA during the events of 1906, however, he had emigrated to the Transvaal, finding work at the Village Main Reef diamond mine. Perhaps touched by a loyal helpmate's distress, Wardill had then offered Mackay a £300-a-year job at Melbourne, part of a scheme the club mooted in May 1907 to encourage rural cricket entailing the appointment for three years of 'a high-class cricketer of standing and experience to act as organiser and advisor to the country clubs'. But the day after receiving a formal proposal, Mackay had been struck by a motorcyclist at Boksburg, near Johannesburg. Regaining consciousness after several days, he discovered his eyesight badly affected.

Assured his vision would return, Mackay returned home. 'He says there is nothing the matter with him now,' reported 'Short Slip' of the *Sydney Mail*. 'It is only a question of nerves.' His appointment was announced at Melbourne's annual meeting on 13 September, and enthusiastically greeted, yet it was soon clear that his powers were gone. His unhappy tenure terminated in March 1908—Melbourne's committee voted him £10 as a goodwill gesture.[*]

That same month, Wardill met misfortune himself, falling from a tram

---

[*] Mackay's eyesight never returned, thwarting any comeback; after his last match for Burwood in January 1909, he returned to his family at Uralla. Yet for many years his name had a magical aura. The *Referee*'s J. C. Davis felt that if Mackay had toured England 'he would have won a reputation with the bat greater than that of Victor Trumper'.

in South Yarra. The sixty-five-year-old secretary had taken some months to resume work, and even then was not fully himself. By May 1910, when Armstrong's future was in the balance, Wardill may have felt in need of further clerical assistance; he assuredly took the lead in trumping the New Zealand job. 'An attempt is to be made to keep Warwick Armstrong here,' he informed committeeman Edward Mitchell. 'He has an offer to go to Auckland. He would take the place offered to J. R. Mackay two years ago.' Additional support came from Armstrong's old confrere Hugh Trumble, by now a club committeeman. The appointment was formally proposed at a meeting of Melbourne's match and ground committee on 23 June, and then awaited only formal committee approval. 'Mr Trumble says he telephoned WWA and told him he could not give any answer until Wednesday next, and he seemed satisfied,' Wardill wrote treasurer Charles Forrester. 'He had not had the expected letters from Auckland yesterday.' Armstrong's recruitment as a 'pavilion clerk' on an annual salary of £250 was ratified on 8 July 1910. Wardill's records contain a duplicate of Melbourne's cable to the Auckland Cricket Association on Armstrong's behalf: 'Unable accept.'

Although Armstrong was nominally Mackay's successor, his duties at Ludstone Chambers seem to have been less defined, broad rather than onerous. He maintained the roll of its 5300 members: several specimens survive, kept in a neat hand, and signed by Armstrong on each page. He also kept the mid-week and club XI fixture lists, which involved almost sixty games in 1910–11, while part of his role at practices was now to 'impart some of his knowledge in a special net to promising juniors'. The *Herald* endorsed this wholeheartedly: 'If Armstrong is half as capable of imparting knowledge as he is of bowling "puzzlers", and making runs, there ought to be some champions brought forward in the near future.'

For this, Armstrong earned as much as his nominal boss, fifty-two-year-old chief clerk and club scorer Joe Taylor, and more than either of the other two pavilion clerks, David Mair and George Mason.* He was

---

* George Mason, described as 'junior clerk' in club records, was on £150. David Mair, at the club eighteen years, only had his pay increased to £175 in February 1911 after getting married. Obtaining better money from the MCC wasn't easy: one ground staffer, E. Morton, had been at the club since 1879, but by 1910 hadn't had a pay increase for twelve years.

also paid a good deal more than his old friend Bob Crockett the umpire, who as 'pavilion keeper' managing the ground staff bowlers and ordering cricket equipment drew only £156 a year. The only staff members paid more than Armstrong, in fact, seem to have been Wardill and curator Tom McCutcheon, with more than half a century's service between them. All Armstrong's duties, moreover, could be put aside when it came to the chance of a game; having not represented Melbourne at all in 1909–10, he did so on a dozen Saturdays in the coming season and in many more mid-week matches. And as his employment contract also specified—'absence in other states playing cricket to be allowed for'— his first-class and Test careers could continue without interruption.

Armstrong took his responsibilities as a representative of the Melbourne Cricket Club seriously: he seldom, for example, failed to meet visiting state teams on arrival at Spencer Street Station. Yet the arrangement was largely cosmetic. Much as English county clubs often employed leading players as 'coaches' and 'assistant secretaries' to preserve their amateur credentials, Melbourne's underwriting not only kept Armstrong for Australian cricket but permitted him the pretence of operating as a 'gentleman'.

Professionalism in all but name was not a phenomenon confined to cricket. So widespread in Australian rules was the 'back-hander'—informal emoluments for a player through arranged job or payment-in-kind—that the Victorian Football League would shortly legalise direct payments: 'over-the-table', they could be monitored. But while the SACA had employed Ernie Jones for a period during his playing days, and the NSWCA with Alick Bannerman and VCA with Jack Worrall were beginning to employ past players as coaches, Armstrong's position in Australia was unique—recognition of his indispensability, and testament to his personality.*

In becoming a Melbourne Cricket Club employee, Armstrong joined a social network of powerful individuals: captains of industry, pastoralists,

---

* Jones sought employment from the SACA in December 1896 and, at the time indispensable to South Australia's cause, became an odd jobs man at Adelaide Oval. But his duties, from bowling in the nets to watering the hedge in front of the members' stand twice a week, lasted only so long as his cricketing powers: he was retrenched in October 1901.

premiers, prime ministers. Overseeing the roll, handling nominations, collecting dues and distributing membership cards, in fact, Armstrong was well placed to make himself useful to such individuals. While Melbourne retains only a portion of its nomination forms from Armstrong's period there, he probably proposed or seconded as many members as any one person in that time: before World War I about one a month; on occasions during and after the war, when the club was shedding numbers, as many as one a week. Among them were many notables. He seconded the nominations, for instance, of two of Australia's foremost industrialists: in January 1914, the Sunshine Harvester's inventor H. V. McKay; in November 1918, BHP chieftain Essington Lewis.

So many did he assist becoming members that Armstrong cannot possibly have known them all: there were probably occasions on which Armstrong seconded a nomination merely as a favour to someone he knew. Yet, in each case, a form of social transaction was taking place, either establishing a friendship, or firming an existing one. Two examples will suffice: gentlemen named Bill Sweeney and Charles Tootell, with both of whom Armstrong became close personal friends.

Sweeney lived with his wife Florence in Elsternwick's Cole Street, and was a wholesale fruit merchant with premises at 420 Flinders Lane. A Melbourne Cricket Club member since 1903 and friend to Monty Noble, Sweeney probably met Armstrong in a cricketing context, for he was a fanatical supporter of his state; in a column in January 1912, 'Felix' toasted him as the man who 'follows the Victorians everywhere they travel, and can tell you the form and capabilities of Australian players with an ease and readiness that is difficult to beat'. Armstrong would second nominations to the club of five of Sweeney's business associates; Sweeney would act as Armstrong's best man.

Originally a stockbroker, Tootell ran MacKenzie Allan, a Queen Street merchant in the liquor trade, and ended up owning a string of Melbourne hostelries: the Supreme Court, Post Office, Mangalore, and Terminus hotels. The cricketer proposed him for club membership in December 1918. Later we shall hear more of him, in his role as Armstrong's business partner.

Thanks to the Melbourne Cricket Club, Armstrong became, in the modern vernacular, a 'networker'. His participation in these rituals of male reciprocity—the club would not admit women members for another seventy years—subsequently served him well. He proposed for membership the secretary of the Silverton Tramway Company; Armstrong would become a sizeable shareholder in that company. He seconded the nomination of the great Essendon footballer Albert Thurgood, and two nominations for VCA president Donald Mackinnon: both Thurgood and Mackinnon would serve on his testimonial committee.

The extent of the club's influence can be sensed from an event shortly after Armstrong's recruitment: the end to his brother's benighted marriage. At 1.30 p.m. on 20 January 1910, Joseph Rich, Jack Armstrong's father-in-law, and Bertram Harlem, solicitor's clerk, entered Collins Street's Federal Hotel. The latter handed Jack a sealed copy of a petition for divorce. In an affidavit Rich swore:

> This took place in the vestibule of the said Federal Hotel and, on the same occasion, I spoke to the said respondent and said to him that I was sorry this had happened and had to be done, but I hoped there would not be any needless disgrace and expense, and the said respondent said to me that he did not intend to defend the application for divorce or words to that effect.

Divorce was an extreme measure: there were only 141 in all Victoria that year. Catherine Armstrong's motive was her wish to remarry; indeed, she was eager to do so, as her intended planned leaving for Scotland. A *decree nisi* was issued on 13 May, a *decree absolute* on 10 September—all very expeditious and discreet. That there was no 'needless disgrace and expense' stood to the credit of the presiding judge in the Supreme Court's Matrimonial Causes branch: Justice Leo Cussen, president since succeeding Roderick Murchison in April 1907 of the Melbourne Cricket Club.

The 1910–11 season offered a novelty act, South Africa's first Australian visit. The five-Test series had been arranged by Peter McAlister and Leslie Poidevin at the inaugural meeting of a new Lord's institution, the Imperial Cricket Conference, on 15 June 1909, though it almost foundered over the board's refusal to offer a guarantee.[*]

---

[*] This decision in July 1910 was probably because of the board's experience with the deficiency it had been left with after England's 1907–8 tour, but invited

The team was an unknown quantity upon arriving in Adelaide on 26 October 1910 aboard the *Commonwealth*. Wiring salutations from the Melbourne Cricket Club, Wardill addressed them to 'the captain' and 'the manager' of the team, apparently unaware of their names.

Other aspects of the summer were more routine: the Australian associations were locked, as ever, in private squabbles. On 3 October 1910, the VCA replaced McAlister as selector with Melbourne's stalwart Hugh Trumble—reversing the result of their deliberations two years earlier. 'The appointment is sure to give general satisfaction,' remarked 'Mid On' of the *Leader*, 'as nearly all cricketers recognise that it should have been made long ago.' But Trumble's election set off a train of intrigue. When the board met a fortnight later, it disregarded his appointment and opted to continue McAlister's tenure as an Australian selector alongside Hill and Iredale (more predictably, the board at the same meeting also rejected Noble's candidature as a selector). 'As McAlister gave them satisfaction in the past,' commented 'Wicket-Keeper' of the *Herald*, with something of a double-meaning, 'they could not very well pass him over.' But it caused peppery exchanges when the VCA reconvened a week afterwards, South Melbourne's Henry Skinner and University's Norman Spiers describing Trumble's rejection as 'an insult to the association', and querying the allegiances of board delegates Ernie Bean and Harry Rush.

Rush: This has nothing to do with the association. It is Board business.
Skinner: Surely we ought to be allowed to express an opinion.
Spiers: Might I ask how the Victorian delegates voted?
Bean: By ballot.

After this exquisitely opaque reply, president Donald Mackinnon ruled the debate out of order. That day, Trumble published his first Victorian XI of the season, generously recalling McAlister, who was then elected captain for the game in Adelaide beginning 29 October. The match was a rout. Against a South Australian side reinforced by Surrey's

---

accusations of hypocrisy. 'Observer' of the *Argus* commented: 'Why should a distinction be made between the wealthy Marylebone club and the struggling South African Cricket Association, whose men like ours have to earn their own living?' Even English critics thought it churlish, E. H. D. Sewell commenting in *Sporting Life*: 'There is a feeling that Australia should not expect all and take none of the risk.'

John Crawford—at loggerheads with his county and seeking sunnier climes—Victoria was 7–27 after an hour. Armstrong grafted 35 but the 111 total could not be protected and a six-wicket defeat ensued. Given McAlister's contribution, 1 and 4, and his age, forty-one, it is unsurprising his name was missing when Trumble's next team was published on 7 November. His playing days were over, but his role in Australia's cricket destiny was not.

15

'Not Quite the Impartial Body It Ought to Be'

T he same board meeting that reinstalled Peter McAlister as a selector was noteworthy for another reason: for the first time, an appointment as Test captain was originated wholly by administrators rather than teammates. Clem Hill was not a controversial choice but here was another effacement of player influence in Australian cricket affairs. In Victoria, by contrast, the old system of team appointment continued—at least for the moment. And the state's next home game, against the touring South Africans, was a form of rehabilitation for Warwick Armstrong; three years after his mysterious dispossession, he was unanimously re-elected captain, presiding over a five-wicket win. Perhaps colleagues detected a dash more maturity in him; one pre-match incident suggests he was becoming a more democratic leader. At the visitors' request, the Victorian Cricket Association did not issue team members their usual ration of complimentary tickets. According to the *Argus*, Armstrong 'interviewed the executive', stating that 'the players would not submit to being deprived of a time-honoured privilege', and 'that unless the players received tickets for the match there would probably be no team'. The perquisite was restored.

His own needs, however, remained paramount. After Victoria's handsome victory against South Australia at the end of November, Armstrong and teammates Bert Kortlang, Jimmy Matthews and Dave Smith were invited by McAlister to represent an Australian XI against the tourists in Brisbane. Alone among them Armstrong inquired about the fee, turning up his nose at the £15 plus expenses. 'Mr Armstrong said he would not go except under Test match conditions [a £25 allowance],' the *Herald* reported. 'Though Mr Armstrong had little to say on the matter he did not seem anxious to make the trip.' He stayed in Melbourne.

Not everything went Armstrong's way. When Queensland visited for their fixture on 16 December, he was diagnosed with mumps, and confined to bed at Arra Glen for a week receiving daily visits from a Dr Rupert Willis of Malvern. Odds were against speedy recovery. 'An attack of mumps is not lightly overcome and takes a lot out of a man,' commented the *Argus*, 'and the probabilities are that Armstrong will not be able to play in the Second Test beginning on Saturday week.' But he arrived at the MCG a couple of days before the match and, though unable to practice, convinced Hill of his fitness. His 75 in two hours and 4–134 from forty-eight overs was a determined resolve in a determined team; Australia, 158 in arrears on the first innings, recovered to win by 89 runs. Six weeks later in the Fourth Test at the same arena, Armstrong compiled 132 with thirteen boundaries, including a rollocking 154-run stand with Hill in 101 minutes.

Percy Sherwell's South Africans proved a talented handful, their inexhaustible all-rounder Aubrey Faulkner gathering 1534 runs and 49 wickets on the tour, but the Australians were demonstrably superior. Lured from self-imposed exile by his state's captaincy, Victor Trumper demonstrated all his old sorcery, the profusion of his 661 runs at an average of 94 detracting not from their natural magic: as South African E. W. Ballantine put it, 'one seldom gets tired of the ocean waves'. There was even a hint of tranquillity about Australian cricket that season. The New South Wales Cricket Association ended it by presenting Trumper with a dressing case in token of his stature as the 'world's greatest living batsman'. Reported the *Sydney Morning Herald*: 'Mr Trumper, in returning thanks, said he appreciated their kindness, because it showed he had their confidence.' Time would prove this a fond illusion.

That season, Armstrong also repaid Melbourne's investment in his talents. Not only did he generate 456 runs at 114 in district cricket, but he travelled widely in his capacity as organiser of the team's off-piste fixture list. Easter, for example, found him in Wagga playing against a local XV; no match being too mean for his endeavour, he took 7–80 and scored an undefeated 117. So often would Armstrong criss-cross the country over the next few years that he became friends with Tom Molomby, then a senior railway official, later railway commissioner, who hosted teams in a special car. Melbourne's matches, too, were often festive occasions with other entertainments laid on; on one occasion at Bendigo Oval, goat races were staged, Armstrong laying 20 shillings on a competitor called 'The Joker' at 20–1. Despite starting with a 50-yard handicap in a 100-yard race, and being guided erratically by a small boy in a sulky, it won; Armstrong declared it one of his shrewdest punts.

It was on this trip to Wagga that Armstrong met the O'Donnells, a wealthy pastoral family with strong Irish Catholic roots who owned 'Mingay', a choice Murrumbidgee property. He got on well with the O'Donnell brothers, John, James and Thomas, and endeared himself further by turning out for their local team—an episode recalled by a Gundagai railway station employee called Akers:

> I was living at Coolac at the time and one Sunday we met Muttama in a cricket match on our own wicket. Muttama arrived a man short, and seeing a big, brawny young fellow drive up in a sulky with a Mingay man, one of the Muttama players asked him if he could play cricket and if so make up their XI. Muttama did not know who he was. None of them knew, in fact. It was Armstrong, then at his best. He said he would be willing to oblige Muttama, but did not think he would be much help—a sweet leg puller is Armstrong.
>
> 'Oh, you can have him,' we said to Muttama, as we sized the stranger up. He looked like a 'half Johnny' kind of chap. His name went down in the scoring book as 'Stranger'; well, 'Stranger' went in, and we felt confident of getting his wicket first over, but he gave us the surprise of our lives. He pasted our bowling all over the ground. Every man in our team bowled at him, but 6s and 4s came off his bat like clockwork. We scratched our heads and began to think, then our tails went down when someone whispered it was Armstrong. He knocked up 84 in a very short time, then he banged a ball very hard, and it flew over the heads of our men in the field, and lodged in Coolac Creek, and we never recovered it. It was the only ball we had, therefore we could not go on with the match.

The O'Donnells were in upheaval, squabbling over the fortune of their patriarch Patrick James O'Donnell—this was a complicated Irish immigrant story three generations in the making. Patrick was the second son of a Limerick couple, James and Mary O'Donnell, but more importantly the nephew of a stocky red-haired revolutionary, James Fitzpatrick, transported in 1822 for 'firing on a British residence'. Fitzpatrick prospered as a farmer in Australia after his release and encouraged his kin to emigrate, which they did in June 1858 aboard the *Castilian*. Patrick showed an immediate aptitude for farming, going on to run Fitzpatrick's Cootamundra property 'Cowcumble'. He was also befriended by a wealthy family, the Hanleys, who presented him with the 10,000-hectare Mingay when he married their daughter Margaret.

Patrick had inherited his uncle's strong nationalism, which fitted well with the Hanleys, a branch of whom owned a Gundagai hostelry called the Erin Go Brae, that resonant Irish battle-cry. He became a generous benefactor of republican causes, in addition to being 'a gentleman of overflowing good nature and hospitality, a staunch and generous friend and a right-minded, philanthropic and public spirited colonist'. Mingay's sixteen-kilometre river frontage made the property robust during drought and fertile after rain. Patrick imported sheep from Tasmania and livestock from New Zealand, became a successful exhibitor, and seemed favoured by the proverbial Irish good fortune; one year of flood, several of his best bullocks were swept downstream to Wagga and deposited in Fitzmaurice Street, apparently none the worse for their journey. Wishing to share his luck, Patrick invited brother James, less fortunate since arriving in Australia, to dwell on the estate.

The luck, however, didn't last. Patrick's favourite among his nine children, Paddy, died at twenty-four—fighting a bushfire at Christmas 1900, his horse tripped in a rabbit burrow. Three years later, Patrick himself was thrown from a buggy while crossing his paddocks. He seems thereafter to have hardened towards his offspring and, increasingly debilitated by diabetes, became wary of their intentions towards the estate. While in Sydney in June 1907, having sold Cowcumble and placed Mingay in the hands of agents, he abruptly redrafted his will. He wanted Mingay's integrity maintained, and the children to derive income from it rather than sell. The will, dated 27 July, is signed in a spidery scrawl suggestive of haste. He was dead, from gangrene precipitated by his diabetes, within a fortnight, leaving an estate worth £186,978.

The children were, indeed, eager to cash out of country life, but the presence of their uncle James on Mingay complicated matters.

Documents were drawn up for a sale in October 1910 but court action to dislodge him from the property failed. By the time Armstrong visited the area, the O'Donnells were clearly wealthy but in the unusual situation of not knowing how wealthy. Not only was much of the estate tied up in Mingay, but a large portion was accounted for by monies receivable on the completion of Cowcumble's sale. Mingay's stately brick homestead consisted of twelve rooms, ringed by a verandah, with three servants' rooms and a coachhouse. A partly enclosed orchard and vineyard occupied an acre. Yet the O'Donnells were now little interested in this symbol of their family's past, or interested in it purely *as* a symbol. When Patrick's widow, beneficiary of a £10,000 annuity, bought a residence in the Sydney beachside suburb of Woollahra, she reminiscently named it Mingay.

Even if he did not realise it at the time, Armstrong had met the woman he would marry: Patrick's twenty-nine-year-old daughter Aileen Veronica. No details of their courtship survive, but as a partner she had several recommendations: she was well-bred, she was Catholic, and like Amelia Flynn when she had met John Armstrong those many years earlier in Kyneton had wealth behind her. One imagines that, for Armstrong, this last was not immaterial.

For Australian cricket, the summer of 1911–12 promised a team from England under Marylebone's flag, and a resumption of internecine strife. Melbourne entered its now annual application to join district cricket ranks on a competitive basis on 11 September and received its now annual rejection with the threat of a further slap in the face. The *Argus* reported that the VCA had contemplated confining its Sheffield Shield team to those players with full-fledged district teams:

> Those who have watched the workings of the association in the past few years have no doubt that, were it not that the two leading Victorian players Warwick Armstrong and Vernon Ransford would thus be debarred from playing for Victoria, even this indignity would be heaped on the Melbourne club.

The writer was 'Old Boy', Reginald Wilmot, first to discern Armstrong's talent fifteen years earlier while covering school sports for the *Australasian*. Now he was first to foresee the impending conflict:

One gentleman expressed himself thus to me on Saturday: 'Cricket is a British sport and its management should be on British lines...This continuous crushing of the Melbourne Cricket Club by the association reminds one of the stories of the treatment by the Romans of the countries occupied by their armies.'

The threat to proscribe Melbourne's Victorian representatives did not materialise, but 'Old Boy' shortly had other grounds for griping. To sit with Trumble, the VCA re-elected to its selection panel not only Peter McAlister but Ernie Bean, overlooking a new but widely fancied candidate in Harry Trott. Though the NSWCA then replaced Frank Iredale with Trumper, it again snubbed Noble. Finally, at the board's meeting on 13 October 1911, the old selection panel was re-elected: Iredale and McAlister to sit with Clem Hill. Just as McAlister had been a Test selector while not a state selector, so too was Iredale; the clear priority was to keep in a minority anyone who might threaten the existing autocracy. As 'Old Boy' commented:

> It seems extraordinary that the best two captains in Australian cricket, Messrs Noble and Trott, should have been rejected by their associations, and that the delegates on the Board appointed by their associations should vote in opposition to the wishes of those associations as voiced in the choice for state selectors.

Billy McElhone's election as chairman at the same board meeting was equally ominous. One last almighty fight had been likely since the truce of July 1906, and probably inevitable since McAlister's appointment as tour treasurer in February 1909. Now it was imminent: its battleground would be the control of the next Australian team to visit England, scheduled for the following year as part of a novel Triangular Tournament featuring the host country and South Africa. The board wanted—needed—the spoils of English tours: it could not otherwise consider itself a true board of 'control'. This, in its way, was perfectly sensible: the profit-share system under which previous teams had operated was archaic, a vestige of the roaring days of the 1870s and 1880s when pioneering colonial players had formed joint stock companies to float themselves to England. Access to those profits would make colossal new revenues available to Australian cricket—or, at least, to Australian cricket as personified by the board. The next move, moreover, had been obvious since 1909's Ashes tour; the VCA had then stated explicitly in its annual report that 'One or two modifications to the Board's procedure relative to Australian XIs may be considered desirable, notably in connection with the appointment of a manager, which should be made by the Board and not by the players.'

Such an appointment, of course, would breach Rule 9 of the board's constitution; but for McElhone, this was mere detail.

The board was now a cricketing Tammany Hall, McElhone its George Washington Plunkitt. Although Hill, Harry Blinman and Mostyn Evan of South Australia were still inclined to resist his will, usually in co-operation with Melbourne's Arthur Aitken, the NSWCA and VCA were bulwarked against them by the delegates of the Queensland Cricket Association. Why the QCA, which did not compete in the Sheffield Shield, had as many board representatives as the VCA is explicable only in terms of its convenience to McElhone.

Both QCA delegates were politicians and freemasons, silver-haired and superbly moustached. One was Joseph Allen, a fifty-year-old grocery merchant, formerly mayor of South Brisbane. He had led his association into the combine and was now deep in the McElhone camp, suborned by the promise of a hometown Test. The other was Colonel Justin Foxton, recently an honorary minister in Alfred Deakin's third adminis-tration, a barrister by training and a bully by instinct. As member for Carnarvon in Queensland's Legislative Assembly between 1883 and 1904, Foxton's electioneering ploys had included persuading a coachman to 'lose' a group of passengers who were political opponents *en route* to the polls, and smashing railway gates deliberately lowered to stop a train of his Brisbane supporters at Stanthorpe station. Yet, for all his bluster and the disdainful tilt of his head, he was an obtuse individual, the willing instrument of abler intellects. 'Everybody who remembers the genial and warlike Colonel when he was in Federal Parliament knows how facile he is to the touch of a strong man,' wrote *Melbourne Punch*. 'He [is] Billy McElhone's puppet.'

The loyalty of Allen and Foxton meant that McElhone could essen-tially do as he pleased: with the seven votes mustered by the NSWCA, VCA and QCA cast *en bloc*, dissent merely agitated the atmosphere. As Joe Darling, who had by now left the board in disgust, recalled:

Everything on the agenda for meetings was discussed privately at a prior meeting of five delegates from Victoria and New South Wales and two from Queensland, who in that period sold their votes for a secret promise of a Test match. Western Australia was denied even one delegate, as the ruling clique were afraid he might vote against them.

McElhone also had at his side throughout the ensuing dispute a new secretary, pint-sized thirty-two-year-old Sydney Smith Jnr. Like McElhone, he was from a political family, his father having been opposition whip in the first federal parliament, being described in terms that would become reminiscent of his son as 'inclined to be fussy' and 'to surround trivialities in a veil of secrecy'. If it is possible to be a prodigy in cricket administration, Smith was one: his first role had been the secretaryship of an Annandale boys' team at age ten. Though by day merely a clerk in the Government Stock Department, he would enjoy a career in cricket's management spanning three-quarters of a century. Here, too, McElhone could hardly have had a stauncher loyalist. Smith felt he had 'never met a stronger man'.

Smith's first act was to renew board requests for Frank Laver's 1909 tour ledgers. Predecessor Colin Sinclair had sought them the year before, but accepted Laver's word that they were outside the board's province, containing entries intimate to individuals, and not books of the team *per se*. Only one imputation can be drawn from Smith's inquiry: that the board wished to embarrass or compromise Laver in such a way as to disqualify him from acting again as Australia's manager on the forthcoming tour. Rather than merely surrender the books, Laver offered to attend a board meeting to answer questions about receipts and expenditures. This the board refused. Then, without explanation, Laver was dropped by Victoria, immediately after claiming 6–111 from 63 tireless overs against the Englishmen at the MCG.

It did not take a leap of deductive reasoning to connect events, and another rumour began circulating: that the more tractable Barlow Carkeek was being groomed to supplant Armstrong as Victoria's captain. Doubtless Armstrong heard it. In Victoria's next game, coming in at 3–59 against South Australia, he batted almost six hours for 250. Studded with 29 fours and a six onto the asphalt in front of the Harrison Stand, it was the biggest innings by a Victorian. The dispute in which he would shortly be embroiled, however, would demand more of Armstrong than mere sporting excellence.

When Pelham Warner arrived aboard the *Orvieto* with his team, his wife and two children, the *Bulletin* fantasised: 'What with looking after them, running his team and keeping up his end as a talker, the captain is in for a busy time. Of course, it is quite possible the wife and two children will look after the old man, soothe his troubled brow when the bowling goes wrong and the batting starts to rot.'

It was a clairvoyant comment. After just one innings, Warner succumbed to a duodenal ulcer, so grave that he was compelled to surrender the captaincy to his deputy. Twenty-nine-year-old all-rounder John Douglas would later be one of Armstrong's greatest—and unluckiest—rivals. But for him, this would be a golden summer, in which he took fullest advantage of Australian disunity.

Australia's campaign began with its own ill omen. Arriving in Sydney just before the First Test, Armstrong attended the Gore Hill funeral of Reg Duff, the bravura strokemaker with whom he had made his Test debut ten years earlier, but whose talents had steadily been sapped by alcohol. 'Some few years back,' euphemised the *Referee*, 'he did not take that care of his health necessary for one wishing to live a normal life in years and in vigour.' Duff had died suddenly in Royal North Shore Hospital, where he was under treatment for alcoholic poisoning, and an XI of state and Test comrades formed a graveside guard along with a contingent of Sydney Harbour Trust workmates.

Duff, a few months younger than Armstrong, had died intestate. Former Australian comrades helped cover the funeral's cost, and appear to have been much moved; perhaps, reminding them of an earlier era, he concentrated their minds on the nature of the new. Even winning the First Test, thanks to a chanceless Trumper hundred and 12–175 from their new googly bowler 'Ranji' Hordern, did not ease their disquiet. Strolling at Manly afterwards, Vernon Ransford and umpire Bob Crockett spied some of the Englishmen ahead. 'Bob,' confided Ransford, 'I think they'll win the Ashes.' Ransford's reasoning was logical: Hordern could not dismiss the Englishmen every time, while Douglas possessed, in the peerless Sydney Barnes and coltish left-armer Frank Foster, two outstanding opening bowlers. But the spontaneous confession seems to betray a psychological frailty among the Australians, an anxiety about the ordeal ahead, both on the field and off. A couple of days later, the board distributed an agenda for its next meeting whose significance 'Old Boy' apprehended instantly:

Colonel Foxton has given notice that he will move that a representative of the Board of Control shall be appointed to travel with the Australian team as a secretary to keep the books and accounts, that such a representative shall be paid the sum of £400 by the Board, and that his expenses on exactly the same scale as the players in all things shall be paid out of the proceeds of the tour; that is by the players.

Wilmot recognised it as a contrivance—'out of all reason'—to circumvent Rule 9. While it theoretically remained open to the players to appoint a manager, the representative would be 'practically a clerk unless the manager's duties are to be largely restricted', and this was clearly not the intention; here was a manager by any other name. The *Sydney Morning Herald* pleaded with the board to reconsider:

> The institution of the Board of Control was…a reform generally due and should have been in the best interests of cricket. It may yet be so. But hitherto it must be confessed the Board of Control has gone about its work not quite as the impartial body it ought to be…but a body possessing grievances and keen on the poor objective of getting the better of certain players opposed to its point of view…What is quite clear is that the representative players really have some rights left. They are not entitled, perhaps, to all the rights they once had, but as the men who call the game they cannot be wholly ignored. The public is mainly concerned with the game after all. It is only faintly concerned with the financial share of the players on tour. It does not begrudge them their due share.

The board did. One suspects, given their long acquaintance, that Armstrong was the source of 'Old Boy's' prescient story on the meeting day: 'A leading member of the Australian XI who is regarded as a certain member of any team to be sent to England said last evening that if the appointment is made there will be at least half a dozen other certainties refusing the join the team.' Thanks to McElhone's gerrymander, Foxton's motion succeeded: that a board representative accompany the Australian XI to England in 1912 and 'keep the books of account relating to the tour and generally supervise all matters relating to, or incidental to, the tour'. Hill, Evan, Blinman and Aitken insisted that the manoeuvre was illegal. McElhone ignored them. And when Evan moved that the players appoint a manager on the same financial terms as themselves, Victoria's Harry Rush countermoved: 'As the Board has already decided to send a representative with the team, the players be informed, as soon as the team is selected, that it will be unnecessary for them to appoint a manager.' Foxton appears to have been a little surprised by Rush's motion; perhaps he imagined that the board's mail fist would be at least clothed in a velvet glove. 'But under Regulation 9,' he interjected, 'the players have the right to appoint a manager.' Rush replied airily: 'Oh, we swept Regulation 9 away last night.'

With the ink barely dry on the board's minutes, the Australians commenced their Second Test at the Melbourne Cricket Ground the following day. They were soon in deep trouble. None were equal to the bowling of Sydney Barnes, who upended four batsmen for four runs within the first hour, including Armstrong caught at the wicket. It was a spell destined for legend, and recognised as such by Armstrong; asked by Warner if the pitch contained some hidden devil, he replied: 'No, it was just great bowling.' By early on the third day, with Australia 43 runs in arrears and only six second innings wickets remaining, the match seemed all but over.

Armstrong chose the moment, the tenth anniversary of his debut on the same arena, to craft a Test innings close to his best, nerveless in defence and poised in attack. Surviving an lbw shout from Barnes on 11, he struck the next two balls majestically for four, then did the same to Woolley. Escorted by Vernon Ransford, he turned the game round so successfully that the crowd began fantasising of an unlikely victory. The *Argus* reported:

> No cat watched a mouse as he watched the ball. With the sight and reach of six feet two inches in stature, he was ready, a big figure, on strong, heavy lines, so big as to seem ponderous and lethargic…[but] when set, Armstrong's enterprise made puzzling balls into loose ones. A quick movement of the feet, a flash of the shoulders, a circle of the bat and Armstrong had the ball in the outfield with the flower of English fieldsmen chasing the hard-hit bowling of the flower of English bowlers.

Boundaries straight and through cover off Barnes took Armstrong to 90 but, after two and half hours and 14 fours, his resistance ended. Foster choked an lbw appeal when he sensed that the ball had pitched outside the line, then exulted when it cuffed the stumps with sufficient force to dislodge a bail. 'When he fell he had given his side at least a chance of victory,' wrote Warner. 'It was a great piece of batting.' It was also insufficient; Hobbs' first Ashes century delivered the visitors victory late on the fourth afternoon.

The game was designated as marking the fiftieth anniversary of the outbreak of Anglo-Australian cricket hostilities: the inaugural game of H. H. Stephenson's trail-blazing Englishmen had begun at the same arena on the first day of 1862. There was a subtle irony in the commemorative smoke concert at the Masonic Hall held on the first evening. That initial tour, bankrolled as a colonial entertainment by caterers Speirs & Pond, had set the tone of commercial adventurism to cricket exchanges between the countries—the very spirit that the board, by annexing financial responsibility for tours of England, intended snuffing.

Tenor John McCormack and the Melba Grand Opera Company's Rufus Ferguson serenaded tables including the lord mayor, the governor-general, the speaker of the Legislative Assembly, the Minister for Customs, and esteemed veterans like Tom Horan and John Blackham. Armstrong volunteered to pass the hat round for Blackham, who had been gifted a testimonial for the season; with Cotter and Victoria's Bert Kortlang, he collected £56. It testified to the prestige Australian cricket had won in half a century that Prime Minister Andrew Fisher was guest of honour. 'Cricket is a manly sport,' he declared, 'and provided it is cleanly played it is second to none of an outdoor character.' Over the next two months, Hill's Australians would come to consider their game in very different terms.

16

'The Big Six'

In the wake of the Second Test, thoughts returned to the brewing storm. McElhone was outspoken, detecting as ever the hidden hand of his old nemesis: 'This attempt to bring certain leading cricketers into conflict with the Board is no doubt done with the object of bursting up that body so that the management of international cricket reverts to the Melbourne Cricket Club.' Laver criticised the board's proposal of a 'secretary' for the forthcoming tour of England as factitious: 'The Board breaks its bond by doing in an underhand manner what it could not do openly. It agreed that the players should appoint the manager yet it practically ignores that agreement, for the secretary is nothing more than the manager.' For their part, the players remained silent, which the *Bulletin* prematurely celebrated as a backdown: 'The Board of Control has made itself respected by proving that it holds the right end of the waddy, and intends to use it with all its might and soul if it comes to a real row.'

In fact, there was a volatile admixture in the air, of unrequited grievance on both sides, reflected in the growing estrangement of selectors Clem Hill and Peter McAlister. Their relations had been sour since McAlister's promotion of himself to the 1909 touring party, but during deliberations over the Australian XI for the Third Test in Adelaide grew irredeemably bitter. The episode is one of Australian cricket's most famous, although historians have seldom probed the fact beneath the folklore.

The scenario was this. Consultations over the team's composition were unusually prolonged because neither McAlister nor Iredale was in Adelaide, necessitating negotiation by telegram. Hill became anxious. If rain fell, he wanted a left-arm bowler—possibly Bill Whitty, preferably Charlie Macartney. On 5 January 1911, however, Macartney suffered a bizarre practice mishap, when a net pole fell on his head. Worried his colleagues were arbitrating in ignorance of events and conditions, Hill wired them on 10 January: 'Impossible fully choose team till Friday, owing Macartney's accident. Suggest Armstrong and Trumper act with me in making the final selection.' But what to Hill seemed a sensible contingency—deputising two senior players to tailor the team to last-minute requirements—struck McAlister as a captain overstepping his authority. He cabled vehemently that he would have no part in such arrangements.

The process resumed next day. As Macartney reported himself recovered, Hill advanced his claims and those of Victorian all-rounder Jimmy Matthews, cabling: 'Macartney all right. Think must have left-arm bowler. Suggest Macartney and Matthews in place of Whitty and Minnett. Minnett twelfth.' Twenty-three-year-old Dr Roy Minnett, however, was a great McAlister favourite, and the selector's response has gone down in infamy: 'My team as forwarded yesterday. Still opposed to Macartney's inclusion. If Iredale agrees with you as to Macartney's inclusion, I favour yourself standing down not Minnett.'

Quoted in isolation, as it invariably is, McAlister's wire seems the utmost provocation: one who'd never made a Test fifty advising a captain with eight Test hundreds to stand aside. In context it is more comprehensible: the response of someone already affronted. Yet it was McAlister's high-handed resistance to the co-option of Armstrong and Trumper in the selection process that irked Hill as much as, if not more than, the final tactlessness. Hill told the *Argus*:

> I think with such an important match in front of us, my co-selectors should have been there so that they might know the probable conditions before they finally selected the XI. In their absence, one might have expected that the man on the spot would be left to make the final choices, and it was only because I suspected that this would be a great responsibility that I thought I might consult such experienced players as Trumper and Armstrong.

The telegrams *do* seem, however, to have galvanised the Australians. The *South Australian Register* reported that 'the older men scorned the suggestion of Mr McAlister and the younger generation were no less indignant'. Hill convened a team meeting to discuss the board's mooted 'representative'. Its details remained confidential, but a broad picture can be painted. Every player was invited save Warren Bardsley: he was felt too cosy with the board. With perhaps one or two abstaining—Hordern, a dentist, had already put his practice before the tour—there was over-whelming disapproval of the board's actions. The chief impediment to responding, however, was the touring party's uncertain make-up. How could players protest about arrangements for a team of which they might not be part? And, if they did, would it militate against their selection? Hill later 'expressed himself strongly' to the *Age* that it would have been unfair to cajole youngsters into jeopardising a trip to England, which 'was an education to every player who had not been there'. It was decided ultimately that six 'certainties' would lead any protest: Hill, Trumper, Armstrong, Vernon Ransford, Albert Cotter and Hanson Carter. In a nod, perhaps, to Ambrose Pratt's popular 1911 adventure novel *The Big Five*, they would be known to posterity as the 'Big Six'.

Australia began the Third Test like a team in disarray: 'persistent ill-feeling,' Macartney wrote later, 'seriously affected the morale of the side.' Only Armstrong passed 30 in a total of 133, to which England retorted with 501, Hobbs being dropped five times in his five-and-a-half-hour 187. Though Hill and Carter rallied Australia on the fourth day, there was no escape. Was there from the board?

After Australia's seven-wicket defeat, the delegated cadre crafted a careful plea for Rule 9's integrity. It began deferentially—'We beg respect-fully to approach the Board of Control'—and was geared to compromise: though believing the board's appointment of a 'representative clothed with the powers of a manager' illegal, the players had no dispute provided that the board paid for this officer, and that they were permitted to select their own manager. Only its conclusion hinted defiance, stating that 'failing compliance with our requests, we have to inform you with much regret none of us will be available for selection or to play if selected.'

The board's 16 January meeting in Brisbane showed no wish to meet the players at this half-way. Not only were seventy applications for the position of 'representative' reported, but Foxton and Allen produced further 'evidence' of the players' improvidence, citing the £400 in tips distributed by the 1909 team.* Smith's reply to the players, meanwhile, was terse:

> In the first place, the team which is being sent to England by the Board as the governing body of cricket in Australia...has nothing whatever to do with the arrangements, the Board taking the whole of the responsibility. Certain terms, which will be communicated to each individual member on selection, have been decided on by the Board, and each member will then have the opportunity of declining the Board's invitation if he is not satisfied.

This was dictation: the players were to be reduced to mere vassals of their board. Smith went on:

> In the next place, the Board has in no sense abrogated Clause 9 of the constitution but has only expressed its opinion that, as a representative of the Board will accompany the team, the appointment of a manager is unnecessary; so it follows that, if this opinion is not voiced by a majority of members of the team, they can still nominate a manager for confirmation by the Board. Personally I do not see why the positions could not be carried out by one person acceptable to the Board as well as to the members of the team.

This was evasion: the board had no intention of permitting the players to appoint their preference as manager, Laver. Harry Rush's airy comment that Rule 9 had been 'swept away', correct or not in fact, was certainly true in effect. Smith concluded:

> While the Board is anxious at all times to send the best team possible, still, at the same time, I am sure it will not permit any number of cricketers to dictate the terms and conditions on which a visit is to be made, or if a manager is appointed the terms and nature of his engagement.

This was a gauntlet: would the players pick it up?

---

* The *Argus* responded amusingly to this claim that, while it reflected 'great credit on the Queensland delegates, or rather on their mothers, who must have brought them up well and guarded them carefully from all contact with the wicked world of hotels, steamers, wharves, railways stations and other places where tips are given and received', it was a shame they didn't know 'a little more about the pains and penalties of travelling'.

What made Laver so unacceptable to the board as a manager? The question is not easy to answer. The players mistook Smith's interest in obtaining Laver's ledgers for the 1909 tour as expressing suspicion about their contents. At one meeting with McElhone in Sydney, Hill suggested that they be assessed by an independent auditor: Laver could surely not be disbarred if a respected third party passed them fit. 'It is not a question of books,' McElhone replied. 'It is a question of Mr Laver having been disloyal to the board.'

This word—'disloyalty'—would recur during the dispute wherever Laver was mentioned, without ever really being defined. Certain misdemeanours were mentioned—Laver's actions *apropos* the bridging loan, his failure to persuade Armstrong and Trumper to sign the tour contract— but the allegation stemmed more from what Bean called the manager's 'inactive antagonism' toward the board on tour. In other words, Laver's 'disloyalty' hinged on that earlier question about who the 1909 Australian team had been playing for: the board or themselves. As Laver himself told the *Age*: 'It has been stated by members of the Board that I was a servant of the Board. That is all rot. If I were a servant, then the players were.' This also explains Laver's reluctance to surrender his documentation: not because there was anything to hide, but because he did not feel it the board's property. What, after all, had the board appointed a treasurer for?

For Laver's six supporters, now hostages to fortune, the strain must have been acute. Even Armstrong sometimes appeared listless. When Victoria played the Englishmen on 2 February, a day of 108-degree heat, he seemed altogether uninterested in proceedings: it was one of only three occasions in eighty first-class appearances as captain in which he did not bowl. 'For some reason or other, Armstrong did not bowl at all,' commented the *Age*, 'although the crowd loudly urged him to do so.' One can speculate why: a 'special meeting' of the board at Sydney's Bull's Chambers that afternoon was the last chance for peace.

The poles of the dispute did not yet seem so opposite. There were hawks, like the *Bulletin*: 'The letter of the six has cleared the air a lot. It has made it possible to drop without any signs of cruelty a number of gentlemen of somewhat avaricious nature who on recent Test form have fallen from the ranks of players to that of hasbeens.' But there were also doves, like the *Sydney Morning Herald*:

> We urge the Board today to set itself toward compromise, to let bygones
> be bygones, to rest the new order not upon the wreck of the old but by

a merging of the one with the other…We think the letter of the players ill-considered in its threat…[but] the eminent players of Australia cannot be ignored in their insistence upon the spirit of the Board's constitution.

As rapprochement remained possible, the three South Australians and Melbourne's Ramsay Mailer remained silent throughout the first part of the meeting. While Hill's letter was read into the minutes, even he said nothing. Finally, when the board commenced deliberations on its 'representative', Mailer made a last bid for the honouring of Rule 9, suggesting that the players be permitted to appoint their own manager and that this choice be bound by agreement to carry out the board's wishes. He was ignored. When it became clear that there would be no compromise, Mailer and the three South Australians asked that the minutes record their discountenancing of what they considered an illegal appointment. The ballot's only surprising outcome was its choice: with Bean angling for McAlister, and McElhone favouring the New South Wales Cricket Association's Ernest Hume, thirty-five-year-old George Crouch of the Queensland Cricket Association, partner in a butter brokerage, prevailed.

The following day in Melbourne, as the Englishmen batted on beneath a pitiless sun, Armstrong remained at slip, as inscrutable as a cigar store Indian. 'Armstrong was playing but either could not or would not bowl,' the *Age* noted. 'Spectators urged him loudly to make the attempt but he took no notice.' Nor did he bat as his team slid to 6–84 at stumps chasing 476. In Sydney, the atmosphere was still more stifling. At Bull's Chambers that evening, a selection meeting convened that would resonate for decades. It was Hill's first encounter with McAlister since the latter's inflammatory telegram and, individually disappointed by the previous day's events, neither was happy. Also present at the outset were Iredale, Smith and a journalist called Davis; although Smith later referred to a Joe Davis, this was probably John Corbett Davis of the *Referee*. Smith's official account recapitulated their exchanges minute-by-minute and blow-by-blow.

Hill began by referring to the match in which Armstrong was playing, criticising Laver's 'strange' absence: a provocation, as McAlister was among the Victorian selectors who had exiled him. When McAlister sniped back that Hill in the Tests had underused change bowlers Minnett and Charles Kellaway, Hill contended that neither was effective on the surfaces of Melbourne and Adelaide, and was clearly in no mood for debate; when Davis also contradicted Hill's high opinion of Laver,

Australia's captain informed him that 'he did not consider that he was any judge of cricket'. McAlister again commented favourably on Minnett, and Hill could barely contain his fury, remarking 'that Minnett had better take over the captaincy, and that he was quite prepared to hand his resignation to the honorary secretary at once'.

Davis left so the meeting could begin, but bickering continued. Hill challenged McAlister to state his captaincy credentials using what were clearly fruits of discussion with Armstrong:

> Hill remarked, was it not a fact that Warwick Armstrong had refused to play under him as captain in the old country? This McAlister denied, and Hill asked him to name any match in which Armstrong took part, and in which he (McAlister) acted as captain. McAlister replied that he played under him as captain at Lord's on one occasion when Mr Noble had to leave the field, but that he did not play under his captaincy in other matches because he always stood down when Mr Noble was not playing.
>
> Hill then asked McAlister what matches he had ever won as captain and asked him to write them down on a sheet of paper. McAlister numerated several, and Hill remarked that they were very second-rate matches.
>
> McAlister said: 'At all events I did quite as well as Victor Trumper had done in captaining the Australian XI against Gloucestershire, when he almost made a hash of things'.
>
> Hill then stated: 'Fancy you comparing yourself to men like Trumper and Armstrong.'
>
> McAlister replied: 'At all events I consider I am as good a skipper, if not better, than the two players you've mentioned.'
>
> Hill then informed McAlister that he had no idea of captaincy and McAlister replied: 'At all events I reckon I am a better skipper than either Trumper, Armstrong or yourself.'
>
> Hill got up from his chair and informed McAlister that he had better take the position of captain and pick the team himself. Hill then sat down and informed McAlister that he knew absolutely nothing about skippering a side, which brought forth a retort from McAlister that he (Hill) was the worst skipper he had ever seen.

Hill's unfailing composure was a byword. 'He was always the same,' wrote 'Ranji' Hordern, 'and no-one would know from his demeanour whether England or Australia had won.' Yet McAlister had ruffled him as no Test defeat. 'You have been asking for a punch in the jaw all night,' he said, 'and I'll give you one'. Leaning across the table, he struck McAlister.

How hard was disputed. Smith saw 'a violent blow on the side of the face'; Hill coyly admitted 'a gentle slap on the face'; Iredale first told the

Argus of a back-handed clip, then amended this by letter to 'a severe blow to the nose and side of the face'. Whatever the force, a fight ensued, for perhaps as long as twenty minutes. Smith tried to interpose, but only restrained Hill from pushing McAlister through the third-floor window by grabbing his coat-tails. 'As soon as I got Hill away,' Smith's report concluded, 'I at once shoved him out of the door and told him he "had better stay outside".' McAlister shouted after his assailant: 'You coward!'

Settling McAlister among the blood-spattered, disarranged furniture, Smith advised Hill to return to his hotel. 'Syd,' Hill replied, 'I will not be a member of the selection committee any longer, as I refuse to sit with McAlister as a co-selector.' Smith asked Hill to put it in writing. Amazingly, bloodied McAlister and befuddled Iredale continued their consultations, naming not only the Fourth Test team, but also the first ten players for the Ashes tour, including the six pro-Laver partisans. The following morning, Hill, McAlister and Iredale all boarded the Melbourne express. They presumably occupied separate berths.

Word of events spread swiftly. There was no prospect of secrecy when the trio arrived on 5 February to find themselves thronged by reporters. 'As he stepped from the Sydney express and walked along the Spencer Street platform, Mr P. McAlister moved with all the grace and assurance of the athlete,' wrote the *Argus*. 'But there was no disguising the fact that he had been engaged in a bout of fisticuffs. His nose was cut and there was a bruise under the left eye and numerous scratches disfigured his face.' Hill was unrepentant: 'When a man is insulted and insulted, well, it must reach a limit.' McAlister was unforgiving: 'It was no open-handed slap. Look at my nose!'

Although the scuffle did not pertain directly to the issue of the management of the Australian XI, it was clearly an indirect outcome. The players had grappled with the board almost six years, and landed not a single figurative blow—now at least, in time-honoured Australian fashion, they could feel they had inflicted a physical one. The telegrams and correspondence that poured in afterwards to Hill—which he preserved—show that it wasn't only his immediate circle who found the incident cathartic: 'Congratulations Clem Hill Offer you £600 fight Jack Johnson'; 'Hip Hip Only regret blighter still living'; 'Congratulations self Armstrong bonzers you beauties'. A letter from 'Jack'—perhaps Hill's former interstate and Test teammate Jack Lyons—strikes a particular note of pugilistic relish:

Dear old Clem,
Just a few lines to say how glad I am that you gave Peter Mac a dashed good hiding. I hope he will take it as a lesson and not try any more of his pranks on people, he struck a wrong 'un when he tried to upset you old boy and he got what he deserved, I hope you put in a few for me because I hate the swab.

Perhaps events also reinvigorated Armstrong. That day and the next, he made 51 and 120, defiantly unconquered in either innings. Yet even as he did so, there was a disclosure that bore heavily on his involvement in the affair.

Hill's opening sally at the selection meeting in Sydney, concerning Laver's continued omission from Victoria's XI, was one of the summer's abiding mysteries. Despite his forty-two years, Laver was still probably the country's cleverest medium-pace bowler. Yet his place was occupied by a procession of nonentities: Ernest Spencer, Harold Hart, Norman Brown and others unknown to fame. A letter to Hill from Hanson Carter survives suggesting that erstwhile Australian teammates were keen to engineer Laver's Test recall. It describes a discussion with Iredale after the Third Test where Carter 'strongly urged that Frank Laver be asked to practice with the players in Melbourne with a view to selection [in the Fourth Test]' and expressing the belief that 'with a little persuasion he [Iredale] could be prevailed upon to give Frank a trial...despite your friend McAlister's vindictiveness'. But one can imagine the difficulties inherent in picking for his country a player not representing his state, especially one whose exile was apparently, as former Test comrade Charles McLeod told the *Argus,* 'not on cricket merit but because the Board of Control has decided he must be pushed out the game'.

The Victorian selectors responsible were Bean, McAlister and Harry Trott, Trott having belatedly joined the panel after Hugh Trumble's resignation six weeks earlier in order to become Melbourne Cricket Club secretary. Such was Trott's standing that Arthur Aitken had withdrawn his own nomination as a selector rather than oppose him. So what was happening? The VCA's intramural machinations would have remained impenetrable but for another Victorian cricketer, Jim Kyle. A hardworking dairyman, his perseverance and economy had just earned him the tribute from *Cricket* that he was 'probably the best fast bowler in

Victoria'. For Victoria's game against the Englishmen, however, the selectors had sprung a surprise by dropping him. Now Kyle sprang a bigger surprise by informing an *Argus* reporter that he had been excluded because of his loyalty to Armstrong:

> Ever since I was picked for Victoria, I have had it drummed into me that Armstrong is a bad captain. I did not agree with that view. He has always treated me well and handled the side well. I have been repeatedly approached, before every match in fact, to propose someone else against him as captain. I refused. I have been asked to propose either Carkeek or Kortlang. These requests have been made to me by leading members of the association, two in particular. They even came to me in the Town Hall in November during the reception for the English cricketers with the same request. I have not the slightest intention of opposing Armstrong if I get into the Victorian team again. In fact, I don't care if I never play again. I won't do that sort of thing.

The story is not quite so simple. His candid remarks suggest Kyle had little idea he would be quoted. Indeed, he was probably alarmed to be, for he shortly wrote to the *Argus* claiming that the coercion to vote against Armstrong had come from within the Victorian XI rather than without, from players rather than officials. Yet this smacks of a clarification he was encouraged to make. The *Argus* took the unusual step of standing behind its report, insisting that the words attributed to Kyle 'express correctly the unreserved statement conveyed to our reporter's mind', and was supported by a letter to the editor from one George F. Pape:

> The thing is that Mr Kyle, in the course of a conversation with me on the second last day of the Victoria v England match, related almost word for word the statement detailed in that report—with this exception, that the two representatives of the association who approached him were Messrs Bean and Rush.

Kyle professed in a letter to the VCA not to know Pape, a member at both Prahran and Melbourne who later sat on the committee of the Melbourne Football Club, while Bean and Rush denied the allegations. But the scenario has the ring of authenticity for two reasons: firstly, it is easy to imagine an irked Kyle unburdening himself freely to whomever would listen; secondly, having probably marked his card, Kyle never represented Victoria again. Indeed, there were several consequences of Victoria's selection squabbles that summer: Laver never reappeared for his state; Trott never picked another team. At the VCA's 18 March meeting, Trott complained by letter that he had on three occasions over summer tried picking Laver, but had on each occasion been resisted by Bean and McAlister. He was dumped as selector five months later.

Kyle seems to have gone on his way without bitterness; perhaps he really didn't care if he played again. Certainly, his regard for Armstrong was unfeigned. Half an hour after being run out in a club match on 11 January 1919, the *Australasian* reported, he had a heart attack and died with his old skipper's name on his lips:

> After his innings he was with some friends and in the course of conversation…said that Warwick Armstrong was his best friend, and then collapsed. At first it was considered that he had taken a fit, but upon medical advice being obtained, it was ascertained that life was extinct, the cause of death being heart failure.

'He was the essence of kindly good nature and a most unselfish cricketer,' pronounced the *Leader*. 'Poor old Jim "played the game" to the last.'

As the Kyle controversy unfolded, the board issued its first nine invitations to join the 1912 tour, including one to Armstrong, requiring reply within ten days—Hill's was held over pending inquiries into his affray with McAlister. Yet because there could be no vote on the manager until the team's completion, and thus no resolution of the Laver impasse, the *refuseniks* could offer no reply. They now experienced the eerie sensation that these might be their final Australian appearances—the Fourth Test, which began in Melbourne on 9 February must have been like attending their own wake. Each of the six was greeted with a sympathetic ovation, the captain being especially moved. 'Old Bob Crockett the umpire told me that when Clem [Hill] reached the batting crease, there were tears in his eyes,' recalled Daniel Reese. 'How could anyone play their best under such circumstances?' Douglas showed scant mercy. Chasing Australia's ragged 191, England's Hobbs and Rhodes piled 323 for the first wicket, batting almost a day. At one point, when a dummy dropped onto the outfield from an advertising balloon, a spectator cried: 'Another bowler for you Clem!'

The day after Australia's seven-wicket defeat, Hill and McAlister entrained for Sydney where the board had scheduled an *in camera* investigation of their brawl. The only hint of the four-hour hearing's conduct was, the *Argus* noted, that 'on two or three occasions, Mr McAlister was consulted by a delegate, and from his demeanour it could be gleaned that he was pleased with the information imparted to him'. The board itself cloaked the affair in official jargon, saying that it had been 'satisfactorily settled'. The *Age* reported:

> Mr Smith was then asked: 'What does "the matter was satisfactorily settled" mean?'
> 'I'm not going to say,' replied Mr Smith.
> 'Has the Board sent an invitation to Hill to go to England?' was the next question.
> 'No,' said Mr Smith.
> 'Is the Board going to give him an invitation?' was the next query, asked in some desperation.
> 'I suppose,' said Mr Smith, 'that he will get an invitation in due course.'
> 'What does "due course" mean?' was the next volley.
> Mr Smith's reply was: 'Well, you can say that Hill will get at once an invitation to go to England.'

But time was short: despite the SACA's recommendation that state selector Charles Dolling succeed Hill on the national panel, the board unilaterally co-opted opening batsman Edgar Mayne, twenty-nine years old and rather more malleable. Armstrong and his confederates were now clearly stalling for time; they wrote on 19 February that they would 'give a definite answer when the selection of the team had been completed'. The board replied that, failing 'definite and unconditional acceptance' within two days, they would be classified unavailable. The letters were hand-delivered, in Melbourne by the VCA's new secretary John Healy: Armstrong was presented with his while visiting the association's rooms on an errand. Again the cricketers sent non-committal acknowledgments.

One wonders what the six were thinking as, the following day, they began converging on Sydney for the Fifth Test. By wire, Laver had advised them to surrender: 'Though I consider the Board has been most unjust, I beg you in all consequence Triangular Contests to accept terms. Insist on your rights to appoint manager, but ignore me.' England's convalescent captain Pelham Warner was egging them on with martial allusions: 'They must be patriotic and fight for the country when called upon to do so.' Two dramatic intercessions at the last tested the rebels' resolve.

The first was by Warner, who visited McElhone on 20 February seeking permission to 'interview' the players. 'All through the trouble, I absolutely refused to take sides,' he recalled. 'But when I knew that the Board would not give in, I begged Hill and the others to accept unconditionally and come to England.' Warner met Armstrong, Hill, Carter and Cotter early the next morning at Sydney's Treasury Buildings. To impress upon them the importance of the Triangular Tournament, he had also roped in New South Wales' English governor: Lord Chelmsford told the players that, much as he admired their loyalty to Laver, their reluctance to tour was 'quixotic'. The players were unmoved. They were persuaded to meet McElhone at Bull's Chambers, but the encounter only roved old ground; the board chairman again rejected the proposal that Laver's managerial credentials be independently assessed.

Another aspiring mediator then approached the players. Harry Hoyle MLA knew Trumper through the New South Wales Rugby League— Hoyle had been its first president, Trumper its first treasurer. He proposed that all six meet New South Wales' Labor premier James McGowen, a man of plebeian roots but patrician attainments, and a skilled negotiator. A gathering lasting some hours convened on 'a balcony in the cool evening air', interrupted occasionally by fierce exchanges in the Legislative Assembly chamber during a censure motion against the speaker. But McGowen found the cricketers as unbending as any political opponent. The premier proposed two measures: that he seek Laver's selection as a player, which the cricketers unanimously supported; and that the players offer two alternatives to the board for the role as manager and agree to accept any decision, which all but one opposed. The *Argus* found no softening among the *sanscullottes*:

> When asked tonight if there was any prospect of a settlement, one of the six players said emphatically: 'No'. When asked if any players would make a move towards a compromise, he replied: 'Not an inch'…The players swear by Laver. The Board figuratively swear at him.

McElhone dismissed McGowen's proposals, and was ready for anything; for the Fifth Test, which commenced 23 February, he had five reserves in readiness for a player boycott. They were unnecessary, though the match's preliminaries were hopelessly disorganised: realising at the toss that his team list did not include a twelfth man, Hill had to find McAlister and Iredale for confirmation that Macartney had been excluded. Those selectors then returned to the business of finding replacements for the six now 'unavailable'. Armstrong, Trumper and Cotter were the first supplanted—by Syd Gregory, Gerry Hazlitt and Queensland's Jack McLaren—which 'Old Boy' saw as symbolic: 'It must not be forgotten that Trumper and Armstrong were the two men who refused to sign the agreement with the Board on the last tour, and that the Victorian cricket caucus has long wished to remove Armstrong as captain of the Victorian cricket XI'. Like McAlister three years earlier, Edgar Mayne now voted himself an Ashes tour despite a season's interstate average of only 30: this from the board that had accused players of nepotism.

The drama affected the dissidents differently. Hill was visibly moved to receive another ovation. Trumper was also distressed; England's keeper 'Tiger' Smith recalled: 'Victor turned to me at one stage and said: "Tiger, they think I'm finished." All I could think of was: "I wish I could play like you Victor."' But Armstrong, who grafted 33 in each innings and claimed 4–78 from 43 niggardly overs, was irrepressible. This game appears the origin of a story imparted to historian David Frith by Frank Woolley, whom Armstrong caught off Hazlitt in England's second innings: 'Armstrong took a ball at slip after I'd cut it towards him. It hit the ground first, but he threw it up. I said: "Now then Warwick, you didn't catch that." He started swearing. But the umpire gave me out.' Perhaps, after all the acrimony of the preceding months, the violation of one more piety about fair play and the game being the thing seemed immaterial.

How *exactly* the six felt during that match, however, is unclear, for a simple reason: aside from a handful of public statements during the affair, not one of them wrote or uttered a public word about it in these or later years. Their position's most eloquent expression, indeed, was non-verbal: Clem Hill's famous punch. Yet even this could be variously interpreted, as expressing defiance, a vengeful sock to authority's jaw, or helplessness, a wild slug from a punch-drunk fighter. When almost nine years later Hill published his cricket reminiscences, he referred to the dispute only by quoting from Warner's tour book: 'Men cannot show their best form amid an atmosphere of trouble, uncertainty and misunderstanding.'

The six's silence was initially a policy: 'We have agreed to say nothing,' one told the *Argus* on 23 January. It subsequently became an attitude. This was what most impressed young leg-spinner Arthur Mailey when he played two years later with Armstrong, Trumper, Ransford and Noble:

> Long before I met these great men I had heard stories about their recalcitrance which, in my innocence, I had believed. But when I toured with them in New Zealand during the early part of 1914, I never once heard them utter a word of criticism against the controllers of Australian cricket...If these men were rebels, they were also gentlemen. And if there was a fault, I doubted that it was on their side.

For now, when the *Age* found Hill and Trumper at the Hotel Australia during the Fifth Test, they seemed exhausted:

> 'The Board did not think it worthwhile to give any statement of the reasons why it did not want Frank Laver [said Hill]. It simply put a pistol to our heads. It was a case of take it or leave it.'
> Any other action? 'Not tonight,' he answered. At any other time? Mr Hill shrugged his shoulders and spoke to Mr Trumper who had just come into the vestibule of the hotel. 'What do you think of it Victor?'
> 'They have got us down to bedrock,' said Mr Trumper. 'It's the end of it as far as I am concerned.'

For New South Welshmen Carter and Cotter there would also have been the additional provocation of the McElhone regime at the association: they had been among the players punished for their complicity with the Melbourne Cricket Club six years earlier. Armstrong and Ransford, meanwhile, were of Melbourne itself, the former an employee at the time, the latter an employee later. And it says much of the board's *idee fixe* about Melbourne that, while perusal of club records today suggests that its committee was not interested in the skirmish, McElhone and his apologists continued to refer to it as the ultimate bogey.*

The 'Big Six' affair, however, transcended issues of the board's constitution; it had the personal dimension of the board's objection to *Laver's*

---

* McElhone and Bean remained steadfast in this view. McElhone confounded a censure vote at the NSWCA with a forceful speech concluding: 'I have my own views as to the party at the bottom of the whole of it.' Bean dismissed the players as fronting for Melbourne, which was making 'a last attempt to salvage its position'. The dispute's only mention in Melbourne's records, however, are letters from Hugh Trumble to the VCA in March 1912 complaining about its policy toward the proxy that Mailer used at board meetings.

appointment as manager. That Laver should have inspired such loyalty expresses, as nothing else, the profound sense of the commonweal among the cricketers of Armstrong's time. Perhaps the dispute's most striking relic is a handsome five-drawer document cabinet which Armstrong and his colleagues later presented to their erstwhile manager. The strength of their solidarity is expressed in the inscription on the sterling silver plaque: 'To F. Laver from "The Six".'

One suspects that Armstrong felt this mutual obligation more keenly than most: Laver was among the selectors who had first picked him for Victoria, was often his Victorian captain, twice his manager in England, even his travelling companion in Asia. Indeed, one illuminating impression of the affair was that of 'Tiger' Smith, who said of Trumper:

> The off-field incidents in the Australian dressing room saddened Victor. Stronger men like Warwick Armstrong pressurised him into supporting the players' demands to have Frank Laver as their manager on the forthcoming tour of England…I think he was bewildered by it all.

The depiction of Trumper as natural moderate and Armstrong as incorrigible militant is sentimentalised: Trumper was perfectly capable of autonomous protest. Yet the view of Armstrong as *agent provocateur* does not seem stretched. Perhaps, for this wilful, stubborn, bloody-minded cricketer, membership of the 'Big Six' was a role he was born to play.

17

'Ruthless War under a Flag of Truce'

The 'Big Six' disturbance was all over bar the shouting but community displeasure now found expression in a series of public meetings, underscoring cricket's cultural primacy before World War I. Aligned with the cricketers were a remarkable cast of individuals, hot with indignation and public spirit.

As the Australian players watched rain fall on the third day of their Fifth Test, Hill received a telegram from Melbourne signed under the auspices of the so-called Citizens' Cricket Committee: 'Public meeting here probably Thursday night protest action Board. Resolutions will be cabled Marylebone. Will you, Trumper and Armstrong select team? Necessary funds already available.'

The campaign had originated with a letter to the *Argus* ten days earlier signed 'A Hater of Tyranny'. Towards his aim that a private team selected by Hill, Trumper and Armstrong be 'sent home', the writer had enclosed a cheque for a staggering £1000. He soon found fellow travellers: an Albury correspondent sent £100, a nine-member Melbourne syndicate £500. The identity of 'A Hater of Tyranny' is unknown, although it was probably one of two men, both comfortably capable of such a gesture: Edmund Jowett, a fifty-four-year-old wool baron owning more than forty sheep stations covering in excess of 2.4 million hectares;

and William Baillieu, the Australian J. P. Morgan, whose newly built Collins House headquartered more than fifty companies, mostly in mining and manufacturing.

Why either should have entered the fray is unclear. Although later one of the Country Party's founders, Jowett was not then active in public affairs; Baillieu had recently resigned as Victoria's public works minister, intending relocation to England. Yet both felt an affinity with the crick-eters, men of action who spoke by deeds not words, and men of enterprise who valued their free trade. Jowett was described as feeling 'a throb of kinship for the gypsy lore of the wandering bohemian'; Baillieu was known to complain during tiresome board meetings about directors 'more concerned with not being wrong than being right'. And both Jowett and Baillieu—it would not have escaped McElhone's attentions—were Melbourne Cricket Club members.

Some of their supporters were probably attracted by prospects of a public barney, like diminutive Martin Hannah MLA, president of the Socialist League and known to *Melbourne Punch* as 'the Microbe of Mischief': 'If he was in a peaceful quaker's settlement he would probably get up indignation meetings about the poke bonnet...You could no more keep him quiet than you could stop a frog croaking.' Others, though, almost certainly joined the protest out of prior friendship with the cricketers, and with Warwick Armstrong in particular. Lawyer Agar Wynne had been familiar to Australian players since at least April 1905, when he threw a dinner in their honour aboard the *Miowera*, and for the past six years had been Armstrong's federal member, holding Balaclava as a protectionist with a reputation for sporting connections; he was said to 'score the vote of nearly every "sport" in Balaclava...through his fra-ternal disposition among the boys, and his accessible chequebook for any object in which a ball was banged or booted.'

With Wynne came Walter Carre Riddell, his former partner in the firm Hamilton, Wynne and Riddell, and chairman of the Metropolitan Board of Works since April 1907. He was another Caulfield patriot, having been shire president for eight years. There was also James Guthrie, Geelong general manager of the pastoral house Dalgety's. Portly, forthright and expressive, he was also surprisingly nimble for one with only a right leg: his left had been amputated ten years earlier in New Zealand to counteract anthrax caught from sheep. He and Armstrong would later become good friends.

Hill was ambivalent about the proposal. Protest was one thing; alternate XIs another. He consulted Armstrong and Trumper before replying: 'If Marylebone approve resolutions, we three willing select team. Many as possible will attend.' It didn't prove possible—the Test, prolonged by rain, still had a day to run on the meeting's scheduled date—but crowds began thronging Collins Street's Athenaeum Hall two hours ahead of the 8 p.m. start. So vast did they grow that hundreds were siphoned to overflow meetings upstairs and in the nearby Baptist Hall, while more were turned away. Jowett had even hired an orchestra to keep the audience amused, inspiring spontaneous choruses of *What's the Matter with Laver? He's All Right!*

Seldom can Baillieu have enjoyed a crowd so concordant. Commencing amid thunderous assent by reading sympathetic telegrams from Monty Noble, Joe Darling and George Giffen, he praised the six as men 'who sacrificed their business careers in order to uphold the prestige of Australian cricket in England', and celebrated their loyalty to Laver: 'The players are told by the Board that they should set their personal feelings aside. What is wanted is that the Board should set aside its false dignity and cease to regard the leading players of Australia as paid servants (loud applause).' Other prominent Victorians joined in. The issue had appealed to the eccentric social democrat Dr William Maloney, federal member for East Melbourne. The first politician in the British Empire to introduce a bill for women's suffrage, he saw the board as infringing democracy itself:

> Would the thousands who crowd to see the Australian team in England crowd to see the Board of Control if they went to London (laughter)? The public would only go to see them as they would go to see a number of freaks (laughter). Who on the Board of Control represented the thousands who paid their shillings and half crowns to see the Test matches? Mr Bean or Mr Rush? (cries of 'no!')

The *Argus* reported special support for Harry Trott, his final salute bringing the house down:

> To say that he was disgusted with the Board of Control was to put it mildly. He would like to shake hands with the six men who had stood out against the Board. They had stuck out for the honour of cricket in Australia…Hill had told him that, though he had wanted a particular bowler, he could not get him. He had much pleasure in proposing his health—(great laughter) He must beg pardon. He had forgotten that he was not at a smoke night.

The fourteen-member committee elected to negotiate with the players and Marylebone about the new tour was a cross-section of Melbourne's elite: in addition to the pastoral and commercial clout of Jowett, Baillieu and Guthrie, and the political and public service connections of Wynne, Hannah and Riddell, there were members from the law (leading solicitor William Riggall), finance (Melbourne Stock Exchange chairman William Roberts) and sport (Norman Brookes, Australia's successful Davis Cup captain, and former Test players Billy Bruce and John Trumble). The meeting dissolved in buoyant mood; it had demonstrated, said the *Leader*, that support for the board 'had been entirely alienated by its unreasonable and unjustified actions'. Hundreds of well-wishers then greeted Hill, Armstrong and Ransford at Melbourne's Spencer Street station on 2 March 1912, and expressions of sympathy poured in from further meetings in Sydney, Hobart and Adelaide; a typical one from Adelaide's mayor Lavington Bonython commended the six on the 'straightforward and manly attitude they have adopted all through the dispute with the Board', and 'appreciation of the great services they have rendered to Australian cricket'.

Sympathy, however, was ultimately all that could be extended. Marylebone decided it could not interfere in Australian affairs. President Lord Desborough did wire the board encouraging reconciliation for the Triangular Tournament's sake, but the 'unofficial' communique was ruled out of order. This was actually one of McElhone's boldest acts of apostasy; tackling the players was one thing, ignoring cricket's *fons et origo* another. Told of it by a reporter aboard the *Orvicta* in Fremantle, Warner was stunned:

> 'What?' answered Mr Warner, clearly amazed. 'Do you mean to say they have taken no notice because of a technicality?...I should have thought,' he continued, 'that Lord Desborough cabling out would have meant something. It is an honour. He is the president of the MCC, the mother of cricket so to speak, the prospective host of this Australian XI in the old country...I really don't know what to say about it. It seems so extraordinary.'

Perhaps, like Armstrong in claiming that contentious catch from Woolley's bat in Sydney, McElhone had run out of courtesy, although in his case from the savour of power rather than the want of it. He stood, in the words of a prophetic *Melbourne Punch* profile, as 'the czar, the despot, the ruler of the Australian cricket world today':

He has found that all his enemies possess one neck and he has severed it at one blow. He has been more fortunate than most tyrants. The coming year's cricket may bring defeat and failure but the new cricketers who will come on will owe all their opportunities, all their rise to distinction, to the Board, or to W. P. McElhone, which is the same thing. They will be his henchmen, who will obey him and work for him.

After a fortnight's rest, Armstrong resumed representing Melbourne. Though he would not enjoy an English summer, this did not prevent his own travels. On 4 April, he embarked again for Wagga as part of a team playing matches over Easter, reuniting him with the hospitable O'Donnells at Mingay, in particular Aileen. It is possible that by this time they were betrothed, for Armstrong appears to have been making plans: on 26 April, he purchased a large vacant lot in the Melbourne beachside suburb of Carrum, with a fifty-foot frontage onto an unmade government road.

The 'Big Six' dispute steadily mutated into a paper war between the board, the VCA, the citizens' committee, Laver, McAlister and the Melbourne Cricket Club—dragged into events by allegations of its involvement from McElhone and Bean. All published lengthy pamphlets—Melbourne's filled thirty-one pages—in tones of varying woundedness. The only interested parties uninvolved were the 'Six' themselves, maintaining watchful distance. Armstrong started building a sand-brick cottage on his new property, younger brother Tom helping clear the tea-tree cover. A period photograph survives, showing Armstrong up a ladder in workman's togs; it is captioned, in an unknown hand, 'Weary Willie at work.'

Not that Armstrong was forgotten. Ahead of the Triangular Tournament, Warner picked his ideal 'World XI' for the *Westminster Gazette*, an innovative notion, in which Armstrong was one of three Australians.* The absences of Armstrong and his kinsmen then robbed the event of much of its lustre, for the team led by last-minute draftee Syd Gregory proved perhaps the puniest Australia has sent abroad: in six Tests, only three batsman posted more than 100 runs at averages

---

* Warner's team also included Charles Fry, Jack Hobbs, Aubrey Faulkner, Reggie Spooner, Charlie Macartney, Frank Foster, Percy Sherwell, John Barton King, 'Ranji' Hordern, Sydney Barnes and Victor Trumper (12th man).

exceeding 20 (Bardsley, Kellaway and Macartney), and one bowler obtained more than 20 wickets (Whitty). Where Frank Laver had never experienced difficulties with discipline, Crouch encountered many. His report on the players was damning, alleging bad language, coarse manners, and drinking so illimitable that, on one trip to Ireland, stewards declined to serve them. 'It may be added here,' said *Wisden*, 'that some of the players were not all that satisfied with Mr Crouch as manager.'

Board members remained convinced of their rectitude: McAlister sympathisers presented him with a wallet containing £100 and an illuminated manuscript; McElhone admirers held a banquet in his honour at Sydney Town Hall. But they also stayed on a war footing. On 29 June, the *Argus* reported sightings of Armstrong in Sydney with Noble and Cotter, Ransford, Laver and John Trumble having also visited recently. What did this portend? 'I would not be surprised at anything so far as the Melbourne Cricket Club is concerned,' commented McElhone. 'They will never be satisfied until they have control of cricket again.' 'Old Boy' reported that board members were taking 'every care to keep themselves accurately posted' on the 'Big Six's' doings. In fact, the conspiracy was a phantom: Laver had passed through Sydney returning from Queensland, Ransford was in town playing baseball, Trumble on business, and Armstrong on a fortnight's leave, probably visiting the O'Donnells. Hill fantasised facetiously about them attending McElhone's banquet.

The final product of the winter's phony war, published by Bean and Rush in early September, was *The 1912 Australian Eleven in England: A Few Facts for Fair-Minded Sportsmen*—an attempt to persuade the disillusioned that Gregory's team hadn't been so bad. As board members, both VCA men knew better: gross tour proceeds were 40 per cent poorer than 1909. This wasn't bad news for Macartney, Whitty, Mayne and Hazlitt, who had wisely accepted a fixed £400 fee, but next to nothing remained for the balance of the team.

McElhone then had a brainwave: the board would waive its cut—5 per cent of the first £6000, 12.5 per cent thereafter—leaving sufficient to reward its loyalists. This was little enough—depending on the players' tour drawings, between £80 and £100—but the *ex gratia* payments showed the board in a kindly light, at least toward those in favour. Some were convinced, 'Not Out' of the *Referee* applauding. 'Felix' of the *Australasian* saw the manoeuvre as fraudulent:

> If the Board had acted generously and in this conciliatory spirit in the past, there would have been none of this serious trouble which had had such a disastrous effect on the prestige of Australian cricket…The fact is that certain delegates of the VCA are saturated with the belief that the Melbourne Cricket Club is aiming to secure control of cricket in Victoria. You say 'There is no truth in it. It is not so'. But you might as well talk to the wall.

Repaying loyalty with loyalty, however, McElhone had been shrewd. Not only did members of the 1912 team owe him 'all their rise to distinction', they now in a sense owed him financially. And the board and its satellites would tighten their grip on Australian cricket still further in the coming season.

Armstrong attended his club's annual meeting on 13 September 1912, looking ever more visible. 'The Melbourne Cricket Club leviathan Warwick Armstrong is shaping well as ever,' reported 'Felix', 'though he looks a shade on the "weighty" side.' But stirrings against him were soon apparent. Harry Trott's failure to gain reappointment left Armstrong with a hostile selection panel: Bean, McAlister and Mat Ellis.

Ellis, adopted son of a Presbyterian clergyman, had played a good deal of cricket with and against the incumbent Victorian captain. On one occasion for Fitzroy, he had teased Armstrong by boasting that he would hit his first ball out of the ground—Armstrong greeted him with a first ball so wide that the wicketkeeper had to shy at the stumps to execute the stumping. Ellis was also famed for his loquacity. 'Mat is never at a loss for something to say,' wrote *Melbourne Punch*. 'A witty rejoinder to every quip slips off his tongue. His fund of anecdotes concerning racing men, cricketers, men of business and the man in the street will outlast any railway journey.' Yet Ellis liked his cricket 'pure', and here his attitude and Armstrong's well and truly diverged. Representing Victoria in January 1903, for example, Ellis had been involved in a record 211-run last-wicket stand with Tom Hastings. But when a public collection was organised in their favour, Ellis recoiled from it and demanded that the funds be returned to subscribers—not an action Armstrong would have taken, or even understood.

From the outset of the season, the selectors were clearly bent on unseating Armstrong as Victoria's captain. Ellis made it obvious when he proposed at the VCA that, as was now custom for New South Wales and

Australia, selectors rather than players should choose captains. Though the motion failed, Armstrong could hardly have failed to decode its intent. The selectors then began making some curious choices, their effect being to isolate Armstrong within his team. Continuing to exclude the likes of Laver and Kyle, Victoria called during 1912–13 on no fewer than eight players from McAlister's East Melbourne. Armstrong was soon leading an XI he would hardly have known, and with whom his relations deteriorated quickly.

On Boxing Day at the MCG, with Victoria set to play New South Wales, VCA secretary John Healy installed a ballot box in the home team's dressing-room for the captaincy vote. Armstrong was proposed by Albert Hartkopf, University's young captain and one of his skipper's chief admirers. 'Felix' said their games were so similar that it was as if Hartkopf had learned cricket by standing behind Melbourne's nets while Armstrong was batting or bowling. Healy ruled promptly that as twelfth man Hartkopf was ineligible to vote. Although Ransford intervened to support Armstrong's nomination, Barlow Carkeek then proposed Arnold Seitz, the twenty-nine-year-old Scotch College teacher who had succeeded McAlister as East Melbourne captain. When the vote was finally held—candidates abstaining—Seitz won six votes to three.

Not all blame for this *coup* can be heaped at the selectors' feet: ultimately, and for the second time in five years, Armstrong's players had toppled him. And, especially if Armstrong felt that he was not getting the teams he wanted, one can suspect why: the 'confirmed growler of the Victorian team'—to use the *Daily Telegraph*'s description—had issued one rumbling judgment too many. For Armstrong could be a harsh judge. Touring with him the following year, New Zealander Arthur Sims found Armstrong's cutting asides a trial: 'Where others would attempt to cheer up batsmen out to a good ball, Armstrong was just as likely to comment on a poor stroke, sparing no feelings.' These habits, too, lasted a lifetime. Postwar teammate Bert Oldfield remembered his silent reproofs for dropped catches and careless errors: 'His look was sufficient to indicate what he was thinking—those sideways glances of his would pierce.' Many years later, Robert Menzies was beside Armstrong when young Jack Fingleton collected a pair in an Adelaide Test. When Menzies reflected on the batsman's horrid fate, Armstrong stated simply: 'Can't bat.'

Carkeek's role is unsurprising. He had been one of the recipients of McElhone's largesse, and he and his captain simply did not get on. Just as Hill nursed doubts about Carkeek's character, Armstrong was dismissive of his cricket, perceiving his two tours of England in 1909 and 1912 to have been entirely undeserved. An incident a year earlier during a Sheffield Shield match reflected their relations. Edgar Mayne had been stranded yards from home and, giving himself up, started for the pavilion. Yet, when Carkeek broke the stumps, the umpire shook his head; the keeper had somehow dislodged a bail before the ball's arrival. Armstrong exhorted him to pull up a stump, which Carkeek did, though by this time he'd lost the ball. Although Laver saved blushes, snatching the ball *and* a stump, Armstrong snapped: 'That almost cost us a wicket!' Carkeek's injured feelings are imaginable.

Seitz's elevation, despite this being only his twelfth game, promised a new dispensation. He appeared an embodiment of the Golden Age ideal: an Ormond Collegian, a Rhodes Scholar, and an Oxford blue who sported a harlequin cap in the university's 'authentic' colours of gold, dark blue and dark red. He was also a serene and decorous character. Club teammate Howard Houston recalled a lecture he received from Seitz after denouncing an umpire as 'a bloody cheat' for denying him an lbw:

> He said: 'Howard, that's very very naughty.' I said: 'What? Querying the umpire's decision? It was out, wasn't it?' He said: 'That's not the point. You must never swear like that.' He was more offended by my saying 'bloody' than calling the umpire a cheat!

Seitz was also capable, in a way Armstrong was not, of the chivalrous gesture. During a game against South Africa, for instance, he had been involved in a misunderstanding while batting with Bert Kortlang, and charitably sacrificed himself. The *Herald* reported:

> While running it became apparent that one of them was sure to be run out. He therefore slackened speed to prompt the fieldsman to throw to the end to which he was running. The fieldsman did, and he was run out...It was a most generous act on the part of the East Melbournite.

Nonetheless, an ambush had clearly been executed. Some even appear to have anticipated it. An *Age* correspondent overheard a visiting player bruiting as he arrived: 'I hear "they" are going to "bump" Armstrong!' The newspaper deplored the 'efforts of a somewhat underhand nature' to displace Armstrong, concluding: 'It was a case of "get rid of the Melbourne Cricket Club man at any price".'

Armstrong went his own way for the rest of the season, compiling an unbeaten 118 against New South Wales in Sydney and collecting 9–121 against Queensland in Brisbane. As part of his Melbourne Cricket Club duties, he was also star attraction in country meetings at Bendigo, Benalla, Wangaratta and Ballarat, never failing to put on a show, albeit after his own fashion.* With its many new caps, however, Victoria finished last in the Sheffield Shield, and Seitz averaged only 19 as captain. Discipline, never tight, also slackened. Essendon's Patrick Shea failed to show for the match against Tasmania until after lunch on the first day, then Melbourne's Gordon Johnstone left the game a day early because of work commitments. Hartkopf, by now exiled from the state side, also declined to play in a colts match at East Melbourne staged at the same time, and was singled out: Bean told a VCA meeting on 24 January 1913 that Hartkopf had not 'realised the seriousness of his position' and the executive had 'decided to recommend drastic action' (not specified in the minutes). The likely explanation did not elude the *Age*: 'The public remembers, of course, that Hartkopf seconded the nomination of W. W. Armstrong when he was proposed as captain of Victoria during the first interstate match against New South Wales.'

The VCA soon had more pressing matters to address. Its selectors were attracting increasingly acid criticism. When they named their last team on 20 February 1913, to play South Australia, 'Old Boy' wrote dismissively in the *Argus*: 'The persistency with which the selectors stick to [leg-spinner Norman] Brown and Seitz…speaks well for their determination and consistency but does not do much credit to their judgment.' The *Herald*, criticising an 'extraordinary list of anomalies', decried the exclusions of Kyle ('the most accurate length bowler in the state') and

---

* Armstrong's minor cricket accomplishments reached a kind of peak this season. On 14 December 1912, he scored 82 out of 162 against Bendigo United. On 15 and 16 January 1913, he took 11–34 against Fourteen of Benalla. At Easter, he made another country tour, making 148 (retired) out of 418 against Benalla, then 45 out of 139 plus 8–45 against Wangaratta. After visiting Mount Buffalo, he then made 99 (retired) against Gold Street Old Schoolboys, and 256 against Ballarat with 27 fours and three sixes.

Hartkopf ('turned down without apparent reason'). Four days later, there was a surprising development. Without explanation, Seitz withdrew from the Victorian team—permanently. He did not play the following season, then accepted a principal's job at Hamilton College in western Victoria. Either from neglect or politeness, no contemporary periodical pursued the East Melbourne skipper's reasons, but circumstantial evidence suggests that Armstrong had not made Seitz's job easy.

Despite Armstrong's respectable statistical record for season 1912–13—402 runs at 40, 24 wickets at 21—closer inspection reveals some absences. He left his preferred number five only once, to open in the brief second innings of the match against Queensland. And only in that game did he shoulder his usual bowling load; in two matches against New South Wales, he delivered only 39 of Victoria's 266 overs, well below his customary output. This becomes material in the light of a letter Ellis sent the *Referee* eight years later, at the height of another selection scandal, in which he enumerated various Armstrong peccadilloes, among them 'complaints from a previous captain that he could not get Armstrong to either bowl or bat when required'. Ellis reported: 'That player asked to be and was relieved of the captaincy.' In all probability, this relates to winsome Arnold Seitz. It may have expected too much for them to harmonise anyway: a cricketer deploring profanity with one who thought nothing of cursing Jack Hobbs and Frank Woolley.

The vote for Seitz's replacement at Adelaide Oval contained potential for another ugly stand-off. In the event, Armstrong rather adeptly averted it. When Carkeek was nominated, Armstrong successfully counterproposed Ransford, who led the state to a comfortable victory. Armstrong was biding his time—the stand-off could wait.

Bean, McAlister and Ellis finally obtained the power they had so long coveted on 10 November 1913. Probably persuaded by the previous season's events, the VCA vested the appointment of captains in the selectors: Bean's motion, seconded by Ellis, was carried nineteen votes to four. Their first choice became of consuming interest—the *Age* viewed Armstrong as the rankest outsider:

> Doubtless the selection will be guided by the reasons—or prejudices—which now dictate the selection of international and interstate teams. After the return of the [1912] Australian XI, the men responsible for the

position entreated their indignant critics to bury the hatchet for the good of the game. Most people agreed to forgive and forget. But the result is that the Board of Control is secretly waging a ruthless war against old opponents under a flag of truce.

The selectors' irritation with recent criticism had also made them wary, with comic consequences which the *Argus* reported when they named their first team:

Messrs Bean and McAlister hurried off to their trains and our representative sought the information from Mr Ellis. That gentleman informed him that the selectors had decided to refuse to give the names to the *Argus*. He urged as a reason that the *Argus* had attacked the methods and the rulers of the association. The consequence is that, though the team was picked yesterday evening, no information can be given regarding its composition this morning.

The selectors had opted to continue with Ransford, although Armstrong tackled the season as if to make an unanswerable case for reappointment. On 3 and 4 December, he made an unbeaten 154 and took 8–73 for Melbourne against Metropolitan League Juniors. On 5 and 6 December, he poached an unbeaten 202 from Queensland in five and a quarter hours. Despite a recurrence of his malaria, counteracted by 'repeated doses of quinine', he towered over the match against South Australia at the Melbourne Cricket Ground beginning on Boxing Day, claiming 5–74 from 52 overs, and spending five and a half hours over 51 not out and 132. It brought reward. On the final day, Armstrong was approached by the VCA—not directly, but through his friend Bill Sweeney. Ransford was shortly to undergo nasal surgery, and Harry Rush had asked Sweeney to ask Armstrong if he would lead Victoria against New South Wales. Either Rush was being coy, avoiding confrontation, or conniving, hoping the cricketer would be unable to refuse a friend. Armstrong coolly told Sweeney to tell Rush that he would act only on condition that the appointment was for the remainder of the season. Merely to be back where he'd been a year earlier was insufficient; he expected reparations.

Bean, McAlister and Ellis seem to have been confounded by this reply. They did nothing. Victorian players arrived at the MCG on New Year's Day 1914 to find that they had no captain. Armstrong asked John Healy: 'Have any of the selectors arrived?' None had. Armstrong said he did not intend to act unless his demand was complied with.

Healy pleaded with him to hold the fort. Armstrong agreed: until the interval. The detailed content of Armstrong's lunchtime exchanges with Bean and McAlister—Ellis, it transpired, was at the races—does not survive. But its substance soon became widely known. The VCA pair claimed that they had no constitutional power to make a seasonal appointment, but pledged that they would 'deal fairly' with Armstrong in future. Unconvinced, Armstrong resigned. Healy had to foist the captaincy on East Melbourne's Hughie Carroll, who accepted with greatest reluctance.

The dispute has many piquant aspects, one being that all three men—Armstrong, Healy and Carroll—were parishioners at Malvern's St Joseph's Catholic Church: one wonders how they greeted each other next Sunday. Yet perhaps strangest about the handover is that the average spectator would hardly have noticed it. Ambling out after lunch as though nothing untoward had occurred, Armstrong bowled for most of the next session: five of his first seven overs were maidens, and his initial 16 overs cost only 19 runs. His team, meanwhile, disintegrated. 'Armstrong assured the new skipper that he would give him every assistance on the field,' reported the *Leader*. 'The result was complete disorganisation.' The 13,717 spectators enjoyed the situation's absurdity, inundating Carroll with advice to change bowlers, move fieldsmen and move himself. At one point, when both Armstrong and his captain were seen adjusting the field, a spectator hollered: 'Let the big fellow do what he likes!' This was echoed by correspondents to the various newspapers. 'Surely a player of Armstrong's outstanding ability was justified in taking such a stand,' wrote 'Disgusted Cricket Lover' of Carlton to the *Age*. 'Why should he help out of a hole the very people who have moved heaven and earth to put him out of cricket? Even a worm will turn— why not a giant?' The only published letter supporting the VCA was from the VCA itself, Ellis somehow tracing the rift back ten years to Armstrong's seasons as a professional: 'It is well known to cricketers that Mr Armstrong has never had any feeling of friendship or loyalty towards our association. His action of demanding and obtaining a professional fee of five guineas for an interstate game may be the cause of his present attitude.' Anyone who had so much as flirted with professionalism was clearly tainted evermore.

The match became farcical. Carroll was burdened with three injured players: Bill Sewart had split a finger, Bert Bracher had wrenched a knee so badly that he needed a runner in both innings, while Bill Cannon remained on the field with a damaged hand only because Victoria had exhausted its substitutes' bench. The second-day crowd of 10,907 was confused. Carroll was accorded a sympathetic reception, Armstrong a rich ovation, to which he raised his cap. The *Argus* lamented:

> If anyone unacquainted with the inner circumstances of cricket had heard the demonstration yesterday, they would have come to the conclusion that it was a great and popular game which stirred people to such emotion…But when demonstrations take place on cricket grounds now they seldom have anything to do with cricket. It generally means, as it meant yesterday, that apart from the man and the moment, one faction is 'rubbing it in' to the other…All the unpleasantness that is taking place in this match is a continuation of the trouble that will apparently never end for as long as men can get up a good wholehearted hate of each other.

Some questions remain. Was Armstrong, for instance, acting on his own account in the affair? Rumours spread that Armstrong's ultimatum had been at Melbourne's instigation and, in attempting to defuse them, 'Observer' of the *Argus* was ambiguous:

> It was pointed out to him [Armstrong] that while they [Melbourne's committee] had no particular desire to interfere in a matter in which he had strong personal feeling, as the olive branch had been held out, it would be well to take it and to accept the captaincy of the side. It is just as well to get to the root of the trouble and to make it clear that, as far as the Melbourne Cricket Club is concerned, the vast majority of its members and executives have nothing at all to do with it.

That 'Observer' chose only to absolve 'the vast majority' suggests Armstrong *did* enjoy an undercurrent of support from militants, perhaps vestiges of the citizens' committee. Yet in concluding that Armstrong's actions were essentially unilateral, 'Observer' was probably right. Perhaps he had adopted the board's approach: never be satisfied by compliance with one's first set of demands.

One wonders, too, what Armstrong meant to achieve. For no sooner had the match ended than Armstrong abandoned his objective. On 5 January 1914, Healy wrote Armstrong with utmost politeness:

> I am instructed to inform you that the VCA selection committee purposes electing you captain of the Victorian team in the forthcoming match against New Zealand which commences on Friday next on the

Melbourne Cricket Ground and I have to ask whether you will be good enough to state by 5 p.m. on Tuesday whether you are willing to accept such a position. I will be pleased to accept your reply at my office by the hour named.

Armstrong replied:

I am in receipt of your communication of the 5th inst and will be pleased to captain the Victorian team against New Zealand.

Suddenly everyone was 'pleased' again. The implication is that Armstrong didn't care about a seasonal *fiat*, that his resignation had been more in the nature of a battle of wills—which he had won. Six years earlier, the VCA had threatened him with a life ban over an expenses chit. Now there was no hearing, no threat, and straightforward confirmation of his status as Victoria's foremost cricketer—as though the VCA could not bear yet another unedifying squabble. Armstrong could feel satisfied: he had tested the association's willingness to court further trouble and, at last, felt its resistance give.

One could criticise Armstrong's behaviour in this affair: he had capriciously deserted his team, and placed Carroll in a dreadful position. Yet in dealing with Bean, McAlister and Ellis, perhaps no option existed. It is instructive to study the fate of more diplomatic methods at an association meeting a week later. South Melbourne delegate John Baragwanath, with acute sensitivity, had mooted a conference of VCA clubs to discuss general issues of the management of Victorian cricket: constant upheaval clearly injured the game. He even invited Bean to attend.

Bean: 'No hope!'
Baragwanath: 'If you are past hope I feel sorry for you.'
Ellis: 'Messrs Rush and Bean have worked hard in the past.'
Baragwanath: 'I am not here to say anything against anyone in the room.'
Ellis: 'No, because you can't.'

Eventually, the chorus of ridicule overwhelmed Baragwanath. He was an admired veteran of state politics who now testily referred to the forum of public opinion.

Bean: 'What is public opinion?'
Baragwanath: 'It is what nineteen out of every twenty people have to say. I will give £100…'

Ellis: '…with a string attached.'
Baragwanath: 'Sandown Park jokes. People regard you as a huge joke.'
Ellis: 'Didn't we hold out the olive branch in the recent struggle?'
Baragwanath: 'No, it was a thistle.' (laughter)

The proposal failed. Baragwanath left wondering how one dealt with such people. Armstrong could have advised him.

18

'When Shall We Have Another Test on the Melbourne Ground?'

Not all Warwick Armstrong's energies were sunk in grim feuds with officialdom. On 13 July 1913, six weeks after his thirty-fourth birthday, he married Aileen O'Donnell at Woollahra's St Joseph's Catholic Church. Armstrong's best man was his friend Bill Sweeney; Aileen was given away by brother Thomas.

> The bride…wore a trained gown of ivory *crepe-de-chine* showing a corsage of Brussels lace, which lace also composed her veil worn over a small wreath of orange blossoms, and she carried a shower bouquet of white roses, hyacinths and asparagus ferns. Miss Susie O'Donnell, sister of the bride as bridesmaid wore mull *crêpe-de-chine* showing touches of Nattier blue and a blue Tadgell hat trimmed with lemon-coloured feathers. She carried a bouquet of violets and her Nellie Stewart bangle was the gift of the bridegroom.

It was not a large wedding, and the reception at Mingay in Darling Point was confined to immediate family. Nor did the couple enjoy an extended honeymoon at Medlow Bath in the Blue Mountains; rather like his father John, who scheduled the Kyneton football club annual meeting the day after his own wedding, Armstrong returned to Sydney five days later for a Paddington Cricket Club ball. Sweeney was hit of the evening, spontaneously donating ten guineas, the basis of a scheme for young cricketers later known as 'Sweeney Colts'. Armstrong's new bride did not attend; perhaps she was already resigned to life as a 'sporting widow'.

Armstrong's belated matrimony may be partly explained by his sport. Many contemporaries believed that cricket and conjugal contentment were inimical. The first Australian team to visit England, in 1878, had been composed entirely of bachelors. Captains like John Blackham and George Giffen had never married, and Noble, who would not do so until early the following year at the age of forty, held strongly that sport and wives did not mix: 'Women are very often keen followers of the game, but their excitement over a match and their sympathetic interest in the players are offset by the uneasiness and disquietude of mind they create in the team's family circle.' Trumble was almost thirty-five when he married, Laver forty-four, and Peter McAlister fifty-eight. One exception, Trumper, perhaps thought marriage at twenty-six acceptable because it was to wicketkeeper Jim Kelly's sister-in-law.

Aileen Armstrong herself was a small, pretty, rather frail woman, the fifth of Patrick O'Donnell's six daughters. Her involuted family affairs had been simplified by the death six months earlier of her uncle James—Mingay station's tenacious tenant. She was something of a Sydney society belle, so marriage to Armstrong entailed the hardship of relocation to Melbourne, away from friends and relatives. Nonetheless, the couple's matrimonial home was a handsome top-floor apartment in a St Kilda block called Majestic Mansions where his former teammate Billy Bruce also lived, with weekends at Armstrong's Carrum cottage. Glimpses also survive of Armstrong in a domestic setting that contrast markedly with his cricketing demeanour.

When the Armstrongs became friendly with the family living downstairs, the Powells, Armstrong exposed an endearing sense of humour. The Powells' son Victor, born in November 1904, recalled:

The Armstrongs' bedroom was immediately above that of my parents. Sometimes, Armstrong returned late at night and presumably sat on the edge of his bed to take off his boots, which were of enormous size…Consequently, they made quite a thump when they hit the floor and invariably woke my mother if she were already asleep. One evening when my parents were having a drink with the Armstrongs, mother jokingly told him about the boots that went thump in the night. Armstrong was profusely apologetic for his thoughtlessness and promised it would never happen again.

All was well for a time, until mother was once again thumped into wakefulness by the dropping of the first boot. Resignedly she settled down to wait for the second before trying to go to sleep again. She was still waiting at dawn. Next morning, Armstrong looked in to apologise for his forgetfulness, but was obviously pleased with himself to have saved her from the second thump. Dead pan, mother told him of her sleepless night. They looked at each other for a moment then burst out laughing.

Armstrong also revealed an unaffected charm with children. Victor Powell, who played cricket in a park across the road with friends, remembered him even at the height of his renown manifesting a keen interest in their doings: 'My lasting memory is of that huge—to us— man solemnly taking guard with a child's bat in his hands in front of stumps of similar size. Our great joy was that he apparently took it all as seriously as we did and treated us as cricketers not children.' When young Powell turned ten, Armstrong even proposed him for membership of the Melbourne Cricket Club, drafting Hugh Trumble as a seconder.

Armstrong seems to have retained an affection for children all his life. Rowland Ryder, son of the secretary of Warwickshire County Cricket Club and later a long-serving official in that post himself, recalled at the age of seven meeting him at Edgbaston:

Father was upstairs in the committee room talking to an alarming, gigantic cricketer, immaculate in green blazer and flannels. Father performed the introduction. I goggled. Warwick Armstrong picked me up from under my shoulders and lifted me above his head so that I was nearly touching the ceiling. At this point I thought he was going to eat me; however, he only gave me a kiss, set me down, and I was able to escape with my life.

Later on the same tour, having become a Clifton College schoolboy, Victor Powell went to watch Armstrong and his team play at Bristol, rather optimistically sending a note of greeting into the pavilion:

It seemed a long wait, but then a beaming Armstrong burst through the pavilion doors and all fears were forgotten. He swept me and the one friend who had been brave enough to accompany me up to the balcony, where he chatted to us for about half an hour. I know we met quite a few of the Australian team but, distinguished though they were, I don't remember any of them. My memory is of Armstrong's warmth and friendliness towards the young.

Peter Murley, now a leading Melbourne silk, relates a similar story of meeting Armstrong at Caulfield Park as a child, shortly after suffering tuberculosis and poliomyelitis, confining him to calipers:

> He was a great, big, gregarious man, but articulate and very interested in everything. Some of the things you see written about him suggest he was a bit of a blowhard, full of himself, but he didn't come across that way. I think he took an interest in me because I'd been in hospital so long and got round in these calipers. One day he said to me: 'Are you interested in cricket?' And the next time he saw me he gave me this album of photos.

In fact, the album was one of those Frank Laver created for members of Noble's 1909 Australian team: a keepsake today of incalculable value.

There are many such stories. Once an undersized boy himself, Armstrong may have seen something of himself in youthful strivings. An admirer might speculate that the cynicism of his adult world caused him to cherish youthful innocence, a detractor that his petulance reflected part of him that never entirely grew up.

Warwick and Aileen Armstrong's first extended holiday was inevitably a cricket trip, a private tour of New Zealand, leaving Sydney on 28 January 1914 aboard the *Victoria*. Arranged by Canterbury's Arthur Sims through Noble and Laver, with both Trumper and Ransford along for good measure, it was reminiscent of the days when Australian players had pleased themselves with help from outside capital—Sims, wealthy from the trans-Tasman frozen meat and wool trades, filled the Melbourne Cricket Club role.

This trip was almost the Golden Age's last burnishing. Bumper banquets were staged, bumper toasts drunk, and runs poured forth in unending profusion: 658 against Auckland, 653 against Canterbury, 922 against South Canterbury. Trumper, often held back to preserve him for the edification of Saturday crowds, batted with cheerful abandon, including 293 in three hours in Christchurch, his eighth-wicket partnership of 428 with Sims still a first-class record eighty-seven years later. Trumper's fame became such that the young googly bowler Arthur Mailey recalled teammates taking it in turns to impersonate him:

> On the train journeys at night, I think every member of the team at one time or other played the part of 'Trumper'. In the middle of the night

there would be a call for him from the platform and everyone from the smallest to the largest, not omitting Warwick Armstrong, each of us basked in the fame of 'the incomparable Victor'.

Again, New Zealanders were in a defeatist mood; Wellington Cricket Association's president said the country wanted 'a good beating to show them they could not play cricket as Australians could'. Again, Armstrong tackled ineffectual opposition in deadly earnest, collecting 96 and 5–80 in the First 'Test' at Carisbrook, an unbeaten 110 and 6–47 in the Second at Eden Park, and squeezing more than 300 overs into eight first-class matches. In fact, Sims found Armstrong's unquenchable thirst for activity and gruff off-handedness 'something of a trial'. When Sims tried to encourage juniors like Mailey and all-rounder Herbie Collins, Armstrong would 'scowl moodily'; it seemed that 'even when he made a century he still expected to bowl unchanged at one end'. Whether it was much of a trip for Aileen Armstrong is also doubtful. For ten weeks, Sims' combine played more or less incessantly, interposing eight minor matches against XVs and XVIIIs; Armstrong, acting as a tour selector with Noble and Trumper, and 'restless when he was not batting or bowling', missed only one. Aileen appears in a team portrait, a demure, petite figure. Her gargantuan husband, arms folded, leans hungrily forward as though keen to be elsewhere. As perhaps he was.

After two years of austerities, the board finally arranged another overseas tour, to South Africa for 1914–15—this time, firmly under its direction. It had struck out altogether that pesky Rule 9, taking full responsibility for appointing managers, and originated a subtly sinister Rule 11, permitting it veto rights over all selections: henceforward, it could disapprove any cricketer selected 'for reasons other than cricket ability'. These were Billy McElhone's final legacy as cricket's overlord: at the board's meeting on 20 June 1914, his retirement as chairman was announced. His energies in future would be devoted, aptly, to the hurly burly of Sydney municipal politics—he had been an alderman for two years and would be mayor eight years later. The decisiveness of his triumph is reflected in the fact that these last constitutional changes caused not a murmur. Perhaps, just as the VCA had recently refrained from action against Armstrong, so had the players wearied of struggle.

The day of McElhone's retirement was for Armstrong also a grand one. With Hill and Trumper unavailable, he was named captain of the party visiting South Africa: showing unaccustomed generosity, Colonel Justin Foxton was his nominee, Hill his seconder. With Bean and Leslie Poidevin, Hill chose a young team: eight of the thirteen, including twenty-one-year-olds Roy Park and Johnnie Moyes, had not played Tests. Armstrong, it was foreseen, would be their model. 'Armstrong is a giant,' commented the *Sydney Morning Herald*, 'not only in stature but with bat and ball, and there are few greater all-round cricketers than he.' Passages were booked aboard the *Themistocles*, and five months of fixtures scheduled, including five Tests.

Was this, for Armstrong, an ambition fulfilled? His response to appointment is unrecorded, but his skirmish with the VCA demonstrates how he valued the office of captain. He could submit to leaders he admired—Darling, Noble, Hill—but to play for those he did not— Worrall, McAlister, Seitz—was purest torment. Perhaps the best circumstantial evidence that he was eager to lead Australia is that he overlooked the £200 tour fee, which among others *World of Cricket* deplored: 'How many crack Australian cricketers can afford to do this? They are not wealthy men for the most part—they cannot afford to leave their occupations for six months or more without adequate com- pensation.' If Armstrong set financial considerations aside, we can probably assume that the tour had other enticements.

Fulfilment, however, would have to wait: the tour never occurred. On 4 August, German troops marched on Belgium, plunging Britain, and its dominions, into war. Prime Minister Andrew Fisher saw Australia's duties clearly: 'To gird up our loins and remember that we are Britons.'

War's thunder emitted at first merely a distant rumble. Although the Board cancelled the South African tour on 17 August 1914, no need was felt to rearrange the scheduled 1916 Ashes tour, or to circumscribe the Sheffield Shield. The VCA, too, continued its district competition: indeed, it was finally enlarged to incorporate the Melbourne Cricket Club. In return, on 30 September, Melbourne renounced claim to sep- arate board representation. The armistice to the conflict that had riven Australian cricket was signed as the world's battle standards were unfurling. The association even showed a glimmer of generosity. It agreed that Ramsay Mailer should retain his board position indefinitely, and only thereafter would this delegate's appointment become a VCA prerogative: a concession later significant.

As pavilion clerk, meanwhile, Armstrong sought a pay rise. His application was considered by Melbourne's committee on 27 October: it decided that the request could 'not be entertained at present'. Armstrong, nonetheless, approached domestic cricket wholeheartedly. He and Trumble had been recruiting: impressed with Queensland's left-arm spinner Bert Ironmonger, they offered him a ground staff job at Melbourne at £2 10s a week. Ironmonger and Armstrong immediately became a compelling slow-bowling combination. And merely because war raged elsewhere was no reason to alter time-honoured tactics—Armstrong had seldom been a more avid competitor. Melbourne lost only one game for the season, and that in Armstrong's absence: he overwhelmed East Melbourne in the semi-final with 195 and Prahran in the final with 11–70. Victoria also lost but once, Armstrong captaining them to a pivotal 16-run win in Sydney, stifling New South Wales with leg theory while Ironmonger winkled out wickets at the other end. He even attempted a cunning run-out at the bowler's end as non-striker Eric Bull backed up. 'Once as he came up to the bowling crease,' reported the *Daily Telegraph*, 'Armstrong very nearly caught Bull napping. He whipped the bails off but Bull detected the move in time.' No-one had tried such a trick in Australia for almost fifty years, and no-one would again for more than thirty: had Bull not been alert, the 'Mankad' might today be known as the 'Armstrong'.

More significant, however, is Armstrong's attitude to what became known as 'the greater game'. Impulsive younger men heard 'the bugles of England blowing o'er the sea'. Armstrong did not. The reasons may be simple. Initial enlistment requirements of the Australian Imperial Force covered men between nineteen and thirty-eight in first-class physical condition. Armstrong was thirty-five, and his health may not have met requirements because of his malaria, of which he suffered another periodic recurrence in January 1915. He also had family obligations, not merely toward Aileen, but towards his parents John and Amelia, sixty-three and sixty-two as 1915 began. As both Armstrong's brothers Jack and Tom would serve, it may have been determined that the family's eldest son would not—an arrangement not uncommon, also applying to future prime minister Robert Menzies.

As Menzies would learn, though, those who did not rush to the colours were often subjected to scorn, and Armstrong doubtless experienced pressures to conform. Sportsmen, suited to upholding national honour not only as premium physical specimens but as lovers of competition, would be a focus of recruitment campaigns. Attorney-general Billy Hughes addressed to 'Sportsmen of Australia' a clarion call: 'As you have played the game in the past, so we ask you to play the greater game now. You are wanted in the trenches now far more than you were ever needed in the football and cricket fields.'

Many responded: Melbourne's 1914–15 annual report enumerated no fewer than 423 members in uniform. When Armstrong attended the VCA's annual meeting on 20 September 1915 to receive the district pennant, he heard a bellicose address from president Donald Mackinnon:

> The president...remarked that the healthy rivalry created in sport had a result in the readiness with which players had come forward in the great fight for national freedom. It was considered at the time of the Franco-German War that it was impossible to improvise armies, and many people of the present time thought it impossible, too, to do what Lord Kitchener had done. Healthy pastimes such as cricket had greatly helped towards the building up of armies.

Armstrong's innocuous reply, meanwhile, did not mention the war:

> Mr Armstrong, in receiving the gifts, said that the pennant matches had been to the Melbourne club hard but enjoyable, and he hoped the same spirit would long continue. It was a good thing for the pennant to go around, and the team that beat Melbourne would be entitled to the pennant and Melbourne would be the first to congratulate the winning team. With so many young players, interesting matches could be looked forward to.

Was he sensitive, then, about his failure to enlist? Surrounded by talk of war, the man without stake in it, for reasons however valid, could hardly have avoided twinges of discomfort. A splenetic editorial appeared nine days later in the *Australian Statesman and Mining Standard*. 'Cricket and Shirking' denounced Victoria as the slackest of the Sheffield Shield states in exchanging flannels for fatigues. The unsigned editorial was probably the work of editor Ernest Oliphant, whose balance as a Shakespearean scholar was belied by his extreme opinions concerning war's conduct. He'd done his homework: eleven players from New South Wales and six South Australians had answered the call, yet the Sheffield

Shield's holders had produced only one soldier, Jimmy Matthews. Some comments especially seemed tailored to Armstrong's specifications:

> We want no-one to be a hero because of his enormous patience in dealing with good-class bowling, because of his skill in turning a ball, because of his mastery of the science of a mere game, or because as a captain he is more tricky or unscrupulous than a rival captain. When the country is at war, its only heroes are those who serve it, not those who, in ministering to the pleasure of the idle and the disloyal, minister to their own vanity and give proof of their own lack of patriotism.

Armstrong kept his own counsel, as indeed those not enlisting tended to: the biographer of Jack Ryder, another of Armstrong's contemporaries not to serve, notes that he 'didn't speak to his family on the subject in later years'. While one can speculate, ultimately it is possible to say only that Armstrong had his reasons and retained them to himself.

As the pall of war hovered, the board cancelled its Ashes tour and curtailed the Sheffield Shield. Melbourne then advocated termination of the 1915 Victorian Football League season: though unsuccessful in obtaining the necessary two-thirds majority of clubs, it made its point by withdrawing from competition in February 1916.* Two of Armstrong's old haunts—South Melbourne Cricket Ground and Caulfield Racecourse—became soldiers' quarters. The greatest arena of all, meanwhile, provoked sombre reflections. 'Only the other day,' 'Felix' mused on 16 October 1915, 'I heard an old man say "when shall we have another Test match on the Melbourne ground?" I am afraid it will be a very long time.'

Ten days later, Australia changed prime ministers, swapping one Melbourne Cricket Club member for another. The appointment as high commissioner in London of Andrew Fisher, a member since 1909,

---

* Five Victorian Football League clubs went into recess in 1916: Melbourne, Essendon, South Melbourne, Geelong and St Kilda. Senior Australian Rules competition ceased in South Australia altogether, and continued in Western Australia only as a 'patriotic competition', gate takings donated to the war effort. Horse-racing and boxing, meanwhile, were circumscribed from September 1917: unregistered race meetings were banned, and important bouts restricted to one a fortnight.

admitted to the premiership Billy Hughes, a member since 1914. The mercurial Hughes saw the war in more drastic terms than anyone on either side of politics: 'We must beat Germany to her knees; there is no safety for civilisation left otherwise.' He entreated Australians to provide more manpower, lectured them on their lassitude, and openly coveted the mechanism of conscription—in time, the country's most divisive issue.

Yet whatever Armstrong's reasons for non-enlistment—and they must by now have been taxed—he continued playing cricket with utmost seriousness. He even strove to keep his weight in bounds, running round the MCG for a quarter or half mile every evening, and two or three times a week having 'a turn at football' with an old St Kilda opponent, Joe Hogan. He dominated the VCA's non-pennant competition, missing barely a game, and only a handful of selection meetings.* After his 842 runs at 93.55 and 29 wickets at 18.2 in 1915–16, the *Australasian* called him 'unquestionably the best all-round player in the world at the present time'. Within two years of war's beginning, twenty-four Melbourne first and second XI players had enlisted, and picking sides was difficult: for a period, Melbourne's wickets were kept by a deaf mute, G. D. Edwards, nicknamed 'Dummy' and 'silently eloquent' in appeal. But Armstrong alone was worth half a team.

He did render the war effort some service, appearing in the 'Cricketers' Tribute', two VCA fund-raising fixtures over the Christmas–New Year period, enlivened by fly-pasts from military aviators and airs from three city bands. For once, too, he entered into an occasion's spirit—he was stumped twice, for 27 and 102. The matches encouraged a noble sacrifice by the great wicketkeeper John Blackham, who vouchsafed for auction a cricket ball used in 1882's landmark Oval Test—an artefact so sacred that £617 was subscribed to purchase it for the Melbourne Cricket Club. Considering their prior bitternesses, the donation list makes piquant reading: the names Armstrong, Ransford and Laver, with erstwhile supporters Ben Wardill, William Baillieu, James Guthrie, Billy Bruce, Agar Wynne, Reginald Wilmot and Bill Sweeney, mingle with those of Ernie Bean, Mat Ellis, Peter McAlister and even

---

* Armstrong had never been a regular at First XI selections, but his record during World War I was irreproachable: from 1915–16 to 1918–19, he attended forty-one of forty-six meetings held.

Arnold Seitz. The 'Blackham Ball' presaged an 'Auction Sale of Cricket Relics', to which leading players and aficionados volunteered various treasures. One of Armstrong's bats was among sixty items sold at Scott's Hotel on 21 January 1916. Oliphant's impugning of Armstrong's patriotism had not affected his market value: the item fetched £27 6s, considerably more than similar donations from Laver, Hill, Gregory and Bardsley.*

There were few such interludes. As if in anticipation of European slaughter, Australian cricket suffered a string of mortalities. Victor Trumper, only thirty-seven, the batsman Armstrong had most esteemed, died of Bright's disease in June 1915: Armstrong was a pall-bearer, with Noble, Cotter, Carter, Gregory and Bardsley, among 200 cricketers who attended the funeral. Tom Horan, who had spotted Armstrong as a junior talent, died of dropsy in April 1916: Armstrong again was a mourner, with Laver and McAlister, perhaps all three on slightly better terms. Former club and Test comrade Gerry Hazlitt, twenty-seven, dropped dead in a Sydney street of a heart ailment. Armstrong's youngest Victorian teammate Jack Souter, twenty-one, perished of 'rapid consumption'. There was the loss of Ben Wardill, *paterfamilias* to Australian cricketers for a generation, the man who had gifted Armstrong with his enviable job: again Armstrong stood graveside in October 1917, again with Laver, alongside Trumble, Ransford and Bruce. His death was followed a month later by the passing of Harry Trott, Armstrong's schoolboy idol.

Then came the casualties: Frank Lugton, a medium pacer whom Armstrong had led in five matches for Victoria, perished at Pozieres; Fred Collins, once arraigned alongside Armstrong by the VCA, fell at Broonseinde; Gother Clarke, the leg spinner whose inaccuracy in a Sheffield Shield match had expedited Armstrong's Test selection, died at Zonnebeke; finally Albert Cotter, another of the 'Big Six', was shot peering over a parapet at Beersheba. All were pages, greater and lesser, from Armstrong's cricketing tale, and all proxies in their way for

---

* Armstrong's bat was bought by Audley Lempriere, an amateur golf champion; of living cricketers only John Blackham's fetched more (£42). Melbourne Cricket Club member Thomas Millear, former shire president of Ararat, lavished £185 on bats owned by Billy Murdoch, Victor Trumper and Clem Hill, and on Tom Horan's scorebook of the 1882 Australian tour of England; generously, he returned it to Horan.

Armstrong himself. In the non-pennant competition of 1916–17, he appeared out of place: Melbourne's team, commented the *Australasian*, seemed 'just a band of boys, with Warwick Armstrong looking like the father of the lot'.

Club matches were suspended on 28 October 1916 as Australians went to the polls for a long-awaited referendum on conscription. President Donald Mackinnon having become director-general of recruiting, the VCA decided that it 'must not place any obstacle in the way where such a momentous question is to be decided'. There is no divining Armstrong's views, though they are intriguing to contemplate.

No issue in Australian history has aroused such bitterness. In this heyday of the public meeting, it provoked flights of brilliant oratory, involving *inter alia* many of those at the forefront of the 'Big Six' dispute, though this time opposed at the barricades. Edmund Jowett, instigator of the citizens' committee, was ardently in favour; William Maloney, who had memorably compared the board with a 'bunch of freaks', was fervently against. At Armstrong's club, meanwhile, although hundreds of its number had answered the call, the institutional position was complex. Melbourne had sanctioned many patriotic events on its ground and approved recruiting posters within its precincts, yet was philosophically resistant to the case for compulsion—an outgrowing, explains historian Alf Batchelder, of its amateur origins:

> The Melbourne Cricket Club was not necessarily opposed to conscription, but it was not in favour of the spirit which compulsory enlistment represented. That was 'the force of consolidated mass, not high elevation'....If an individual was to go to the War, he must do so because he freely recognised that it was his duty to answer the empire's call—compulsion should not be his reason for being involved in the 'game'.

Where Armstrong's family was concerned, influences were further complicated. For loyal Britons *and* practising Catholics, interlocutors on both sides of the question had force: pros asked, 'How would the Kaiser like you to vote?'; antis asked, 'How would Christ like you to vote?' They would have endorsed Hughes' view that 'the country must not fail', but could scarcely have ignored Archbishop Daniel Mannix's insistence that 'conscription is a hateful thing and almost certain to bring evil in its train'. One suspects the Armstrongs leaned slightly to the negative, as indeed did the country, which voted narrowly against Hughes' brain-child; they may even have enjoyed Mannix's acid wit when he dismissed allegations that Australian Catholics were not pulling their wartime weight: 'Apparently not enough nuns are joining.' Such allegations were in their case baseless: by this time, both Armstrong's brothers were not only in uniform, but abroad.

On 19 May 1915, Jack Armstrong married again, to thirty-three-year-old Leonie Spangler. It was a low-key ceremony at her family's East Malvern home, conducted by a Congregational minister, but undoubt-edly happier than his first wedding nine years earlier. Family lore has it that he chose to marry in expectation of enlisting, guaranteeing Leonie's pension entitlements in the event of his casualty; perhaps craving for redemption in his parents' eyes also played a part. Photographs of Jack after his enlistment on 24 January 1916—posing at Arra Glen, petting the family dogs—hint at prior sins forgiven. Among his personal effects were listed a crucifix, prayer book and devotional book—probably gifts from his mother. Jack's departure for Plymouth on 20 May with the 8th Brigade Australian Field Artillery perhaps served as an example for twenty-four-year-old Tom. He joined 3rd Division Artillery Corps a week later.

Withal Jack's ambitions, no glories impended: instead, the rigours of uniformed life and a northern winter took rapid toll. An army Christmas card to Arra Glen survives—signed 'from Jack, with fondest love to all the girls'—but he lasted only a fortnight in France before evacuation with bronchial pneumonia, which became pleurisy. Not until 8 September 1917 did he rejoin his unit. Eleven days later he received a severe shrapnel wound in his left foot during the barrages preparatory to the Battle of Menin Road. At Orpington's Ontario Military Hospital, a doctor scrawled the case note: 'Condition too poor to amputate, delirious.'

After Jack's condition had stabilised sufficiently for amputation, the Armstrongs were advised on 26 October that he was 'dangerously ill', and his official file is fat with subsequent cable traffic: 4 November, 'seri-ously ill'; 24 November, 'condition improving'; 2 December, 'out of danger'; 6 December, 'slightly improved'; 18 December, 'progressing favourably'. Two days later, the Armstrongs voted in Australia's second conscription referendum. So many more families had by now endured similar experiences that the proposition was this time soundly defeated. The war which had begun as a patriotic adventure was now ending in drab squalor—like Jack Armstrong's military career. For contrary to optimistic reports, his infection had spread, and meningitis set in four days after Christmas. After complaining of headaches and vomiting, Jack drifted into semi-consciousness, and died at 9 a.m. on New Year's Day 1918. The Armstrongs' next bulletin concerned details of Jack's burial in Orpington Cemetery, including the casket ('good polished elm coffin with brass fittings') and the ceremony ('coffin draped with Union Jack', 'several beautiful wreaths').

Warwick joined the family mourning. He was amid a game against North Melbourne straddling Christmas, but when it resumed on 5 January he opted out. Nor did he play for another three weeks—quite a tribute from such a compulsive cricketer. But beyond newspaper reports of Armstrong's absence, few traces remain of his younger brother. The only surviving family correspondence, dated 21 May 1918, is from John Armstrong to Victoria Barracks' Base Records Office: financially fastidious, he inquired about 'particulars of his deferred pay and when it will be available'. And in future years, his sisters seldom spoke of Jack beyond that he had 'died during the war', while Leonie Armstrong became a curious family adjunct. She converted to Catholicism—being baptised at St Joseph's on 29 June 1918, with Olivia Armstrong as sponsor—but was never entirely welcome in the family circle. She found a small house in East Malvern's Tollington Avenue. She subsisted on her war widow's pension, and didn't remarry. 'Leonie was a nice sort of person,' recalls Patricia Armstrong, who married Armstrong's nephew Warwick Francis. 'But the sisters tended to look down on her a bit.' Perhaps she also reminded the family of the past, and of Jack in particular—the prodigal son who never came back.

19

'There Never Was a Captain to Equal Warwick Armstrong'

Keeping 'the lesser game just alive while the greater game is being played': thus did president Donald Mackinnon explain the Victorian Cricket Association's wartime mission in September 1916. Sometimes, a pulse was nigh undetectable. Crowds dwindled in poor weather that summer, and there was no cricket at all some Saturdays, once for the first conscription referendum, once for a Win-the-War procession, once for the rescheduled Melbourne Cup. Warwick Armstrong and Edgar Mayne led teams in another MCG match on Boxing Day raising funds toward cricket equipment for Australian troops abroad: despite Armstrong's undefeated 125, less than £50 was taken.

Armstrong himself was doing it hard at the Melbourne Cricket Club. With the ground barren of sport and so many members in service, revenues had shrivelled. Much of secretary Hugh Trumble's correspondence now involved entreaties to clubmen considering resignation. 'We quite recognise that under the shadow of the war the club has little to offer members in the way of attractions at the ground,' reads a typical one from August 1917, 'but surely the good times will come again.' Though Armstrong continued playing cricket ceaselessly—his 1917–18 season was worth 419 runs at 139.7 and 42 wickets at 8.9—austerity programs the club implemented left him running its office virtually alone. It was a burden; one incident suggests he did not bear it with equanimity.

Prior to committee elections at the club's September 1918 annual meeting, a candidate called Albert Manfield entered the office seeking to inspect the members' roll. Armstrong found him in the act, informed him that this was against club policy, then repossessed the roll—and did so, it would seem, in rather unparliamentary language. Manfield complained bitterly to president Leo Cussen, who sought an explanation from Trumble. Not surprisingly, Trumble stood by his old pal:

> On Mr Armstrong's returning from lunch he informed Mr Manfield that he considered he had no right to come into the office without permission and inspect the paid-up roll, and in any case he would have to obtain authority from the secretary. He therefore took possession of it. He explained to Mr Manfield that, by scrutinising the paid-up register, he was obtaining unfair advantage over other candidates who had never sought such a privilege.

'Mr Armstrong does not admit that he was discourteous to you in any way,' Trumble told Manfield. 'He simply thought you had no right to inspect the list in question without authority and informed you to this effect.'

By that annual meeting, there were better tidings. The war's final German offensive, at first successful, had been stunningly reversed. A sub-committee was mandated to review club sports 'so that when peace is declared they may be vigorously pursued'. Vigorous pursuit was also the Board of Control's first thought when the Armistice was signed on 11 November 1918. As 30,000 jammed Melbourne's Spring Street for a thanksgiving service six days later, the board met to celebrate an 'honest admiration for those cricketers who so nobly responded to the call of the empire', and resolved to take 'the earliest opportunity of arranging for the resumption of international cricket'. The board reconvened on 6 December to schedule three interstate matches. When Victoria named its XI, Armstrong was appointed captain.

Forty-three months had elapsed since Armstrong's—and Australia's—last first-class match. He had played uninterruptedly for Melbourne, continued his laps of the MCG, his 'turns at football', and boxed in his club's gymnasium. But he was now in his fortieth year and unmissably huge, displacing about 130 kilograms, and as manoeuvrable in the field as a Pullman carriage. On the eve of the Boxing Day match against New South Wales, indeed, Armstrong does seem to have experienced misgivings about his ability to bridge the war. 'Not Out' of the *Referee* reported a conversation where Armstrong confided 'his conviction that he had lost form in spite of assiduous practice'—a rare pang of self-doubt. He need not have worried. Armstrong compiled a sterling 68 in difficult conditions on the first day—he 'shaped with steady certitude from the first ball' and 'moved with astonishing agility between the wickets considering his huge physique'—then took three crucial wickets in Victoria's 216-run win. On the first day of 1919, Armstrong's powers then came flooding back: arriving at 6–100 against South Australia, he stormed to 162 not out in three hours with eighteen boundaries, the last two wickets helping him add 173. 'Although careful at the outset,' reported 'Observer' of the *Argus*, 'he seemed to have a special stroke ready for every ball bowled, and...not for an instant did there seem a note of doubt or indecision.' Making his first-class debut was twenty-four-year-old Victor Richardson, a future Australian captain and grandfather to two more in the Chappell brothers. He was struck by 'the effect of a really great player on a team', and awed by the batsman's command: 'Armstrong took charge of the game. He hit threes when he wanted the strike for the change over. He belted fours when he wanted them. I believe he bent every picket on the Melbourne ground.'

Things were looking up. The Melbourne Cricket Club's decline was reversed. Membership numbers, virtually halved during the war, began expanding again; president Cussen was soon referring to the club's 'splendid financial position'. That meant an upturn in Armstrong's fortunes. His office burden was eased by a young junior clerk, and he was awarded pay rises in January and August 1919—his first since joining the club—taking his annual salary to £350.

For Australians in general, however, 1919 was a disorienting year. Fighting had ended, but austerities and shortages persisted. Separations and casualty announcements continued. And this eerie diminuendo to the war had, on Armstrong's career, two far-reaching effects. For the story behind one, we must return to his very first Test, at the MCG eighteen years earlier.

During England's innings, Archie MacLaren had fallen into conversation with umpire Bob Crockett. How strange that Australians did not grow cricket-bat willow, MacLaren commented. Strange indeed, Crockett replied; perhaps MacLaren could send some cuttings? Five of the six died while transiting the tropics, but the survivor became mother tree to 5000 more at Shepherds Flat, near Daylesford in Victoria. Nothing changed overnight. Australian cricketers continued using English equipment, to the vexation of the nationalist *Bulletin*: 'Why should Australia flog an English-made cricket ball with an English-made bat?'* But four years of wartime isolation had their effect; by the cessation of hostilities, inventories of English equipment in Australia were almost exhausted. Having bestowed hundreds of bats and balls on military camps and struggling clubs, the Melbourne Cricket Club was by January 1919 'desperately short'. It placed a huge order for bats, balls, stumps, pads, gloves and keeping gauntlets with John Wisden & Co in England through a club member at London's Royal Bank, but the consignment had still not arrived at the beginning of the following season. So parlous were supplies in general, indeed, that senior grade competition in both Sydney and Melbourne recommenced with a relaxation of the law requiring a new ball at the start of each innings.

As a result, several Victorian players began using bats from R. M. Crockett & Sons, made from Daylesford willow: the first of Australian manufacture used in first-class cricket. Honour of the first Sheffield Shield hundred with a bat of indigenous *Salix alba* fell to Edgar Mayne, in December 1919 against South Australia; unfortunately, it broke during the next game. But the landmark of the first Test century made with a local product, fittingly, appears to have been Armstrong's: the bat he used in his 158 not out at Sydney in December 1920, displayed at the Melbourne Cricket Ground, is stamped 'Crockett'. Nativists could finally be satisfied that their cricketers, in effect, were all-Australian.

The logistics of concluding the war effort also influenced Armstrong's postwar career. For Australian families, there were no speedy reunions after the war: tens of thousands of servicemen and numberless tonnes of *materiel* overseas required retrieval and demobilisation. Armstrong's

---

* One South Australian batmaker Ewald Kumnick presented Monty Noble's 1909 Australians with examples of his product, although they do not appear to have been used in first-class matches. Kumnick, a Lutheran, had started bat-making as a sideline to carpentry at Lobethal in South Australia in the 1890s, using a local willow (*Salix x rubens*) grown in the Adelaide Hills rather than the traditional bat willow (*Salix alba* var *caerula*) propagated at Daylesford.

brother Tom was typical: not until 17 August 1919 would he finally arrive home aboard the *Karmala*. Others staying longer needed diversion; for young, fit men far from home, the obvious recourse was sport.

When AIF Order No. 1539 on 31 January 1919 instigated a Sports Control Board to 'encourage sport in all units and supervise organisation and selection of representative teams', cricket was a priority. Under Australian arms in Britain were a host of handy players, including two Test all-rounders in Corporal Charlie Macartney and Lieutenant Charles Kellaway. Lance-Corporal Herbie Collins, Gunner Johnny Taylor, Lieutenant Ted Long and Gunner Eric Bull had represented New South Wales before the war. Major Gordon Campbell and Captain Clarence Pellew had played for South Australia. Some had experienced very hard wars indeed. Macartney had won the Meritorious Service Medal for gallantry in June 1918. Kellaway had been wounded four times. Young keeper Corporal Bert Oldfield had been blown up at Polygon Wood by a shell that had killed three comrades. Nor could one in all conscience stop a man who, with the opportunity to do so, simply wished to return home. Macartney, Kellaway and Campbell all eventually fell into this category; Campbell, originally envisaged as team manager, had a three-year-old son he'd never seen. Yet here in embryo was a body of rare talent, and the basis of the great Test XI that Armstrong would command. Collins proved an unflappable captain. Bold Pellew and boyish Taylor batted with panache and fielded electrically. Oldfield moved with such ease and grace behind the stumps that his feet seemed scarcely to touch the ground.

The emergence of one team member, however, was most remarkable of all. Lieutenant Jack Gregory was cousin of Syd, and thus part of Australia's most fecund cricket family, seven members having represented New South Wales. But as a youth he had shown no particular aptitude for cricket: though he had captained Shore's first XI in 1911 and 1912 as a batsman, he impressed at least as much as a track athlete and rugby player. His decision to go jackerooing in Queensland had then been a 'sad blow' to relations. Enlisting as an artillery gunner in January 1916, he toyed with bowling fast in regimental cricket between two tours of France, but also hurdled, sprinted and played tennis.

A chance encounter changed everything. England's Pelham Warner spied Gregory playing for the Artillery Officers' School against the Red Cross. The family name induced a *frisson* of recognition. 'His name is

Gregory, and he is from cricket stock,' Warner told the AIF selectors. 'I'm sure he can play.' It didn't seem so at first: early on, he reported having cut his hand by stepping on it at fine leg, and was ironically nicknamed 'Pavlova'. But while convalescing at slip, Gregory proved a close catcher of uncanny reflex and reach, and when tossed the ball in an emergency, an intuitive and natural fast bowler. In the tour's third match against Cambridge University, Gregory claimed 6–68, not merely disarranging stumps but scattering them like ninepins. On a benign surface at Lord's a few days later, he struck a batsman's chest so hard that the victim was lifted off his feet—the ball then trickled cruelly onto the stumps.

Gregory could also bat, with bare-headed and bare-handed abandon. And while the AIF XI travelled in uniform and subsisted on army pay, they played with anything but military rigidity: their carefree *elan*, as intended, put thoughts of war to flight. A mixture of officers and enlisted men, they cribbed from the Regent Street flat of Australian actress Dorothy Brunton the motto 'abandon rank all ye who enter here'. The team journeyed also to South Africa for six weeks, where it accomplished further prodigies, especially Gregory. Having claimed 9–32 against Natal at Durban, he threw the last man out for good measure. Wrecking the stumps of a South African batsman in Johannesburg, he sent a bail flying more than forty metres. Just before landfall at Fremantle, the team was wired by the Board of Control: homecoming matches had been arranged for them against Victoria, New South Wales and Queensland, a chance for them to return in style, and for Australians to glimpse their cricket future.

For Warwick Armstrong, the past was steadily sealing itself off. In September 1919, he attended the funeral of Frank Laver, who had died in East Melbourne's Crathie House Private Hospital after falling ill some months earlier while visiting a family property in the Northern Territory. Of prewar cricket's chief personalities, only Armstrong remained at the forefront: Trumper and Cotter had also died, Hill and Noble had retired, Ransford and Carter had faded. Could he, at forty, find a place in the postwar game?

Perhaps the inspiriting sensations of becoming a father helped. The Armstrongs had been trying for a number of years to continue the family line, but Aileen is believed to have suffered at least two miscarriages.

When finally they succeeded—their son Warwick Geoffrey was born on Melbourne Cup Day 1919—it may have been a complicated birth.* While it is difficult to be definitive, however, something of a change does appear to have come over Armstrong in the summer of 1919–20, or at least change grew more noticeable. Once Victoria's renowned 'growler', the cricketer who 'spared no feelings', Armstrong revealed a streak of beneficence, even generosity. He was increasingly content to indulge younger teammates, saving himself in the event of need: in the Boxing Day derby against New South Wales, for instance, he let his charges do the bulk of work until the match was in the balance on the last day, then as seventh change bowled Victoria to a 116-run victory. He could even be found bestowing praise. After making 143 against South Australia in four and quarter hours, he commended the bowler of the sharp leg-break that dismissed him, Norman Williams: 'If I had known he could bowl such a ball, I certainly would not have let him bowl me,' he told the *Australasian*. 'But good luck to the young fellow. It will do him no harm.' From his comrades he now received a reciprocal indulgence. When the VCA executive queried his charging them a bottle of whisky to entertain visitors to Victoria's dressing-room, keeper Jack Ellis retorted, 'Why get his back up for the sake of two lousy bob? Give him two bottles.'

Armstrong reserved particular favour for two rising Victorian players. One was Dr Roy Park, twenty-seven-year-old son of a Methodist minister and a member of Armstrong's 1914–15 Australian team that never was. Park had been a cricket prodigy at Wesley College; schoolmate Robert Menzies recalled that one of the chief pleasures of his youth had been reading Shakespeare behind the school practice nets, so that he could partake of the bard whilst watching Park bat. Park had then been awarded one of the exhibitions that Melbourne settled on promising public schools talent, and became the youngest man to lead the club's batting averages. 'The Little Doc', as he became known after commencing medical studies at Melbourne University, also filled in winters as a nimble forward in Australian Rules football: a lithe 60 kilograms and 165 centimetres, he 'came through packs like smoke through a keyhole'.

---

* Newspaper notices of Warwick Geoffrey's birth were delayed more than a week, and replying a fortnight later to a Melbourne member who had sent Armstrong his regards, Trumble wrote: 'Mr Armstrong thanks you for your congratulations. The recent arrival is doing well now.' As Aileen was thirty-seven, it would not surprise if there were complications.

At Melbourne, Park had been one of the youngsters sent to the 'special net' for Armstrong's attention. Armstrong had been impressed, Park awestruck, later crediting Armstrong with 'most of my cricket brains'. They were an odd sight in partnership, like a planet and its satellite, but their simpatico was deep. During the match against South Australia, for example, Park joined his captain with an hour left of the second day and shared a thunderous stand. Over lunch on the third day, with Park 226 and himself 101, Armstrong recalled his own eight-year-old record score for Victoria: 'Parky, you haven't far to go to beat my 250. I promise to do my best to stop there while you make them.' Park did not make it, but always remembered the gesture.

Armstrong's other protege was also a noted all-round sportsman. Twenty-eight-year-old Ted McDonald had played fifty-two games of football for Richmond, Essendon and Fitzroy, including a winning Grand Final in 1916, but had now renounced the winter game in favour of his improving pace bowling. A tinsmith's son from Launceston, he had arrived in Melbourne in March 1911 in somewhat mysterious circumstances: research by journalist Nick Richardson suggests that he left home hurriedly after an embezzlement case. His bowling was also enigmatic, sometimes fast and penetrative, sometimes casual and innocuous. Nonetheless, perhaps because McDonald was a protege of Frank Laver's at East Melbourne, Armstrong had used him with care, favouring him with the new ball, and in short spells suiting his slender physique. Their relationship was unusual. McDonald was a self-contained man devoid of small talk, who held himself aloof in company. Yet, detached from his family, he perhaps found in Armstrong a proxy paternal figure. As McDonald's future teammate Cec Parkin put it: 'He always maintains...that there never was a captain to equal Warwick Armstrong.'

Though he may not have appreciated it, Armstrong was now in a special sporting category. Among teammates who had admired him as boys, he enjoyed automatic stature and authority—akin to the positions occupied by Sir Donald Bradman and Allan Border toward the end of their careers. When he met members of the newly arrived AIF XI at Scott's Hotel in Collins Street on 9 January 1920, his presence meant more than that of any of the other dignitaries assembled. None of the AIF XI knew him personally bar Collins—they had toured New Zealand together in Arthur Sims' side six years earlier—but all knew him by reputation. Interested as Armstrong was to meet Gregory, Gregory was still more abashed to meet Armstrong, 'the big man of cricket'.

The AIF XI's game at the MCG then allowed them to demonstrate all their exciting skills. Gregory was not deployed until Armstrong had added 43 for the first wicket with Edgar Mayne, but at once 'drew a chorus of admiring ooohs', and his spell of 7–22 included the electric thrill of bowling to the great man:

> In my first over, I got them flying high, and had to grin when I saw Warwick Armstrong draw himself up to his full height as one whipped past his chin. Possibly the grim smile on his face as he faced up for my next ball was due to the fact that he knew he would not always be opposed to my bowling.
>
> It was indeed a pleasure to find that my first over should be a maiden, and perhaps I shall be forgiven for saying that I was elated to have one for none, particularly as my victim was none other than my ideal cricketer, Warwick Armstrong. Armstrong went for an off ball and turned it to second slip where Cyril Docker took a beautiful catch.

Bert Oldfield flushed with similar pride in the second innings when he caught Armstrong at the wicket:

> Armstrong turned to me with a smile and offered a word of congratulation. It was to me a thrill to be able to share in the dismissal of one of Australia's greatest all-rounders and also to receive acknowledgement from him in the field, especially when it was the first time that I had played against him, or even met him.

Armstrong closed the match with an unusually chivalrous gesture, hurrying Victoria through its overs so that the AIF XI should have a chance of winning by 6 p.m. Fielders and umpires actually ran to their positions. To the crowd's delight, the visitors prevailed with a ball to spare. Pipe in mouth, Armstrong was seen shaking Collins' hand as the teams adjourned from the ground, doubtless pleased with the mettle of this new generation—the more so because, in Gregory's words, they 'would not always be opposed'.

By now it was known that Test cricket would resume the following summer with the visit of an English team. It was a matter in the interim of sustaining performance. Jack Gregory rolled on, collecting twin hundreds and eight wickets against New South Wales. Armstrong's season concluded with 86 not out and 9–93 against Queensland, plus 699 runs at 99.86 and 25 wickets at 14.08 while leading Melbourne to the VCA's so-called 'Victory Cup'. Generously overlooking Armstrong's role in the end of his career seventeen years earlier now that he'd been rehabilitated as the *Australasian*'s cricket correspondent, Jack Worrall decreed that there was 'no other man playing capable of such a performance'.

While today it appears that Australia's powerful postwar XI gathered like iron filings to a magnet, its composition was debated freely. In his 1920 memoir *Thirty-Three Years of Cricket*, Frank Iredale was typically equivocal. He felt modern players 'interesting' but lacking 'the brilliancy of some of our men in the past'—Macartney was 'a bit of a puzzle to most', McDonald 'hard to gauge' and 'not physically fit', and leg spinner Arthur Mailey 'not as dangerous as he was some years ago'. Nor was Iredale enamoured of Armstrong: 'While he retains his power of scoring, his fielding is not so good, and his bowling especially in representative matches does not cause the anxiety to batsmen it used to.' Armstrong might not have disagreed. When the new governor-general Lord Forster arrived in spring, he indulged his fondness for cricket by entertaining several favourite players: Armstrong was a guest in Melbourne, with Trumble, Worrall, Ransford, Billy Bruce and John Blackham. Worrall heard Armstrong admit that Australia was 'not as strong as we might be in Test talent', and of himself 'that he had lost part of his bowling, the ball coming more slowly off the pitch than a few years ago'.

Then there were Australian cricket's masters to deal with. Though relations between administrators and players were no longer a tinderbox, Armstrong's incendiary past had not been forgotten. The first shot across Armstrong's bows came at the Victorian Cricket Association's annual meeting on 13 September 1920, when it rejected his nomination as a state selector. 'In the opinion of officials' he was, on the basis of his job at Melbourne, a professional—a harsh judgment considering that he was not receiving professional fees from the association. When the board met in Sydney eleven days later to elect Australia's captain, proceedings were more opaque; indeed, one suspects deliberate obfuscation. An inauspicious thirteen were present at the meeting, but according to historian Johnnie Moyes, at the time a VCA delegate, it turned out to be lucky for Armstrong: in *Australian Cricket*, Moyes says that Armstrong was elected only on the odd vote.

Of this we cannot be sure. The meeting's minutes state merely that 'it was resolved that the Captain of the Australian Team be elected only for the first Test match', and that 'Mr Armstrong was elected' after his nomination and that of Herbie Collins. But, given that board minutes were usually scrupulous in documenting who moved and seconded what, the imprecision is suspicious. The scenario Moyes describes was perfectly possible: with the inclusion of a West Australian representative on the Board, Harry Gregory MHR, the old McElhone gerrymander no longer functioned. The narrowness of the decision, too, appears to have been no secret. It was specifically referred to, for instance, in a letter to the *Age* three months later by a correspondent signing himself 'Disgusted': 'It is well known that two of the Victorian representatives on the Board of Control fought tooth and nail to prevent Armstrong's selection as Australian captain. They were defeated by one vote, it is said, because the South Australian, West Australian, and Tasmanian delegates were prepared to forget past squabbles.' Writing six years later, Joe Darling went further, insisting that 'everyone knows how Bean & Co tried to drive him [Armstrong] out of the game', and claiming that Armstrong scraped into office on the vote of the Tasmanian Cricket Association's secretary Clyde Smith.

What is beyond doubt is that the board—quite against previous policy—appointed Armstrong only for one Test. The feeling that he was captain *pro tempore* would have been deepened by the composition of the selection panel chosen at the same meeting: South Australia's captain Algy Gehrs, New South Wales' captain Collins and none other than Ernie Bean. The outcome was, the *Age* noted, that Warwick Armstrong had no say in his team's selection, while Collins, appointed his vice-captain, did:

> He is captain of the Australian XI, but he must take no part in the selection of the team. He must do as he is told. That is characteristic of Victoria's attitude towards its cricketers. Armstrong has not even a word to say in the selection of the Victorian team...It is said that because Armstrong is a paid official of a cricket club, he cannot hold any office in the association. Evidently this rule was introduced to clip the wings of the professional cricketer, but Armstrong is not a professional cricketer.

It was a bad start to any reign as captain, and worse followed. Armstrong contracted what was feared at first to be the malign Spanish influenza, but proved to be whooping cough—usually a complaint of children, and possibly contracted from his infant son. The timing could not have been less opportune. Armstrong determined to play

Melbourne's first game against Essendon on 16 October, but despite taking 5–56 was clearly labouring and spoke of 'going to the country for a couple of weeks'. He was still suffering during the season's opening Sheffield Shield match in Adelaide: after two days, he was too exhausted to continue, and prescribed bedrest by a doctor. When the English team reached Melbourne on 9 November 1920 ahead of its fixture with Victoria, Armstrong sent apologies for not being among the welcoming 2000—he had gone for a week's rest cure at the Hermitage, near Healesville, about 70 kilometres from Melbourne.

The Hermitage, a collection of chalets and crow's nests among giant gums and lily ponds 100 metres below the summit of Black's Spur, was a popular destination for nature lovers. 'Its neighbourhood is a paradise for the angler and to the scientist,' wrote a visitor. 'For the poet and the artist, it furnishes an endless diet of subjects for inspiration and study.' But it was no place for a restless cricketer, who now had but a single first-class match at the MCG to ratify his primacy. Returning to town, Armstrong roped ground staff bowlers Charlie Over and Herbert Fry into lengthy practices. It did the trick. Against South Australia on 26 November, he produced a performance of such vastness and willpower that all doubts were dispelled.

For his first trick, Armstrong bludgeoned an unbeaten 157 out of 204 runs scored while he was at the wicket for two and three-quarter hours. 'Onlooker' of the *Referee* applauded him as 'a colossus with his six feet and more of height and his immense stature, his bat held like a feather', and compared him to 'some great sturdy oak'. The *Argus*'s 'Old Boy', having watched Armstrong man and boy, thought he had never been greater:

> Armstrong had come down from the ranges a good deal improved in health but still far from fit. Yet he made others who are not by any means neophytes look cheap and unfinished by contrast, and his 157 was another one of those efforts which vividly marks the difference between the master and the prentice hand.

Nor was Armstrong finished. In the second innings, he pushed on unmolested to 245 in five hours and twenty minutes. This time only thirteen boundaries were launched from his bat; belying his forty-one years and 130 kilograms, he ran 78 singles, 35 doubles and 15 trebles. Not that, 'Old Boy' noted, he ever appeared impatient. Armstrong took no liberties with the brilliant AIF man Pellew at cover: 'Whenever the ball went near him, he held up a warning hand as though to say "don't—they've a policemen there".' Nor did confidence stir him to extravagance: 'An old international cricketer watching said: "I'd like to see him go mad now, for just about five minutes." So would many others. But Armstrong is not that sort of batsman.' Nor would he prove that sort of Australian captain.

20

'The Big Ship'

Three significant artefacts on display celebrate Warwick Armstrong in the Australian Cricket Hall of Fame, to which he was elected in January 2000. The Crockett bat we have already mentioned; the other two beggar belief. One is a pair of boots, white kid leather with iron spikes, possibly of the 'Warwick Armstrong' brand, marketed by W. Abbott & Sons of London's Ludgate Hill. Thirty-two centimetres long, and eighteen centimetres wide, they resemble small canoes, or the footwear that anchors divers to the sea bed. The other is the shirt, perhaps the most famous of its kind anywhere. It is not of flannel but of wool, probably designed for the northern hemisphere, and measuring ninety-six centimetres by eighty-five centimetres would hang on most people like a smock. Fitted today on a large tailor's dummy, it seldom fails to arrest passers-by: how, one wonders, can a man so mountainous ever have played cricket?

This is a reflex response, of course, conditioned not only by what we feel cricketers should look like, but what people should. The parameters of what we now define as 'fit', indeed, are extremely narrow. We regard the tapered shapes of our Olympic athletes and swimmers as the embodiment of health and grace—yet, strung to their pitch of perfection, how frequently are they laid waste by the slightest cold or virus.

Maybe Warwick Armstrong was not 'fit' as we understand it. He smoked, he drank, he carried at his top weight 140 kilograms and probably would have puffed if asked to run a hundred yards. Yet, studying his achievements over the next year in first-class cricket alone, our preconceptions are challenged. He would bat fifty-two times, scoring 2282 runs at an average of almost 56. He would bowl 5420 deliveries, claiming 117 wickets at a cost of 15.47 runs each. For the purposes of comparison, consider that, in Test, first-class and one-day cricket during the year from October 1999, Steve Waugh batted forty-two times, and Shane Warne bowled 4572 deliveries. Armstrong, in other words, did more than both put together—going on forty-two, what is more, and despite two recurrences of malaria. The comparison is inevitably far from perfect, but the arenas on which they played are of equivalent size, and pitches have always measured twenty-two yards. Armstrong was, then, 'fit', in its original sense: preternaturally strong and durable, he was 'fit' to do what he had to.

In this respect, Armstrong's weight is immaterial: it curbed his effectiveness not a jot. A newsreel of him batting and bowling in all his vastness against Surrey at the Oval in June 1921 is surprisingly impressive: although his crouching stance is ungainly, the few strokes featured are fluent and wristy, and the leg-break action could barely be improved on. Yet precisely because Armstrong's bulk has become eighty years later almost the only reference point to him that we retain, it invites our consideration. Before charting the events of 1920–21, let us contemplate what it meant to be Warwick Armstrong.

In his *Never Satisfied: A Cultural History of Diets, Fantasies and Fat*, American writer Hillel Schwartz contends: 'Between 1880 and 1920 gluttony would be bound to fatness, fatness to inefficiency, inefficiency to lack of energy and loss of balance, and imbalance to overweight.' When sixty-two-year-old Teddy Roosevelt died in 1919, for example, *Physical Culture* magazine asked openly: 'Did Mr Roosevelt's extra weight in any way lessen the length of his life?'

Yet Armstrong's postwar eminence was not in spite of his bulk, but in large part based on it. 'Armstrong's very immensity as a cricketer and as a personality,' felt the *Age*, 'makes him extremely popular with the whole cricketing public.' This suggests either that the kind of moral judgments about weight that Hillel Schwartz describes were not being made in

Australia and England, or that Armstrong's postwar appeal was based on something else, that as a growing point in a shrinking world he bucked the trend. Because settling flesh in no way compromised his effectiveness, perhaps, he became a glorious exception to the new rules. 'He is living proof of the truth,' asserted E. H. D. Sewell in the *Captain,* 'that size does not matter so long as the individual concerned is active.' In the hundreds of thousands of words written about Armstrong's cricket, it is surely of significance that he was never referred to as 'fat'—wherever size is at issue, he is always 'big'. He evoked another age, and another champion, still fresh in memory; as Englishman Edmund Blunden put it in *Cricket Country*: 'If I were to write a dictionary of cricket, I would enter in the index: Armstrong, W. W., see Grace, W. G., and Grace, W. G., see Armstrong, W. W.' Frank Iredale, who had played against both Armstrong and Grace, saw similarity even in their mannerisms:

> He does a lot of things that WG used to do, for instance, when he looks like missing the ball in the field, he grabs it at the last moment, and seems to say: 'I know it will surprise you.' He has got the old man's happy knack of picking out the vacant spots in the field, and also that irritating habit of turning the ball out of his wicket just when a bowler thinks he has got him…He is the last link with those great men that kept the flag flying prior to 1902.

Armstrong's unbeaten 162 against South Australia in January 1919 was a vital validation, both for himself and onlookers. Those who might have harboured doubts about a cricketer of such tonnage rushed to praise and explain. 'He gets himself into rare physical condition,' wrote Jack Worrall in the *Australasian*, 'and can bat and bowl all day, irrespective of how fierce the sun's rays may be. It seems safe to prophesy that he has many years of usefulness yet to his credit.' 'Short Stop' of the *Leader* thought that he had imbibed of 'the elixir of perpetual youth':

> Warwick Armstrong shows no diminution of his magnificent powers and for a man of his colossal physique is wonderfully active. The secret of his condition is that he regularly exercises all through the winter by indulging in boxing and football on the Melbourne ground. He is of the build for a 'white hope' and would match any of the big Americans such as Willard and Fulton in size if not in science.

The press now relished writing about Armstrong. Having found his cricket hard to describe before the war, journalists found his displacement a far richer source of inspiration, especially in England. The *Observer*'s Harry Altham saw him historically: 'In bulk greater than any cricketer since Alfred Mynn, the captain is today as great a batsman as he ever was, possibly in a real crisis the greatest in the world.' The *Daily Mail*'s Herbert Henley saw him whimsically: 'Anyone meeting Armstrong in the street might imagine him a retired merchant with a rooted objection to exercise of any form and a taste for cigars and good living.' Most famous is Edmund Blunden's word picture in *Cricket Country*: 'He made a bat look like a teaspoon, and the bowling weak tea; he turned it about idly, jovially, musingly. Still he had but to wield a bat—a little wristwork—and the field paced after the ball in vain. It was almost too easy.' Perhaps even better were the lambent lines of Neville Cardus, a brilliant young wordsmith recently baptised 'Cricketer' in the *Manchester Guardian*:

> Armstrong—how well the name befits his composition!…He is elemental, of the soil, the sun and wind—no product of the academies. Nature has by herself fashioned him—he has grown on the cricket field, like the grass. Someone has called him a cricketing Falstaff. The simile will not do. There is no kind of alacrity about Armstrong, no apprehensiveness, nothing 'forgetive'. His composition is of the humours, shrewd instincts and most likeable flesh…Australian cricket is incarnate in him when he walks from the pavilion, bat in hand. Consider the huge man's bulk as, crouching a little, he faces the bowler. He is all vigilance, suspicion and determination. The bat in his hand is like a hammer in the grip of a Vulcan.

There is some powerful imagery here: boxers, businessmen, characters from fact and fiction, even Roman gods. Yet the metaphors that clung were maritime: it appears to have been shortly after the coming of peace that Armstrong collected a nickname to accompany him the remainder of his career.

For some years before the war, both 'Felix' and 'Short Stop' had enjoyed describing Armstrong as the 'Leviathan of Cricket', a popular appellation of the period for anything large. Melbourne's biggest department store, at the corner of Swanston and Bourke streets, was The Leviathan Pty Ltd; Melbourne's biggest racehorse owner, Sol Green, was known as 'the Leviathan of Australia'; and the company for which Armstrong would later work, Distillers Company Ltd, was described as 'the Torpichen Street Leviathan', after its Edinburgh address.

During the war, another Leviathan then hove into view: the world's largest ocean liner. More than 300 metres long, displacing 55,000 tonnes, and capable of holding 3300 passengers, she was originally the Hamburg American Line's *Vaterland*. Interned in New York after her maiden voyage and redeployed as the troopship *Leviathan*, she then returned to the Atlantic service under that name as part of the United States Line: thousands greeted her when first she visited Southampton. This may explain why, too much of a mouthful for laymen, the 'Leviathan of Cricket' appears to have been simplified as 'the Big Ship'. The nickname was certainly in use by the aforementioned match against South Australia, for Victor Richardson recalled it tripping from Bill Whitty's lips when Armstrong was dismissed in the second innings:

> Bill Whitty was in great glee. He rolled over and over on the grass in his delight. I can still see him. As Armstrong lumbered from the wickets—and 'lumbered' described it best—Bill called after him: 'And the "Big Ship" sailed safely home again.' He lay there laughing until I thought he would swallow his tongue. It was the first time I had heard Armstrong called the 'Big Ship'. I thought how appropriate it was... 'Big Ship' he looked as he made his way home that afternoon.

Appropriate indeed. Before the war, the great Atlantic liners had been symbols of national pride and accomplishment; after the war, they would be fungible currency in the settlement of Germany's war debts. Australia, of course, had no such nautical expression of itself, but it did have in Armstrong the largest cricketer afloat. The epithet does not seem to have been used in print until December 1920, when Leslie Poidevin profiled Armstrong in the *Sydney Morning Herald*: 'He is, in fact, the "big ship" of our cricket today—in physique, in performance and in possibilities.' But variations on the theme soon proliferated. When Armstrong almost fell over while trying to field a ball at Adelaide Oval in January 1921, Charlie Turner of Sydney's *Sun* reported an onlooker's interjection: 'The wreck of the *Armstrong*!'

'Big ship' after the war, moreover, was a potent political phrase. The huge dreadnoughts in which Britain and Germany had invested before the war had proven ineffectual; they seemed set to be among the first casualties of the peace. This caused alarm among Australians, conscious of Alfred Deakin's warning that 'but for the British Navy there would be no Australia', about who would secure the Pacific. They looked to Britain, but found little encouragement. 'From the British viewpoint, the end of German seapower has fundamentally altered strategy,' lectured the press baron Lord Rothermere. 'Australia believes the Pacific may be the next storm centre and she is particularly concerned about what to us are far off waters. If Australia wants big ships, she may be prepared to pay for them.'

Scaling down military expenditure, however, Australia could not even afford to run the tiny existing fleet it had begun building in 1907. One casualty of peace was its flagship HMAS *Australia*, turned into a training ship; another was its senior officer Commodore John Dumaresq, who resigned in December 1920. 'The flagship is gone,' commented the *Argus*. 'It seems that the flag is likely to follow.' There was a need for new ships, new commanders. And Armstrong, it happened, could fill both roles.

Not everyone overlooked Armstrong's corpulence. He was built for bar-rackers' sport. Ray Robinson, just old enough to have seen Armstrong as Australian captain, recalled him being 'subjected to barracking as heavy as his own tread'. In *On Top Down Under*, Robinson wrote: 'If he failed to reach an edged ball, they would yell, "You big jellyfish" and coarser terms of endearment.'

Australian spectators have always induced strong reactions; those of Armstrong's career were no exception. England's Drewy Stoddart had deplored 'the evil of barracking' after his tour of 1897–98 as 'no good to man or beast'; South Africa's Percy Sherwell had opined after his 1910–11 visit that 'to play without the accompaniment of cheers and groans and advice gratuitous would be to eat an egg without salt'. English leg-spinner Cec Parkin found fielding before a packed Australian house eighty years ago an experience like no other:

> A crowd of fifty thousand sits in the terrific sunshine. To see a Test match, Australians have been known to travel a thousand miles. Work is suspended in the afternoons, and a contrast with the packed ground is the quietness of everywhere just outside. Sometimes when the heat is unbearable, you will see thousands of spectators sitting in shirtsleeves, even without their waistcoats. Boys go round the field all day long selling ices and iced drinks and there is a great demand for 'tonsil varnish'. If you make a mistake, you have to go through it. I remember during the First Test match I somehow got fielding in the long-field. The crowd just behind me kept shouting: 'What's your name, cocky? Who said you could play cricket? It's a rumour.'

In the forthcoming series, in fact, there would be occasions where the visitors felt as though violence might break out, which Patsy Hendren recalled his teammate Harry Makepeace responding to directly:

> When E. R. Wilson was approaching the pavilion at the end of his innings it seemed likely there would be a real demonstration. So Harry Makepeace sidled down near the gate and, when a spectator rose up as though to strike the Yorkshireman as he came in, Harry stood up, looked very fierce, and the spectator decided that discretion was the better part of valour.

In defending local mores, apologists for Australian crowds viewed it as significant that they were prepared to chaff their country's elephantine captain. After the Second Test, Melbourne's *Truth* spoke out on locals' behalf: 'Perhaps the most predominant notes in Australian barracking are cheerfulness and impartiality…How often during the two Test matches when Armstrong happened to misfield a ball was he told to "get work", yet Armstrong is the idol of the crowd.'

Armstrong himself did not see it the same way. Though he was a spectators' favourite, there were times when crowds vexed him sore. 'The effect on young players is sometimes disastrous,' he said. 'We do not mind barracking but too often it is personal—disgustingly personal.' On at least one occasion, a match for Melbourne against South Melbourne in December 1919, he was irked enough to complain. Melbourne's secretary Hugh Trumble wrote to South Melbourne's committee in high dudgeon: 'It has been reported by the captain and other members of our team that the behaviour of a certain section of the onlookers…was very bad indeed. Most objectionable language was made use of to some of our players.' He advocated empowering police 'to have such people ejected from the ground when conditions warrant'.

The irony is that the same bulk that made Armstrong barrackers' bait was also his best defence. His feelings as a skinny youth might have been injured by the imprecations of St Kilda supporters, but nobody intimidates a man of 190 centimetres and 140 kilograms. Armstrong had taken a leaf from Noble's book—his advice to cricketers about the barracker was to 'betray no sign that you even know he is there'—and his very size made barracking seem mere noise: as effectual, in English writer Alan Gibson's phrase, as 'a peashooter on the Great Pyramid'. If anything, the larger Armstrong grew, the more wilful he became in the face of spectators' interjections. Having refused to bowl at Trent Bridge in May 1905 while the crowd was in uproar, he actually sat down on the pitch at Old

Trafford in July 1921 while awaiting the subsidence of jeering. Jack Fingleton recalled a flavoursome vignette from a Sheffield Shield match, when Armstrong retrieved a ball from the fine leg boundary:

> The big fellow ambled out after it, recovered the ball, and was raising his arm to return the ball when a spectator at his back shouted: 'Come on Armstrong! Throw it in!' Armstrong at once dropped his arm, walked slowly back to his position in the slips, then softly lobbed the ball back to the bowler.

In a thorough survey of opinion on barracking by the *Herald* during Victoria's MCG match with New South Wales at Christmas 1921, Edgar Mayne claimed that several visiting players had confided their reluctance to play again before such uncouth demonstrations: 'Is it British fair play for mobs to get on to one man?' Armstrong, the newspaper reported, was more defiant: 'Mr Warwick Armstrong thinks that he gets most of the barracking while he is on the field. "Perhaps they do it," he said, "because they know it has no effect on me."'

What did it mean for Armstrong, in a physical sense, to be such a huge man? If many distinctions between the obese and the non-obese today are made through the eye of the (non-obese) beholder, the overweight do lead different lives to those of normal weight. Obesity is recognised today as a health risk, being associated with coronary heart disease, high blood pressure, diabetes and osteoarthritis. This is not actually the full story. Research by Cornell University's Paul Ernsberger has also demonstrated that the overweight actually enjoy some blessings, being less prone to infectious diseases, chronic obstructive pulmonary complaints, osteopeorosis, scoleosis and even suicide. Nonetheless, playing sport while overweight must for Armstrong have entailed considerable willpower. You can approximate his experience by a simple experiment: if you weigh 70 kilograms, try piggybacking a person of the same weight. Hefting 140 kilograms on a daily basis, let alone in the context of a cricket match, requires enormous effort; profiling Armstrong for the *Captain*, Laurie Tayler revealed that 'in his native land he [Armstrong] perspires so much that a pool is often formed at the crease which seriously interferes with the bowling on the wicket'. The quotidian strain on legs and feet alone would have been enormous.

Armstrong in fact had many problems with his legs after the war, and

'A body possessing grievances': Billy McElhone of New South Wales (above left) and Colonel Justin Foxton of Queensland (above right) engineered the reorganisation of Australian cricket that placed the Board of Control at the heart of its affairs. When Warwick Armstrong and five teammates held out against them, they were exiled from the Australian team. Armstrong also had implacable enemies in the Victorian Cricket Association, including Ernie Bean, Donald Mackinnon and Harry Rush (third, fourth and fifth from left in front row), against whom he would be pitted for another decade.

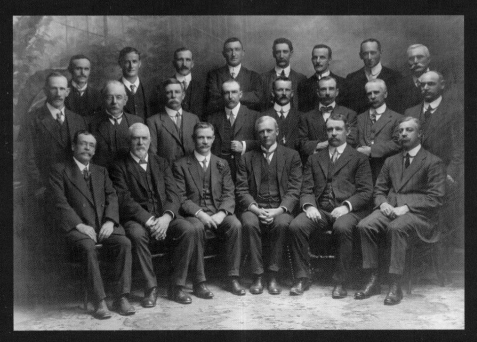

'Even a worm will turn—why not a giant?': sacked then reinstated as Victoria's captain in January 1914, Warwick Armstrong resigned when selectors refused to guarantee his tenure for the rest of the season. He looked on from the stands during the game against New South Wales with his father (above). Yet he had staunch support from teammates like young fast-bowler Ted McDonald, and friends like Melbourne businessman William Sweeney (right).

E. McDONALD, W. SWEENEY, L. KEATING (Victoria's 12th man).

'There is no sounder player in the state': in the team photo of the Australian XI that met England at Brisbane in December 1920, Dr Claude Tozer sat placidly behind his unmistakable captain. A fortnight later he was dead, shot by an estranged lover during the First Test: the Australians won their first game under Armstrong's captaincy wearing black armbands in his honour.

'The right temperament for all occasions': Warwick Armstrong led Australia to England in 1921 with a 130-kilogram air of authority. Laying a wreath at London's Cenotaph on Anzac Day (above), he towered over his grey-haired manager Syd Smith next to him, physically and figuratively. Leading Australia out for the tour's first match five days later (below), he seemed to be captaining a team of boys.

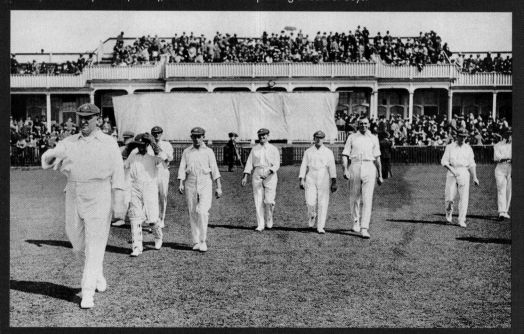

'The popular Australian': English hero-worship took many forms on the 1921 Ashes tour. Armstrong paid his respects to the Prince of Wales at Bristol (above) and King George V at Lord's (below), and was the embodiment of charm with children. Administrators, opponents and even teammates saw a different side to him.

not only as a result of the weight they bore. Now such a big target, and in an age when thigh guards were not *de rigueur*, he suffered ceaselessly from incapacitating bruises. As we shall see, one severe set of knocks precipitated perhaps the gravest controversy of his career, and Armstrong's dressing-room complaints of discomfort were whimsically recalled in the team song of the 1921 Australian side (written by Arthur Mailey to the tune of 'Mademoiselle from Armentieres'):

Of men the cricketing world has known
Parlez-vous
There's one whose record can hold its own
Parlez-vous
And Warwick Armstrong may fluke a score
Although his leg is terribly sore
Inky pinky parlez-vous

Bruising is, of course, an occupational hazard of cricket, but Armstrong's sufferings possibly had another cause. Descriptions of his injuries are consistent with purpura, a rash caused by many tiny bleeds into the skin, which may in his case have been a complication of malaria. Quinine, which Armstrong used regularly, is a fast and short-acting drug, with a number of dangerous side-effects, including ringing in the ears. Another, pervasive in long-term users and in Armstrong's time little understood, is a low platelet count, platelets being the tiny blood cells responsible for clotting. It is possible that sustained use of quinine, while ameliorating Armstrong's malaria, also impaired his ability to recover from injury. This would explain why, when Armstrong fell ill *en route* to South Africa in October 1921, newspaper reports spoke both of a recurrence of malaria and a leg injury.

The psychobiology of the overweight, meanwhile, is a field of research in itself. John Dryden's dictum that 'our minds are constantly wrought on by the temperaments of our bodies' has been investigated in hundreds of scientific studies devoted to how increasing weight affects behaviour. In most ways, of course, all are brothers and sisters under the adipose. As Anne Scott Beller explains in her cultural history of obesity, *Fat and Thin*: 'First in answer to the question implicit in many of these studies as to how crazy the obese actually are, the only fair answer is not very, and if anything perhaps on the whole a little less crazy than the population at large.' But there are divergences. It seems, for instance that, while slower to respond to a single uncomplicated stimulus, the overweight are significantly quicker absorbing complex stimuli like lists than those weighing less. Beller also describes an aspect of the overweight resonant in Warwick Armstrong's case: the heavier the person, the more 'perseverative' their behaviour:

> This means that once they have committed themselves to a given activity, no matter how dull or intrinsically unrewarding that activity may be, fat people will tend to persevere at it more doggedly and for significantly longer periods of time than controls…In the classical layman's view of the characterology of the obese, the happy fat man is an imperturbable fellow, pacific and hard to arouse except when there is food on the table. The image of the phlegmatic fat man may have firm roots in the unedited phenomenology of everyday life, but it has a corollary that has received much less attention, to wit that once aroused, the originally unexcitable fat person may be more difficult to 'turn off' than his more easily excited brothers and sisters.

As an identikit of Armstrong's nature—slow to rouse but undeviating when moved—this does not seem inexact. It may be that Armstrong's notorious obstinacy was more deeply engrained than anyone suspected.

Perhaps the most striking aspect of Armstrong's postwar dimensions is an effect evident in group photographs featuring him. His is the face and physique on which the eye naturally alights; even surrounded by teammates, the 'Big Ship' possesses a unmistakeable magnetism. In the context of Armstrong's time, this identifiability is noteworthy. Even today it requires practice for a cricket spectator to distinguish between sundry whiteclad figures. In an era when photography remained primitive and news was vested in word rather than image, it was still more difficult.

There were some interesting manifestations of this during the summer of 1920–21. On 10 December 1920, one Henry Beasley was convicted by a Brisbane court on a charge of fraudulently obtaining goods. He had been passing himself off as England's Harry Makepeace, cadging gifts from the gullible—apparently with considerable success, as he was sentenced to six months hard labour. Clearly, few Queenslanders at the time had any idea what Makepeace looked like. There was also a delightful episode when the Australian team was crossing the continent four months later to catch the *Osterley* in Fremantle *en route* to England. Their train stopped at Quorn in South Australia where the crowd, while listening to a speech from the manager, suddenly issued a cry for dynamic

Jack Gregory. But when a deputation boarding the train in search of him was immediately confronted by Gregory himself, nobody recognised him. No limelighter, Gregory confided that the object of their search had slipped off the other side of the carriage, sending his disciples off in comic pursuit.

It was sometimes complained after the war—the Golden Age already taking on mythic qualities—that cricketers were more homogenous, lacking their former individuality. In 1922's *Cricket and Cricketers*, Philip Trevor complained that not once between 1897 and 1914 had he ever needed a scorecard to identify a batsman; now all were alike. But never at any stage in Armstrong's career was there risk of his misidentification, and postwar pictures of him scarcely needed captioning. The 12 February 1921 edition of *Pals*—'the Australian Paper for Australian Boys'—featured Armstrong on the cover beneath his Melbourne cap. That was all it featured, too: there was no name, no identification on the inside cover, not even an article in the magazine concerning him. He was simply, totemically, there. Even in Scotland, when Australia visited four months later, the *Watchman* stressed that introduction was needless:

> Armstrong is so big that he will be easily identified. Six feet in lineal measurement and 20 stones in bulk is not easily lost sight of...Big, jovial, good-tempered, but shrewd and obstinate (if necessary), Armstrong is a butt for those who like fun. To see him bend to pick up the ball—a mountain in labour—the mob chortles and 'Armstrong' smiles. Not a bit does he mind being chaffed. Armstrong does not mind anything so long as his side keeps winning.

In November 1920, that winning streak was still to begin, although its hapless victims had arrived—the English team led by Johnny Douglas. The auguries were all against them. A typhoid sufferer having boarded the *Osterley* in Naples, they were immediately quarantined at Fremantle, bunking in army huts at Goodman's Point for a week. Fishing, swimming and playing football amongst themselves was scarcely ideal preparation; Jack Hobbs felt the interlude 'a trifle "red-tapish"'.

Hobbs was among four players who had previously toured Australia. Others found conditions overpowering: the brightness of the light, the hardness of the grounds, the noise and irreverence of the crowds. Injuries and illness then began mounting; Parkin suffered a boil on the neck, paceman John Hitch strained leg muscles, and Jack Hearne succumbed to lumbago. Douglas maintained a superb outward demeanour—perhaps partly because he was accompanied by his wife and parents—but must at times have felt the strain acutely.

Who would meet the Englishmen was surrounded in mystery. On 8 December, the three selectors disappeared to decide the Australian team's make-up, their whereabouts secret even from board secretary Syd Smith who knew only to expect a 4.30 p.m. telephone call. When it came, he reeled off the XII to the pressmen around him: eight New South Welshmen, three Victorians and a South Australian, half of them members of the AIF XI in the persons of Collins, Kellaway, Taylor, Gregory, Pellew and Oldfield.

None surely have greeted Test selection with dismay, yet what ecstasies there must have been for this half of the team. Three years earlier, Bert Oldfield had been a shell-shock victim, narrowly spared by an artillery explosion. Now, having as a boy slept beneath a picture of Jim Kelly, he was Australia's first-choice keeper:

> We were at our evening meal when Charlie Kellaway…called and told the good news. My mother, whose face was wreathed in smiles, rushed back into the dining room and the members of the family wondered what it was all about. After a while she came over and kissed me and loudly whispered: 'How wonderful, Bertie, you've been picked for the First Test!' I was so excited I could not finish my meal…I saw myself wearing the much-coveted green cap bearing the Australian coat of arms and walking out onto the field in the select company of such celebrities as Noble, Armstrong, Macartney, Kellaway, Bardsley, Cotter, Ransford and others whose skill had won for them international fame.

Interestingly, Oldfield's fantasy involved a tradition rather than a specific team, encompassing Noble, Golden Age glass of fashion, and Cotter, fallen warrior: almost nine years without a Test in Australia had little weakened his sense of historical continuity. Yet in other senses it was a decidedly new age. Despite the presences of Macartney, Kellaway and Bardsley, Armstrong's forty Tests represented almost half the team's accumulated Test experience; he was an old character in a new play, like the Falstaff of *Henry IV* reappearing in *The Merry Wives of Windsor*. The members of Armstrong's team had played only under the board's jurisdiction, which must have seemed to them the natural state of affairs. But their captain, raised in different times, bred with different habits, was accustomed to giving orders rather than obeying them.

21

'I'll Show Them'

Australians had often fantasised during the war of the resumption of sporting hostilities, but 1920 was not a banner year for their athletes. The *Sun*'s Claude Corbett described it as 'close to disastrous to the prestige of Australian sport in many respects', enumerating the loss of the Davis Cup, failure at the Antwerp Olympics to win a single event, and successes in Australia of English sculler Ernest Barry and American swimmer Norman Ross.

Cricket was a different matter. Mood was buoyant. 'Time was when England taught us the game,' declared Sydney's *Telegraph*. 'Today the lion's whelp is a full-grown lion himself and a troublesome one at that. Bonds sealed with the blood of battlefields have made us close friends, but nonetheless close contestants in the realm of sport.' For the First Test, both the *Telegraph* and *Melbourne Punch* ran contests where entrants were asked to guess the winner and the correct margin of victory: the former alone received 40,000 entries, 25,000 backing the hosts, 15,000 their guests.

Newspapers were replete with reports manifesting 'Test match fever': a clergyman on the south coast of New South Wales who ended his sermon with 'here endeth the first innings'; a costumed cricket match between The Stage and The Jockeys at Sydney's Hampden Park; workers idling during a lengthy waterside strike immersing themselves in a spontaneous match on Sydney's Lime Street. Businesses also hurried to associate themselves with the craze. Two cricketers toasted one another's health in a promotion of Abbots Lager, 'the drink of all true sportsmen'. A batsman executing a cleanly hit drive attested the effectiveness of Pinkettes, a laxative, the figure's vigour being ascribed to 'a healthy stomach, well-regulated bowels, perfect digestive organs'. The First Test itself attracted commercial sponsorship from Sydney liquor distributor M. Moss & Co. Seeking prominence for their Wolfe's Schnapps—'The public appreciate bright cricket as they do a good invigorating stimulant'—the firm offered 2s for every four, £1 for every six, and £5 to the greatest wicket-taker.

Test eve brought Sydney to a standstill. Despite twenty bills awaiting its attention, state parliament convened later than usual to permit members their full day's cricket watching. The press sought both captains for their forecasts before the toss: Armstrong volunteered that he was 'very confident of winning', Douglas that 'I hope to win under equal conditions'. Confidence versus hope. Armstrong then fished out a favourite American silver dollar, and was observed to smile when his rival called incorrectly.

Not everything unfolded to plan. Though Collins made an impressive 70 in two and a half hours, Australia's 267 was anti-climactic. Armstrong himself was strangely dilatory: greeted by a reception to which he 'had to raise his cap repeatedly', he pottered half an hour over 12 before being stumped from Woolley. Yet Armstrong was taking his responsibilities seriously. Gregory, disconsolate to have been caught at the wicket cheaply in his first innings, recalled being reassured:

> I felt that I had made a poor start, and Armstrong evidently felt he had to put me at ease. 'Don't worry about the runs; you are in for your bowling.' It was just the kick I needed and, although I knew my skipper was trying to buck me up, the words of encouragement were not wasted.

Before his team took the field, Armstrong then gathered them in the dressing-room and laid down his few laws: 'I want you to realise you are playing for Australia. I want you to do your best and above all keep an eye on me in the field. I don't want to be clapping my hands to draw your attention and so give our plans away.' This was a custom he had learned from Archie MacLaren, but his first on-field manoeuvre was entirely his own. With Gregory at his disposal, Armstrong surprisingly allotted first over at Charlie Russell to Charles Kellaway, who didn't even take the new ball for his state. 'JFT' of the *Telegraph* wrote:

> Who will bowl? Kellaway! Why the devil doesn't he start with Mailey and Gregory? At that moment, Armstrong was the subject of nasty censure. Whiz! The ball, the first of the innings, speeds to Russell. There is a click and a shattering of stumps. A great batsman has gone for nothing. Armstrong is the most popular man on the ground.

Not merely for its immediate success was this a notable gambit. As we shall see, Armstrong was not a captain of abrupt hunches; he preferred to strangle his opponent slowly. When Gregory got his chance and bowled Hobbs, the captain smiled: 'Any complaints?' Gregory recalled loyally: 'No player could complain at his treatment from Armstrong.' When England lost its last seven wickets for 47, the public also seemed persuaded of Armstrong's credentials. Coming in alone after consulting the groundsman he was 'cheered in a most enthusiastic way', reported Donald Macdonald of the *Argus*. 'He had done things which in a moment seemed to be caprice and which turned out to be captaincy.'

Not everyone was convinced, however, especially in the Sydney press. Since the start of the season, 'Not Out' of the *Referee* had been advocating the claims of Collins, ten years Armstrong's junior, as a more inspirational leader. Now he captiously found fault with Armstrong's field placings: 'No-one wishes Armstrong greater success in the position than I do, but I have not the least glimmer of doubt that Collins is the finest captain among our active first-class cricketers in Australia.' Armstrong, too, was still seeking the eye-catching individual feat that would compel his reappointment for the Second Test. And by now, privately, he had other things on his mind.

At 7.20 that morning, wharf labourer James Rooney had been travelling on the Rose Bay cable tram line. Near the intersection of Mona Road and New South Head Road, he later told police, he had watched a passenger try to board, miss his hold, and be dragged beneath the car. Rooney alerted the conductor, who ordered the driver to stop. They found a figure trapped beneath, unconscious and badly maimed. The civic ambulance conveyed the unconscious victim to Sydney Hospital.

The casualty was fifty-two-year-old John O'Donnell, Armstrong's brother-in-law. He had been intending to attend the day's cricket with other family members. As Australia's openers extended the home team's lead to 123 that evening, Armstrong left the ground to join distressed in-laws at Sydney Hospital where O'Donnell was hovering between life and death, suffering concussion, a fractured left leg and internal injuries.

The evening also contained a test of Armstrong's stomach. He was among fifty-five guests at a vice-regal dinner hosted by Lord Forster at the Hotel Australia, which adjourned to the Sydney Stadium at Rushcutters' Bay for some decidedly male-only entertainment: a feather-weight title bout pitting Victorian Bert Spargo against Frenchman Eugene Criqui. A night at the fights eighty years ago was a rude and ramshackle affair. Sydney Stadium enclosed crowds of up to 16,000 in wooden seats beneath a tin roof, the atmosphere thick with cries of boys selling peanuts, chocolate and gum from wicker baskets. This evening was a classic: Criqui, a legendarily tough and resourceful fighter, finally battered a bloodied Spargo into submission in the sixteenth round.

After such a blood-soaked Saturday, Armstrong did not join the teams on their rest day picnics at Manly and Newport beaches, probably returning to Sydney Hospital where John O'Donnell had recovered consciousness long enough to tell police: 'There is no-one to blame. It was my own fault.' When play resumed on Monday, as Collins completed a watchful hundred on his Test debut in cahoots with Macartney and Bardsley, Armstrong was loath to bat himself, promoting Taylor and Pellew. He loitered instead in the bar.

In *On Top Down Under*, Ray Robinson reports his appearance in a jocular fashion: 'In the second innings Armstrong, padded up, had whisky with his mates at the members' bar.' While the image is one of male bon-homie, it may be that Armstrong needed cheering, and not only because of John O'Donnell's mishap. Collins' hundred would have caused him mixed feelings; much as it strengthened Australia's position, it hardly consolidated his own. There does seem that day to have been a good deal of pavilion talk about Australia's captain, overheard by Frank Iredale of the *Age*, to the effect that 'not only has he lost his dash in batting, but his general movements are not in keeping with the position in which he finds himself today'. So a January 1928 item in the *Australasian's* 'Notes from a Sportsman's Diary', while doubtless embell-ished, seems more indicative of Armstrong's state of mind than Robinson's cheery jotting:

Just before he went in in the second innings, there were further prophecies of his impending failure, and people did not hesitate to pass remarks in his hearing. A friend said to him: 'They have a poor opinion of you, Warwick.' The big man smiled—a trifle wanly it must be admitted—but replied: 'I'll show them. I'm going to make a hundred.'

Taylor having fallen to the last ball of the third day, Armstrong had his chance to 'show them' immediately the fourth began. He seized it. Kellaway, 23 at the day's beginning, was rapidly overhauled, comfortably beaten to a half-century, occasionally almost run off his feet. All Armstrong's experience came to bear. He expertly assessed each fieldsman. Though he'd not previously encountered the brilliant outfielder Patsy Hendren, Armstrong soon figured that his was not an arm to challenge: 'It was amusing to watch the fieldsman walking in to meet the ball, the batsman just as quietly walking a run. Each apparently oblivious to the other, but alert, the batsman for the chance of a second run, the fieldman for the chance of a run out' ('Observer', *Argus*). Others, however, could be taken on: 'They got singles to the off with strokes which the previous day had brought no runs to others. Armstrong for such a big man showed astonishing initiative and pace in this direction' ('Not Out', *Referee*). At one stage, he even called his partner for a fifth to take advantage of a laggardly chase: 'Armstrong, running with the abandon of a two year old, accomplished five sprints between wickets, almost exhausting Kellaway in the process' ('JFT', *Telegraph*). Above all, there was power; when a gap could not be found, Armstrong simply hit through the man, to every quarter of the ground, and from every bowler. Hendren recalled Armstrong's maltreatment of his team's pace attack:

> I have never seen a man treat fast bowling the way the mighty Armstrong treated ours. In these days, fast bowlers carry on, quite confidently, without any man fielding behind the wicket at his end. But it was not so that day in Sydney so far as Warwick Armstrong was concerned. He went for our fast bowlers—John Douglas and Harry Howell—and by sheer strength of wrist drove the fastest and best back over their heads.

Bob Crockett remembered Armstrong's manhandling of England's slow bowlers, thinking that 'even the great Victor Trumper in his heyday had shown us nothing better'. He recalled leg-spinner Jack Hearne pleading with Douglas—'Don't take me off, captain, I think I can get him'—but that 'Armstrong seemed to relish his slows and quilted him quite unmercifully'. Armstrong sailed blithely through the nineties, the force of his blows making up for any imperfections. Mid off retreated rather than advanced on a possible chance when he was 98, Parkin could not hold a red-hot return catch at 99, then a subtle single forward of point raised the captain's hundred in two hours. In the *Sydney Morning Herald*, Leslie Poidevin enjoyed the crowd's interjections:

'Hit him on the head Johnny and be done with it,' came a drowsy but powerful voice. Australia was making it too hot even for the 'hill'. It was too much for Armstrong whose big jovial face rippled with laughter…Armstrong had got well past his century and was well on the road to his second when another despairing voice lifted itself out of the crowd for England's sake: there was only one way to dethrone Armstrong and it was to strike him in the most vulnerable part. Armstrong had unsympathetically ignored the advice to take it upon the head; the jocular suggestion now from the 'hill' was that the attacking bowler should hit him in the abdomen and crumple him up that way. It was not cricket, but one had only to glance at Armstrong's very generous proportions to appreciate the humour of it.

Kellaway succumbed for 78, his contribution 55 to a 187-run partnership in two and a half hours. Armstrong pressed on. 'JFT's' excitement was heightened by thoughts of the schnapps cash being amassed: 'At one stage, he was earning £8000 a year excluding Sunday and working only eight hours a day.' Not until a tired waft at Parkin with his score at 158 was Australia's now firmly established captain done with. Exhausted fieldsmen dragged themselves off. 'I have an impression that their trouble with Armstrong has only begun,' wrote Donald Macdonald of the *Argus,* 'and I have an impression, too, that they have exactly the same impression.'

The week's catalogue of incident, however, was still incomplete. In contrast to his agitation about Armstrong's batting, 'JFT' struck a sober note the following day when he reported the sudden death of New South Wales's talented opening batsman Dr Claude Tozer: 'How he died does not matter. He was dead.' It mattered, though, much indeed.

Nephew of a former Queensland agent-general, Tozer had earned nothing but golden opinions all his life. He was a schoolboy star at Shore, first appeared for New South Wales while still at Sydney University, then won the DSO in World War I. Now in practice at

Roseville, his performances over the two preceding seasons had suggested a Test player in the making. 'I don't suppose that at present there is a sounder player in the state,' wrote Frank Iredale in the *Sun*.

After beginning the season with grade scores of 110, 211 and 131, Tozer had made a brace of half-centuries for an Australian XI in Brisbane under Armstrong's captaincy. But the photograph of that team, in which a youthful Tozer sits behind his captain beneath a broad-brimmed sun hat, is the last image of him alive. After attending the Test's third day, Tozer was asked by one Harold Sutcliffe Mort, a surveyor in the Railway and Tramway Department, to visit his Lindfield home: Mort's wife Dorothy was complaining again of 'nerve trouble'.

Mort was at work when Tozer called in late morning, but his wife's female companion told the *Telegraph*:

> I showed the doctor into Mrs Mort's bedroom where she was lying in her bed. I closed the door and went to another room in the house. A few minutes later I heard a noise which I took to be the sound of shots. I don't know how many. They seemed to come from the drawing room.

She inquired about the disturbance through the drawing room's bolted door, but Dorothy Mort quavered that nothing was wrong. In fact, she had shot the doctor in the head and torso, propped his lifeless body on the couch, tried to shoot herself in the chest, then somehow propped a Colt automatic pistol on her victim's hand before beginning a dazed and disoriented vigil. Not until 7 p.m. was this scene disturbed when, purporting to comply with a request for iced water, the companion forced entrance, discovering her employer 'covered in blood' and 'in a state of collapse'. The *Telegraph*'s report was replete with polite ambiguities:

> They [police] obtained a certain letter from Dr Tozer to Mrs Mort. This, the police state, revealed certain facts in regard to the personal relations that had existed between Dr Tozer and Mrs Mort. There were other letters, too, which aided detectives in arriving at a certain decision as to who had fired the shots.

Tozer and Dorothy Mort had indeed been star-crossed lovers, a relationship the former had chosen to end, precipitating its bloody climax. She would be charged with murder, but judged unfit to stand trial. As the SCG's flags fluttered at half-mast on 22 December, Australian players wore black armbands in Tozer's memory.

The Test wound to a doleful conclusion. Once the captain had removed Hobbs with his trademark 'straight break', only Hendren and Rhodes detained the Australians long, although Armstrong was not expansive after his first Test victory. 'What can I say?' he told journalists, adjusting his tie in front of a dressing-room mirror. 'We won. I am satisfied the better team was successful.' Returning to Melbourne the following afternoon with much of the Australian team—New South Wales and Victoria being due to meet at the MCG on Christmas Eve—he did not savour the 'three cheers for Warwick Armstrong' from well-wishers at the station. 'Armstrong…did not wait for any congratulations,' reported the *Herald*. 'As soon as the train pulled up, he hurried away.' In fact, he had apparently just learned of John O'Donnell's death overnight in Sydney; he withdrew from the first day of the Sheffield Shield match, citing a 'bereavement'. Tozer and O'Donnell were buried in the same cemetery, Waverley, on consecutive days.

At the end of one of the most tumultuous fortnights of his life, nonetheless, Armstrong found himself a hero of greater proportions than ever. A meeting on 29 December at the MCG instituted a testimonial for him, twenty-two notables in Melbourne, Adelaide and Sydney volunteering for its organising committee, from former football star Albert Thurgood to erstwhile teammates Monty Noble and Clem Hill, with the VCA's Donald Mackinnon as chairman. The same day, most importantly, the board extended his tenure as captain for the remaining four Tests. The minutes state for the record this time that the motion of South Australia's Mostyn Evan was 'carried unanimously'.

The Second Test at Melbourne went off with few hitches. As Gregory revealed the full measure of his talents in a two-hour stand of 173 with Pellew followed by 8–101, Armstrong could rest on his laurels a little. He was disappointed at the unlucky Test debut of his Victorian protege Dr Roy Park: summoned the previous evening to attend a prolonged birth, Park suffered the misfortune of being bowled first ball. He was also annoyed that his bowlers could not do more with a rain-damaged pitch. But taking up the cudgels himself, he collected 4–26; good for his country, and good for himself. By the time Australia's victory was secure by an innings and 91 runs, his testimonial fund had swollen to £1500.

On the fourth day of the Third Test at Adelaide Oval, circumstances called for a greater contribution: Australia trailed by 22 with seven second-innings wickets to fall. Armstrong stepped in. Swiftly overtaking the dour Kellaway, he had his half-century by lunch and his century by tea, meting out heavy punishment to England's slow bowlers. 'Goodness only knows what would have happened to Australia if Armstrong had gone over that morning,' wrote Clem Hill in the *Referee*. 'I consider that Armstrong gave the best knock I have ever seen him contribute in my life, and at the present moment he must surely rank as the world's greatest all-round cricketer.' The fourth-wicket partnership of 194 between Kellaway and his captain in three and a half hours might have been the only event occurring in Australia during the day. Thousands assembled outside the *Age* and the *Sydney Morning Herald* to watch scores being updated on improvised boards, cheering each landmark. In a dispatch to London's *Star*, Hobbs conveyed local passions anecdotally:

> In a country centre a wedding ceremony was being performed. Just as the question 'will you etc' was about to be put, a telegraph messenger came in and handed a telegram to the bridegroom. He read it and handed it to the bride, who read it and handed it to the best man, and it went round the whole immediate group. 'Something's happened, the wedding's off,' whispered one of the onlookers. Nervously clutching the paper, the officiating minister said, 'Armstrong 100, Kellaway 80, total 3 for 300-odd!'
>
> 'Too much public attention is given to the Test match!' exclaimed a severe-looking gentleman on a tram car. 'It disorganises everything. We should keep our balance and not allow sport to sway us so much.' Presently a man jumped on the car and remarked, 'Armstrong has got his century.' 'Ah, I thought he would!' said the severe-looking gentleman.

Another resolute Hobbs hundred checked Australia's final thrust, but Armstrong successfully bartered wickets with Mailey's sometimes expensive leg spin. By now, everything seemed to be going the captain's way, his slip catch of Douglas off Gregory being suitably preposterous. 'The ball went to the Australian captain like a bullet and, hitting him in the stomach, stopped dead and rested on his arm,' Oldfield recalled. 'As he passed Armstrong on his way the pavilion, Douglas scowled, tearing off his batting gloves in a spasm of annoyance, but Armstrong apparently remained quite unconcerned.' Six days of record crowds and record totals ended with the Ashes in Australia's possession and salaams at each end of the globe. 'It must always remain a great feat when one of the Dominions defeats the Mother Country,' said *The Times*. 'But if we did not know it before, the war showed us how it is they do it. They are a magnificent fighting stock, these brothers of ours beyond the seas, and they play, as they fought in France and Gallipoli, to win—but to win like gentlemen.' And it was perhaps because Australians were savouring this special moment that Armstrong's next action took them so unawares.

Armstrong's usual terseness could not disguise his underlying pleasure on 20 January 1921: 'I do not think there has ever been a better Test match. It was a hard fight throughout and the result was uncertain until after lunch today.' Leaving Adelaide the following afternoon with the players of Victoria and New South Wales, he even shared a long and apparently not unfriendly dialogue with Ernie Bean on 'cricketing matters'.

Yet Armstrong had paid a price for victory: bruises to his right leg from thigh to ankle inflicted by England's Harry Howell. Among Test comrades, this was probably common knowledge. Not only are dressing-room secrets hard to keep, but it was also material information: the group was transiting through Melbourne to an SCG Sheffield Shield match. During the journey north, too, others seem to have been taken into their captain's confidence. Armstrong had a long talk with Johnnie Moyes—the Essendon delegate to the VCA was in the process of moving to Sydney—while an unnamed state teammate later told the *Age*: 'You ought to see them. Howell made an "Aunt Sally" of him during the Test match at Adelaide and he got many bad knocks.' Victoria's Carl Willis gave the most decorative description: 'Armstrong's legs are like a futurist painting. They are a chaotic welter of clashing colour. Howell proved himself a great artist with the ball.'

The forthcoming game was more than usually prestigious: styled the Centenary Match, it was the one-hundredth meeting between these rivals since intercolonial days. But by the time participants arrived in Sydney on 23 January, it was in the wind that Armstrong was an uncertain starter; the *Referee*'s 'Not Out' commented later that 'it was common talk that some of the Australian XI knew that Warwick Armstrong was not going to play here'. The NSWCA's acting secretary Edwin Tyler subsequently advised the VCA that he had also been 'unofficially informed' to this effect when the teams arrived, but 'refused to believe it as he had just spoken to Armstrong'. The origin of this intelligence is unknown, but it is probable that Armstrong replied non-committally to inquiries because he had not made up his mind.

Although a room had been booked for him at the Grosvenor Hotel, Armstrong stayed in a flat Aileen had rented, and was conspicuously absent from practice the next day. This seems surprising until it is realised that he was not part of the team executive. Bizarrely, in what appears another Bean initiative to limit Armstrong's influence in state cricket, Australia's captain was not among the players deputised to select the final Victorian XI—Mayne, Park and Jack Ryder were to decide the twelfth man. The effect, however, would prove important. Manager Bert O'Brien, University's delegate at the VCA, appears to have been entirely ignorant of Armstrong's condition, and puzzled merely that his calls to the Grosvenor were unanswered.

Armstrong actually spent the day at Coogee for the purposes of taking a hot saltwater bath in the hope of counteracting his condition. He later met Park, who in his professional capacity conducted an examination. The prognosis was discouraging. When they met again in the dressing room at the SCG at 11.10 a.m. the following day, Armstrong recalled, a decision had to be made:

> I opened my bag where the players were dressing. Dr Park was dressing just opposite to me. I went across and asked him if they had picked the team yet. He said 'not yet' and I said 'well my legs are no better than when you saw them last and I think for the benefit of the side it would be better for me to stand out'. I said: 'What do you think about it yourself, Doctor?' He said: 'My advice is you are very foolish if you do play.' I said, on that understanding, I would sooner be out of the team.

When Park fetched Mayne, Armstrong advised that he would be unable to run up to bowl and would find running between wickets difficult. With only twenty minutes remaining before the scheduled start, there was no time for a formal selection meeting: Mayne and Park promptly agreed, without consulting Ryder, that Armstrong should be rested. The decision, however, clearly unsettled the team. A player poll had to be held to elect captain and vice-captain, delaying the toss, and a substitute fielder unearthed. Johnnie Moyes accepting the job. The press, meanwhile, learned of Armstrong's non-involvement when he was accosted by a reporter at about 11.25 a.m. and asked for the twelfth man's name. 'I am,' Armstrong replied. The reporter suspected a jest: 'I want to know for my paper.' Armstrong confirmed: 'That is so. My legs are badly bruised all over. I must give them a spell. They are in a very bad state.'

Without Armstrong, the Victorians crumbled in 42.1 overs. The hosts were only six runs behind with seven wickets in hand at the close. But the press was sympathetic. The *Age* thought him 'tired after the recent strenuous Test match', the *Sydney Morning Herald* that he had 'decided to rest after the strenuous campaign in the southern states'. Nor were there recriminations when he appeared that evening at Sergeant's Cafe to attend a Centenary Match dinner. It was quite a glittering assembly— full of cricketing identities like Noble, Iredale, Syd Gregory and Rowley Pope—but 'the idol of the hour was Mr Armstrong'. His short speech praising Collins was greeted by 'echoing cheers'.

The cricket fraternity saw little of Armstrong for the rest of the week: Melbourne's *Herald* reported him 'resting in Sydney'. Ever conscious of entitlements, he attended the game's last day, 28 January, to claim his expenses from O'Brien, but did not accompany the Victorians on their homeward journey. Rumours spread that he had been seen at Randwick's AJC Anniversary Races, even that he was on a drinking binge—though rumours, and probably pernicious ones, they remained.

Out of sight, Armstrong was never out of mind. In his absence, the VCA's executive committee met twice with O'Brien and Mayne. Statements were taken from both. Disappointed at the six-wicket defeat sustained in Sydney, they held Armstrong partly responsible. O'Brien alleged that 'the players were incensed by the action of Mr Armstrong in not playing', Mayne that 'the incident upset the team and accounted for the bad start'. The executive refrained from recommending specific sanction, but turned the matter over to the three of their number who formed Victoria's selection panel 'for any action they saw fit'.

Bean, McAlister and Ellis convened at 5 p.m. on 1 February. For this trio, so often at loggerheads with Armstrong in the past, his latest action must have seemed the bitter end. Feuds over money, ultimatums over captaincy, his defiance during the 'Big Six' affair—now he had taken them to the brink once more. Yet axing him would be difficult. The *Argus*'s report suggests that the selectors knew precisely what they were doing:

> After a few minutes, Mr Ellis left the committee room and said that the Victorian team had been picked, but Mr Bean when he left the room volunteered no information. When asked 'have you the Victorian team?', he gave out the list of players and walked towards the door. 'What about Armstrong?' he was asked, and replied: 'The selection committee will make a statement. I am going home now and if you ring me up after I have had my dinner then I will make a statement.'

Subsequently Mr Bean was communicated with by telephone, but refused to make any statement. When it was recalled that he had promised to make one he said: 'It is not customary for the selectors to make any statement or to give any reasons.' When asked if Armstrong had been available he said: 'I decline to discuss the matter at present.'

By this stage, Armstrong was *en route* home. He was discovered late in the evening by an enterprising *Sydney Morning Herald* correspondent, in the unlikely setting of a platform at Goulburn in country New South Wales:

Shown the telegram regarding his omission from the Victorian team, Armstrong said: 'I have nothing to say.' Pressed for a statement, Armstrong said: 'I would sooner say nothing about it.' Asked if he had wished to rest for the Fourth Test, Armstrong said he had nothing whatever to do with the omission of his name.

Melbourne was about to go slightly crazy. At Spencer Street station the following morning, surrounded by hundreds of supporters informed of his exile by their newspapers, Armstrong guardedly explained his decision not to play in Sydney as a consequence of the Third Test and desire to save himself for the Fourth: 'Bruises on the right thigh spread down the leg and…if I had played and got another knock I might not have been able to take my part in the Test match.' But he could barely be heard amid the cheers and shouts; the *Herald* reported that not until a telegraph messenger forded the crowd could he thread a way to his car in the yard without. Then:

'Warwick!' With an exclamation of pleasure, a grey-coated young athlete sprang forward and grasped the hand of Armstrong as he took his seat in the car. 'You're surely causing some fun,' he remarked to the veteran. Armstrong smiled—a little warily. A whispered conversation followed. 'It's all one way,' the grey-coated friend assured Armstrong. He was evidently referring to the tide of public opinion. With a look of relief and satisfaction, Armstrong sank back in his seat.

The report suggests that Armstrong was bemused by the reception, and unsurprisingly so. While acclaimed for his cricket feats, never had he been truly a popular hero, like Trumper in Sydney or Hill in Adelaide. Yet now he had been singled out not for something he had done, but because of something done to him—and seldom in the history of popular causes has there been a less likely martyr. But his grey-coated confidant was correct: opinion was 'all one way'. Newspapers were deluged with letters denouncing Armstrong's persecutors, under pseudonyms like 'Sport', 'One Who Pays' and 'Anti-Victimisation', sometimes shaded by world events. 'Even the worst criminal when caught red handed is called before a tribunal and asked to state his case before he is sentenced,' wrote 'Ex-Kaiser Bill'. 'Our Lenin and Trotsky know a better way of meting out justice…Long live bolshevism.'

The press interpreted the affair as continuing the old, old feud. 'It is not necessary to go back to the details of the dispute which culminated in six members of the last Australian XI withdrawing from the team in 1912,' wrote 'Old Boy' in the *Argus*. 'It may be well, however, to recall that, of that six, Warwick Armstrong is now the only cricketer representing Australia in Test matches.' Clem Hill was well credentialled to state in the *Referee*: 'It is the old trouble cropping up again and the sooner the men responsible for it get out of the game, the better it will be for all concerned.'

Battle lines blurred by passing years were suddenly re-established. That evening, nine years after it been a 'Big Six' forum, Melbourne's Athenaeum Hall again resounded with the name Armstrong. Despite only three hours' notice, 400 'lovers of sport' gathered at 8 p.m. to execrate 'the treatment meted out to Australia's greatest cricketer Mr W. Armstrong, who has been omitted from the Victorian XI without even an opportunity to make an explanation'. Henry Westley, a prominent Queen Street barrister and Melbourne Cricket Club member, accused the VCA of 'the most dastardly outrage ever committed in the history of cricket'.

22

'You Will Never Be Forgiven!'

What exactly was this dispute about? The answer is not straightforward. As in December 1907 when the VCA had proposed banning Warwick Armstrong for disobeying an ordinance of which he was unaware, so now it had punished him for an infraction it declined to define.

What Armstrong's crime would boil down to was not withdrawal from the Centenary Match *per se*, but withdrawal without informing team manager Bert O'Brien. Here there were resonances with the 'Big Six' affair. Armstrong and his association represented antagonistic models of the management of Australian cricket. He stood for the foundation system, in which players had pleased themselves; by his lights, he had fulfilled his obligations in Sydney by speaking to teammates Park and Mayne. The VCA represented that system's replacement, in which administrators held the ring; to them, O'Brien had been the deputed authority, which Armstrong had failed to recognise.

Unlike the 'Big Six' dispute, however, this was not an argument to assert the combatants' principles. That fight had been won and lost. Armstrong wasn't crusading to restore the old order, nor were Bean, McAlister and Ellis campaigning to establish firm government. The political had become the personal—the fight for control of Australian cricket had become the fight for control of Warwick Armstrong. It is also probable that this agenda had a specific objective, one noted at the time by the *Age*:

> It has been obvious throughout the current cricket season that a section of the Australian cricket authorities has done its best to harass the Australian captain in every possible way. As illustrations of this one need only point to the action of the Board of Control in appointing Armstrong originally to be captain of the Australian team for the first Test match only…and also to the withholding of his selection as captain of the Australian team due to leave for England in March next. The 'powers that be' have also refused, for reasons nothing more than 'quibbles', to find a place for Armstrong on either the state or Australian selection committees. Could a position of captain be more humiliating?

The 'withholding of his selection as captain' for the forthcoming Ashes tour would prove increasingly significant. Armstrong had been among eight 'certainties' named on 4 January 1921 for the trip—Bardsley, Collins, Mailey, Gregory, Macartney, Taylor and Pellew being the others—but the board would not deliberate on the touring team's captain until 25 February. This had provoked speculation that Collins was being groomed as successor. 'Not Out' in the *Referee*, for one, had never desisted in running Armstrong down, stating even after Australia's huge Second Test victory that he was not 'up to the old standard' of Australian captains: 'An old international cricketer, in whose judgment I have much faith, tells me that, in Melbourne, Armstrong's leadership was not inspiring, nothing like it ought to have been.' The speculation, too, had a foundation of which only board and selectors were aware: alone among the 'certainties' Armstrong had delayed answering his tour invitation. Several explanations are possible. Was Armstrong stalling his acceptance, making it conditional on appointment as captain? Were the VCA selectors trying to destabilise his position? With the remainder of Australia's touring party to be selected shortly, there were rumours to this effect, which the *Herald* voiced under the headline 'Will Armstrong Go to England?':

> After the Fourth Test match, which begins in Melbourne next week, the team for England will be announced, and the possibility of Armstrong's not being appointed captain has been mentioned. In the event of this occurring, Armstrong might not go to England, and as he has very firm friends in the Australian XI, including J. M. Gregory, the effects of the trouble might be very far-reaching.

Eighty years later, such questions are unanswerable. In speaking at the Centenary Match dinner, Armstrong did stress his high regard for Collins, a laconic, leathery character with a deadpan wit and a flair for baccarat: he would, he said, 'be prepared to commit himself to Mr Collins if he were captain'. Yet touring England merely as a player would scarcely have appealed to him, as indeed did anything smacking of compromise.

As press and public kept the affair percolating, Armstrong had business to attend to. The morning after returning to Melbourne, he drove to seaside Mentone, honouring a promise made a fortnight earlier which must by now have seemed a distant memory.

Just before the Third Test, Armstrong had been entertained at the Mentone home of John Fogarty, president of Victoria's Wine and Spirits Association, and principal of spirits wholesaler Fogarty Doyle & Co. It was another friendship of Armstrong's either created or sealed through the Melbourne Cricket Club—Fogarty had been a member since October 1915. Also present was Armstrong's friend Charles Tootell, now on his testimonial committee.

Whilst there, Armstrong had struck up conversation with Fogarty's two boys, during which they had challenged him to a game of cricket. Armstrong replied that he'd happily play them wherever they chose. From this *obiter dictum* sprang one of the strangest matches in which an Australian Test captain has been involved. Fogarty set to training lads from the local grammar school, eighteen being chosen from the fifty aged between six and fifteen trialled during a fortnight's practices. Armstrong was permitted two helpmates: Tootell's boys, eight-year-old Bill and six-year-old Tom. The *Herald*, which alone seems to have known of the event, described Armstrong's arrival at picturesque Mentone Reserve:

> They cheered the laughing champion to the little shelter that served as a dressing room in the corner of the reserve and permitted him to disrobe. They stood about him in silent awe while he drew from his nicely-creamed flannel trousers his famous American dollar…and invited Billy Godby, the smallest boy in the team, to declare for head or tail. 'Have a look, Billy. It's got two tails,' suggested a voice from the crowd. And to the entertainment of the gathering, little Billy stepped forward and gravely inspected the coin.

Armstrong sent his opponents in, though the game was probably a little more elaborate than he had envisaged: 500 spectators were present and, with only two tiny fielders to help, the big man's considerably gentle bowling was rather punished. Nonetheless, he kept smiling under the summer sun, while Fogarty began insinuating additional children into the field. By the time the eighteenth boy came out—accompanied by a cry of 'That's the last!'—Armstrong was supported by a full eleven. His final figures were 16-144.

It was a curious diversion for a sportsman sunk in career-threatening controversy, and the *Herald* reporter attempted over lunch to draw Armstrong on matters more pressing. 'You understand I have had no explanation of my exclusion from the Victorian team,' Armstrong replied. 'So I cannot discuss the "reason".' Then it was back to the game. The Tootell boys made just three runs between them, leaving Armstrong to chase 143, and he had advanced only 13 runs himself when he was bowled, or allowed himself to be so, by eleven-year-old Godby. Indeed, Armstrong gave Godby the ball, which proved one of his own souvenirs: 'It's a long time since any man bowled me for so small a score. That ball you bowled me with is the ball that was used in the Test game played at Nottingham, England, in 1909. Keep it boy, to remind you of the day you got me cheap.' When Armstrong was presented with a pipe, he responded: 'Thank you boys. I'll never forget you, nor the happy time we have had together today.' He left to the accompaniment of 'three cheers for Mr Armstrong'.

Though never intended as such, the game was a publicity coup. The *Herald*'s report, headlined 'Australia's Champion Beaten by Boys at Cricket', was illustrated with a photograph of a beatific Armstrong flanked by the tiny Tootells, bats reaching their armpits. A *Sun* columnist chortled that, in Godby, Armstrong had unearthed a great new talent: 'A bowler who can bowl Armstrong for 13 and get a whole team out for 16 may be the medium curly bowler for which Australia is looking.' What a contrast to the VCA's tight-lipped tyrants. When Victoria's match with the Englishmen began the following day, 7354 spectators made their allegiances clear. Mayne was booed, Park cheered, Bean mercilessly heckled, while the *Herald* likened proceedings to 'Hamlet without the prince'. Armstrong himself kept a low profile. Arriving after work, 'Old Boy' related, he 'came in unobtrusively in order to avoid any possibility of a demonstration'. But he was unmissable while attending *Maid of the*

Mountains at the Theatre Royal that evening as J. C. Williamson's guest; when the house lights at interval revealed him in one of the boxes, the audience exulted. Armstrong, momentarily unsure of the correct response, advanced a few steps and bowed.

While the tour match continued on Saturday, selectors met at the MCG to pick Australia's team for the Fourth Test. There were no shocks: Armstrong, already confirmed as captain for the series, was named as expected. Shocks, instead, resounded from outside. Shortly before 3 p.m., huge sections of the crowd began exiting for a 'monster indignation meeting' scheduled on the city side of the arena. Although the VCA was refusing to issue pass-outs, almost half the 17,000 tore themselves from Patsy Hendren's brilliant batting to listen to a succession of prominent orators. 'The ranks of the members in the enclosure,' reported the *Herald*, 'were depleted as suddenly and as drastically as if a machine gun had been sprayed upon them.'

Speaking from the back of a lorry were old cronies of Armstrong's from previous disputes, like Edmund Jowett and Dr William Maloney MHR, and new allies, like John McKenzie, state president of the Returned Sailors and Soldiers Imperial League, and Edmund Cotter MLA, president of Richmond Cricket Club. The ubiquitous Henry Westley began proceedings with an expression of regret to the Englishmen:

> I desire to apologise to the English cricketers for the indignity placed on them by the holding of an indignation meeting outside the ground where they are playing. But the Englishmen are true sports and I am sure they are in sympathy with the objects of the meeting.

He then assailed the selectors with a bitter fury, inciting a noisy crowd of about 10,000 to pass a string of resolutions:

> A specific charge had not been made against Mr Armstrong and it would not be made because it could not be made. The selectors had flouted the public for so many years that their actions were beginning to recoil upon them. The public was now going to have its say and express its opinion in no uncertain manner (hear hear).

As Maloney inveighed against the VCA, the audience was in an ecstasy of rage:

It was an old axiom that those whom the gods wish to destroy they first make mad...Whom would they have on the selection committee? Would they have Bean? (No!) Would they have Ellis? (No!) Would they have McAlister? (No!) Would they have Armstrong? (Yes! and great cheering).

Inside the ground, as Hendren blasted a path to 262 not out, barrackers bawled 'Put Armstrong on!' and 'Why don't you give Ernie Bean a bowl?' As the day closed with the Englishmen 5–455, a disconsolate wail echoed round the arena: 'Oh, where's Warwick?' Departing patrons heard a blind man playing 'Will Ye No Come Back Again?' on a tin whistle.

Events were also moving on an unexpected front. Although the Melbourne Cricket Club was loath to become involved, the South Melbourne Cricket Club had taken up the fight, foreshadowing a no-confidence motion in Victoria's selectors.* The involvement in the affair of Roy Park, who had joined the club that year, probably inspired the gesture. But prime mover was club president John Baragwanath, perhaps recalling the ridicule Bean and Ellis had heaped on his mooted peace conference of association clubs seven years before. Baragwanath was a determined character, an impoverished country boy made good. A bootmaker, printer's devil and brush-factory foreman before entering politics thirty years earlier, he had thrice presided as South Melbourne's mayor, and was admired in Victorian politics for having no known enemies; even adversaries used his nickname 'Barry'. That he was unafraid to court enmity in worthy causes, however, would here be amply demonstrated.

At 7 p.m. on 7 February 1921, the twenty-eight VCA delegates convened at their Nicholson's Chambers headquarters in Swanston Street. For many, the affair was already unhappy. President Donald Mackinnon's position was especially invidious: he was also chairman of Armstrong's testimonial fund. Tensions did not take long to express themselves. When Baragwanath dissented a motion to expel the press, Bean exploded: 'You will never be forgiven!'

---

* When Bean later accused Melbourne of instigating protests, Trumble wrote the VCA bitterly: 'The miserable dispute referred to is no concern whatever of the club, and why it should be drawn into a private and personal matter of this kind the committee quite fails to understand.'

'Not by you,' Baragwanath retorted. 'I ask that the threat be withdrawn. That is the sort of prejudice the meeting is opening with?'

Though Bean withdrew the remark, Ellis then irrupted: 'You have made a very insulting remark to him. I have known both of you for twenty years, and he is a much better man than you are.'

Baragwanath wasn't having that: 'If he is no better than you, he is not much.'

'You are worse than the rebels of Ireland!' Ellis exclaimed. Appalled cries caused him to withdraw the remark, but delegates voted narrowly to exclude reporters, then listened to the statements collected from O'Brien and Mayne. Finally, Armstrong walked in.

Had he been looking forward to this moment? He began with unmistakeable relish: 'I have very much pleasure in giving you a statement of what occurred in Sydney. I will tell you exactly what did happen in Sydney.' In recalling events, he sounded like someone expecting vindication:

As for saying I refused to play, I can tell you it was nonsense. I was very keen to play in this game for two reasons: one was it was the 100th match, two my testimonial was just starting in Sydney and it meant a big thing to me to play in that match…As for the players being upset and one thing or another, I do not think they were any more upset than I was.

When Armstrong was examined by delegates, two dilations were notable. The first was Armstrong's view of managers: 'I do not think it is the usual thing to tell a manager you are not going to play, or anything like that, and in regard to the practice, I do not think it was my duty. That is what the manager goes with the team for, to arrange the practice.' One can imagine Bean's inner fury at this view of the VCA's representative as no more than a practice factotum.

Armstrong denied, however, discourtesy toward O'Brien himself, a rumour he charged the VCA executive with spreading, and gained unlikely support from the manager:

Armstrong: There have been some very grave statements that have come to my hearing, and to my father and mother, the way some of the executive have spoken that they had the manager's report to go on, as much as to say they had a terrible lot 'up their sleeve'. A lot of people assumed I was insulting to the manager. I have not in any way been insulting to him. As soon as I met the manager, I asked was there anything I could do to help him? That I would do anything to help put him up to any hint and do anything I could.

O'Brien: That is quite right.

Armstrong: Another statement has come to my parents' ears, and probably to my wife's ears, and that is that I was drinking in Sydney.

Howlett (North Melbourne): That is quite untrue, Warwick.

Ellis: That is not in the report.

Armstrong: No, it was not in the paper, but I am only saying what has been read between the lines...

O'Brien: While Mr Armstrong is here, I would just like to state that, while it has been asserted through the press that while in Sydney there were differences between Mr Armstrong and myself...[I] emphatically deny that there was any difference between Mr Armstrong and myself.

It is not difficult to imagine Bean's satrapy, in attempted self-justification, spreading rumours that they had information 'up their sleeve'. They had faced pressure from public and press before, but never like this: South Melbourne's no-confidence motion threatened a whole administration and way of ruling. As we shall see, though, their sleeves' contents were decidedly odd.

Testimony completed, Armstrong withdrew. Mayne, Park and Ryder were examined. Park's testimony was crucial—indeed, it was courageous. He described examining Armstrong the night before the match, finding his injuries serious, but favouring the delay of any decision until next morning because 'there was always hope': corroborating Armstrong's recollections. The trio then joined Armstrong to await deliberations. It was after 10 p.m., but the meeting was in full swing. Teeth probably clenched, Bean was next obliged to read South Melbourne's motion:

That the action of the Victorian selectors in omitting Armstrong from the Victorian team against England without first giving him an opportunity to being heard as to his reasons for not playing in the Sydney match is contrary to the best interests of cricket and in so acting the selectors have lost the confidence of this association.

Bean then began reading a statement on the selectors' behalf, revealing finally why Australia's captain was unfit to represent his state:

With every desire to judge the evidence favourable to a distinguished player, and with a full appreciation of the gravity of the situation, the committee felt that some form of censure was imperative. Certain statements of the manager in the report could not be ignored. It seemed indisputable that Mr Armstrong had not intimated that there was any improbability of his playing...Mr Armstrong's actions were deliberate and were designed to flout the manager and, through the manager, the association.

The wounded *amour-propre* of this statement still beggars belief. How did Bean know Armstrong's actions were deliberate? Where was it stated that players were obliged to report injuries to a manager? For what had Mayne, Park and Ryder been deputised but to deliberate on such questions? Tried thirteen years earlier for breaching a rule he didn't know, Armstrong had now been punished for transgressing one that didn't exist.

Armstrong's actual misdemeanour, of course, was absence of deference. And perhaps his actions in Sydney *had*, subconsciously, been coat-trailing. But even Bean knew that this hardly justified the selectors' caprice, for he suddenly changed tack. If Armstrong *was* injured, Bean continued, then surely he required rest: 'If these [injuries] were of sufficient seriousness to warrant his recent absenteeism from the game, they would also justify the committee relieving him from playing in the following match so as to facilitate his recovery for the Fourth Test.' This was a rather desperate rationalisation after the fact: it was hardly a favour to omit someone for an injury of whose extent they were unaware.

Lest this be interpreted as a softening of the VCA position, however, Bean tacked again, commencing an extraordinary declamation:

> The committee were...influenced by the fact that, for every year past, all unknown to the public, there has been in progress a subtle movement to undermine the authority of the Victorian Cricket Association. The measures of the selection committee to combat this hostility have worked out most successfully...We are ready to justify to the members of the clubs not only our present actions, but the actions of the association since it participated in the establishment of a Board of Control some fifteen years ago. In the event of an adverse vote this evening, we shall ourselves submit the entire matter for the arbitration of the clubs...The consequent full exposure of the inner history of Victorian cricket might prove extremely embarrassing to those who have precipitated the present crisis and, in the event, we have no intention of swerving from what we believe to be our duty.

This was what Bean had been keeping 'up his sleeve': the 'inner history of Victorian cricket', with Armstrong as chief troublemaker. At best, it was an act of self-preservation by one watching his world crumble: we should remember that Bean was a devoted servant of cricket who had given it thirty years of his life without financial reward. At worst, it was blackmail, and unhinged blackmail at that, driven by a paranoia rooted in the great crusades of 1906 and 1912. As the minutes ticked away to midnight, Bean was threatening to plunge the VCA into a battle to end battles. Now he played what he would have fancied his strongest card: the showdown of December 1907. 'The committee,' he began, 'would point out that it is not by any means the first time it has had trouble in connection with this player...'

Melbourne's Edward Cordner would hear no more. 'I entirely disapprove of bringing in anything that took place in 1907,' he interjected. 'Let us deal with the facts as they are. I think any reference to past disagreements should be excised from the report.' Mackinnon, anxious for compromise, agreed: 'That is what I would like to see take place.' But Bean continued his peroration, speaking for the selectors:

> They have no desire to stir the ashes of past controversies but perhaps they may be permitted to refer to the decision in 1907, when Armstrong refused to play for Victoria against New South Wales because he was not paid more than the maximum allowance fixed by the rules. A special meeting of the association was called to deal with the matter and the motion was tabled that he be suspended from playing cricket in Victoria. The passing of that motion was rendered unnecessary by the reading to the association and signing in the rooms of the following promise and apology: 'I now see that my action in connection with the New South Wales match was utterly inexcusable and detrimental to the best interests of cricket and as far as I am concerned nothing of this sort will occur again. Signed Warwick Armstrong.'

This was ludicrous. Armstrong's withdrawals from the two matches thirteen years apart were not remotely similar: the former had been precipitated by a dispute over expenses, the latter by an incapacitating injury. The only similarity was that, in both cases, the VCA had adjudicated before hearing evidence on Armstrong's behalf. Yet Bean now quoted Armstrong's thirteen-year-old letter like a detective flourishing a smoking revolver.

To the meeting's outcome, Bean's disconnected ramble was probably irrelevant; delegates had arrived knowing which way they would vote. And when the no-confidence motion was put, the selectors had the numbers 17–10: Baragwanath, Dow (South Melbourne), Bird, Broughton

(Richmond), Cordner, Simmonds (Melbourne), Hatch, Meagher (St Kilda), Delves (Carlton) and Moore (University) wanted the selectors ousted; Bean, Howlett (North Melbourne), McAlister, Nodrum (East Melbourne), Ellis, Bussell (Fitzroy), Rush, Wyles (Prahran), O'Brien (University), Yeomans, Butler (Northcote), Moyes, Plummer (Essendon), Melville (Carlton), Roberts, Connor (Collingwood) and Browne (Victorian Junior Cricket Union) stood firm. The vote of Sub-District Cricket Association representative Hammond is not noted in the minutes.

It might, however, easily have been otherwise. Somewhat surprisingly, all three selectors were permitted to vote. Two clubs were split, including University: O'Brien, essentially obliged to support the selectors, did so; colleague Moore wanted them expelled. Also notable is the stance of Johnnie Moyes, later one of Australia's foremost cricket historians. He recalled Armstrong's omission in *Australian Cricket* thirty-eight years later as 'a foolish action which caused a tremendous stir and much trouble', and travelling from Sydney to attend the VCA meeting with its 'argument and counter-argument of extreme bitterness'. Yet at the time he backed the autocracy responsible. For this was more than a vote about a selection decision. It was a trial of the authoritarian management model entrenched in Australia for almost fifteen years. Victoria's selectors had sacked a successful Australian captain for a misdemeanour so vague as to be almost indefinable. If this could occur, there was genuinely no limit to administrative power.

Why did delegates agree that evening to management by oligarchy? For one, through the VCA's share of the summer's profits, the clubs would shortly receive a bounty they would not have wished to jeopardise. Although many had supported the Board of Control in expectation of more money, there had been more thin years than fat in the preceding fifteen, while war had pushed many clubs to the brink of extinction. Yet one suspects that the overwhelming motive was simply to contain damage already done; when 10,000 gathered outside the MCG to cry *sic semper tyrannis*, it was almost a matter of public order.

Once immediate danger to the association's authority had passed, everyone relaxed a little. When at 12.30 a.m. they voted on Armstrong's actions in Sydney, Charles Nodrum had a motion ready, a barb in the tail to maintain appearances:

That this association having heard Mr Armstrong, Dr Park and Mr Mayne consider that Mr Armstrong was justified in not playing in Sydney. It regrets that the manager of the team was not informed earlier of the likelihood of his being unable to play. Had this been done the present trouble would not have arisen.

With a majority in favour, Armstrong was summoned after a two-hour wait to learn of the status quo's restoration. At the MCG twelve hours later, he was 'overwhelmed by congratulations in regard to the outcome of Monday night's meeting'. Bean, meanwhile, was hosting a VCA luncheon, but found many seats unoccupied: irate at exclusion from the previous evening's deliberations, the press had boycotted. If he had imagined this matter easily resolved, he was mistaken.

Armstrong was gratified by the outcome of the VCA hearing: he wrote to the board on 8 February 1921 accepting his tour invitation. He would also have been pleased to learn that supporters were maintaining their vigil: they convened the following day to plan another meeting, this time at the Town Hall six days hence. When the Fourth Test began, Armstrong's every deed inspired storms of approval, even losing the toss. '"Good old Armstrong" was the favourite, if somewhat trite, form of address during the day,' reported the *Age*, 'and the Australian captain could not even stop a ball without inciting the crowd to applause.'

But while Armstrong's legs had recovered, his malaria had recurred. Craving respite when England's first innings ended at 284 after an hour of the second day, he demoted himself to number seven, hoping he would not be required that afternoon, and could convalesce on the rest day following. It didn't work. Collins and Bardsley commenced Australia's reply with 117 in an hour and a half, but the loss of five wickets for 36 left him no choice but to join Jack Gregory.

Glimpsing his hulking frame at the Grey Smith Stand gate, 31,979 spectators rose as one. It was a quarter-century since Armstrong had first played at the MCG. He was older than any of the structures now composing its skyline, like a monument in himself, built from his 5000 first-class runs and 10,000 deliveries there. Now there was cheering, clapping and stomping from every quarter, prolonged every time it seemed about to fade by another stand or section, resonating like a choral round. It was the greatest ovation anyone could recall, stirring even Jack Worrall:

As the figure of Armstrong emerged from the pavilion, bat in hand, there was a demonstration the like of which had never been seen on the famous old ground, even outrivalling the ovation accorded Clem Hill at the time of the old trouble, which is also the new. There was cheering and counter-cheering by over 30,000, which the champion courteously acknowl-edged…The precipitate actions of the selectors had made a martyr of him, and the crowd showed its resentment in a manner unmistakeable and unforgettable.

Armstrong later admitted to have been 'slightly unnerved' and 'glad he made a few straight away': he clipped his first ball for two, struck his second for four, and was swiftly into stride. He might have been run out at 22, but the keeper fumbled a return, and he continued unmolested, so vast that to the English leg spinner Percy Fender he appeared impassable: 'To the bowler, he seemed all bat, and one seldom seemed to see any of the wicket to bowl at.' With Gregory, felt 'Onlooker' of the *Referee*, Armstrong enjoyed an instant rapport.

In the first place, the physique of both appealed to the crowd, who love big men, especially good big men, and it was a pleasure to watch the per-fect understanding and the utterly unselfish attitude of each. It seemed that they revelled in each other's company, interchanging mutual confidences as the runs were piling up.

The pair added 106 that evening, narrowing Australia's arrears to 17, although Armstrong was almost exhausted. Despite a day's rest in St Kilda, he worried about resuming on Monday. Though a gentle southerly off the bay encouraged him, he was soon labouring, and by the time Gregory was caught behind for 77, had stopped to a walk, visibly distressed. Douglas asked solicitously if he wished to retire. Armstrong said he would review his condition at lunch, and was 88 when the session's last over began.

Fender was bowling: an all-rounder from Surrey with a quizzical air and inquiring mind, he had grown friendly with Armstrong during the summer and just spent several days as a houseguest of Armstrong's friend Senator James Guthrie on the Barwon River. Now, he understood the need to keep his opponent quiet, preferably marooned. But Armstrong would not be inhibited: he bridged the gap to his hundred in a trice, with two boundaries and two twos. 'The big crowd stood up as one and cheered again and again for two or three minutes,' wrote Carl Willis in the *Sun*. 'The game was delayed, and even when Armstrong took strike again, cheers were still ringing around the ground.' The reception acted like a reviving draft, and in a quarter-hour after lunch he added another 23. As he lumbered in, a spectator jumped the fence and ran to shake his hand—an unusual incursion. Nobody intervened: perhaps it expressed a universal wish.

This was one of Armstrong's finest innings: at forty-one years, eight months and twenty-two days, he was the oldest man to break three figures in a Test match, and ill into the bargain. 'We are doing well—and then comes the old, old story,' lamented the *Manchester Guardian*. 'Just when we are safest, there's an Armstrong touch. What a man he is in moments of trouble and responsibility! The severer the ordeal, the mightier Armstrong he.' His innings held still greater significance in Melbourne. 'Old Boy' of the *Argus* described it as 'the big man's answer to the small man's affront,' and 'infinitely more effective than speech or protest'. The legend developed, indeed, that the innings was expressly for Bean's vexation.

This story's original pedlar was Ray Robinson, then fifteen but already alive to the telling anecdote. He described Armstrong fortifying himself with whisky before batting, then spying Bean in the crowd:

> As a youngster who had no right to be listening, I heard later that, as Armstrong walked in to bat, he saw among the sea of faces the countenance of Bean, wearing an expression that seemed to say 'I've got him now!' The sight of the teetotaller, seemingly gloating, sobered Armstrong if he needed sobering...The punchline of the story was that when Armstrong came out Bean was drunk.

This is probably one of those many Armstrong stories where the priorities of legend have turned something of doubtful authenticity into solid fact: it is unlikely Robinson intended it to be regarded as other than folkloric. But that it was uttered at all conveys the spirit of the times. The protest committee's Town Hall meeting the following evening was fierce. Slides of Armstrong during the Fourth Test provoked a spontaneous rendition of 'For He's a Jolly Good Fellow' from more than a thousand. Westley's motion calling for the sacking of Bean, McAlister and Ellis—to 'give new life to cricket, not only in Victoria but in the whole of Australia'—was carried unanimously. Others then took turns lambasting the VCA, including no fewer than five politicians: William

Maloney, Alexander Parker MLA, Western Australia's Sydney Stubbs MLC, and two veterans of the 'Big Six' days, Senator James Guthrie and Martin Hannah MLA. Guthrie railed:

> They had said it was no place for an Australian senator. But his reply was this. He did not tie himself to any section of the community. His job was to stamp out persecution and injustice wherever it occurred and that night at the Town Hall they were all present for one reason: because they refused to stand for the persecution of one of their leading citizens by a clique of dictators...He had once played against one of the selectors and had caught him out; on this occasion he was going to help boot him out.

Hannah continued in similar vein:

> The Armstrong incident was a resurrection of the old vendetta, when the selectors wiped out six of the finest sports ever seen on the cricket field. Now they thought they could use their tyrannical power to crush another great player. Kaiserism was not dead. It still lived in Victorian cricket.

Superficially, this sound and fury signified nothing. Bean, Ellis and McAlister would survive: McAlister had another seventeen years' selecting ahead. But it probably persuaded board members when they finally chose Australia's captain for the Ashes tour that straightforward reappointment of Armstrong was the line of least resistance.

At the last moment, Bean appears to have tried tilting the balance against Armstrong. He, Harry Rush and Melbourne's Ramsay Mailer were Victoria's three board delegates. Mailer, however, was at that stage sailing for England intending a summer's cricket watching, and Bean moved at the VCA's 21 February meeting that Johnnie Moyes act in his stead. The Melbourne Cricket Club was displeased. Although its board seat was only a vestige of its former power, it wanted Edward Cordner as Mailer's proxy: Moyes' nomination was, at least, a breach of good manners. Cordner was reinstated. When the board convened in Sydney four days later, Armstrong's appointment was moved by South Australia's Mostyn Evan, seconded by Queensland's Roger Hartigan, and 'carried unanimously'. Which may well be the case: once Cordner was present, there was no danger of the odd vote that had installed Armstrong going against him.

Armstrong had little chance to savour the Sydney crowd's tribute: anticlimactically, he was caught at slip first ball. But his side marched to its fifth consecutive victory, built round Charlie Macartney's four-hour

170, on 1 March.* A fortnight later, Melbourne granted Armstrong nine months' leave on half-pay with 'best wishes for a successful and enjoyable tour to yourself and the team'. At last, he could set about making that happen.

What did Armstrong himself make of the protests? Sensibly, he said little during their currency, but there is little doubt he was of a mind with supporters. Sydney's *Sun* reported him surveying the situation with satisfaction while visiting the protest committee's office on 12 March:

> He knew the object of the committee was to force the resignations of the selectors of the Victorian team and he considered that, if it attained that object, the committee would do much in the interests of the game. He did not think that the selectors had the game of cricket as much to heart as they should have. In his opinion they had done and were doing the game a good deal of harm. He hoped to hear before he returned that the selectors had been deposed, and if the committee brought about their resignations he would be the first to congratulate it.

Ultimately, public ardour cooled, and recalcitrant clubs were placated by distributions from the summer's Test gates. Writing to Syd Smith in May, Bean crowed: 'The opposition to our association has apparently fizzled out. We have had two meetings and dished the bolsheviks badly.' But Armstrong had reason for gratitude, especially to South Melbourne, which had risked the VCA's wrath by its stand. Indeed, the association made displeasure plain by leaving Baragwanath off the guest list of a farewell dinner for Douglas's Englishmen. 'I was informed on the night of the Armstrong inquiry that I would never be forgiven,' Baragwanath told the *Argus*. 'Probably this is the first instalment of that threat.'

The South Melburnian who probably suffered most by allegiance to Armstrong, however, was Park. Since the war, he had batted outstandingly, averaging 53, and was still only twenty-eight. Yet in the Ashes touring party, he was displaced by none other than Edgar Mayne, ten years his senior, and with a postwar average of 41. The selection seems explicable only in terms of Park having crossed the association, and

---

* In the crowd that day was twelve-year-old Donald Bradman, his experience of Armstrong's batting thus confined to a single ball. His consolation was watching Macartney and Gregory add 198 for the fourth wicket in 133 minutes.

Mayne's record of loyalty extending back to the 'Big Six' dispute. Armstrong felt so. Early the following year at a South Melbourne function honouring Park, he regretfully suggested a causal link: 'I wish I'd never had that bad leg in Sydney last summer, for...I cannot help feeling that that had a deal to do with your not being a member of the Australian XI.'

As a result of his growing Footscray medical practice, Park last represented Victoria in November 1924, never adding to his solitary Test cap. He is remembered today only for having scored a golden duck in his sole international innings—folklore having it that his wife dropped her knitting when he took guard and missed his entire Test batting career— but a worthier memorial would be his resistance to an association bent on Armstrong's destruction. The VCA, meanwhile, closed the affair perversely in its 1920–21 annual report: this contained a 'vote of thanks to Mr A. O'Brien who so capably managed the team to Sydney' but, beyond his appearance in scorecards, not a single mention of a Victorian who had led his country to a 5–0 Ashes victory. In the corridors of Australian cricket power, Warwick Armstrong had mutated from the intolerable to the unspeakable.

23

'A Cricketer with No Use for the Ultra Modern Methods'

No Ashes captain before Warwick Armstrong had swept a five-Test series clean, nor has one since. How had he done so? In short: carefully, prudently, remorselessly. The examples of Harry Trott, Joe Darling and Monty Noble were his for the following, but Armstrong drew on none of them. He shaped his captaincy, rather than the other way round.

As a tactician, Armstrong was orthodox. Like his batting, which banished risk, and his bowling, which starved batsmen out, his captaincy gambled nought. Percy Fender, later a shrewd leader himself, noticed how Armstrong happily went long periods where he simply bottled opponents up:

> Armstrong seemed to divide his bowling into two very distinct groups, attacking and defending. Directly a batsman came in, he was attacked along whatever line previous experience seemed to have shown him most vulnerable. If this did not succeed after a time, the attack changed and the batsman was made to go after the ball if he wanted to score. Armstrong seemed to be taking a breather during these periods…while giving away as few runs as possible.

Like Armstrong's all-round cricket, this was in its own way unsettling, as though he was dictating events rather than adapting to them. Cec

Parkin thought that Armstrong 'never dazzled you with a flash of strategy', but that 'his captaincy was all the better for his safety first methods'. Patsy Hendren even detected a sort of mystery to it: 'Somehow, one always had the impression when Armstrong was captain, that there was something out of the ordinary in everything he did.' Rather like one of his leg breaks which did not turn but burrowed straight on.

So what was Armstrong like to play under? The most perceptive observations about his leadership were made by Arthur Mailey, whose belated entry into Test cricket during the 1920–21 season had been an unqualified success: his 36 wickets at 26 would remain an Australian record for almost sixty years. Mailey had also prospered off the field, supplementing his income from the Sydney Water Board with cartoons for the *Referee* under the pen-name 'Bosey'. Armstrong contributed a cheerful preface to a book of Mailey's caricatures published in March 1921: 'All of the pictures are very good, and I must say that his idea of me combines just enough mercy with veracity to make me feel very pleased with myself.' Yet as captain and bowler, they did not always hit it off. A free spirit, Mailey spun his leg breaks hard, tossed them high, and varied them freely: qualities that scarcely endeared him to a skipper who was an apostle of economy. Mailey wrote:

> Tremendously tenacious and a relentless fighter, Armstrong bluffed rather than cajoled the opposition out. When he couldn't think of an answer, he smiled blandly and lumbered away. But nobody could deny his courage, his capacity for hard work and his determination. These qualities were more pronounced when he was in conflict with somebody he didn't like. Armstrong had strong dislikes and cast-iron convictions. To him reciprocity was a coward's weapon and he didn't have much time for arbitration unless he himself could act as the arbitrator…He belonged to the older school and appeared to treat newcomers to Test cricket as being beneath his notice.

This identification of Armstrong with 'the older school' is highly significant. Much separated Australia's captain from the players in his charge. With an injury to Oldfield, Hanson Carter had made an unexpected comeback in the final two Tests of the 1920–21 series, but only Macartney and Bardsley among the remainder of the team visiting England had sampled prewar Test cricket. To Armstrong's mind, this did indeed diminish them; for the rest of his life he would retain an acute loyalty to the generation with whom he had begun the game. This seems strange: the Australian teams he led were accomplished by any measure. Yet Armstrong avowed that he never played with a team superior to his first. 'The 1902 side,' he said, 'could play twenty-two of my chaps and give them a beating.' He told Archie MacLaren, too, that Australia's postwar XI was 'fifty per cent weaker than the Australian elevens of the nineties'. MacLaren, with similar prejudices, described 'my old friend Armstrong' as a cricketer with 'no use for the ultra modern methods'.

One minor incident during the 1920–21 season manifests both the march of time, and Armstrong's resistance to it. For the first two decades of Armstrong's first-class career, as we have seen, pitches were uncovered—something commonly held to enrich cricket by testing techniques under a variety of conditions. But because matches on rain-ruined pitches could be over in trice, forfeiting days of takings, financial arguments were made in favour of covering, and the 1920–21 season had seen the first steps in this direction. Armstrong's response to an agreement about overnight protection in Sheffield Shield matches was characteristic: discovering that covers had been lain during Victoria's game with South Australia at the MCG, he told newly appointed curator Bert Luttrell to remove them at once.

This was an outrageous overstepping of Armstrong's authority; Bean, infuriated, remained at the ground on subsequent evenings to ensure the offence wasn't repeated. But at the time, Armstrong found several supporters, including an ironic one. His old nemesis Jack Worrall of the *Australasian* deplored covering as 'against all laws and precedents and sport'. 'Although the pampered batsman is being further advantaged,' he wrote, 'it is purely incidental, the chief reason being a financial one. Cricket as a sport has been relegated in favour of the commercial side.' Which was Armstrong's own opinion: that the old ways were better. He saw the Second Test on the same ground a month later as validating his views. When rain turned the uncovered pitch into a mire, England appeared doomed to a huge defeat. In fact, they fought doggedly, Hobbs making a virtuoso hundred. Australia's bowlers seemed at a loss: the *Sun*'s Charlie Turner, so irresistible on damaged pitches in the 1890s that he had been dubbed 'Terror', described it as 'unquestionably the poorest bowling I have seen on a wet wicket in a Test match'. Armstrong, umpire Bob Crockett recalled, was appalled:

Armstrong remarked to me in somewhat pitying tones, 'what do you think of them, Bob?' Of course, it would not have been the done thing to answer his question. But I can answer his question now...Not one man could take advantage of the conditions and, without wanting to detract from the batting of the Englishmen, I feel certain that, had they faced our bowlers of other days, Turner, Trumble, Noble and others of the time, they would not have made the 251 and 157 they did.*

The old umpire had officiated in Armstrong's very first Test, not coincidentally at the same arena and on a wet wicket, nineteen years earlier: few were better qualified to understand Armstrong's grievance. But who else could comprehend? The product of an earlier time and earlier ideas, to which he held with increasing tenacity, Armstrong seemed increasingly a man apart.

This conception of Armstrong as an 'old school' cricketer should not be construed as making him 'old-fashioned'. On the contrary, some of his values appear strikingly up-to-date, far more so than those of the players he now led. At the risk of getting ahead of our story, let us examine several happenings on the 1921 Ashes tour which resonate deeply with the modern game.

Armstrong's behaviour where umpires was concerned was a product of his prewar upbringing: good ones he respected, poor ones he was not above intimidating. He had always been an imaginative appealer. After Melbourne was dismissed late one day against Northcote in October 1908, for example, Armstrong led his team onto the field at 5.57 p.m. and claimed a wicket 'timed out' on the grounds that the hiatus between innings had expired. As no batsmen had appeared, it would have been a difficult arbitration: fortunately the clock struck six as Armstrong was making his point and the umpires hastily drew stumps. He was more successful against St Kilda in February 1913 when a slip catch he claimed was refused. It was the last ball of the over and, as the field changed, Armstrong upbraided the umpire: 'That was a catch. Why did you not give it out?' When the umpire replied that the ball had struck the batsman's pads, Armstrong reissued his appeal: 'How is it for leg

---

* This sentiment was echoed in the *Manchester Guardian* six weeks later when rain fell during England's match with New South Wales: 'True lovers of cricket will be dismayed to read that, although rain fell in Sydney overnight, the wicket was not affected, owing to protection. Cricket is an outdoor game in which the glorious uncertainty is the greatest fascination that can be attributed.'

before wicket?' The umpire raised his finger. The following season, Armstrong also took the unusual step of reporting an umpire after a match against University. A letter survives dated 29 October 1913 from Melbourne's secretary Hugh Trumble to the VCA's John Healy:

> In reply to yours of 28th inst regarding report sent in regarding Freeman's umpiring, Mr Armstrong, the captain of the XI, states that Stevens (the University batsman) was palpably caught at the wickets and given not out. In fact, on the appeal being made, the batsman started to walk away, also that several wide balls were in the opinion of our captain incorrectly called by the umpire in question.[*]

That Armstrong brought these attitudes to his Test captaincy, Mailey recalled, resulted in some tense discussions with his own team:

> On the 1921 tour Armstrong would not accept certain English umpires—one in particular had cheated some years before, he maintained. Always skeptical about adverse opinions of umpires, I, with other members of the team, thought the 'Big Ship' was nursing one of his many grudges; and when matters appertaining to the tour were discussed in caucus, the vote invariably went against our captain.

The umpire in question was John Carlin, a former Nottinghamshire wicketkeeper. It appears, too, that contrary to Mailey's pious recollection Armstrong had his way: minutes of an Imperial Cricket Conference meeting on 6 June 1921 refer to 'Carlin's case' and 'the non-selection of J. Carlin'. Carlin did indeed have an interesting record: England had won all four of the Tests he had umpired, including two during the 1905 Ashes series involving controversial decisions. The conference was clearly peeved by the protest, for they moved that 'the principle should be laid down that those playing in International contests should not have any authority to interfere...in the appointment of umpires', but this would not have bothered Armstrong: he had achieved his objective.

More explicit articulation of Armstrong's attitudes then occurred during Australia's second innings against Sussex; according to Arthur Gilligan, it unfolded when Jack Gregory 'walked' with his score on two after snicking a catch to the keeper:

---

[*] District cricket umpiring standards were poor, many umpires being elderly. Responding to complaints, Mat Ellis convened a conference at East Melbourne on 5 October 1914 testing umpires for sight and hearing. While Bob Crockett's faculties were proven excellent, many scored low, three umpires not at all.

When he [Gregory] was nearing the gate, Armstrong turned to the umpire and said: 'What did you say, umpire?'

'I said not out, sir,' replied the umpire.

'Come back, Jack, come back,' bawled the Australian heavyweight skipper. 'He's given you not out.'

Gregory returned, and guiltily commenced slogging, actually racing to 53 in twenty-five minutes before holing out. Armstrong snorted to Gilligan: 'Chucked his wicket away, that idiot did.' When Gilligan demurred, saying he thought Gregory had 'played the right game', Armstrong scoffed again: 'The more you play this game, the more you will find out that you will be given out many times when you are not out and vice versa.'

Protesting umpires' competence, counselling colleagues not to 'walk': it all sounds very modern. Yet the antecedents are prewar. Joe Darling disputed English umpiring appointments in both 1899 and 1905. Victor Trumper himself advised Charlie Macartney to accept smooth umpiring with rough. The significance of Mailey's and Gilligan's recollections lies, meanwhile, in the image of the older Armstrong on the side of ornery pragmatism, while younger comrades lean to nobler notions. Cricketers of the Golden Age, it would appear, could be more robust in attitude than those who followed. This stood out with still greater clarity on issues of pay and conditions.

Australia's 1921 Ashes party came firmly under their board's control. Their contract contained no scope to choose their own manager: the board, as always intended, were masters. Nor were the players to share the tour's profits: the board offered each player a non-negotiable £466.

This was, of course, somewhat less than prewar players had earned on tour—which would not have eluded Armstrong. It was also rather less than the £600 being paid manager Syd Smith, something generating comment in the *Referee*: 'Cricketers are asking: why the difference? They do not contend that £600 is too much for the manager, but that £466 is too little…and the *Referee* agrees with them.' During the tour, the *Argus*'s Donald Macdonald devoted several columns to the players' allowance, which he thought 'emphatically not enough'.

Armstrong, not surprisingly, agreed. And in a letter to the *Argus*— responding to one Macdonald outburst—board chairman Harry Rush revealed that Armstrong had proposed before the tour a quite extraordinary incentive deal for his men:

> At the last meeting of the Board of Control, the honorary secretary [Syd Smith] reported that the captain of the team had waited on him and asked him to place before the Board a proposal that, if any profits resulted from the tour after the payment of the players' allowances, the Board should take the first £1000, and then distribute the balance equally amongst the players and the Board. He said, if the Board would do this, the players could string the matches out, the same as all Australian teams used to do. Otherwise most of the county matches would be finished in two days. The honorary secretary asked him to reduce his request to writing and it would be placed before the Board: this was done, the letter being signed by the captain and vice-captain.

This plan—which the board's minutes confirm was received on 25 February 1921—is assuredly one of the strangest ever presented to a cricketing authority. It was essentially a proposal to 'fix' matches, with the implication that this was an old Australian custom. Collins' involvement is significant—it emphasises that he and Armstrong were indeed a tight unit—but there seems little doubt that Armstrong conceived of it. In a way, it was an attempt to restore the old days of private enterprise tours, different only in that the board was to be treated as a partner taking a preordained share then participating equally in additional spoils.

In another way, however, the plan is not so old-fashioned: if one ignores how Armstrong envisaged enhancing the tour's financial success, it is another case of him taking from the past to point the way forward. After the Australian Test team's threatened strike in December 1997, their representative body the Australian Cricketers' Association agreed with the Australian Cricket Board a scheme involving the splitting of surplus profits between the board and the players. With cricketers positioned less as board employees and more as partners, this deal broke with the master-servant relationship of the past in a similar fashion to that Armstrong mooted eighty years ago.

At the time, Armstrong's plan went nowhere: the board had no interest in going halves with anyone, least of all in the idiosyncratic manner their captain proposed. On the motion of South Australia's Bernard Scrymgour seconded by Queensland's Roger Hartigan, members decided it 'be not entertained'. Nor, it seems, did it strike a chord with Armstrong's team. Rush informed the *Argus*: 'As far as the Board could ascertain, the captain and vice-captain did not consult any of the other players before making their request. The majority of the players stated that they were satisfied to leave the matter in the Board's hands when the financial result of the tour was known.' No wonder the players of 1921 were apt to disappoint their skipper.

Thwarted on the issue of pay, Armstrong next set his mind to the issue of conditions, and once out from under the board's nose staged a little coup. The team's itinerary had been designed by A. M. Latham, acting secretary of Surrey; unsurprisingly in view of his position, he had folded fixtures into the county season's contours. This entailed piling three-day tour matches on top of one another, scheduling three-day Test matches without a day's rest beforehand, and often absurd amounts of internal travel. In the second week, for example, a three-day match in London against Surrey was followed by a 306-kilometre overnight journey to a three-day match in Bradford against Yorkshire, then a 442-kilometre overnight trip to Portsmouth for a three-day match against the Services. All this amid a ten-week national coal strike which from 15 April threw train timetables into chaos.

Armstrong protested. He wanted playing hours restricted to between noon and 6 p.m. He also wanted several tour matches to finish early so that the Australians could enjoy lay days before each Test. There being no central authority for English first-class cricket, each county had to be approached individually. Test case was Surrey. With Smith, Armstrong met their committee on 8 May. 'Armstrong spoke on behalf of the entire team,' the *Herald* reported. 'He said that the two major objections were the heaviness of the program, and the hardships of travel which were aggravated by the coal strike.' None too happily, the committee consented to shortened hours. After receiving letters from Smith, most county secretaries agreed.

The ambit claim did not succeed. Only Warwickshire and Oxford University consented to two-day games. Yorkshire was furious even to be asked. Marylebone felt the cessation of play at 6 p.m. to be 'not in the best interests of cricket'; secretary Francis Lacey consented only with greatest reluctance. Armstrong, moreover, was pilloried for his stand. As the *Evening Standard* commented:

It is conceded that Armstrong is correct in saying that the Australians are under a big strain here but, if the visitors wish a day off before the Tests, it is hardly right simply to send what is practically an ultimatum to the county clubs. A two-days match at Yorkshire is simply a futile waste of time which could not attract the public.

'An Australian in London' even wrote the *Morning Post* urging Armstrong and his team to reconsider for the sake of his country's reputation:

A decision which reduces the playing hours of the cricket day to roughly five hours did not flatter the Australian national energy, and it is taken here as not showing consideration for the English public. Even if it does make a heavy demand on Mr Armstrong and his mates to observe the English playing rules, I am sure they are equal to it, because Australians when put to it are equal to any effort. Will they not in the cause of sportsmanship and good imperial feeling think over the matter again?

Armstrong's gunboat diplomacy on this issue, willingly courting unpopularity in order to achieve his ends, testifies to his strength. Few captains would have been capable of playing shop steward in front of cricket's bosses; few Australians would have had the nerve to challenge the English on their own turf. At the same time, there may have been a root to Armstrong's intransigence on this subject deeper than his players' welfare. The thirty-eight-match Latham program was a tough one, entailing 7500 kilometres of overnight train and coach travel. But it was shorter, for example, than the thirty-nine-match program of Armstrong's first tour. The difference, of course, was in the beneficiary of this hard work. Packed schedules in olden times had meant more money for sharing. Packed schedules now merely meant more profit for the board.

Again, too, Armstrong's stance evokes about him that mingling of ancient and modern. Like the prewar Australian cricketer he was, Armstrong insisted on his rights to suitable terms. Yet he also behaved as a leading athlete might today. Being out of step with the times once more caused friction in his own camp for, despite Armstrong's claims of Australian unanimity, some of his players agreed with English critics. Mailey, Edgar Mayne, Jack Ryder and one other were all opposed at least to curtailing the Yorkshire match. And Mailey suspected that his dissidence was later held against him:

When I and a few others crossed swords with him in connection with a Yorkshire fixture, which had been arranged against Armstrong's will, I felt that the 'Big Ship' nursed that incident for a considerable time. To be frank, I thought his subsequent reactions were not exactly favourable to me.

From mild-mannered Mailey, this was plain speaking. One notes that despite his successes in Australia, he was omitted from the First Test, while Ryder and Mayne played no Tests at all. Armstrong's response to back-sliding? We cannot tell. What *is* clear is the friction between generations, the contrast between the abrasive Armstrong and his players.

It would be wrong to conclude, though, that Armstrong estranged himself from his players. Some team members were intensely loyal, including the pair chiefly responsible for Australia's success: Jack Gregory and Ted McDonald.

The latter's selection had been a surprise. He had played in three home Tests, swift in his first spell, less penetrative and sometimes expensive later. Yet several sources contend that his selection was at Armstrong's specific request. 'There had been some objections to McDonald's inclusion,' Daniel Reese recalled, 'but Armstrong insisted that, without the fast bowler, Australia could not bring back the Ashes.'

The novelty of this intuition should not be underestimated. It is a platitude today that 'fast bowlers hunt in pairs', but this was scarcely so in 1921. Australia had taken individual bowlers of great speed to England before—Ernie Jones in 1896, 1899 and 1902, Albert Cotter in 1905 and 1909—but never two. Prevailing wisdom held that opening bowlers should contrast—one quicker, one slower. In their own ways, however, Gregory and McDonald *were* different, and complementary. Where Gregory's approach could look awkward, McDonald's flowed like a river. While Gregory was always favoured with the wind and swung the ball mostly away, McDonald didn't mind breasting a breeze and possessed a sinister backbreak. Where Gregory brought the ball down from altitude, McDonald skidded it through. In the case of McDonald, Armstrong also foresaw his suitability to English conditions: reviewing his success in *The Art of Cricket*, he commented that it had been 'anticipated by the closest judges of the game'.

Armstrong's conviction about Gregory and McDonald, for once, owed nothing to his prewar experiences, although his management of it may have. In his book, Armstrong warned repeatedly against overusing fast bowlers, and described deciding 'to nurse' Gregory and McDonald with the 'greatest possible care'. Gregory later recalled: 'He impressed on E. A. McDonald and me that we were to give him the wink when we were feeling the slightest bit tired. He always told us that we could recover from tiredness quicker than strain.' This was not a consideration exercising other captains at the time: Collins, for instance, extracted 830 overs from Gregory in twenty-five English matches on 1919's AIF tour, Armstrong 655.4 from him in twenty-seven matches two years later. It echoed, however, a conviction of Monty Noble who, describing Ernie Jones, asserted that unthinking captaincy often ruined fast bowlers:

> Because he was the great, reliable, hard-working, wicket-taking, willing horse of the team, he was frequently bowled to a standstill. He frequently occupied the bowling crease from noon till 1.30 p.m., and after lunch he was again in harness until nearer four o'clock than three, tired out and reduced to mediocrity for the rest of the day. Jones was a physical marvel, as active as a racehorse and chockfull of fight and stamina, yet his term of usefulness was shortened by years.

In apprehending that his fast bowlers would be better for short bursts and recovery time, Armstrong was again years ahead of the game. And again, he may have gotten the idea from looking back.

In the light of recent events, another unpopular stand Armstrong made seems astoundingly relevant today. It involves a meeting of England's Board of Control for Test Matches on 10 May 1921 at which Armstrong proposed to the English cricket potentate Lord Harris that Test umpiring appointments be delayed until shortly before each match. Ray Robinson's version runs:

> Armstrong said, 'The umpires are paid little for their services and, as there is a lot of betting on Tests, it would be wise to remove them from temptation.' Lord Harris thought the matter so serious that he suggested holding it over until next day, until inquiries were made. Next day he said, 'I can find no evidence of betting on cricket—people don't bet on cricket.' Armstrong drew deeply on his big bent-stem pipe, then he leaned across and said, 'You don't think so, my Lord? If you'd like £500 on the next Test, I can get it on for you.'

Robinson's account is incomplete: Armstrong's remarks formed part of a general discussion of the umpiring appointment system in which Harris, Lord Hawke and F. S. Jackson from England largely consented to proposals from Armstrong, Syd Smith and Ramsay Mailer from Australia.* But one can imagine how his implication that umpires were not above suspicion affronted Lord Harris, who viewed cricketers as 'ministers of a high moral and educational medium'. The history of administrative inaction on cricket corruption begins here. Harris's inquiries consisted of contacting the Victoria Club, a London gentlemen's gaming establishment, and asking if they carried bets on cricket. No, they did not: QED.

Little research has been done on the incidence of betting during cricket's Golden Age. Yet if we look generally at gambling during that period, especially in Australia, the question soon changes from 'Was there betting on cricket?' to 'Why would there not have been?' This was an era of huge speculations. At the 1904 Caulfield Cup, John Wren won a record £51,000 backing his Murmur. Three years later, Sir Hugh Denison won £100,000 by backing his Poseidon for the Caulfield Cup and Apologue for the Melbourne Cup. It was also the era of a huge subterranean betting world, the subject of rumour and innuendo. The period's most celebrated cycling event, the Austral Wheel Race, was permanently tarnished by the pervasion of bookmaking. A couple of weeks before Armstrong's Test debut there, the MCG hosted a notorious Austral where one rider was disqualified immediately and nine others charged with having tried not to win. In a letter to the *Argus* 'Country Visitor' wrote:

> Outside the grandstand, as if by way of a grim joke, was a notice prohibiting betting, but on emerging from the corridor under the stand the place was simply alive with bookmakers...Where I sat, the din was

---

* Smith's report to his Board reads: 'On arrival in England, Mr Armstrong and myself consulted Mr Lacey about the appointment of umpires. Mr Lacey told me that they wished to adhere to the English custom of appointing the ten umpires to the five Test matches straight away, but we asked if the English Board of Control could not see its way clear to give special consideration to the Australian method in this connection. A special meeting of the Board of Control was held which Mr Armstrong, Dr Mailer and myself attended and, after hearing our view on the subject, the board decided to alter their system and agree to the umpires being appointed for each Test just before same.'

unbearable, and the smoke like that of a bushfire. Boys were betting as well as adults. There was one free fight that lasted over ten minutes.

There were no equivalent scenes at Australian cricket matches, of course, but anecdotal evidence suggests that cricket and gambling were far from complete strangers. Describing Armstrong's first Test soon after, for example, 'Felix' alluded to bets on the game while describing smoke from the nearby railyards that shrouded the MCG while Australia batted:

'Bother that smoke,' said Jack Blackham. 'It must affect the batsmen's sight.' 'Of course it does,' chipped in the old Jolimonter, E. P. Hastings, 'you may rely it was done on purpose with the railwaymen about to have their little bit on the Englishmen.'

At least three great players of the period are known to have been involved in bets on their performances. Gilbert Jessop confessed to backing himself at 20–1 to make a century in the Oval Test of 1902, albeit with 'the laudable object of raising drooping spirits'. Percy Fender recalled that teammates of Ranjitsinhji would sometimes 'stimulate his interest in the form of small bets', Clem Hill that Victor Trumper was consciously involved in a big collect for an Australian punter at Pretoria in November 1902:

One South African had a bet of £20 at long odds that Victor Trumper would not make a 200 on the tour. The bets were taken by an Australian at Johannesburg. Victor immediately obliged by doing the trick in the second contest. When Saunders, the last man, came in, Trumper was 160. Trumper knew of the bet and set out to get those other 40. He got them. Out of the next 60 runs he scored 58. Saunders scored 1 and there was one extra.

This was, of course, quite distinct from making a pre-determined score or conceding runs deliberately to advantage a bookmaker or gambler. But from a recollection of Sydney Barnes in the *Daily Chronicle*, recalling England's dramatic one-wicket victory in the Melbourne Test of January 1908, it appears that stakes could be sizeable: 'A businessman at our hotel told us afterwards that England's victory made £600 difference to him. He asked that Humphries, Fielder and myself should join in his celebration. We thanked him but declined.'

This subject merits far greater attention than we can give it here, yet it seems credible that betting did not simply vanish from cricket in the 1830s when bookmakers were expelled from Lord's, but merely went underground. After the tour, indeed, Armstrong enlarged a little on his earlier comments, replying in the *Argus* to assertions by Lord Hawke that 'there is not the least foundation for the assumption that betting takes place on the game of cricket in modern times'. Armstrong stated:

> In regard to betting on cricket in England I can speak with some authority. I have no hesitation in contradicting Lord Hawke's statement that there is no foundation for the assumption. Personal friends of mine resident in England and Australia won quite large sums on the Test matches that were played during the last tour.

At the time, of course, after his recalcitrance concerning the itinerary, Armstrong's allegations provoked merely disdain. Few Australian teams have been denounced as bitterly as Armstrong's in the *Observer* of 29 May:

> The fact that the Australians objected to the publication of the names of the umpires for the First Test on the wholly absurd grounds that these men may be 'got at' is unworthy of Australia as a great cricketing people. We in this country know nothing of umpires susceptible to such a thing…England has one decided and final way of dealing with guests who do not cheerfully conform to rules prevailing in its own house, and will not hesitate about it in future.

Syd Smith went into damage control. At the subsequent Imperial Cricket Conference meeting, which he attended with Mailer, Smith protested the tenor of the *Observer*'s comments, but appears in his captain's absence to have apologised for any aspersion cast on English umpires. When Harris referred to Armstrong's remarks about betting—claiming that they 'could not be substantiated' and 'were very much resented by English cricketers'—the minutes note: 'Mr Sydney Smith and Dr Mailer said that they were not prepared to support the Australian Captain's views'. Harris, indeed, was still scoffing at Armstrong's comments during a Middlesex dinner four months later:

> He had had certain business relations with Armstrong, from whom he understood there was a great deal of betting on English cricket which affected the game. A leading betting club denied that. The fact was that what Armstrong knew about English cricket was worth nothing.

The day would come, of course, when the nexus of cricket and gambling would compel authorities' attention. But it is unlikely any of the breast beating worried Armstrong. He took a simple precaution against distraction; as he told the *Daily Chronicle*: 'I never read the newspapers so I do not know what the critics have said about me.' Daniel Reese thought this extraordinary: 'It was in this way, like Pitt and Balfour in their political worlds, that the Australian captain was more out of touch with public opinion than any of his predecessors.' Yet perhaps only a captain so inclined could have led Australia as he did.

24

'England Are Really Scared of Armstrong'

The fifteenth Australian cricket tour of England began with a tour of Australia. The team's 3500-kilometre rail journey from Melbourne to Fremantle aboard the three-year-old Trans Australian took almost a week. The monotony of the landscape was interrupted for the cricketers by wayside receptions in isolated townships and hamlets, as though they were tourists in their own land. At Riverton, they met Clarence Pellew in his farming togs: it being harvest time, he had requested a delayed passage to England. At Eurelia, they stopped for a corn-beef supper in a barn lit by oil lamps. At Tarcoola, they were greeted by a dusty schoolmaster with his class of twenty boys. Quaintest of all was the sight of Warwick Armstrong tossing for innings in a Perth friendly with local skipper Harold Evers—between them, they weighed almost 300 kilograms.

With the prospect of so much cricket ahead, Armstrong appears to have been contemplating his condition. At Fremantle, Johnny Douglas told reporters that he had advised Armstrong 'to get three stone off his weight and he would be able to continue forever', and his example may have stirred the Australian captain's novel response. Douglas himself had kept in trim on tour by stoking railway engines between destinations; once the teams began their passage aboard the *Osterley* on 22 March,

Armstrong established a similar fitness regime. He made regular descents to the ship's engine room over the next few weeks—usually, according to Daniel Reese, with Ted McDonald:

> After leaving Fremantle, McDonald, who knew it was largely due to his captain that he had been selected, took the opportunity to thank him. He then said: 'Is there anything you want me to do, Warwick?' To which the big fellow replied, 'Yes Mac, I want you to put the "peg" in until we have won the rubber, and this means getting fit.' For the rest of the voyage, Armstrong and McDonald each morning went down to the stokehold of the P & O liner and for two hours worked as firemen. They planned to rid themselves of superfluous fat and became as hard as nails.

Fitness being the chief question mark over McDonald, this makes some sense. It coheres also with McDonald's acute loyalty to his captain and advocates.[*] The other player for whom Armstrong looked out was uncapped twenty-five-year-old Hunter Hendry, a last-minute inclusion after Charles Kellaway's withdrawal. A Paddington product, Hendry had been recommended to Armstrong by Monty Noble. In a privately published memoir, Hendry recalled how 'he would look forward every night to the time when he and Warwick Armstrong played deck quoits with the captain and chief officer. Afterwards, they would adjourn to the captain's cabin for drinks.'

A twin-screw vessel of 12,323 tonnes, the *Osterley* was the pride of the Orient Line. The Australians dined in evening dress in the first-class section of the dining room, joined the ship's sports committee organising deck games, and learned the new-fashioned foxtrot at dances held every second evening in the ballroom. 'Even our skipper was enticed to this form of amusement,' Syd Smith recalled, 'after he had heard the special jazz band comprised mostly of members of the team.' The Suez Canal was threaded on 10 and 11 April and the team disembarked at Toulon, separating momentarily for some sightseeing on the continent before reuniting in Paris. Collins led a group to the casino of Monte Carlo, and parlayed a pot of 100 francs into 3700. Others revisited sights familiar to

---

[*] Percy Fender could not recall Armstrong working as a fireman, but a passage by Laurie Tayler in the *Captain* appears to confirm both the story and its sequel: 'During the voyage to England, and in the hottest weather, he tried working down the stokehole, but alas! stoking must suit his constitution. When he weighed in afterwards, it was found that he had gained four pounds. They say the machine died of a broken heart almost immediately.'

them as servicemen, Macartney meeting a Boulogne family who had befriended him during the war. Armstrong travelled overland through Milan to Paris with McDonald and Hendry, the latter's recollections evoking their innocence abroad:

> One night, Hendry and Ted McDonald visited some of the same Paris nightspots, which Hendry recalls were packed with elegantly-dressed ladies. No sooner had they sat down at a table when two beautiful young women joined them and began to talk to them. When a stunning looking woman came down the stairs from the entrance, Hendry inquired, 'Surely she's an artist.' The women replied, 'Yes, like us, an artist on the bed.'
>
> Somewhat taken aback, Hendry and McDonald told the girls they would 'pay their charge' if they promised to go home and stay off the streets that night. They brought them back to their apartment and watched them go inside, however, they waited some little way up the street behind a telephone booth to see if they would keep their promise. The women soon reappeared...and proceeded to look for further business.

Armstrong was not quite so callow when a tour guide led the team to a bordello:

> There was a queue of men some thirty yards long outside; however, the guide must have had a contact, as the team was soon inside and taken up to a huge room with a piano in it. Hendry particularly recalls this occasion because of the extraordinary sight of a tiny woman, doll like, perched stark naked upon the knees of the twenty-stone captain Warwick Armstrong. His memory of ensuing events was somewhat vague.

With the exception of Smith and Carter, who had in advance daringly flown from Paris aboard a Handley-Page airliner, the Australians arrived at London's Victoria Station on 22 April 1921. Armstrong was confident, but gave little away. Asked if he had any 'new theories' in mind, he replied: 'If I have, they cannot be disclosed.' He wasn't quite so pleased with the advice of a railway station weight machine, which rather mocked his exertions aboard the *Osterley*. 'Shall I ever forget the look of disgust when he saw the hand racing round to twenty-one?' recalled Oldfield. 'Instead of taking off a stone, he had added one.' That weight, however, he was free to throw around.

A key issue at the tour's commencement was Armstrong's rivalry with Smith, the board's staunchest functionary, whose trip was a reward for nine years as secretary commencing during the 'Big Six' dispute. As the team settled into the Strand's Hotel Cecil, he was determined that the tour should bear the board's imprint; Armstrong's responded predictably.

Smith had a variety of ideas for reducing the tour's overheads. He proposed that the team stay during some fixtures with wealthy English cricket devotees who had offered their hospitality. Armstrong dismissed the idea: 'I am opposed to the proposal…We appreciate the kindness, but members of the team prefer to have their evenings to themselves, and will stay at hotels.' Smith also wanted to limit meal allowances. Armstrong, Hendry recalled, dismissed that too:

> The manager Syd Smith came up to me and said, 'Hunter, if you have an entree at dinner you cannot have the main course.' I was absolutely stunned and immediately made my way to Armstrong's room and told him about it, and he said: 'Ignore what he said and have what you want.' Which I did throughout. Mr Syd Smith was evidently out to make something on the side but he had no chance of doing so with Armstrong as captain.

This low-level feud between captain and manager would last the whole tour. Armstrong would subtly twit him again and again, whether requesting that liquor be served in the Lord's dressing-room, to Smith's embarrassment, or ordering champagne to refresh his bowlers, at Smith's expense. In Australia, Armstrong had been required to observe at least a few protocols. In England, he was in charge. When the Australians attended Anzac Day ceremonies at the Cenotaph, their captain laid the wreath. When they were guests the following day of the Australia and New Zealand Luncheon Club at the Connaught Rooms, their captain was 'received with prolonged cheers' and told the audience he was 'looking forward to hard games'. It suited him they be as hard as possible. His old friend Archie MacLaren watched Armstrong take his first practice hit of the tour at Lord's on 27 April, and warned *Daily Express* readers what was to come:

> Armstrong went in practically last and I wondered whether that terrific straight drive would retain all its force. Something told me that it would, for his increasing bulk is only normal with the passing years; in spite of his extra weight there is no superfluous lumber. At any rate the schoolboys who were standing twenty yards behind the bowlers were removed at my request, and only when the decks were cleared for action did he begin to open his shoulders.

War's end had not ended the empire's travails. Ireland and India were in upheaval, the British economy in recession and almost a million unemployed. Yet the resumption of elite sporting contact, twelve years since the last visit of a full-strength Australian team, seemed a tradition stronger for interruption. 'The Empire's intense love of sport survives all things,' commented *The Times*. 'Perhaps it is a manifestation of the spirit which used to prompt British teams to dribble a football across the unhealthy wilderness of no man's land when it was for many the last hour of life.' In the opinion of a new English periodical, the *Cricketer*, Armstrong would be among the first chosen to 'represent the World against Mars should the inhabitants of that distant and interesting planet ever think of challenging us at cricket'.

The Australians began their tour at Leicester on 30 April. The weather was balmy, the excitement palpable. The Australian share of the gate at the corresponding fixture nine years earlier had been £37. Now the brimful ground offered up £637, and the toss had to be transacted twice because some of the small army of photographers had missed it the first time. There was curiosity and foreboding in the air—how good was this all-conquering team? Reviewing England's defeat in Australia, *Wisden*'s Sydney Pardon had written: 'In the face of the almost complete overthrow of the English team it would need the most sanguine person to view hopefully England's prospects for the coming summer.' Yet some remained optimistic. F. J. Sellicks of *Illustrated Sporting and Dramatic News* thought Armstrong would 'find his task appreciably more difficult here than it was in Australia'. Familiar surfaces, supportive audiences, wider selection choice: all might play to English strengths.

War, however, had taken toll of English cricket. The country's annihilated generation had included more than sixty first-class cricketers, and many more who might have succeeded them. County cricket had resumed unsteadily, reliant on prewar talent stretched past its prime. Leicestershire's Harry Whitehead, who took strike to Gregory that day, was an example: a thirty-six-year-old professional who'd played almost 380 games, but who would probably have been superannuated had it not been for his county's paucity of reserves. As it was, he met a hasty, symbolic end: Gregory's first delivery reared from short of a length, took an edge and was accepted behind. It was a harbinger: this Australian team was playing a new brand of cricket, ushering the old order into extinction. Poor Whitehead represented Leicestershire only once more.

Ultimately, it was McDonald's day: Armstrong's Victorian protege claimed 8–41 as Leicestershire were routed for 136 in two and a half hours. By stumps, thanks to a vehement Macartney hundred, Australia were 1–234, and their 7–430 took just four hours. Victory was consummated late on the second day by an innings and 152 runs. Armstrong, ironically, had a frightful game, dismissed first ball and missing four catches. When one of these rebounded to the prehensile Gregory, 'Wanderer' of the *Sportsman* thought it a great joke:

> Once when a ball jumped out of his hands at slip from a chance given by Sharp, Gregory and Carter both went for the catch. Gregory being much the taller secured the ball and simply sat down on Carter. It was remarked at the time that, if the ball had gone out of Gregory's hands into Armstrong's, the Australians would have had to call on their second wicketkeeper for several weeks.

Somehow, though, the mere sight of Armstrong's vastness, counterpointing the lithe keenness of many of his team, was intimidating. Elsewhere, 'Wanderer' was more deferential: 'He is now so greatly increased in bulk, without becoming the least corpulent, that he dwarfs all his neighbours. And at Leicester, no-one could think of any cricketer of the past or present who could be compared with him.' Even in failure, thought the *Leicester Mercury*, Armstrong oozed confidence: 'He walked back to the pavilion after his dismissal for a duck as though it was one of the jokes of the day. Happy the cricketer with the right temperament for all occasions.' By Armstrong's own account, indeed, his minimal contribution to Australia's huge win was 'the merest trifle when compared with the success of the side'. And his players looked on in undiminished regard. After the game, Armstrong's body was 'covered with big round black marks' from the impacts of chances he'd missed. 'Heavens!' thought Hendry. 'Lots will pay for all this!'

The Australians' host at their next stop was another Australian, the swashbuckling financier Lionel Robinson, his fortune built on the mining stocks of Broken Hill. Robinson had acquired an 800-hectare estate in the Norfolk village of Old Buckenham in 1906, and built a £1 million mansion there containing no fewer than fourteen bathrooms. In fact, he had built it three times, twice ordering its demolition out of dissatisfaction with the result. Now by hosting cricket matches and employing Archie MacLaren as a personal assistant, he indulged a love of sport and aspirations to enter English society—unsuccessfully, it happened, for he was dismissed as an *arriviste*. How he had insinuated a traditional country house match into the Australian team's crowded schedule is a mystery; it is a fair guess money played a large part.

It became one of the Australians' sterner fights; in wintry conditions, against a talented XI including Hobbs and Douglas, their batsmen amassed only 136, thanks mainly to Armstrong's unbeaten 51 in 100 minutes. Local hopes rose a little. 'Yesterday proves that the Australians can be dismissed cheaply,' chirped the *Daily Express*. 'The plain fact is that they were fairly and squarely outplayed.' Perversely, however, the match tilted the balance of power more firmly Australia's way. Hobbs strained a leg, scratching himself from the first two Tests. Australian momentum was also unaffected; when Armstrong claimed 12–77 against Surrey at the Oval, Australia won their second massive victory.

Amid the arguments over playing hours, it seemed that Armstrong was proving his point on the field. After routing the Services at Portsmouth by 198 runs, the Australians needed less than two days to overcome Essex by an innings and 75 runs. Their batting was balanced: the daring Macartney, Pellew and Taylor complemented by the dependable Collins and Bardsley. Their bowling covered all contingencies: Gregory and McDonald to concuss, Mailey to confound and Armstrong to constrict, all supported by fielding of athletic elasticity. The captain also provided a final bulwark against trouble, as in the showpiece match at Lord's against Marylebone. The hosts actually obtained a 93-run first innings lead, but Armstrong kept the match under control with 4–51 from 38 overs, his every action striking *The Times* as full of menace and cunning: 'His length was wonderful and he bowled only two bad balls. Which probably were not bad at all but sent down with some method dictated by that clever brain.' Armstrong was struck above the eye by a bouncer from Middlesex's towering paceman Jack Durston, but ignored medical advice not to resume batting, and interposed again when Australia's last-day run chase stumbled. Melbourne's *Herald* reported:

> The huge crowd was thoroughly alive to the prospects of English victory and there was a buzz of excitement as Armstrong's burly form appeared at the gate. His left eye was stitched, his left temple covered in plaster. He looked hurt and sore. But the side truly depended on him. This was a dramatic moment—the big captain coming out to save his side.

Which he did, with a neat cameo of 15 not out in ten minutes including the winning runs; although only one run was required to win the match, he insisted on running two off the winning hit. The press had still more to conjure with when it emerged that Armstrong had received a sympathetic telegram after his injury from King George V. Armstrong's celebrity was sealed. One cartoonist depicted the monarch sweeping aside a litany of imperial woes—'Irish trouble', 'Coal strikes', 'Poverty', 'Silesian Affair', 'Alexandria Riots'—with the words: 'Yes yes, but I must find out how my friend Mr Armstrong is first.'

Despite campaigns for Charles Fry and Archie MacLaren, the role of England's captain for the First Test at Trent Bridge fell again on the hapless Johnny Douglas. He had no more luck than in Australia. The match was essentially decided by the seventh over, when Gregory dynamited the defences of Donald Knight, Ernest Tyldesley and Patsy Hendren. No resistance remained once Douglas had played a demoralised shot at his rival skipper; indeed, the browbeaten Englishmen could scavenge only 33 runs from Armstrong's 30 overs in the match. With Gregory and McDonald collecting eight wickets each, Australia had achieved a ten-wicket triumph by the second afternoon. It was almost too easy, even for Australia's captain. 'I am proud we have won,' he told the *Daily Mail*, 'but surprised our victory was so decisive.'

On the face, Trent Bridge was a victory for speed. Gregory and McDonald were a force without precedent, sapping English spirit where the Kaiser's U-boats and Zeppelins had failed. Armstrong had kept his word, lightening their burden wherever possible, and McDonald in particular had proven a revelation. His economical run and silken action cost him nothing in effort; with supernatural energy, he could bowl at high speed for a session on a glass of water and a few puffs of a cigarette. Frank Woolley felt McDonald was 'probably faster than Larwood ever was'. Yet Australia's invincible aura radiated chiefly from its captain. A *Times* leader exalted him as 'the greatest match winner in the world'. Warner commented in the *Morning Post*: 'We accept the discomfiture in the true cricketing spirit, and are left in admiration of Australia's fielding and bowling, and Armstrong's genius for captainship.' Melbourne's *Herald* was represented at the Test by no less than Keith Murdoch, shortly to become the newspaper's editor-in-chief; the journalist whose Dardanelles dispatches had echoed round the world found more to admire in Armstrong's leadership than he had in the generals of Gallipoli:

> There was an unmistakable mark of quality about it all, and Armstrong's wise captaincy was evident, not only in his judicious use of the bowling but in his quiet but firm domination over his men, and the easy way in which he moved them to just the right places for catches and run saving...Yes, Armstrong is an astute fellow. Sharp wisdom is hidden beneath that big, slow, quiet exterior.

The spell Armstrong cast emerged most clearly when he took the ball himself. Once he had used leg theory to constipating effect; now he needed no such trickery. As he struck his perfect length, even attacking batsmen like Woolley and Hendren bobbed like clippers in the doldrums. The routine was perennial: an over or two of leg-breaks, then the straight one, leaving the stumps disturbed or the umpire granting an lbw. And the longer the tour lasted, the deeper would be batsmen's contemplations and the spectators' chagrin, for there appeared nothing to that easy amble and gentle arc: 'He bowls rather like a fat uncle, not altogether unlike a fat aunt,' recalled Robert Lynd in the *Sporting Life*. 'This is not the first, second or third time that Armstrong has done this kind of thing during the present tour,' lamented the *Daily Telegraph*'s Philip Trevor after Armstrong's 8–33 in a two-day rout of Middlesex shortly after the First Test. 'There is no doubt that at the moment there is not a single batsman in England who faces with any appearance of confidence his innocuous slows.'

Armstrong was actually as puzzled as anyone by his bowling success. Sir Home Gordon recalled meeting him at a post-tour dinner thrown by H. D. Swan, Essex County Cricket Club's shipbuilder president. Armstrong 'expatiated gleefully on the way he had "spoofed" England...by taking many wickets with what he called his own adjectivally innocuous bowling'. In the meantime, however, all he allowed himself was a little slow-dawning smile as each maiden and wicket accreted and brought victory closer.

Seldom have a country's cricket plans been so disarranged by a single setback as England's after the two-day Nottingham nightmare. Its bowlers were no better than triers, its batsmen plainly spooked.

Syd Smith would recall in *Australian Cricketer* the appearance of one particularly miserable county batsman: 'As Gregory started his kangaroo-like bound, this batsman commenced to gradually move away from his wicket and, by the time the bowler delivered the ball, the three stumps were all exposed and, needless to say, they were knocked over.' Even Wally Hammond, then a rising Gloucestershire star commencing a brilliant thirty-year career, had not the stomach for the fight: 'Jack Gregory had cultivated a fearsome stare and gave me the treatment. With knees trembling and hands shaking, I was relieved when he bowled me first ball.'

England's selectors were Reggie Spooner, a Golden Age batsman of famous charm, Harry Foster, oldest of the famous Worcestershire cricket family, and John Daniell, Somerset's captain. The last was a famously unconventional character, a former rugby international prone to sweeping damnations like: 'If you look at the hind leg of a syphilitic chicken, you will see a better cricketer.' The cowardice they had perceived at Trent Bridge had appalled them. When, having resisted honourably for ninety minutes, Yorkshireman Percy Holmes was bowled by McDonald while shrinking towards square leg, Foster fumed to Home Gordon: 'So long as I have influence in choosing England, Home, that man never bats in another Test.' He did not.

Which was all very well, but who would replace them? No fewer than six changes were wrought to the XI for the Second Test at Lord's beginning on 11 June. Like a line officer dismayed by the follies of his headquarters, Douglas exclaimed: 'What's this damnable side of pic-nickers they've given me?' His conscripts were simply swept aside. It was the Test debut of Johnny Evans, a sound player who had made an unde-feated 69 against the Australians for Marylebone, and a courageous man. As a wartime airman, he had won the Military Cross and bar. As a pris-oner of the Germans, he had organised escape attempts of such reckless derring-do that he had recently published a popular book, *The Escaping Club*, describing how his mother had sent him maps and compasses con-cealed inside cakes and jars of anchovy paste. Yet in the face of Gregory and McDonald, he was 'so nervous that he could hardly hold his bat, and his knees were literally knocking together…His nerve had gone and the first straight ball was enough for him.' It was Evans' only Test.

Such craven capitulation was too much for the selectors, who advanced as one to accost another of their new men, Middlesex's Nigel

Haig, instructing him to attack the Australian bowling. Writer Ian Peebles described the sequel:

At the top of the steps, Nigel met his defeated and highly disgusted captain. 'John,' he said. 'The selectors have told me to have a bash. What shall I do?' The reply was scarcely in the 'captain's hand on his shoulder smote' tradition, but, delivered in thunderous tones and sulphurous terms, it clearly indicated that, so far as his captain was concerned, the in-going striker was free to exercise his own judgment.

Haig succumbed to Gregory for 3, and in the second innings to McDonald without scoring. He didn't play another Test for almost a decade.*

Despite Woolley's princely 95 and 93, Australia secured an eight-wicket win at 1.35 p.m. on the third day, its captain having again proven himself the game's most paralysing bowler: McDonald's 8–147 from 43 overs had grabbed the ascendancy, Armstrong's 1–28 from 30 overs had secured it. 'GWP' of *Sporting Life* expressed English awe:

To see Armstrong lumbering up to the wicket…and then to watch him toss high into the air a weirdly slow and occasionally hanging ball is one of the engrossing spectacles of present-day cricket…Armstrong puzzles me. The mentality of this man is of no ordinary character and yet his appearance belies this. I can imagine Armstrong with his huge pipe in his mouth surveying with satisfaction the results of a good season's farming. I cannot visualise him as the chief cause of the decadence of English cricket. And yet it is so.

Only one of England's draftees emerged creditably from the debacle. The Honourable Lionel Tennyson was grandson of the poet laureate, and son of Australia's second governor-general. The defining experience of his life had been three years as an officer in the 60th Infantry Brigade; he had been wounded thrice, mentioned in dispatches twice, and lost both brothers. 'The war,' he commented euphemistically, 'was not exactly a circumstance to encourage the growth of moral precepts or to instil

---

* England's selectors would become such an object of ridicule that summer that an acting troupe called the Co-Optimists would in August introduce to their Royalty Theatre revue a skit called 'Choosing the Team'. A typical joke involved the selection of the postmaster-general 'because of his peculiar delivery'. Foster wrote to producer Davy Burnaby threatening legal action for such 'impertinence'; Burnaby responded by offering the teams free tickets.

the maxim of "safety first".' And, while his bereaved father transformed the Farringdon family seat into a shrine for his lost boys, Lionel tackled peacetime life with abandon. A compulsive gambler, he bought himself a black and white Rolls-Royce, then had to sell it three weeks later after losing £7000 at roulette. He thought he'd recovered an equivalent sum shortly after, only to have the debtor explain that he would need to commit suicide to raise the necessary funds. A belligerent batsman, Tennyson hit hard off the front foot with a rudimentary technique. 'He received the fast bowlers as the oak receives the storm,' recalled Raymond Robertson-Glasgow. 'And, when he fell to them, he went down with no grace or compliancy, but with a sounding, defiant crash.'

Tennyson had been notified of his selection while 'smoking my second cigar' at 1 a.m. at Bond Street's Embassy Club, and returned from failure in the first innings cheerfully dauntless: 'Never mind. Next time, I'll get 50 for sure.' He did better, hitting ten fours during an unde-feated 74, convincing *Wisden* that 'he, at any rate, was not afraid of the fast bowlers'. When Tennyson joined the Australians travelling to Southampton that evening for the tour match against Hampshire, Armstrong warmed to him. The Australians sailed to 5–569 by stumps on the first day, but Tennyson was cheerfully indomitable. When the cap-tains visited a music hall that evening, Armstrong promised to declare at 870. 'In that case,' Tennyson interjected, 'Hampshire will make 871.'

With Tennyson, Armstrong would form one of the more unusual kin-ships of his career: unregenerate roundhead and laughing cavalier. Armstrong liked Tennyson's 'gift of striking the right note'; Tennyson found Armstrong 'a mountain of geniality'. Yet there was nothing so unusual about it. To Armstrong, Tennyson would have seemed an incar-nation of the old English amateur spirit he admired, a spirit he could see that wartime austerities had endangered. Over the tour's duration, in fact, this would harden into prejudice, and precipitate yet another controversy.

By now, the Australians' tour had become more like a pageant, their games like social events. They were watched by the King, the Prince of Wales, Prime Minister Lloyd George, even members of the guard accompanying Prince Hirohito on his first visit to England. They were entertained by the Duke and Duchess of Portland, the Duke of

Newcastle, and Lord Saville. Armstrong was plied with gifts: Lord Lonsdale, entertaining the team at Cumberland's Lowther Castle, presented him a huge box of cigars bearing the Hohenzollern crest, a prewar gift from the Kaiser himself. He could neither visit theatres without provoking a chorus of 'For He's a Jolly Good Fellow', nor move in public without a gaggle of schoolboy admirers forming round him. Even a visit to a boxing bout with Johnny Douglas's father was news. 'He was attired in evening dress and really looked more formidable than any of the heavyweights,' the *Evening News* reported. 'The popular Australian…expressed the opinion that boxers earned their money far harder than cricketers.'

Some might have found such constant attention a strain; Armstrong was unembarrassed, perhaps unembarrassable. He told against himself a story of strolling round Southampton as his batsmen made merry, and offering his autograph to a child dogging his heels; the boy replied that he was actually following because Australia's captain was 'the only decent bit of shade in the place'. During a day's golf at Gleneagles a large gallery gathered to watch Armstrong tee off. It trickled a few inches. 'Even this catastrophe,' noted Oldfield, 'did not seem to worry him.'

Armstrong could obey the forms. He was a self-effacing Australian at a dinner in Skinner's Hall hosted by Surrey's president Sir Jeremiah Coleman: 'Sir Jeremiah made some reference to "barracking" in Australia. I think that "yours truly" has gotten most of it (laughter).' He was a loyal Briton at a House of Commons dinner with Lord Privy Seal Austen Chamberlain: 'We have come a long way to play this game and we hope you will find that we know how to play it. It is only a game after all. If we lose, we hope that we will take it in the same fine way that you Englishmen took it in Australia (cheers).' But of losing, Armstrong harboured no thoughts. His team was not merely beating opponents, but extirpating them, taking two days each to dispose of Northamptonshire by an innings and 484 runs (Armstrong claiming 6–21 from twenty overs) and Nottinghamshire by an innings and 517 runs (Macartney bludgeoning 345 in less than four hours). It was as though no man's land had been relain over twenty-two yards, but patriotic antipodeans liked it that way. After the Australians had attended her final concert at Covent Garden, Nellie Melba wired Armstrong instructing him 'not to be beaten on any account'. In London for the Imperial Defence Conference, Billy Hughes reminded the team at

Australia House that they were 'a very great advertisement for Australian trade and its development from a settlement to a colony to a common-wealth with an equal voice in the Empire'. Also visiting England that summer, the dramatist Louis Esson thought Armstrong's team more rep-resentative of his country and 'superior in character and temperament' to his generation of writers. He wrote to Vance Palmer:

> England are really scared of Armstrong and the fast bowlers…They are not pleasant players. A good English journalist described them as 'hard-bitten', 'grim' and pitiless. We shouldn't be a soft, mushy, maudlin race. In politics we're a shingle short, a nation of grinning village idiots. The cricketers fill me with great enthusiasm. They can lose, for there is luck in the game, but they'll never crack up like the English.

The Englishmen were indeed cracking up, an air of desperation clinging to their selections for the Third Test. Only four players were retained from Lord's, and the luckless Douglas was replaced as skipper after seven consecutive Test defeats by the Australians' new pal Tennyson—not so much an investment in tactical know-how as in breeding and education. 'Tennyson is not a great captain,' admitted the *Daily Mail*. 'But he is an optimist and likely to have a stimulating influence.' Tennyson himself remained incurably sanguine: 'If depression had settled like a blanket on the minds of most players, my cheerfulness seemed the proper antidote and the best chance of charming the fates.'

The fates went uncharmed. An English player confided afterwards to novelist A. A. Thomson: 'Everything happened but an earthquake.' After an hour, Tennyson split the webbing between his left thumb and fore-finger while at short leg. Then Hobbs, finally over his leg injury, doubled over with appendicitis. Complementing Macartney's 115, Armstrong hit a six and ten fours during his 77 in an hour and a half, and England fol-lowed a well-worn course to 2–22 at stumps on the first day chasing 407. It was like watching the armies of succeeding generations in combat, artillery and tank against sword and horse. Gregory bowled the next day with such fury that Andy Ducat's bat broke in his hands, a frag-ment breaking the stumps while the edge ballooned to slip. Tennyson emerged with a featherlight bat in his healthy right hand to slash 63, while the disinherited Douglas lingered four hours over 75. But Australia's victory margin was as conclusive as those at Trent Bridge and Lord's—219 runs—and the Ashes became incontestably theirs.

25

'The Lion Tamer'

Eight consecutive Test match triumphs, on both sides of the world: this was the unprecedented achievement the Australians toasted on 5 July at Leeds' Victory Hotel. Nor had these been chance's blessings; Melbourne's *Herald* believed that Warwick Armstrong's men 'exerted some hypnotic influence' over their opponents:

> The theory…only puts in a mystic form what many keen observers noticed the moment the Australians appeared in the field. Their easy confident bearing, their smiling exchanges of badinage, and their fielding practice…rather fascinates the crowd, which feels that here is a team that is pretty sure of itself and scarcely so much as a thought of meeting its equal.

Generally, the *Herald* was right: the team functioned smoothly. They bestowed nicknames on one another, from 'Ginger Mick' for Jack Ryder (thought to resemble Hal Gye's rendering of C. J. Dennis's famous character) to 'The Pirate King' for Tommy Andrews (allegedly the team's ladykiller). They had lucky totems, including a horseshoe trimmed with green and gold ribbons, and 'in a prominent position in the dressing room' an inflatable rubber kangaroo presented to Armstrong by his old friend Walter Brearley. The team's cricket, too, was distinguished by an indifference to individual accomplishments, a continuation of the AIF

XI's ethic. Philip Trevor, who claimed to have seen 'obvious signs' of personal glory-seeking in previous Australian teams, thought: 'Armstrong's Australians are not prone to that kind of selfishness. Perhaps if they were they would be severely reminded that this sort of thing does not pay.'

There were, however, frictions. Like every team, Armstrong's possessed members with exasperating habits. Bardsley was infamous for wishing to play every match, and according to Oldfield strongly protested his omission from one minor fixture 'because, as he said, he was the type of batsman that needed all the practice he could get'. Macartney was a notorious hoarder, who would stockpile in his 'home' chest the complimentary cigarettes the team received from the Army and Navy Store then cadge others. Eventually, Armstrong chided him; distributing green and gold scarves received from Jaegers, he teased his champion batsman: 'Now wear this, or I'll give it back.' But tensions Armstrong experienced were less with stars than with supernumeraries. The scenario is a familiar one. English footballer Rodney Marsh once remarked that managers need keep only eleven men happy: 'The eleven in the reserves. The first team are happy because they're in the first team.' The aggrieved here were chiefly Ryder and Edgar Mayne. Ryder, a Test regular in Australia, now found himself restricted to tour games; Mayne played still less, appearing in only fifteen of the tour's thirty-four first-class fixtures. Nor was he pleased about it, fuming when others complained of tiredness: 'You fellows should never have played cricket if you hate it so much! If I were Syd Smith, I'd bundle you moaning cows off straight away.'

Was this one of Armstrong's famous grudges? It cannot have been his decision alone: he had as co-selectors Collins and Pellew. Yet, as mentioned, neither Ryder nor Mayne had endeared themselves to their captain on the issue of playing hours. Mayne, a sound batsman but a clumsy fielder, and as fortunate to be in England as he had been nine years earlier, had also taken the place Armstrong felt Roy Park deserved. While playing the Australians, Raymond Robertson-Glasgow sensed subtle ill-feeling between the Victorian teammates: 'At Oxford, I thought I saw Warwick Armstrong look at Mayne once or twice as if wondering why Edgar hadn't stayed at home in Australia.'

Whatever the case, it became known after the Third Test that some team members were dissatisfied by their treatment. The *Herald* reported that letters 'received privately in Melbourne indicate that the players concerned hold strongly to that view'. Perhaps the only reason it did not become a serious issue was, as Donald Macdonald commented, because it was difficult to decry Armstrong's Test formula:

> Mayne and Ryder may have some grounds for complaint but I can't quite see it in regard to the first three matches...Mayne no doubt thinks he has a bit of a grievance because in cricket he is a bit self-absorbed and tremendously wrapped up in the game. That is a good quality in an international player but here again crops up the old human factor in the case—the defects of the quality.

The *Register,* meanwhile, allayed suspicions of discontent by publishing a letter from Armstrong to South Australian administrator Mostyn Evan: 'The boys have upheld Australia splendidly on and off the field. They are all happy and are feeling well, and I am vain enough to think they have entire confidence in me.' Not until 17 August 1921 was more explicit intelligence disseminated by the Press Association—publication after the rubber's completion, presumably, not being thought injurious to Australia's chances:

> Now that the last Test is finished, the Australian Press Association is in a position to divulge the fact that the team has not been a happy family. Apart from the disputes over hours of play and a day off before Test matches...it is openly stated that Ryder and Mayne are so disgusted with their treatment by the selection committee, especially regarding the Test matches, that they are unlikely to play further for Victoria under the 1920 conditions, and they have decided upon a certain course of action immediately they arrive in Melbourne.

Which was, one imagines, to relocate, although neither eventually did so. And the story, as such stories do, blew over; the proof of the pudding was in the Ashes.

Ryder and Mayne also belonged to a somewhat larger faction in the Australian team: its teetotallers, who at that time also included Macartney, Bardsley, Taylor, Andrews, Mailey and manager Smith. It is difficult today to gauge how the presence of this unit of abstainers influenced the team's collegiality, although Bill Ferguson later testified that it was a cause of considerable tension:

> Warwick Armstrong scathingly referred to his players on the 1921 tour as 'the lemonade crowd' just because they could not consume whisky on the scale of their skipper; Sydney Smith, teetotal manager on that trip, had to

put up with plenty of abuse from Mr Armstrong because he repeatedly resisted Armstrong's appeals to buy large quantities of champagne.

Baggageman and scorer Ferguson had since 1905 been a loyal bondman of Australian teams abroad, and of visiting teams in Australia, having at twenty-four ingratiated himself with Monty Noble by buying 'enough gold fillings to last me a lifetime' from the great man's dental practice. He would fill similar roles until 1954, his copperplate score-books and record of one lost bag (his own) in half a century winning him widespread renown. Yet in his 1957 autobiography, *Mr Cricket*, he confessed a detestation of Armstrong that Ernie Bean could scarcely have outdone:

> Armstrong is the skipper I liked least of all, and I am sure that any players unfortunate enough to have toured with him had identical feelings... Sydney Smith was a real friend to me, and I certainly needed a pal while Warwick Armstrong was throwing his considerable weight around; yet this same Armstrong had taken the trouble to promise Monty Noble before leaving Australia that he would make a point of looking after me on tour. I wrote later to Monty telling him how my 'friend' had taken every opportunity to snub me and impress upon me the fact that I was nothing better than a servant.

Ferguson gripes about Armstrong incessantly in *Mr Cricket*, even citing an instance where the team boycotted an invitation out of sympathy for their scorer, presenting possibly the most unattractive portrait of Armstrong ever published; proof, perhaps, that 'no man is a hero to his valet'. It smacks, in fact, of a grudge that deepened over time, and the flavour of the memoir implies its cause. Ostentatiously puffed with pride at the barest brush with celebrity—the book includes sentiments like: 'Whenever I hear people talking about the Royal Family being aloof and out of touch with ordinary people, I make a point of contradicting them, because I...have found them charming folk'—Ferguson was irked by anyone not sharing his self-estimation. It may be that Armstrong aroused his scorer's ire, at least in part, merely by not treating him as 'Mr Cricket'.

One should not overestimate tensions within the Australian side under Armstrong's captaincy. He managed the disparate personalities as well as could be expected. He kept a light hand on the disciplinary reins, requiring only that all players attend official functions. Hendry also testified that while Armstrong 'certainly could hold his grog in 1921', he was never incapacitated: 'Often after a very late night he would bowl right through to lunch and never put the ball off the right spot.' It may have been as well that Australia was such a vastly superior team, and that they won so consistently. But then, perhaps, that was the point.

As the Australians left the field at Headingley, Ted McDonald turned to his captain. He had poured his lifeblood into the Australian effort, shedding almost 10 kilograms from his pre-tour 80 kilograms. Now, mindful of their shipboard discussion about his 'putting in the peg' until the series was decided, he inquired: 'What about it, Warwick?' The captain replied expressively: 'Go for your life, Mac, and I'm with you!' It was time for fun, and a little profit.

When the Australians proceeded to Manchester, McDonald was contacted for the second time on tour by Lancashire League club Nelson. They had approached him at Nottingham about becoming their professional on a three-year contract worth £1650 with house, passage money and the expectation of testimonials thrown in: more than his tour fee, and far more than his clerk's wages with the Victorian Producers Association, an agricultural co-operative. It was this sort of enticement Donald Macdonald had foreseen in the *Argus* while musing on the board's 'policy of meanness', fearing that 'players with other outlooks in life, to whom the trip is no longer a novelty and a pleasure tour, will conclude "the game is not worth the candle"'. The *Herald* reported the fast bowler's intent to consult his captain and manager about the offer. Though no evidence of these discussions exists, McDonald's subsequent acceptance may be attributable to Armstrong's counsel. Few cricketers of the time more clearly saw financial security as a goal; and by now Armstrong was contemplating his own.

He had been joined on tour by his friend Charles Tootell, the liquor merchant, who planned to watch the remaining Test matches—and given the team's next destination and host, one suspects this was more than coincidence. The Australians arrived in Glasgow on 8 July, and were welcomed by the West of Scotland club, and its patron Peter Dawson. They were staying a week, playing some cricket and enjoying the vistas. Before 10,000, Australia piled on 540 convivial runs in five hours. Armstrong made an even-time 87. Afterwards they were Dawson's guests, motorcading through the scenic grandeur approaching Loch Lomond,

Armstrong sharing a saloon with Dawson and his sons Alexander and Rupert. And Dawson, it happened, was an exceedingly wealthy man—the third generation of a distilling dynasty whose whisky was world-famous, to the extent of having been the preferred tipple on Captain Robert Scott's ill-fated Antarctic expedition of 1912.

Armstrong knew all about Dawson. The Scot had entertained Noble's Australians royally at the end of their 1909 tour, placing six chauffeured automobiles and valets at their disposal for a week then picking up their expenses. His reputation as a benefactor of antipodean causes—the *Leader* described him as 'the well-known distiller who admires everything Australian'—had been secured two years earlier by his sponsorship of aviators Raymond Parer and John McIntosh in the Royal Aero Club race from England to Australia. Parer's biographer describes how colleague John Thornton steered them in Dawson's direction:

> 'The only Peter Dawson I know is Peter Dawson's Whisky,' said McIntosh.
> 'That's the very man. He's a millionaire they say, and he likes Australians, too. Had 'em in his home hundreds of times and he's a friend of Billy Hughes.' Thornton became more enthusiastic telling McIntosh and Parer that the least they could do was try. 'He'll listen to you at least. He'll listen to anyone. There's no snobbery about old Peter, for all his money.'

Dawson said simply: 'Buy your machine.' He asked only that they convey a bottle of Dawson's to Hughes, which they did, as well as painting a grateful 'PD' on their DH9's fuselage and dedicating to him their *The Adventures of Parer and McIntosh*. With Armstrong's team, Dawson again lived up to his reputation: it is easy to imagine fraternal feelings developing twixt captain and capitalist over dinner at the Hotel Tarbet, and on a Sunday steamer journey through the Kyles of Bute, taking in such sights as the Harland and Wolff shipyards and the Fort Matilda torpedo factory. A photograph of Armstrong with Dawson journeying down the Clyde captures their easy rapport. Too soon it was time to part, but they would meet again.

The Fourth Test at Old Trafford began under inky skies on 25 July, but there are hints that Armstrong's planning for it began a month earlier at sunny Southampton. During that Hampshire match, onlookers had watched a painstaking hundred from Philip Mead, a thirty-four-year-old left-hander who epitomised the dour county pro: Robertson-Glasgow saw him as possessing 'the air of a guest who, having been offered a weekend by his host, obstinately decides to reside for six months'. Gregory was resting, McDonald bowled only fourteen desultory overs, and Mead enjoyed the respite offered by Mailey, Ryder and Hendry. Almost a gift. Perhaps it was.

This appears nonsensical: Mead was having an outstanding summer, and would surpass 3000 first-class runs. Yet in three-day Tests, mere weight of runs could not carry the day. Teams had to move smartly: the Australians, indeed, would bat and bowl at hourly rates on tour of 66 runs and 118 deliveries. Mead's selection would have the opposite effect on the English effort. He could exasperate even his county captain Tennyson, who once wired Mead while he was batting: 'Get on or get out—signed Tennyson.'

Did Armstrong want England's selectors to pick Mead? He was certainly alive to the cost of slow batting. Talking with the *Argus* later, Armstrong stated that his team sometimes let less enterprising county professionals remain at the crease in order to kill games: 'On occasions when I knew we had no chance of winning a game but when there was a possibility of losing it, I directed my bowlers to let them stay there knowing the players would not force the pace.' More explicit still was a recollection of Home Gordon: he related that Armstrong told him of bidding his men at Southampton to let Mead have his hundred 'so that he should be included in the last two British XIs, believing that his soundly deliberate batting methods would ensure inevitable draws'. A boast? Or Armstrong at his most Machiavellian?

If it was the latter, Mead played his part to a tee. The Test's first day was lost to rain, turning the match into a two-day affair in excellent batting conditions, but Mead pottered 136 minutes over 47: 'With his side in a very strong position,' *Wisden* grumbled, he 'carried caution to an extreme.' 'England had a splendid opportunity,' agreed Smith, 'but they played scotch instead of going for the bowling.' Until Percy Fender joined Ernest Tyldesley in late afternoon, England were squeezing out less than two runs an over. The match's contraction, too, had a subtler effect. At tea, with Australia ticklishly placed if compelled to bat on a damp pitch the following day, Armstrong was approached by Hanson Carter.

Recalled to Test cricket in Australia when Oldfield broke a finger, forty-three-year-old Carter had been enjoying something of an Indian summer, fully nineteen years since being Armstrong's teammate on their first trips. Now he proved his worth by demonstrating an intimate knowledge of cricket's statutes. 'If they don't close before ten to five,' he confided, 'they can't close today.' For there was a wrinkle to Marylebone's 1914 revision of cricket's Laws. Law 55 (1914) stated that 'when there is no play on the first day of a three day match, Laws 53 and 54 shall apply as if the match were a two-day match'. The applicable section of Law 54 stated that declarations in two-day games 'may not be made on the first day later than one hour and forty minutes before the time agreed upon for drawing stumps'. With stumps scheduled for 6.30 p.m., Tennyson could not close after 4.50 p.m. Carter placed a *Wisden*, open to the relevant page, on his locker when play resumed.

'There is something important going on,' commented Archie MacLaren after tea. 'Those Australians keep looking at the clock.' Yet he, two other former English captains Warner and Douglas, and most importantly Tennyson, were oblivious to the declaration deadline. The clock passed 4.30 p.m., 4.40 p.m., 4.50 p.m.; still at 5 p.m., nothing had happened, and Hendry recalled his comrades' 'great sighs of relief'. Armstrong had just completed an over when Tennyson finally declared at 4–341, but it was 5.50 p.m.—an hour too late.

The next twenty minutes rank among the most chaotic, and comical, in Test cricket's 124 years. Motioning his men to remain on the field, Armstrong sauntered towards the pavilion. Preparing to put Australia's openers through an uncomfortable last half-hour, Tennyson was surprised to be interrupted by his *Wisden*-toting friend. As Tennyson hurriedly consulted Douglas, Warner and MacLaren, Armstrong re-emerged briefly to summon his fielders and warn the groundsman against rolling the pitch, then adjourned to his dressing-room balcony where he puffed impassively at his briar. Finally, amid universal mystification, Fender and Tyldesley resumed batting.

On the face of it, history had been made: Australians had reminded Englishmen of their own rules. Most correspondents took Armstrong's gesture in good part. 'The Australians were perfectly correct in sending us out again,' said MacLaren in the *Daily Express*. 'The game must be played according to the Laws of Cricket.' The *Daily Mail*'s Herbert Henley felt 'the fault really lay with our own captain'. Yet Fender's recollections, imparted to biographer Richard Streeton, lend events a different colouration. Agreeing the debate 'a bit abstruse', Fender nonetheless believed Tennyson's declaration lawful:

> Tests were stipulated as being of three days' duration; nowhere that I could find did it specify that a Test could become a two-day or a one-day match if rain prevented it starting on time…Or putting it another way, if it was a Test, was not the Monday the second day and Lionel, therefore, entitled to declare?

When seven years later Fender shared a locomotive compartment with Armstrong in Australia, he taxed his friend about that day's events. Armstrong admitted that his protest was a 'try-on'; he was unsure of Carter's advice, but content to 'use up some time'. In this light, the incident is less an example of Australian shrewdness and English ineptitude than Australian bluff and English credulity—bluff coming, of course, from perhaps its foremost antipodean exponent. And what occurred next sealed Armstrong's renown. Amid uncomprehending demonstrations from spectators who had expected Australia to bat, Armstrong took the ball to recommence bowling. Indeed, he seemed keen to do so, moving in before fielders had taken their positions, though he stopped when the crowd's agitation intensified, and sat down.

There Armstrong remained, like a medieval Lord of Misrule pausing to admire his handiwork, while umpire Jim Street detoured to the fence to inform more boisterous patrons that England's declaration had been rescinded. Then as the official hurried back to his position, Armstrong brought the chaos to a fitting finale by commencing what was, of course, his second successive over. 'To the utter consternation of the observant,' reported the *Sportsman*, 'Armstrong actually went on to bowl thereby BREAKING LAW 14 as he had bowled the last over himself. Whether his action was intentional we cannot say.'

'The observant' excluded many newspaper correspondents: most failed to report the happening next day amid argument over the annulled declaration. As to whether the action was deliberate, Armstrong never let on. His sly response to the question from Fender later—'He would not answer this, but smiled and looked away'—implies either that it was, or that he enjoyed people thinking so.

When Australia survived the last day, it was their twenty-sixth consecutive match either won or drawn. Thirteen remained. A question now arose. Could Armstrong bequeath to posterity the unprecedented achievement of a tour unblemished by defeat? Could he live up to his family's motto: *invictus maneo*, 'I remain unconquered'?

With this landmark in view, the Australians tackled their programme with renewed purpose. Essex and Warwickshire were routed by an innings. Only bad weather prevented facile victories against Glamorgan and Lancashire. Armstrong arrived at Canterbury in an ungiving mood; he added 194 for the fourth wicket in less than two hours with Macartney, allowed Australia's 676 to run deep into the second day, then cold-bloodedly killed the game by declining to enforce the follow-on when Kent's reply petered out after two and a half hours. When a few players looked askance, he drawled: 'Put 'em on and do as you're told. There's a Test coming on and I'm not overworking my bowlers for any-body.' Australia's meaningless second innings commenced amid slow hand-clapping from the 2000 spectators, which only ceased at the request of Kent's skipper Lionel Troughton. 'The chief object of a team involved in a cricket match,' griped the *Daily Mail*, 'used to be to win.' But spectators hadn't seen anything yet: in the Fifth Test, beginning the following day, Armstrong came as close as any captain to simply deserting a match.

Any rain in a three-day Test markedly lengthened odds on its completion. This game had much; fifty minutes late beginning, three further hours were lost after lunch. By 4.30 p.m., spectators were restless. Noisy hundreds invaded the field, marshalling around the pavilion. 'The Oval crowd is more—shall I say?—outspoken than the Lord's crowd,' reported the *Daily Sketch*. 'And when it surged across the ground to the pavilion, I thought that Armstrong, with whom it was very very angry, would need as much of that heftiness of his as he could muster.' An impasse developed. Tennyson wished to inspect the pitch. Armstrong wanted the kibitzers dispersed first. Tennyson pleaded with the protestors: 'If you people will get back to your places, Mr Armstrong and I will inspect the wicket.' Nobody budged. Armstrong lit his pipe and waited. Robert Lynd wrote:

> One youth went so far as to suggest that the Australians were afraid to face England. Imitating the voice of a newsboy he yelled: 'Speshul! Australia runs away!' Others contented themselves with bellowing: 'Come out of it!' 'Be sportsmen!' 'Play up!' One youth every now and then interjected a wonderful: 'Cooee!' Like the cry of a shriekowl, prolonged and a hundred times magnified.

Not until 5 p.m. did the siege dissolve, permitting examination of the pitch. The *Herald* reported:

> Armstrong's close inspection evoked jeers and hoots. He often flicked dirt from his fingers to the accompaniment of cries of 'Get a towel'. Applause mingled with hoots, greeted the Australians when they came onto the field again. A favourite cry was 'windy' intending to signify that the Australians were guilty of cowardice.

Five hours of what Neville Cardus described as 'intolerably ugly batting' from Mead against bowlers whose interest was manifestly slight became the match's centrepiece. Australia's reply did not begin until 4.15 p.m. on the second day, and their 389 in five and a half hours proved ample to ensure stalemate. Nothing was at stake for either side when England began its second innings at 3.24 p.m. on the last afternoon, and Armstrong's attitude soon became obvious. Gregory and McDonald were relieved after a few overs by Mailey, then by part-timers Pellew, Andrews, Taylor and Collins, while the captain retreated mulishly to the long field at the Oval's Vauxhall End. Once only in next three hours did he stir: when Fender attempted to enliven events with some big hitting, Armstrong could not resist lumbering twenty metres to catch his friend. Otherwise he allowed bowlers to rotate as they pleased and fielders to configure themselves, his presence merely a concession to the obligation of a full XI. Cricketers can, of course, become bored with games they are involved in, yet few can have radiated such utter indifference to events round them, and to more than 10,000 spectators. 'If the finish of the match does not increase Armstrong's popularity on English grounds,' decreed *The Times*, 'he himself is responsible.'

The notion has developed subsequently that Armstrong's *ennui* was somehow an expression of contempt, even a sort of republican irreverence, for Tennyson's English team. This owes itself to a gesture of Armstrong's reported by among others 'Throw In' of the *Daily Express*: 'He is a very monument of boredom. He stoops to pick up a piece of newspaper as it flutters across the ground in a freshening breeze and calmly proceeds to scan its crumpled page.' This image was enriched in Arthur Mailey's 1958 autobiography to include Armstrong's explanation: 'I wanted to see who we were playing.' The story of Australia's colossus perusing a newspaper in the outfield with a Test in progress has since passed from generation to generation.

Sadly for the legend, the story has improved in the retelling: as soon as it appeared, it was contradicted. 'The story that Armstrong picked up a newspaper blowing across the ground and actually read it while play was in progress during the Test match at the Oval is perfectly untrue,' reported *Town Topics*. 'Armstrong picked it up, looked to see what newspaper it was, and tossed it aside.' Armstrong himself denied it when talking to journalist J. C. Clegg at tour's end. 'All that happened,' wrote Clegg, 'was that while in the "country", a leaflet containing photographs of cricketers blew on to the ground, and after picking it up and glancing at it to see what it was, he rolled it up and threw it off the field.'

There is weight, however, to the view of Armstrong's demeanour as Australian self-assertion; perhaps also an expression of Australian sporting mores. Australians had long grumbled about the three-day Tests that England's county program compelled, proclaiming the superiority of timeless cricket. 'We have all along contended that Test matches should be played out,' stated Joe Darling after the Ashes of 1905. 'They are not Test matches if you don't.' Describing the 'enormous interest' aroused by 'the greatest sporting event in the British Empire', Monty Noble commented: 'If the incentive is big and important enough to induce such devotion, it should be big enough for the authorities to produce a definite result.' The issue now became the subject of a fascinating debate between two former English captains, Pelham Warner and Charles Fry, in the *Morning Post*. Traditionalist Warner deplored Armstrong's dog-in-the-manger attitude, claiming that 'his entire lack of interest was a bad example to the many young men and boys who were watching the match'. He concluded: 'Perhaps I am old fashioned…but England v Australia is the greatest cricket match in the world and as such should be played in a great spirit.' Having sixteen years earlier annoyed Armstrong with his critique of leg theory, Fry now supported him, laying blame at his own cricket establishment's door:

> Armstrong is as good a sportsman as Warner and cares as much for the good of the game; but he is bold and unselfish enough to risk being misunderstood, to risk his reputation for sportsmanship, in an effort to obtain rectification of the glaring irritating absurdity of a team travelling 13,000 miles to the possibility of five drawn Test games, by taking the only possible means to bring it under the serious consideration of our cricket authorities. There is excessive pseudo-heroic, silly solemn nonsense in our treatment of what we are pleased to call our sportsmanship.

This was a penetrating remark. On one level, Australia's games at Canterbury and the Oval were indeed demonstrations—Armstrong's way of influencing people, if not winning friends. And to a degree, they worked. *Wisden* felt the time had come to consider a 'very differently arranged' program: 'A day must be kept clear in advance of each Test match. We do not want a repetition of the farcical cricket seen in the match with Kent at Canterbury.' *Sporting Life* likewise lent support to timeless cricket: 'Every Test ought to be played to a finish. This would be possible if the counties would withdraw their opposition.' Yet the means, and the philosophy they expressed, were as significant as the ends: the game was not 'the thing', but for winning, and if this was impossible scarcely worth playing. Australians had always played hard, but never before Armstrong's captaincy with quite such disdain for 'pseudo-heroic, silly solemn nonsense'. It can only have been with Armstrong in mind that Cardus thirteen years later wrote his exquisite estimation of the antipodean sporting ethic: 'The Australian plays cricket to win; he has usually left it to Mr Warner to make Empire-binding speeches.'

Scenes at Canterbury and the Oval little blemished Armstrong's public standing—rather, perhaps, much as the occasional 'courageous' or 'unpopular' decision can enrich a politician's reputation, they completed the image. 'If history and the British Empire mean anything at all, something ought to be done about him,' thought 'GP' of the *Manchester Guardian*. 'Epstein could hew him in Cornish granite…directing the field to his liking with one arm steadily and unmistakably outward, and which once uplifted moves not.' Tribute verses were published, caricatures commissioned, the most famous by *Punch*'s Frank Reynolds. In 'The Lion Tamer', a supplicating British lion surrenders his autograph book to Armstrong with the words: 'I know a good man when I see one. Sign, please.' At a London dinner he threw the team, Donald Mackinnon stated: 'The big man seems to have in his personality and in his temperament quite caught the public eye. Armstrong is not merely a successful captain. He is an Australian institution.'*

* *Punch*'s caricature was viewed as such an honour that MCC secretary Hugh Trumble wrote to the magazine's proprietors 'for the purpose of having it hung in our pavilion here'. In the meantime, however, it appears that Reynolds had offered the sketch to Armstrong. The Melbourne committee minuted on 29 November 1921 that it had been 'presented by artist to W. W. Armstrong', and it later featured in *The Art of Cricket*. (For samples of verse tributes, see pp. 420–21).

Not everyone felt warmly, of course. For Australians in England, Armstrong's success could be a sore point. A young naval rating, J. E. Hewitt, later an air marshal, was joining a new ship that summer, and recalled his 'curious' welcome: 'I liked the engineer, but he had many words to say about Warwick Armstrong's trickery as captain of the Australian XI...My elation over the success of the Australian XI touched a nerve spot.' Others, however, competed for the honour of hosting Armstrong and his men. They were received by the Shakespearean actress Madame de Navarro, the queen of popular romance Marie Corelli, and the distinguished novelist J. M. Barrie. 'Barrie "tremendously wee", sat beside the huge, amiable, invincible Armstrong,' recorded his private secretary Cynthia Asquith; 'I, to the dazzled envy of my small son, between Collins and Gregory.' Mailey demonstrated googly bowling on the village green, before a more serious exhibition, claiming all ten Gloucestershire wickets for 66. By the end of August, when they met an 'England XI' in seaside Eastbourne, only four opponents stood between Armstrong and an unprecedented clean sheet.

This XI had become the plaything of Archie MacLaren, now in his fiftieth year, who all summer in the *Daily Express* had boasted of formulae to beat the Australians. 'Archie,' Armstrong teased him, 'you haven't a bolter's chance.' But MacLaren had taken his task seriously, characteristically vesting his hopes in amateur talent: specifically Cambridge University's Hubert and Claude Ashton, Clement Gibson, Percy Chapman and Michael Falcon. He had also recruited thirty-eight-year-old South African Aubrey Faulkner, no stranger to Armstrong after touring Australia a decade before. And Faulkner's suggestion in the *Westminster Gazette* was that Armstrong entered the match warily: 'Curiously enough, the Australians were a little uneasy over the game before it started...There is always something a little unsettling in tackling an unknown quantity and our side was nothing if not an unknown quantity.'

Nothing occurred to trouble the Australians at first. Amid the scattered spectators was only one reporter: the *Manchester Guardian*'s Cardus, bidden by a letter from his idol MacLaren. The England XI's innings was then curtailed in an hour and a quarter for 43, and when Australia cruised blithely to 1–80, the game appeared a pushover. But there, Armstrong commented ruefully afterwards, was the rub: 'If they had scored 143 instead of 43, we should have won the match.' Falcon and

Faulkner benefited most as Australians squandered their wickets, limiting the England XI's arrears to 131. Cardus, having lavished 150 words on MacLaren's first-ball duck in order to cheer himself up, was persuaded to remain, although he stowed his luggage with the station master in case a quick getaway proved necessary.

When the 'England XI' subsided to 4–60 early on the second day, this appeared a wise contingency. In his famous account of the game in *Autobiography*, Cardus recalled at this point edging towards the exit once more, then again being beguiled by Faulkner and Hubert Ashton, 'their quiet strokes making echoes in the deserted place'. He stayed: 'By the time I had reached the exit gate, I had seen enough. I retraced my steps a little; I sat on a bench facing the pavilion. I did not go to London that day. Or the next.' Australian opposition reawakened all Faulkner's dormant talents. He added 154 for the fifth wicket with Ashton, layering his chanceless 153 with twenty fours and a six. Chasing 175 with nine wickets remaining on the final day, the Australians faltered, against an XI mostly unknown to fame. Twenty-one-year-old Gibson would truncate his career by emigrating to Argentina; now he overthrew the obstinate Bardsley. Twenty-one-year-old Falcon would renounce first-class cricket in favour of a House of Commons seat; now he bowled the magnificent Macartney. White-haired MacLaren at second slip seemed possessed of magical qualities. At 103, Pellew top-edged a pull that hovered over the catching cordon. MacLaren folded his arms, turned his back and advised first slip Hubert Ashton: 'I think you may have that one.' With effort, Ashton got there. 'Well done,' the sage averred, 'but I never had any doubt.'

Armstrong, by contrast, was suddenly invisible. With Australia an anxious 5–106 at lunch, requiring 87 for victory, he had still to bat. Teammates were puzzled. Hendry recalled: 'Edgar Mayne and I were not playing and had been to the local race meeting, and were dumbfounded on returning to the ground to find the side in dire straits and Armstrong had not yet batted, eventually going in seventh or eighth [actually ninth].' Syd Smith ascribed it to arrogance: 'Personally, I think our skipper took too much for granted on the last day, thinking that defeat was out of the question.' Yet, in his *Follow On*, E. W. Swanton recalled: 'Of this game Arthur Mailey told me more than once how acutely nervous Armstrong was on going out to bat in the second innings: "shaking like a great jelly" was the phrase, if I remember aright.' If so, it was the only occasion in Armstrong's career when his nerve was other than steely. But Eastbourne's sea air that day was saturated with tension and emotion. When Ryder miscued to cover, leaving Australia 6–143, Smith was accosted by some agitated Australian women. 'Are we going to be beaten, Mr Smith?' asked one. When Smith admitted there was a solid possibility, she protested: 'Oh no, don't say that!' The crowd promptly erupted again: Gregory had fallen lbw. The woman was escorted away in tears.

MacLaren now played his last card: Faulkner. Cardus saw a 'profoundly sombre expression' cross Armstrong's face when the South African promptly bowled Andrews: 'Gone was the old geniality. Where were his quips and oddities now?' Armstrong himself was then lbw, hesitantly offering no stroke, and Mailey's fall on the dot of 3.30 p.m. meant the Australians had lost by twenty-eight runs to the greybeard MacLaren and his youthful companions.

For MacLaren and Cardus, involvement in one of the century's most celebrated matches was a profound validation.* For Armstrong, it was perhaps his bitterest blow. Englishmen certainly enjoyed its infliction. 'Rip's' *Cricketer* cartoon depicted MacLaren puncturing a pneumatic Armstrong, the deflating figure muttering: 'Et tu MacBrute.' 'A Cinder from the Ashes!' exulted the *Evening News*. 'Armstrong's Waterloo' decreed the *Morning Post*. Nor did absence from the match prevent E. H. D. Sewell, in *Log of a Sportsman*, describing Armstrong's making a truculent exit: '…a well-known cricketer who was there informed me that Armstrong was simply livid at the result. He galumphed down to the station alone like a wounded bear with a very sore head, extremely tired of life, and scarcely on speaking terms with the rest of his team!' Perhaps, however, Sewell's was wishful thinking; Armstrong seems afterwards merely to have been stunned. A *Westminster Gazette* correspondent found him dejected and wistful as he left: 'He looked, as he said, a disappointed man and, in the course of a few remarks with the *Gazette* representative, he could only reiterate: "I am disappointed."'

---

* The victory amply restored MacLaren's credit in English eyes. He was shortly appointed coach of Lancashire on a salary of £550: a godsend for one who had always had difficulty living within his means. Attendance was also a coup for Cardus: 'At this incredible match, at this consummation of a great cricketer's life, the *Manchester Guardian* was the only notable newspaper represented. By my faith in MacLaren I achieved this, the only "scoop" of my career.'

Armstrong demonstrated at Brighton next day he had no intention of losing again, setting Sussex 260 to win in 105 minutes, although Mailey hastily routed the hosts by 197 runs. It was in this match that Armstrong so irked Arthur Gilligan, and the pair tangled again when Australia then met South of England: an incident, in its way, subtly revelatory of the tour. Armstrong had added 43 with Andrews in a reviving partnership when, Gilligan recalled, he nudged to leg:

> I was on the ball like a flash and Warwick Armstrong—five yards out of his crease—was within a yard of me. I picked the ball up and was throwing it under arm to Strudwick the wicketkeeper when I received a heavy blow on my right arm...Armstrong easily regained his crease. I was livid with rage, and this was increased when Armstrong said: 'Do you think I did that on purpose?'

A recrudescence of Armstrong's competitive nature? One cannot say. The protocol is that batsmen may hold their line while running, and that it behoves bowlers to take evasive action, but Gilligan suspected more to it, unleashing a retaliatory bouncer that removed the Australian captain's cap. And though Armstrong probably felt he had the last word by adding 248 in 158 minutes with Andrews in the course of an undefeated 182, the definitive utterance was from Jack Gregory to Gilligan at tea: 'Arthur, the boys are mighty sick about what happened out there; it was too bad of Warwick. After all, he might have remembered that it was not a Test Match!' Although this appears another occasion on which Armstrong's obduracy embarrassed younger colleagues, there is a dual edge to Gregory's apology, and Gilligan's face value acceptance of it: that what was unsuitable for a lazy day at Hastings might be condign in the context of a Test. After fifty Tests over twenty years, Armstrong's had become the way forward.

26

'Alas, Poor Warwick!
He Was Slimmer Then!'

Hopes of an unbeaten record foiled already, Australia lost its last first-class game also, at Scarborough against an Invitational XI, albeit narrowly by 33 runs and with five minutes to spare. For Warwick Armstrong, there was also the *memento mori* of a pair. But his team's record, and his own, remained imperishable: twenty-three of thirty-nine matches won, the captain third in batting with 1213 runs at 41.82, and first in bowling with 100 wickets at 14.44. Nor had merely deeds impressed. The *Daily Telegraph*'s Philip Trevor was struck as much by their insouciant accomplishment:

> Macaulay has said of Warren Hastings that he was tried by both extremes of fortune and never disturbed by either. Something of the kind may be said of Armstrong the cricketer. A superficial observer might mistake his repose for indifference. Some of us always knew better than that, and practically all of us know better now.

Former rival Frank Foster saw Armstrong as having spooked the whole country:

> I honestly think that Australia have got to thank one man, one man only, for their success. That man is Warwick Armstrong, probably one of the best captains ever sent to England from Australia…He yawned and drawled, he

played 'doggo', he finessed, and while finessing he picked the cricket brains of England…Armstrong the general, the man our men actually feared, the man who introduced post-war *fast* bowling to England, and the man who had the confounded cheek to commence his attack with *two* fast bowlers! No wonder England gasped and quailed, shuddered and fell, and then expired.

It would, however, have been unlike Armstrong to depart England's shores without leaving one final flaming public row in his wake.

Armstrong skipped the Australians' final game, a social match at Cumberland on 13 September, taking Charles Tootell to stay in Manchester with Walter Brearley: team members now had almost three weeks of rest and recreation ahead of their South African sojourn. One entertainment Brearley provided was a game of bowls at Fallowfield's MAC Club, Armstrong challenging long-time member John Studd. Also present in photographs of the occasion is a stout, moustachioed, bowler-hatted figure: J. C. Clegg, a prominent *Manchester Evening News* journalist. Between ends, there was time for talk, and for Clegg to interrogate Australia's captain. 'Many subjects were discussed,' recalled Tootell. 'And, as was inevitable, cricket was one of them.' By the time the game was finished—Studd winning 11–8—many issues had been explored. Clegg, catching Armstrong off guard, had a juicy story.

With Tootell, Armstrong then enjoyed a week in Scotland as Peter Dawson's guest. They visited his firm's distillery in upland Dufftown, went shooting and fishing, and talked business. By the time they had finished, Armstrong had been appointed an agent for Dawson's 'Special' Scotch Whisky: a precious benefaction to which we shall turn later. On 18 September, however, as Australia's captain supped at Dawson's table, Clegg published his 'interview', including a passage to excite howls of condemnation:

> 'Why do you think the England Test teams were unsuccessful?' was a question I asked him and his reply was as terse as it was to the point.
> 'The players were too old and you had too many professionals,' he said.
> Enlarging on this expression of opinion, Armstrong remarked that some of the players chosen by England gave way as many runs in the field as they made with the bat. More than anything else, however, the methods of the professionals were all against England's chances of winning a three-day Test match. The time was much too short for men who, being

professionals, would play for themselves and not for their side. 'You never have got, and never will get, the average professional to play as he should do in a match restricted to three days,' said the Australian captain with quiet emphasis.

These typically trenchant views were unsurprising. Armstrong's closest English cricketing friends were gentlemen: notably Archie MacLaren and Walter Brearley, latterly Percy Fender and Lionel Tennyson. And while Australians might be of a more democratic temper, looking askance at the customs separating amateur and professional in hotels and dressing-rooms, they respected English cricket's bloodlines. Armstrong was doubtless thinking in this case especially of Philip Mead, but the Australian view was general and abiding; Arthur Mailey expressed it in his autobiography thirty-seven years later:

> The average professional cricketer is purely and simply a tradesman, and in most cases has to learn his trade in a pretty grim school. He has a six-day-a-week job and the regularity of his work is likely to drive him into a groove. Unless he is a very exceptional man he stays in that groove for security, and the result is loss of incentive, the spirit of adventure and ambition.

At the time, however, Armstrong's words touched a nerve. Marylebone president F. S. Jackson was outraged ('Armstrong's views regarding professionals are a gratuitous insult not only to professionals but to cricket itself'), Lord Harris dismissive ('I do not think Mr Armstrong's view of English cricket is worth listening to'), Jack Hobbs hurt ('His slight is not easy to understand'). Still more censorious were responses from Yorkshire, its greatness erected on a bedrock of professional endeavour. Secretary Frederick Toone commented: 'The professionals resent the insinuation as a serious calumny.' At its annual meeting, president Lord Hawke turned an appreciation of the Australians into a wholesale denunciation of their captain:

> The personnel of the Australian side was excellent, being marred only by the indiscreet remarks of their captain who attempted to decry the tone of the English professional, and actually asserted that betting took place, and also that if umpires were appointed early for the whole series they might—I say might—be influenced by such betting…Further, I saw the other day a letter from a very prominent Australian cricket official who strongly deprecated Mr Armstrong's observations on this point as well as his unfair criticisms of the English professional, adding that Australians were ashamed of his tactics in the Fifth Test at the Oval which this great

cricketer and general—for no-one can gainsay that he is a great judge and player—endeavoured by his attitude to reduce that match to a farce.

The identity of the 'prominent Australian official' who had written to Hawke so unctuously is unknown, though one suspects Syd Smith. Certainly, Smith was mortified by the Clegg interview's contents, and pressed Armstrong about them. The captain did not recant; he merely complained that he had not known Clegg intended to publish. Clegg retorted that the interview was 'authentic to the last comma'.

The irony of the condemnation is that many of Armstrong's critics shared his assumptions about amateur superiority—it was merely that one did not, as it were, utter such remarks in front of the servants. The furore had a piquant sequel when England next toured Australia under the captaincy of Arthur Gilligan, a competent cricketer though scarcely outstanding. Some began questioning the taboo on professional captains, disbarring the likes of Hobbs from office. In the *Weekly Dispatch*, Lancashire's Cecil Parkin then proposed that the optimum arrangement for the Australian tour would have been to nominate Kent's amateur Percy Chapman 'under the supervision of Hobbs'. This provoked Lord Hawke to one of cricket's most famous—and infamous—orations, again at a Yorkshire annual meeting:

> If it had been a Yorkshire professional and my committee were of the same mind as myself, I do not think Parkin would ever step on another Yorkshire cricket field…For a man who calls himself a cricketer to write an attack on the English captain and at the same time to say that the best cricketer he ever played under was Hobbs is beneath contempt. I trust no professional will ever captain England.

Suddenly the boot was on the other foot. Hawke's outburst was widely damned by, among others, Armstrong. Demanding abolition of 'snobbish distinctions', the *Daily Sketch* reported: 'Warwick Armstrong did not mind coming out and without the slightest hesitation said: "It would be a good thing for cricket if Lord Hawke were out of the game." Such remarks as these were "repugnant to cricketers in Australia".' Armstrong would have enjoyed that.

So Armstrong left England trailing a comet tail of controversy. Not that this would have meant much to him: as the Australians boarded the

Balmoral Castle on 30 September, he quietly foreshadowed retirement at tour's end. Even old critics like Pelham Warner of the *Morning Post* issued fond tributes: 'He has been a great cricketer and a great personality, and his pleasant smile and happy figure will be missed on every English ground.' Likewise John Corbett Davis, never chief among Armstrong's admirers, struck a respectful note in the *Referee*:

Many other noted cricketers have made similar announcements only to come forth again more than once. But in this case it looks as though the announcement will be realised in fact when the time comes. Armstrong has had a wonderful career and though he has not always seen eye to eye with the controllers of cricket in his state or acted with uniform tact, he has been a very wonderful player, the greatest ever produced by Victoria.

The curtain fell sooner than expected. By the time the *Balmoral Castle* arrived in Cape Town on 17 October, Armstrong was ill, afflicted in concert by malaria and bruising on his legs. He remained cabin-bound as Smith and Collins greeted the mayor, then continued round the coast to Durban's Royal Hotel. As his leg remained 'troublesome', he moved into the town's sanatorium for a fortnight, and was destined to play no cricket at all on the visit; Collins assumed the captaincy, leading Australia to a ten-wicket victory in the only Test concluded. Instead, 'the Big Aussie' became a kind of celebrity guest, his doings occupying the society rather than the sporting pages. 'There has probably never been an individual member of any team that has toured South Africa,' enthused the *Natal Mercury*, 'who has had the admiration of all so much as Warwick Armstrong.' At Wanderers, he sat in the royal box with Prince and Princess Arthur of Connaught. At Newlands, he was accompanied by Mr and Mrs Percy Day, the latter in 'a smart check coat and skirt and a mastic straw toque trimmed with clusters of grapes'.

Not that Armstrong courted popularity, even with his own team. There was a curious incident at Johannesburg when Springbok Dave Nourse was given out caught at the wicket and walked ten metres towards the pavilion before the umpire changed his mind. Oldfield recalled being 'chastised' by Armstrong for not removing a bail, and thought his captain 'was expecting a lot'. Nor did Armstrong shrink from expressing opinions of local cricket. At Durban's Banqueting Hall just before his team's departure, he voiced an old Australian complaint that matting would have to give way to turf if the South African game was to progress. 'He had heard numerous excuses as to the difficulties in the way, but they were all tommy nonsense,' reported the *Cape Times*. 'People in South Africa were getting into a groove the same as in England. He had gotten into trouble for making these remarks in England but if he went back he would say the same again.' South Africans accepted criticism rather more calmly than Englishmen. Western Province's secretary Vollie van der Bijl commented appreciatively: 'Mr Armstrong told me that he had seen the desired soil all over the country, although I have not seen it myself. Still it must be here, for Australia's leader is not a man who talks lightly on such matters.'

Armstrong's other recreation, while convalescing in Durban and aboard the *Ascanius* home, was literary. While in London, he had contracted to write an instructional work for young cricketers. Methuen had an eclectic list: not only did they publish Joseph Conrad, Arnold Bennett and R. S. Surtees, but the jungle adventures of Edgar Rice Burroughs and the works of Albert Einstein. The firm had just enjoyed great success with *The Art of Lawn Tennis*, written by the American Wimbledon titleist 'Big Bill' Tilden in three weeks. *The Art of Cricket* by 'Big Warwick' Armstrong was a natural companion; the 30,000 words probably took him little longer.

As remarked, it is today more a book of interest rather than an interesting book. The voice is authentically Armstrong's, though mainly because so little of direct relevance about the writer is imparted; which may also be why Methuen included a celebratory epilogue, 'W. W. Armstrong', by Archie MacLaren, to remind readers of the author's stature. But the book was assuredly a novelty, only the fifth by an Australian Test player, and the second primer.[*] Given that cricketers turn authors today at the merest provocation, perhaps this was another trail Armstrong helped blaze.

More than a thousand well-wishers lined the platforms of Spencer Street station in Melbourne on Christmas Eve 1921, and they were impatient: the express ferrying the Australian team's Victorian and New South Welsh members arrived an hour late. They grew still more impatient

---

[*] The other four were Billy Murdoch's *Cricket* (1893), George Giffen's *With Bat and Ball* (1898), Frank Laver's *An Australian Cricketer on Tour* (1905), and Frank Iredale's *Thirty-Three Years of Cricket* (1920).

when Armstrong remained coyly out of sight: they were, the *Herald* explained, 'waiting for the "big man"':

'Good on ya, Warwick!' This and a thousand other greetings resounded as the Australian captain stood quietly at the aperture and hats were waved. Armstrong merely smiled, raised his hat and moved backward into the car. But this was not enough for the crowd. The din became greater, and Armstrong was asked to come out and let the crowd have a proper look at him...So the genial captain returned and three cheers were given for him and repeated. Then with a huge portmanteau...he finally stepped onto the platform. The crowd struggled off the platform and followed Armstrong to his car, surrounding which were hundreds of people. 'Good stuff Warwick', 'We're all pleased to see you' and eager inquiries as to the state of his health were some of the expressions voiced in the walk along the roadway.

Aileen and two-year-old Warwick Geoffrey, there with Charles Tootell, had been surrounded for some hours by curious onlookers: 'The little boy took the mute admiration without affectation for he knew it was all meant for daddy, to see whom he was naturally all the more eager than the strangers.' Placing his son on his lap, Armstrong was driven to Scott's Hotel in Collins Street for the official reception, 'dodging up to the back entrance' to avoid another crush. There he was welcomed— probably in a strained fashion—by Ernie Bean, Mat Ellis and Harry Rush—and in speaking could not resist a snipe at the board:

I am one of the happiest men today. We have had a very hard time. In fact, it is one of the hardest tours I have experienced for the reason that we ran into a dry season. Bad arrangements were made regarding the programme. We travelled thousands of miles unnecessarily. This is due to the fact that the arrangements were put into the wrong hands.*

---

* Reporting to the board on 4 January 1922, Smith foreshadowed a new practice for the organisation of fixtures: 'There is no doubt that the program could have been better arranged and the travelling of the team minimised but I do not think the Board's representative was wholly to blame in this matter, as several counties, I understand, selected their own dates and then Mr Latham had to fill up the vacancies among the other county clubs. This is undoubtedly the wrong procedure, and at the Imperial Conference I was successful with my co-delegate Dr Mailer in getting them to agree to future programs being drawn up by the Board of Control in England.'

Bean, Ellis and Rush sniped back, excluding Armstrong from the day's luncheon for players involved in Victoria's game against New South Wales. Still nursing his leg, Armstrong had ruled himself out of the match, but the VCA's action smacked to Donald Macdonald of churlishness: 'An invitation to lunch is a small matter but one still wonders why the association overlooked an ordinary courtesy to a man who has done so much not only for Victoria but for Australia.'

Thus did Armstrong's career as an Australian first-class cricketer more or less conclude. He could perhaps have been more graceful; the VCA could certainly have been more grateful. Armstrong's team had made the board a fortune, its £35,644 revenue more than compensating for the financial disaster of the previous English venture. That 1912 flop—undermined, of course, by the 'Big Six's' absence—was much in mind when the board agreed on 4 January 1922 to apportion its £12,822 spoils on the basis of monies foregone to reward the board's loyalists during the dispute: Armstrong would not have known it but, ten years after, he was helping to pay the costs of a dispute in which he'd been lynchpin.

Similarly strange was that in expressing gratitude to Armstrong's men by voting a £300 bonus to each player and the manager, the board ensured that the touring party's best-paid member was Syd Smith: the players received their bonus on top of a £466 allowance, Smith his in addition to an original £600 fee. Little wonder that when Smith published his tour book, *With the Fifteenth Australians,* team members were peeved to learn they had to pay for copies.

That, however, was behind Armstrong now. Never of course a board captive, he was now a free agent. That same day, he spoke at a South Melbourne gathering: 'He had been in all the squabbles of the last few years and had come out all right, and he intended to stop out (laughter and cheers).' His valedictory was in Sydney a month later as captain of an Australian XI against the Rest of Australia, where he compiled a sedate 77 not out in 139 minutes; on the game's final day, he formally resigned his Melbourne clerkship in order to work for Dawson's.

All that remained were the obeisances, chiefly the culmination of his testimonial, and 500 guests gathered at Melbourne's Town Hall on 31 March 1922 for a smoke social in Armstrong's honour. He was surrounded by a host of supporters spanning his whole career: from Monty Noble and Clem Hill, teammates from his Test debut, to John Baragwanath, so staunch during Armstrong's sacking from the Victorian team a year earlier. There was Victoria's governor the Earl of Stradbroke, lieutenant governor Sir William Irvine, and the presidents of the Melbourne Cricket Club, VCA, SACA and WACA. After the loyal toast, tenor Joseph Foster sang 'Drake Goes West' and 'Give a Man a Horse He Can Ride', while Will Elder recited 'Cricket At Rednose Flat' and 'Why Doherty Died'. But it was Prime Minister Billy Hughes who, presenting a £2500 cheque, captured the *Argus's* imagination:

> Mr Hughes in making the presentation said that it was very fitting that they should do honour to their friend Mr Armstrong, for Australians were a sport-loving community. Sport was to us a national manifestation of our character. Whether sport had made us a great nation or whether being a great nation we had naturally taken to sport, he looked to them and to the metaphysicians to decide. It was certain that in sport, as in war, we were easily first (cheers). There were other games, but cricket was 'par excellence' the Australian national game (hear hear). We were loyal subjects, and we sang 'God Save the King', and dutifully cheered the banner of Old England, but we sometimes got mixed over the names and dates of the kings of England. Over the names of the kings of cricket, what they did, and what they stood for, we were in no doubt whatever (laughter)...
>
> If ever there was a man singled out as a king of sport it was Mr Armstrong, who had gone out to give the people of England a chance to regain the Ashes, and who had returned, like Imperial Caesar, who 'came, saw and conquered' (cheers)... It was a fact that when Warwick Armstrong went into the field, the English team were half beaten, and when he took the ball they were wholly beaten. He rejoiced in that, because, when one set out to teach one's grandmother to suck eggs, it was well that she should be thoroughly taught. Warwick Armstrong had done more good for English cricket than a library of books or a cohort of expert teachers. He showed them where their weakness lay.
>
> 'This Australia of ours wants advertising,' remarked Mr Hughes. 'Two things have advertised us in the past—the ANZACs (loud cheers)—and this was admitted even by the Americans who won the war (laughter)—and the Australian cricketers (hear hear).' Clean sport was doing more for the moral welfare of the community than anything else. A nation was tested not by numbers but by character. They had before them a man who was hailed as a king in the world of sport—a great cricketer and an example to the whole community where his influence was very far-reaching (loud applause).

It was a classic Hughes oration, blatant populism blended with strutting nationalism, from the airy allusion to high-falutin 'metaphysicians' (of which he, a man of common sense, had no need) to the subtle puncturing of imperial conceits (rendering England as egg-sucking 'grandmother' rather than as succouring 'mother'). Celebrating sporting achievement in the same breath as military accomplishments, it sought continuance of the patriotic strides Australia had taken through blood sacrifice in wartime. So here it was: Armstrong's night, Armstrong's forum, an event at which one might have anticipated some gesture at an account of himself and his career. He chose instead the simplest of farewells:

> They did not want him to say much about cricket—probably he had already said more than he ought. He was sorry that the time had come for him to pass out of first-class cricket and international cricket, but he had many happy recollections of twenty years of the game. He took the testimonial as an indication that he had 'played the game'.

Next morning, Armstrong rose and played the game again. Two months from his forty-third birthday, he joined Noble in a minor match for Melbourne against Combined Public Schools at the MCG. He then enjoyed Melbourne's annual Easter trip to country Victoria, taking 5–41 against Echuca and 107 off Kyabram. Perhaps, for this compulsive cricketer, life without prospect of the game—a game, any game—was unthinkable. Aileen Armstrong had probably hoped her husband's withdrawal from big cricket would cause him to follow more conventional patterns. They had, after all, an infant son, and recently rented a new St Kilda apartment at 15 Fitzroy Street. Yet their life together would continue for some years yet to be shaped by cricket, and spent in the society of cricketers. Armstrong remained a big name—indeed, they came no bigger. 'Where will you find nowadays,' asked Hugh Trumble in *Life*, 'the hero worship that made every small boy, a few years ago, treasure Victor Trumper's photograph and put Warwick Armstrong's under his pillow? Alas! Poor Warwick! He was slimmer then!' Publication of *The Art of Cricket* in May 1922—'A Practical and Enlightening Book by the Popular Captain of the Successful Australian Team'—brought further tributes. Business commitments delayed Armstrong's start to the following season, but he was conspicuous among the welcoming committee for an English amateur team led by Archie MacLaren on 14 November. His return as captain of Melbourne on 9 December was headline news in *Sporting Globe*.

Armstrong was still more than capable—over five more years with Melbourne, he would average 51 with the bat and 21 with the ball—and unsoftened by age. Playing Northcote, he upbraided teenager Hans Ebeling for misfielding at mid off: 'Bend your back! Anyone would think you were forty instead of seventeen.' On another occasion against Collingwood, Armstrong commandeered the ball to dismiss a batsman called Griffiths. 'Give me the ball,' he snapped. 'I'll get Griffiths.' Having done so, he tersely returned the ball to Ebeling: 'You ought to be able to get the rest.' Armstrong could even be short with old colleagues. Hunter Hendry, lured from New South Wales by the offer of Armstrong's pavilion clerkship in April 1924, recalled the captain rounding on Vernon Ransford during a game against Richmond. Ransford had been involved in a productive partnership, then appealed the light when a dust storm blew up. 'When Vernon came into the dressing-room,' Hendry remembered, 'Armstrong absolutely castigated him, saying he should have capitalised on our great start...I was shocked!' It was, indeed, a rather unmannerly display towards someone who had recently seconded Armstrong's honorary life membership of the Melbourne Cricket Club.

Perhaps the cheeriest match of Armstrong's post-Test career was at the MCG on 11 February 1925, when he joined Noble, Hill, Carter, Ernie Jones and Billy Bruce for 'Old Internationals' against an ex-servicemen's XI to raise funds for unemployed soldiers. Some of the old guard had not aged well—Bruce was frail from influenza, Jones hampered by 'aldermanic girth'—but Armstrong had lost nothing. He claimed 2–20 and struck six fours in his 63 in eighty-six minutes, scoring the winning runs before being caught at slip by Bob Grieve, winner of a Victoria Cross at Amiens. Most poignant, 'Mid Off' of *Australian Cricketer* thought, was the sight of Hill batting with Peter McAlister:

> One of the happiest outcomes of the match was the reconciliation between two veteran players, Hill and McAlister, between whom there had for many years been an estrangement due to the incident arising in the torrid days of the trouble between prominent players and the Board of Control.

Whether there was a similar rapprochement between McAlister and Armstrong is unrecorded; perhaps 'Mid Off' knew better than to ask.

The date of Armstrong's last competitive game of cricket is uncertain, though it appears to have been in February 1931, for a Melbourne club XI against officers and cadets of the Flinders Naval Depot: a suitable locale for the 'Big Ship's' final dry dock. He was in his fifty-second year, and appeared as it were by popular demand. A participant in the game survives: Hugh Trumble's son Charles is probably the only man living to have batted with Armstrong. Now resident in a Melbourne home for the aged, he nonetheless recalls Armstrong vividly, both for being 'enormous in girth' and unshakeably confident:

> During our innings I had gone in to bat, about number four or five and, my partner losing his wicket, who should emerge with a bat over his shoulder but the great Warwick Armstrong? Apparently everyone there, anxious to see him in action, had prevailed on him to 'don flannels' (I've no idea from where these came). The flannels were a bit tight fitting. Before taking stance, he moved past me and, waving his bat, said: 'Listen son, I'm not doing any running, so no calling for singles or anything else!' He hit two or three fours, a six, then, having had enough, scooped up an easy catch to first slip. He stalked back to the pavilion to a highly appreciative ovation...Although it was ten years since he had captained Australia there was a big crowd of naval trainees all waiting to obtain 'Armstrong's' autograph as he left the field.

27

'Staunch, Strong Sort
of People'

With the cessation of big cricket, Armstrong moved into the world of big money. Based at 43 Queen Street, he was registered Melbourne agent for Peter Dawson 'Special' Scotch Whisky, using Charles Tootell's MacKenzie Allan as distributor. In May 1922, he set off on the first of many business trips, three weeks in Western Australia—not coincidentally, one imagines, the Australian state then with the highest per capita whisky consumption.

The spirits trade was a logical post-cricket career for Armstrong, and not merely out of personal taste. Several contemporaries whom he knew well were in the business. Archie MacLaren had dabbled in it, while Percy Fender ran a wine merchants in which he later took Lionel Tennyson as a partner, and even marketed a scotch labelled with his initials 'PGH'. Armstrong also had established relations with leading locals in the business, including John Fogarty—instigator of that unlikely Mentone Reserve contest in February 1921.

Big British spirits firms had long recognised Australia as a significant market: before the war, Australia had consumed more than a fifth of the 10 million gallons of scotch they exported. With the introduction of prohibition in the United States in January 1920, its importance had increased further. Australia consumed half as much whisky again as

Canada, and as much whisky as India, South Africa and New Zealand put together. Despite continuation of six o'clock closing, introduced as a wartime measure in October 1916, Victoria alone imported more than 300,000 proof gallons of spirits per annum.

Peter Dawson's 'Special' fared well in the Australian market, differentiating itself as 'a genuinely old whisky'; its trademark Scottish warrior raising a toast with a ram's horn conveyed that it was 'The Brand of Historic Lineage'. But imports in general were dominated by four companies—grain whisky giant Distillers Company Ltd, and the so-called 'Big Three' blended whisky makers, James Buchanan Pty Ltd, John Dewar & Sons, and Walker & Sons—which controlled about 60 per cent of British production. Australian market share, moreover, was difficult to increase, because prices, fixed by the United Licensed Victuallers Association, were uniform: every imported whisky in Victoria in 1922 cost 11 shillings a bottle. Importers were not so much in competition amongst themselves as against cheaper indigenous spirits, foremost among their manufacturers the Federal Distillery in Port Melbourne's Rouse Street: brainchild of perhaps the most controversial Australian entrepreneur of the age, John Wren.

Even today, Wren's name has a disreputable ring, having been model fifty years ago for Frank Hardy's grasping and venal John West in his novel *Power Without Glory*. Such notoriety was probably always inevitable, given not only the defiantly demotic nature of his business ventures (gambling, horseracing, boxing, gold mines, newspapers) but his Catholicism. As biographer Niall Brennan put it: 'Wren succeeded at the thing that the average Irish Catholic was hopeless at: making money, which enabled them to fill an enormous vacuum in their culture largely at the price of his own reputation.'

For such a hate figure of morals campaigners, and one so often suspected of corruption and gangsterism, Wren was a private and ascetic man. His distillery, a partnership with friends Pierce Cody and Frank Leith, was a characteristically opportunistic venture, selling whisky about 30 per cent cheaper than imports. The plant was small but efficient, and integrated vertically with the Cody family's distributorship Austral Wine and Spirits. It also achieved economies of scale in May 1923 by merging with four other small operations to create Federal Distilleries, with Wren the largest individual shareholder.

There is something apt about Armstrong finding Wren a business rival—two rugged sports-loving co-religionists. Their paths would almost certainly have crossed at cricket occasions, where Wren was known for generosity: he had organised a testimonial race meeting for the great bowler Harry Boyle in September 1907 and been the biggest contributor to the 'Blackham Ball' subscription of January 1916. Wren was also friends with Mat Ellis, who had bought for the Wren stable the Caulfield Cup winner Murmur. And even where whisky was concerned, Wren understood the value in Australia of the sporting image. Advertisements for Federal's Captain Cook Whisky at one stage juxtaposed line drawings of Cook and a giant crouching batsman whose identity was betrayed by the legend 'Two Great Captains—Breaking All Records': Warwick Armstrong.

Armstrong's success as an agent during his three years with Dawson's is unquantifiable, but he appears to have established himself effectively. The firm exported about 50,000 proof gallons to Australia and New Zealand annually, one large client being the Melbourne Cricket Club, which agreed to stock Dawson's as one of four bulk whiskies: nothing but the best for Armstrong's old club. Certainly, Armstrong was doing well enough by February 1924 to undertake a lengthy business and pleasure trip to England, leaving aboard the *Osterley*.

Englishmen were happier to have Armstrong as companion rather than competitor. He watched several of the summer's Tests against South Africa. He chummed up again with Walter Brearley on a visit to Wrekin College in the Shropshire market town of Wellington, where Brearley's son was enrolled, and spent a pleasant three days coaching and playing in a twelve-a-side game. Always indulgent toward children, he not only allowed himself to be bowled by a boy called Tom Withers, but a couple of weeks later sent him the ball as a souvenir engraved with a silver plate.* Appetite whetted, he also played several times for Bickley Park Cricket Club in south-east London, helping them win their annual derby against Bromley by taking four wickets and making 93, and took

---

* The engraving reads: 'With this ball, T. N. Withers bowled Warwick Armstrong at Wrekin on 23rd May 1924.' The story of the gift is recounted in the school's history, which concludes: 'Such are the acts of great men.' It records another visit by Brearley three years later with Archie MacLaren, who at fifty-seven made 42 in a social match, declining the offer of a runner. MacLaren is reported to have dozed

The bat in his hand is like a hammer in the grip of a Vulcan': Neville Cardus's simile seems apt for this image of Armstrong at practice in 1921.

THE LION TAMER

Drawn by FRANK REYNOLDS

British Lion (to Mr. Warwick Armstrong) : " I know a good man when I see one. Sign, please."

'The Big Man has quite caught the public eye': caricaturists like 'Quip' of the *Johannesburg Star* and Frank Reyno[lds] of *Punch* revelled in the opportunities Armstrong afforded them. Armstrong (below) was less popular with Yorkshir[e] secretary Frederick Toone (left) and Australia's manager Syd Smith (right), with both of whom he skirmished in 19[...]

'The well-known distiller who admires everything Australian': in July 1921, journeying down the Clyde with distiller Peter Dawson (with beard, seated next to Armstrong), Australia's captain struck up a rapport that flowered into a business relationship. When Dawson's company was taken over, Armstrong became an employee of James Buchanan & Co, undertaking a final cricket tour of New Zealand in March 1927 with Melbourne in order to further its interests (below). Aged forty-seven and weighing 140 kilograms, he was still a formidable cricketer.

'Not embarrassed by the ties of personal friendship': as a pundit in the 1930s (left), Armstrong's outspoken writings made him as unpopular and widely discussed as at any stage of his cricket career. He was a mellower and thinner man by the time he met the English cricket team in November 1946 (below), with his old vice-captain Herbie Collins and England's captain Walter Hammond.

eight wickets in a guest appearance for Marylebone in a game on the Channel island of Jersey.

The trip's chief focus, however, was the state of the British whisky trade. It was disquieting. Profits were suddenly shaky, the industry burdened with substantial surplus capacity. What temperance movements and excise duties had set out to achieve, shifting demographics were now bringing about: younger people were losing the taste for what was increasingly seen as an old man's drink. Armstrong visited the Empire Exhibition at Wembley, where Dawson's was one of forty whisky firms sponsoring a huge stand promoting their wares. The pavilion had been decorated as a medieval Scottish keep, complete with portcullis, over which was blazoned 'Alba Gu Brath' ('Scotland forever')—the famous war cry of the Gordon Highlanders as they stormed the French at Waterloo. Defiant shouts, however, were no defence against this secular shift in consumption; more drastic measures were required.

It is probable that, on this trip, Peter Dawson confided his intention of selling out. Old whisky was then in short supply, and Dawson's 2.75 million proof gallons would fetch a premium. Armstrong was home by the time the transaction was consummated in December 1924, the assets of Peter Dawson's Ltd being acquired jointly by Buchanans, Walkers, Dewars and DCL for about £2 million: 'a further step', commented *The Times*, 'toward the consolidation of the whisky trade'. But the grandest scheme would emerge three months later when, after two years of discussions, Dawson's four acquirers announced that they would themselves amalgamate, under the name Distillers, through a share swap. The merger promised to restore fortunes all round: DCL's dour managing director, William Ross, was acclaimed by Lord Dewar as 'our new Moses', leading the new combine 'out of strenuous competition into a land flowing with respectable dividends'. Doubtless Armstrong was sorry to lose his first business patron, but he above all understood the power that scale conferred.

---

off during the sermon, and was stirred from slumber only by the padre's announcement of hymn number 200. Nudging his comrade, Brearley said: 'Wake up Archie. This is where we take the new ball.' A picture of Armstrong at Wrekin is still in the possession of his grandson Warwick, and signed: 'Your old pall [sic] Walter Brearley.'

The merger terms were such that each constituent retained its identity beneath the Distillers canopy. From 1 January 1925, Armstrong became an employee of James Buchanan. Curiously, while new to the firm, Armstrong was well known to its eponymous founder, whose quest for 'a blend sufficiently light and old to please the palate of the user' had obtained him the royal warrant. A lifelong sporting enthusiast, Buchanan had in July 1905 entertained Joe Darling's Australians at his 1214-hectare Sussex estate, Lavington Park. The visitors were overwhelmed by Buchanan's successful stud farm and hospitality: as souvenirs of their visit, each received a gold matchbox engraved with his name, the flags of Australia and Britain, and the symbol of hands clasping across the sea. This was more than a gesture: though raised to the peerage in 1922 as Lord Woolavington, Buchanan retained a regard for Australians that would later manifest itself in a most remarkable way.

Momentarily, the scotch whisky industry faced some unpleasant obstacles, not only in Britain but in Australia. John Wren—'the master wire-puller', as New South Wales' premier Jack Lang called him—had been busy: Australia had just imposed preferential duties on imported product. The preference on local whisky in Australia amounted to 9 shillings per gallon, a sizeable differential given the average export price of 26 shillings per gallon. This time the response came from whisky wholesalers: they decided to try distilling themselves. In June 1926, representing the so-called Whisky Merchants of Victoria, Armstrong's friend John Fogarty arrived in Britain to solicit DCL's interest in a joint venture to counteract the punitive duty. DCL sent directors Sir James Calder and Peter Dewar to Melbourne to conduct their own review, and by year's end agreement had been reached for a greenfields venture at Corio, 70 kilometres south-west of Melbourne. DCL would own 51 per cent of the venture, which with capital of £250,000 and annual output of 750,000 proof gallons would be considerably larger than Federal. The balance of funds was subscribed by merchants under a March 1927 agreement to take 80 per cent of requirements for Australian whisky from the plant for ten years. Perhaps as a gesture of good faith, Armstrong himself had a small financial exposure to the project, buying 800 shares in MacKenzie Allan at a cost of £1000.

The enterprise opened under bad omens. DCL's Ross, en route to Australia in November 1928, suffered a shipboard fall, significantly impairing his eyesight. Opening the plant in March 1929, he gave a strangely querulous address to the effect that 'it could not hope ever to produce a whisky even approximating to scotch'. As Ronald Weir remarks in *A History of Distillers*, it was 'more like a curse than a blessing', and it worked. The project's strategic sense was validated when, after further lobbying of new Prime Minister James Scullin by Wren, the preferential duty on imported whisky increased to 17 shillings a gallon. But the wholesalers found their whisky hard to shift. Without the Vicker's and Burnett's Gin that the Corio plant produced under licence, the investment would have been a fiasco. To save face, DCL chose to snuff out competition. Fortunately, with the economic climate clouding after the Wall Street crash of October 1929, Wren was suddenly a willing seller.

One wonders how these negotiations transpired. Perhaps they took place at Wren's poky and inconspicuous office at the corner of Bourke and Russell streets, described by Hugh Buggy as 'austere as his habits—almost bleak', adorned only by a few faded photographs of favourite pugs and thoroughbreds. Perhaps there were meetings in Armstrong's more commodious quarters at Henty House in Little Collins Street, which he shared with Dewar's agent Thomas Campbell. It would have been a study in contrasts: small, bandy, abstemious, tight-lipped Wren; tall, vast, bibulous, inscrutable Armstrong.

DCL acquired Federal Distilleries in March 1930, and the end of Armstrong's brush with his era's most notorious businessman is embodied in a notification of a change in directors dated six months later: as Wren and three colleagues resigned from Federal's board on 13 September, Armstrong and three DCL colleagues joined. For Armstrong, this was a new sort of competition, success measured in pounds and shillings rather than runs and wickets. Yet in another sense, he had scarcely moved at all, for he remained part of the same social, sporting and commercial networks as before.

Despite his increasing business obligations, Armstrong maintained throughout this period a strong sporting profile: doubtless the latter helped the former. He continued playing cricket. He started playing golf.* He was regularly seen at the races, both at Flemington and

---

* The *Herald* reported on 10 December 1926 that Armstrong had been playing golf the previous day at 'a course just outside Melbourne', probably Woodlands. He had 'not long taken up the game seriously', which may explain why he was attired in cricket flannels and boots.

Caulfield. Most importantly, at the Melbourne Cricket Club's annual meeting on 11 September 1925, he was elected to its committee.

The club was still cordially detested by the association of which it was part. Leo Cussen used the same meeting to issue yet another 'unqualified denial to any suggestion that the club as a member of the VCA was spending its time devising schemes to undermine the association'. Armstrong's identification with Melbourne also probably told against him when he was nominated as an Australian selector at the board's annual meeting three weeks later: he was unceremoniously booted out at the first ballot. As Joe Darling commented sadly:

> It is absolutely amazing to find such fine cricketers as Hughie Trumble, Warwick Armstrong and Vernon Ransford at the present time being debarred by the Victorian Cricket Association from being appointed as selectors on behalf of Victoria and Australia simply because they are all members of that fine old body, the Melbourne Cricket Club, which made Victorian and Australian cricket.

Withal, the club was faring well. It was bigger than ever, with 5500 members and a waiting list of 3000, and more prosperous, planning a new £50,000 grandstand. It also maintained its reputation for generosity. One of Armstrong's first tasks was to compose a testimonial committee with Trumble, Ransford and Ramsay Mailer for the indestructible Bob Crockett, which Melbourne endowed with 100 guineas.* A year later it also agreed to tour New Zealand, to help the New Zealand Cricket Council bankroll its inaugural Test tour of England. Armstrong volunteered to lead a team.

This seems an instance where, for Armstrong, business dovetailed with sport. Buchanan's was pushing Black and White whisky—Britain's second-largest selling whisky, distinguished by its black bottle and white label—into the New Zealand market. Under what better circumstances could a salesman visit than at the head of a cricket team? In fact, Hunter Hendry believed that business was Armstrong's sole purpose in making the trip, recalling that much of his free time was devoted to courting locals who might be of future assistance. Hugh Trumble confirmed to

---

* Cussen presented Crockett with a £1043 cheque during the tea interval of the district final in March 1926. Deeply moved, Crockett nonetheless truncated his acceptance speech by glancing at his watch. 'Well,' he said, 'it's time to get out there again.'

the *Dominion* that Armstrong's presence had been endorsed by the DCL board: 'We owe a good deal to Mr P. Dewar that Mr Armstrong was able to come as this trip might have fallen through without him.'

'We have come over to help New Zealand cricket as much as we can,' Armstrong told the *New Zealand Herald* when his team arrived on 1 February 1927 aboard the *Marama*. 'I personally will give all the advice possible to advance the game.' The paper described him as 'a household name throughout the cricket world, the most perfect length bowler the world has known and the first man to introduce the famous leg theory'. Some must have found this hard to believe: now in his forty-eighth year, and recently revisited by his malaria, Armstrong weighed about 145 kilograms. When he met a Black and White agent at Dunedin railway station and found him of similar dimensions, he mischievously proposed a bet on who was heavier. The local's weight was 130 kilos; Armstrong's was not precisely determined, because the scale buckled beneath him. He could also still be cantankerous. Hendry recalled that, on joining the team late in New Plymouth, he found a couple of younger teammates concerned about their relations with the captain:

> I guessed there was something wrong when the two said: 'We want to see you urgently.' It appeared Armstrong spoke to them about drinking too much…So I said: 'Have you asked the Big Ship to have a drink?'
>
> 'Oh no,' they said.
>
> 'You start straight away'. And it was the usual custom from then on for all the team to go straight to the bar of the hotel on returning from the ground each night and in turn buy Armstrong a Black and White. No more trouble.

Armstrong, nonetheless, retained remarkable powers as a cricketer. In the course of thirteen matches, he maintained an average of 53. In the second game against Waikato at Hamilton, he scored 166 with twenty-two fours and a six. In the first 'Test' against New Zealand at Christchurch, he bowled 41 overs and winkled out six wickets. Outwardly, too, Armstrong was all charm. With Trumble and Ransford, he met members of the New Zealand team to tour England at Daniel Reese's home, briefing them about English conditions and talking up their chances: 'You are sending the right boys away to England. There are four or five of them who will come back champions.' He even took a personal interest in a teenager from New Plymouth, O. M. Naismith, who made a spirited 94 for Taranaki against Melbourne on 18 February.

Armstrong was complimentary about the innings—'he had the correct stance, sound defence, picked the right ball and hit it hard'—and the youth wrote him gratefully:

> Please permit me to express to you my sincere thanks for your kind remarks regarding my play. I am very fond of the game and desire to further my knowledge of same but, in a small town such as this, one has not the opportunities afforded one in a larger centre. I would deem it a great favour if you would give me your advice as to the advisability of my going to Australia where I would have every opportunity of bettering my play.

Melbourne found Naismith work as a linotype operator at the *Herald & Weekly Times* through cricket writer Ern Baillie, and its annual report forecast a bright future for him, reporting that he was 'desirous of settling in Melbourne and possibly will be here before next season starts'—ultimately, though, Naismith did not accept the invitation.

Armstrong's New Zealand hosts reciprocated this generosity, sometimes to a fault. At one function at Christchurch's Winter Gardens, they presented him with a kaiapoi rug; at another at Wellington's Wellesley Club where Hendry recalled Armstrong 'trying to further his Black and White interests', they even drank him under the table:

> We had to sail that night for Lyttleton. I happened to be behind Armstrong when we reached the gangway and I could not help noticing his face—it was blood red like a full moon—and he certainly made heavy weather of climbing aboard. After about ten minutes at sea, Hugh Trumble came up to me laughing, saying: 'I must tell you this, Hunter. The purser came to me saying Mr Armstrong was in the wrong berth and would I get him out?' Trumble told him the only way that would be possible would be by using the derricks.

Armstrong's final cricket tour was also the only occasion on which he played regularly with brother Tom, ten years his junior. His Waikato exhibition actually encompassed a New Zealand record last-wicket stand with his brother of 226, Tom contributing an unbeaten 89. Tom's left-arm spin also accounted for 39 wickets on the trip at 23.

A bank officer with the Wales, Tom had been bowling successfully for Melbourne's Second XI since returning from active service. Another big man—as tall as his brother, though lighter at 110 kilograms—he bore on the field a more than passing resemblance to his relative. Studying him against Northcote in November 1927, *Sporting Globe* saw 'very little between them':

> In Tom one saw again all the methods and many of the mannerisms of Armstrong—the same walk, almost the same run to deliver the ball, a very similar action in delivering the ball, the same rolling of the head to one side at the time the ball was delivered—and even the same mannerism of giving a tug at his cap when about to bowl. In build he is but a smaller edition of Armstrong, and one who did not think of the difference in their sizes might easily make the mistake of thinking it was the former Australian XI man who was bowling...For some years he has been getting wickets for the Melbourne Second XI and, judging by his success this season, his promotion to the First XI has been delayed longer than it should have been.

A fair point: in January 1928, Tom bowled himself into a Victorian team that visited Hobart, though his 8–112 ultimately counted less than his thirty-eight years and he never reappeared. But one wonders why Tom was so long confined to Melbourne's Second XI. According to the widows of Tom's two boys, Warwick Francis and John Arden Armstrong, perception later grew in the family that Armstrong had either told against Tom's elevation, or shown him no favours—that 'Armstrong wouldn't have him' and 'wasn't going to have his baby brother in the team looking at what he was doing'. True or not—and it seems unprovable—the claim reflects an estrangement between Armstrong and his family during the 1920s.

Since the war, Armstrong had been something of an absentee brother and son. He had been in England when his sister Olivia had married Arden Armstrong on 27 April 1921 and when Tom had married Molly Young on 30 August 1924. He had also missed lengthening periods of ill-health experienced by father John, who since George Major's death in October 1921 had soldiered on alone at Major and Armstrong in spite of heart problems.* This may have resulted in part from tensions between Armstrong's wife Aileen and her in-laws, whom she found puritanical and dull. She missed her Sydney social circle, and had little interest in sport, even in her husband's accomplishments. A note survives in the hand of Armstrong's mother Amelia which appears to be

---

* Arden Armstrong was unrelated, though he added another cricket branch to the family tree: his brother Charles had successfully captained St Kilda. Arden met Olivia through his sister Ruth, with whom Olivia played tennis.

a certificate of authenticity for an inventory for her estate. It reads: 'Warwick's silver set which Aileen would not have. Warwick then said I was to have it. I have bequeathed it in my last will to my daughter Amelia Goldsmith.' This was Armstrong's tea and coffee set— Melbourne's reward for his record score against University in April 1904.

The Armstrongs, meanwhile, found Aileen testy and shrewish. They sometimes expressed the wish that Warwick had married another of the O'Donnell daughters, and rather cruelly ascribed her miscarriages to a refusal to renounce alcohol and tobacco during pregnancy. And, according to Patricia Armstrong, widow of Tom's son Warwick Francis, such asperities were not unusual:

> The Armstrongs could be snobs. They looked down on Leonie, who'd married Jack. And they never thought that Molly was quite good enough for Tom. They thought she was a bit common. They were staunch, strong sort of people, which they got from their mother. Amelia was a terribly hard woman, bossy, stiff as a ramrod.

It was under Amelia's influence, of course, that Armstrong's spinster sisters, Amelia, Muriel and Lucia, remained at home at Arra Glen. The household's atmosphere appears, indeed, to have been oppressively religious; not only were Sundays devoted to the new St Aloysius Church in Balaclava Road, where Muriel was sacristan for many years, but Thursdays were spent sewing vestments at a Franciscan monastery in Surrey Hills. Still more hurt by deteriorating relations was Olivia Armstrong, the oldest of the daughters and closest to Armstrong since childhood; they now seldom saw one another. 'I never met Aileen, and I don't think I'd like to meet her now,' recalls Joyce Taylor, an orphan raised by Olivia and Arden Armstrong. 'It was a terrible thing she did. Auntie Ol loved Warwick, and spoke to me about him often.'

Family tensions may have come to a head shortly after Warwick and Tom Armstrong returned from New Zealand. In their absence, their father had suffered a heart attack. He lingered for three months, but died on 17 July 1927, and was buried at Burwood Cemetery the same day. Most of his £2818 estate went to Amelia and the daughters remaining at home, the three married children being catered for thus: Tom received £100 and a gold watch and chain, Olivia £100, Warwick £20 'to purchase a ring or some other token in remembrance of me'. It is a surprisingly parsimonious bequest given Armstrong's achievements and, in a family where money had always mattered, probably implied reproach.

Whatever the case, Warwick Armstrong had by now left his kin far behind. The household at Arra Glen survived another twenty-five years, holding on grimly to middle-class respectability. A letter exists dated 13 September 1930 from Amelia to her daughter of the same name:

My dearest daughter,

In the event of my death, which I feel is not far off, I wish to have my body buried with the least expense possible. I do not want my death advertised unless it must be so. Let me leave this world quietly and unknown. I hope my dearly loved daughters and sons will both love and be good and true to each other, honorable and honest in every way, [with] a sincere trust in God whom I hope will watch over and bless them. Mel, you will be kind to my dear boy [a reference to Tom's son Warwick Francis, on whom she doted]. May God bless my grandsons.

One can only wonder at how Armstrong's sister responded to such valetudinarianism, both plaintive and manipulative. In fact Amelia lived another eleven years. The letter was discovered amid documents relating to her funeral, including an invoice for a 'polished casket mounted with silver and lined, upholstered and finished throughout with embossed swansdown slipset, sidesheets and breasting'.

A final area of personal speculation involves Armstrong's attitude to his brother Jack, now dead a decade. It involves one of the most haunting expressions of Australian grief at its 60,000 war dead: Will Longstaff's painting *Midnight at Menin Gate*. Longstaff, an official war artist, was present at the opening of the memorial, which overlooks the Ypres salient, on 24 July 1927. He was deeply moved to find the names of old friends among the 6000 commemorated on its walls, and haunted by the words of Field-Marshal Lord Plumer: 'They are not missing. They are here.' In his London studio, Longstaff rendered a striking vision of the scene. The memorial, sharply delineated under a deep blue sky, forms its backdrop. In the dreamlike foreground, ranks of spectral soldiers move through fields of corn and red poppies.

The painting was acquired for £2000 in November 1927 by Armstrong's seventy-eight-year-old boss Lord Woolavington. Sensing its significance to Australians, he generously donated it to their government; it arrived from Buckingham Palace in July 1928 to undertake a nine-month tour of Australian cities and provincial centres. Few single images have so captivated Australians, its powers of evocation enhanced by careful spotlighting and the cadences of Schubert's *Unfinished Symphony*. In Sydney, the *Bulletin* saw the depth of its appeal affirmed by the breadth of visiting pilgrims, from 'the most blatant militarists to mystics of the most ethereal type', peering as if 'searching the spaces between the shadowy helmeted figures…for someone there'. For the Armstrongs, it may have been especially poignant; Jack Armstrong received his fatal wound nearby the location depicted.

Warwick Armstrong's involvement in his boss's philanthropic gesture is unknown—James Buchanan's Australian records were destroyed when its office closed in 1970, while Australian War Memorial files shed little light on the artwork's donor. But Armstrong received one of a thousand signed prints of *Midnight at Menin Gate* from his company, which today hangs in his grandson's Sydney home. Perhaps he also searched its spaces for the brother who had left his kin behind still more completely than he.

28

'Bradman Was Scared'

Sporting greatness confers a lifetime's celebrity, and cricketers of Warwick Armstrong's generation enjoyed theirs. They were men become monuments, almost objects of local interest. Once when visiting Adelaide, Sir Malcolm Sargent was asked if he would like to visit Clem Hill. 'Certainly,' the great English conductor replied. 'How tall is it?' A terrible error. And while he had made successful headway in business, Armstrong was not above exploiting his residual fame: he would shortly enjoy a cricketing reincarnation as columnist for London's *Evening News* covering the 1928–29 Ashes series.

This was an outcome of developments as long as Armstrong's lifetime. By the time of his birth, Australia and Britain had been linked by an undersea telegraphic cable for almost seven years. As its cost was prohibitive for anything but short items, however, it was ill-suited to lengthy descriptive matter such as reports of sporting events. Accounts of Test matches travelled to-and-fro as slowly as the mail steamers navigating imperial sea routes: Australia's first Test in England on 6–8 September 1880, for instance, was not reported in detail by the *Australasian* until 30 October.

That was changing by the time Armstrong watched his first Test series in 1894–95. Taking an expensive gamble, London's *Pall Mall Gazette* published for the first time long cabled reports of the action within a day of its taking place; suddenly, commented *Wisden*, English cricket devotees were 'in closer touch with cricket in Australia than ever before'. By the middle of Armstrong's career, cables fairly hummed whenever a Test was in progress, though keeping foreign readers informed remained costly: during the Adelaide Test of January 1908, for instance, the 68,149 words of press reports sent interstate in 1495 messages cost £172, the 5865 words sent to England in 276 messages £449.

Increased wartime cable traffic enabled further reductions in costs per word, and when Armstrong first led his country against England at Sydney in December 1920, Leslie Poidevin of the *Sydney Morning Herald* found the idea that faraway Australia was a focus of imperial attention compelling:

> At small tables are half a dozen operators. Telegraph boys, rising to the occasion with excessive zeal, are bustling in and out. In front sit two serried ranks of newspaper men—twenty or more of them. There is silence, then the little machines on which fingers are beating a sort of rat-tat, start to talk…Those little machines are flashing out the news to an Empire. Wherever the Union Jack flies, the news is spread.

Those writing for foreign consumption, however, were largely agency men producing basic match reports; the idea of a visiting press corps was far off. For perspectives of their own during the 1920–21 Ashes tour, English readers relied on writings by amateurs Rockley Wilson in the *Daily Express* and Percy Fender in the *Daily News*, while Jack Hobbs sent dispatches to the *Star*. Australian readers following the 1921 tour of England had not even enjoyed this luxury: their news came mainly through two agencies, the Australian Press Association (owned by the *Argus, Sydney Morning Herald, Register* and Sydney's *Evening News*) and the rival Sun-Herald Cable Service (run by Melbourne's *Herald* and Sydney's *Sun*).

Armstrong's *Evening News* appointment manifested another stage of development: like Monty Noble, who had described the 1926 Ashes series in England for Sydney's *Sun*, he was to provide readers on the other side of the world with daily views on the fortunes of Percy Chapman's English team. The only English correspondent actually sent to Australia was Armstrong's old crony Percy Fender, representing the *Star*, and also writing what became *Turn of the Wheel*.

The *Evening News* was a cash cow of the Associated Newspapers empire, bought for a song by Lord Northcliffe in 1894. Editor Frank Fitzhugh—a towering, nonchalant figure favouring silk toppers and lilac waistcoats—was always eager for stunts to excite his 680,000 readers. Armstrong's front page introduction to his new public on 27 November 1928 savours of Fleet Street at its most sensational:

> Warwick Armstrong, who a year or two ago dominated Test matches like the giant of players and captains he was, will be watching every minute of the great Test matches…this winter. Each day he will cable his comments on the day's play to the *Evening News*, his criticisms on the captaincy, his impressions of the men, his thoughts on the deciding features of the game. He was the bogy man of cricket to the Englishmen against whom he played…He will be able to judge the struggle as no other man could, and readers of the *Evening News* will be able to follow the thoughts that pass through his mind.

Armstrong saw as little of the first day's play as his editors, being confined to his hotel room with phlebitis. But he was soon talking the game as he'd walked it, without equivocation, sometimes without courtesy. Before lunch on 4 December, Armstrong watched England potter an hour and a half over 52 runs despite a lead in excess of 500. It was 'one of the worst exhibitions of batting I have ever seen,' Armstrong felt. 'From the point of view of the prosperity of the game as a whole the English tactics were blighting…repetition of these tactics would kill the game in Australia.'

As England was cruising to an overpowering victory, Armstrong's remarks infuriated readers. Even Australian actor Oscar Asche complained: 'Surely we can take a licking fairly and squarely…and it will do us a lot of good. We were getting too cocky about cricket.' Others dismissed him as an advocate of brighter cricket: 'It is not for Warwick Armstrong of all men to complain of tedious tactics. I remember seeing him bowl over after over at Lord's many years ago against England's greatest bats which "Ma" Kelly took wide to leg.' In other words, Armstrong was a hit. The *Evening News* rushed to promote its 'frank and fearless' controversialist: 'Every day during the First Test, every cricketer asked: "What does Armstrong say about it?" For every cricketer knows that Mr Armstrong says exactly what he thinks.'

His views came as no surprise. His contempt for modern mores, for bloated totals on doped wickets, was absolute. He thought both Ashes contestants mediocre; England, despite Walter Hammond, Patsy

Hendren, Maurice Tate and Harold Larwood, were merely less bad. This led him to extremities of opinion sometimes comic in retrospect. In one column before the Third Test, for example, Armstrong consigned both Clarrie Grimmett ('great things though he has done, I feel he is finished for Test cricket') and Donald Bradman ('who will probably be a good player later but, I think, is not a Test player at present') to oblivion; when Bradman made 79 and 112, he was unabashed: 'He is a fine batsman, and will be a still finer one.' Nonetheless, Armstrong was nothing if not consistent in his themes, which he saw as vindicated by England's over-powering victory. 'We Australians have not the goods now, and it will be many years before we have,' he summarised. 'This beating is going to do Australian cricket a lot of good. It has shown the folly of covering wickets and thereby commercialising the game.'

Armstrong's words carried authority they would not today. *Evening News* readers following England's fortunes in Australia did not see a picture of the Test in which their team retained the Ashes until nine days after the event. The newspaper was not breast-beating when it insisted that 'no-one in cricket can afford to miss what Armstrong says'. Most resonant of all his reflections during that summer was one of England's fastest bowler, twenty-four-year-old Larwood, who during the second innings of the Second Test in December 1928 bowled two spells aimed at leg stump, with two short legs, including a number of short deliveries. Fender was merely unimpressed: 'Leg theory in Australia, and to Australian batsmen, is not a paying proposition'. Armstrong was severe, and far-sighted: 'If he continues with these tactics the spectators here might think there were more sporting means of getting results. It would be a pity if a player like Larwood ran the risk of unpopularity when he has the talent to send the ball up differently.'

Not all looked favourably on Armstrong's wanderings, both as newspaper correspondent and businessman; seldom seen at the Melbourne Cricket Club, and often absent from committee meetings, he lost his seat on 16 August 1929 in a vote of the 6900 members. Amid scenes at the Colonial Mutual Life building which the *Sun* likened to 'a fierce Federal election fight', he polled only 477 votes. Rumours circulated that he would leave Melbourne for Sydney, amplified when he and Aileen abandoned their St Kilda apartment for rooms at the Menzies Hotel.

The Menzies was Melbourne's most famous hostelry. Its immigrant founders had built it from the proceeds of a Rushworth gold mine, and hosted many of the day's greatest celebrities: film stars, aviators, politicians, plutocrats. Anthony Trollope thought he had never lodged at 'a better inn in any part of the world'. Mark Twain had stoked its furnaces to keep fit. Now a crossroads for members of Melbourne's elite, it would be here in April 1931 that Labor's Joseph Lyons was persuaded to lead the new United Australia Party, which eight months later routed James Scullin's beleaguered administration at the polls. The establishment reflected its conservative clientele. The kitchen contained a English retainer whose sole task was to carve the beef. Dining-room napkins bore the royal crest on finest Irish linen. On one occasion, two guests nearly came to blows over whether it was correct to stand for 'God Save the King' at a function at which one was not present but could hear. An Australian stood, an Englishman not; the matter went to Government House for a ruling, and the former had to apologise.

Probably the chief reason that Armstrong and his wife moved into the Menzies was their son: when ten-year-old Warwick Geoffrey went to board at Sydney's Saint Ignatius' College in January 1930, there was little reason to maintain in Melbourne more than a *pied-a-terre*. But hotel environs suited Armstrong. He had spent most of his cricketing days in them, and was as a businessman doing the same; so often was he in Sydney during the early 1930s that he maintained a semi-permanent suite at Petty's Hotel in York Street. Perhaps his sportsman's restlessness was being carried into his private life. The vacant lot he owned neighbouring Arra Glen remained undeveloped. The Carrum holiday home was never in his lifetime more than a seaside cottage.

Armstrong's chief business preoccupation had now moved from manufacturing. In March 1931, DCL created a new Australian entity subsuming its distribution and marketing. Armstrong became Buchanan's representative on the Distillers Distributing Agency board, mustering a group of travelling salesmen and holding the combine's advertising purse strings—probably tightly. Continuing rumours that he intended moving to Sydney, however, prompted the *Herald*'s 'In Town and Out' column to report:

> Hero-worshippers of the last generation will be interested to learn that Warwick Armstrong, one of Australia's greatest cricket captains, intends to live permanently in Melbourne. Mr Armstrong, who is a member of the

Distillers Distributing Agency, is standing for election to the Melbourne Cricket Club committee.

After succeeding in regaining his seat on 21 August 1930, in fact, he would help retain for Melbourne—and Australia—one of the best cricketers of the day.

Few of Armstrong's cricket forecasts in 1928–29 came to pass. Bradman and Grimmett, whom he'd maligned, had underwritten Australia's 1930 recovery of the Ashes in England. Enthused despite himself, Armstrong travelled to Essendon Aerodrome to welcome Bradman when he arrived aboard the 'Southern Cloud' as part of his homecoming triumph.

At the same time, Ted McDonald's acceptance of the Lancashire League shilling after the 1921 Ashes series had created an threatening precedent. McDonald had proven a gilt-edged investment worth more than 1000 wickets to Lancashire, and the spectre of wealthy leagues taking their pick of emerging talent had since hovered over the Australian game. A number of cricketers had already defected, others would follow, and there was panic in August 1931 over Bradman's future when it emerged he had been offered an unprecedented £1000 a year to join Accrington.[*]

This fuelled anxiety in Melbourne, meanwhile, about the future of Australia's other star batsman, Bill Ponsford. He had succeeded Armstrong as Victoria's champion, twice scoring centuries in three consecutive innings, twice exceeding 400. In January 1927, he had been offered terms by Blackpool, most attractive to a twenty-six-year-old bank clerk, but widely deplored in Australian cricket circles: Billy McElhone demanded that the 'shabby and unfair scheme to pick the eyes out of Australian cricket…be stamped out immediately'. The *Herald and Weekly Times* had interposed, guaranteeing Ponsford a job for five years, but the leagues' siren song was bound to be heard again when this arrangement ended.

---

[*] Defectors included Frank O'Keeffe, who'd scored 177 and 144 against Armstrong's Australians in Sydney in February 1922, and Arthur Richardson, maker of 100 at Headingley against England in July 1926. Two further Test players relocated in 1932, Bill Hunt joining Rishton, Alan Fairfax taking Bradman's place at Accrington.

The first meeting which Armstrong attended during his second Melbourne committee spell, on 17 September 1931, tackled this issue. Armstrong was in a curious position. Ted McDonald's defection had occurred during his watch as Australian captain. But he could also look back twenty years to the time Melbourne had stepped in when his own services had been under bid. Now in a position to ensure that a fellow cricketer benefited from the same largesse, he endorsed a pre-emptive strike. On 28 October, Ponsford accepted a position on the club's staff at £6 a week: he would receive half-pay while touring England, and full pay while playing in Australia, commencing 1 April 1932. Sydney business interests had by this time also clubbed together to make remaining in Australia worth Bradman's while, and between them these intercessions significantly strengthened the cause of Australian cricket in the 1930s: two years later, Bradman and Ponsford topped Australia's averages in England with 3800 runs between them.

In 1932–33, though, the cricket world was turned on its head. No summer has boiled more tempers than the Bodyline season. The unbending captaincy of Douglas Jardine, the unwavering hostility of Harold Larwood and the heated diplomatic cables have assumed mythic, even telegenic, qualities. The series was fought in print as vehemently as on the pitch, the very word 'Bodyline' being a catchy construction of newspaper 'cablese'. And Warwick Armstrong would be remarkably influential.

For their ball-by-ball reports, English newspapers relied on either a versatile Reuters correspondent, Australian Gilbert Mant, or a seasoned Exchange Telegraph Company reporter, South African E. W. Ballantine. Only three Fleet Street organs were directly represented in Australia, and not very effectively at that. The *Evening Standard*'s Bruce Harris was a tennis writer whom Mant thought 'knew more about *Alice in Wonderland* and Gilbert and Sullivan than cricket': his subsequent book *Jardine Justified* is the shallowest of apologias for England's captain. The *Star* had sent the equally partisan Jack Hobbs, who was actually convinced that England's approach was 'not in the best interests of the game', but never let on in print; he found Australian complaints so irksome that he 'did not wish to embarrass Jardine or his men by giving the Australians another peg on which to hang their fierce attacks'.

Then there was the *Evening News*, which had again retained

Armstrong. For various reasons, he loomed large. He had as a bowler been heavily associated with leg theory, as Jardine was wont to describe his ploy; he had as captain deployed a powerful pace battery, Gregory and McDonald; he was Australian, and the embodiment of combative Australianness at that. Who better to call the shots for English readers? Percy Fender even ascribed to him the coining of 'Bodyline' itself, writing later that he had 'heard that the actual word was first accredited to Warwick Armstrong, who had control of McDonald and Gregory in 1921'.*

Armstrong's *Evening News* reports were again launched amid fanfare, his impartiality as a 'just but blunt judge' their selling point:

> He is not hampered by the thought that he may have to take the field himself with a player he criticises. He is not embarrassed by ties of personal friendship…Indeed it is not too much to say that on each day of the five Tests, a reader of the *Evening News* will understand more of the real truth of a day's play than most of the people who have watched it under the Australian sun.

The bluntness of Armstrong's first dispatch on 1 December 1932, nonetheless, probably took his employers by surprise. In Larwood's line and Jardine's preliminary trials of a leg-side catching cordon, Armstrong had detected the shape of things to come. Beneath the headline 'England's Bowling Tactics Unsportsmanlike', he warned of their likely consequence in the First Test:

> As to England's attack I say frankly that there will be trouble if the fast bowlers go for the body instead of the wicket. In Australia, bowling at the batsman is considered unsportsmanlike—I consider it so myself. Against the methods which have been employed, the batsman's job is reduced to a defence of himself rather than defence of his wicket. He is forced to use his bat as a shield.

Such soapboxing nowadays would be of secondary importance: media consumers would already have predigested a phenomenon like Bodyline through television. Seventy years ago it burst on an English

---

* Fender's attribution of the word 'Bodyline' to Armstrong—in his *Kissing the Rod*—seems hard to support. The construction is usually ascribed to Hugh Buggy, a Runyonesque reporter on Melbourne's *Herald*, whose report of the first day of the First Test includes the phrase 'bodyline bowling': apparently telegraphic shorthand kept intact.

public only dimly aware, and frankly unwelcoming, of Australian feeling.
But Armstrong wasn't finished. He also found fault with Jardine's habit
of playing in a harlequin cap, in which Australians detected unpalatable
connotations of class and breeding: 'The Australian public honestly consider that he should wear the colours of his team, and it is my serious
view that the English authorities should cable him with instructions to
wear the MCC uniform tomorrow.' Armstrong's harshest damnation,
however, was reserved for Bradman, who had ruled himself out of the
Test on medical advice that he was 'run down' after several unsuccessful
outings against Larwood in the tour's early matches: 'Bradman was in
good form. Make no mistake about that. He had all the shots of the last
year and the year before. To put the matter bluntly he was frightened of
the fast bowling.'

An attack on English sportsmanship from Warwick Armstrong was all
that readers could comprehend. Half a page was devoted to letters of
complaint. A. H. Baker of Wimbledon thought of 1921: 'Condemnation
of the English bowlers' actions as unsportsmanlike comes straight from
the man who led the Test Australian team in this country. Was not the
McDonald–Gregory combination guilty of bowling at the batsman?'
C. Richardson of Clapham had a longer memory still: 'I recollect a certain Australian bowler deliberately bowling wide of the wicket in a Test
match so that our batsmen could not score. They should complain of
unfair tactics!' News of reader response obviously reached Armstrong, for
he sturdily defended McDonald and Gregory:

> Let me ask this question: did anyone in England while these bowlers were
> touring with Australian sides ever see them bowling leg theory at the same
> time? Or either of them bowling with a leg side packed with fielders. I
> am not complaining. I have never complained before in my life about the
> bumping ball pitched on the wicket or outside off stump. That in my view
> of cricket is quite legitimate. But to bowl at the man, no.

Armstrong was soon writing in a more familiar vein, lampooning
Australia's batsmen in the First Test who 'with the exception of [Victor]
Richardson and [Stan] McCabe played like children', failing 'to attack
the leg theory bowling from the right angle'. He lamented the Sheffield
Shield's ineffectiveness as a nursery of talent: 'It has suddenly dawned on
the people of Australia that no matter which way you approach it,
Australian first-class cricket is in a deplorable state.' His position on
Bodyline, meanwhile, evolved subtly. Most notably, he was against the

most popular and obvious response: that of Australia adopting leg theory itself.

> It has been suggested that Australia's only way out lies in taking a chance by retaliating with leg theory bowling…I am against all retaliation. In my view if our side retaliated it would tend to kill interest in the game for spectators. And which matters most? The game or the Ashes? There can only be one answer.

'Unsportsmanlike' might have raised English hackles. The judgment that Bradman was 'frightened' might even today raise Australians'. Yet here after the First Test was probably Armstrong's most revelatory sentiment of the summer: the most naked competitor of all had actually put a value on 'the game'. But the objection was aesthetic rather than spiritual—cricket where two sides practised leg theory would in his opinion 'kill interest' in proceedings. And it proved a momentary effusion; the pragmatist soon reasserted himself.

Writings about and representations of Bodyline abound, but more has usually meant less. It is now commonly imagined that there was a monolithic Australian position on Jardine and Larwood that summer, the country unswervingly behind its captain Bill Woodfull. The most cursory examination of the evidence shows otherwise, even when the campaign reached its spiteful height in the Third Test in Adelaide, beginning on 13 January 1933, inflamed by the body blows that Woodfull, Ponsford and Oldfield absorbed, and the famous gauntlet that Woodfull flung at Marylebone's manager Pelham Warner: 'There are two sides out there. One of them is trying to play cricket.'

By the time England had won the Test, the Board of Control had entered into its famous cable exchange with Marylebone, flourishing Armstrong's potent word 'unsportsmanlike'. But it didn't speak for everyone. Arthur Mailey, writing in London's *Sunday Dispatch*, thought Australians were making excuses:

> Leg theory bowling is threatening, but any type of fast bowling would have this effect on Australian batting…After the Test at Melbourne, the Australian public thought that Larwood had been mastered, but now they have returned to abuse, which is a form of squealing, and many are saying we wish we had Gregory and McDonald.

Armstrong broadly supported Woodfull: 'My own opinion is that Woodfull, whether he spoke in the heat of the moment on Saturday or not, spoke with some truth.' But he opposed the cables: 'The South Australian delegates to the Board are against it, and I am strongly of the opinion that delegates from the other states should adopt the same line.' Escalation of the conflict through official channels did not appeal to him; while he felt leg theory doing 'infinite harm', he did not consider it decisive in terms of the series:

> As leg theory is looming so large, I am impelled to remark that England could have won this Test match without recourse to the tactics that have left so bad an atmosphere for future Tests, bowling at the man. It would be entirely wrong to leave the impression that they won by leg theory.

Armstrong's main bugbear henceforward would be what he saw as second-rate Australian batting, especially Bradman's controversial expedient of drawing to leg in order to exploit the depopulated off. He was annoyed when Bradman popped to short leg at Adelaide—'It was a poor stroke. Both Bradman and McCabe were undoubtedly frightened out'— and by the Fourth Test in Brisbane was writing in outright condemnation. When Larwood bowled Bradman for 76 in the first innings, Armstrong commented: 'I have to say candidly that Bradman showed unmistakable signs of fright when facing Larwood today and that his last shot was shockingly bad.' And when Bradman was caught for 24 from a wild stroke at Larwood in the second innings, Armstrong went still further:

> There was no doubt whatever in my mind that Bradman was scared of Larwood…The plain truth about Bradman is that he is a class bat, but can never be described as a champion while Larwood is bowling to him. I also feel that he must learn to play for his side instead of for himself. On the form shown in this series of Tests, Bradman is nothing more than a cricket cocktail.

The dismissal of Bradman as a 'cricket cocktail' was a lively metaphor for Armstrong, generally a plain stylist; Larwood himself thought it a 'rather uncouth sneer'. But the tone of Armstrong's criticisms grew even more exasperated in the Fifth Test. 'As for Bradman, he had made some fine strokes but looked like getting out in every over,' he lectured when the Australian champion was bowled by Larwood in the first innings for 48. 'There is no doubt whatever that he cannot stand up to Larwood.' And while Bradman top-scored with 71 in the second innings, his response to Larwood brought further scorn from Armstrong: 'I have to say…that against Larwood, Bradman's performance for a man of his ability was staggeringly bad. One had hoped that he would master his fear of Larwood during the season but it seems his nerves have become worse.' In his summary of the series, Armstrong was crushing:

> To those whose Test careers are virtually finished, I must regretfully add the names of Ponsford, Woodfull and Ironmonger, and while 'body bowling' continues, Bradman…Had Bradman been built with more back-bone, it is possible the whole story might have been different. The rubber hinged largely on Bradman and Larwood, and Larwood conquered him.

The concern here is not to reopen the long-running and open-ended debate about Bradman's resolve during Bodyline, first voiced by Jack Fingleton in *Cricket Crisis,* and challenged by Johnnie Moyes in *Bradman*, and by Bradman himself in *Farewell to Cricket*. It is to illustrate the complexity of Armstrong's position on Bodyline, where flirtation with morality quickly gave way to critique of method. His general feeling that Larwood's leg theory would 'spoil cricket as a spectacle' competed with and was eventually swamped by a specific sense that Australia's defeat was explained as much by its inferiority to Jardine's team, and by implication to the cricketers of his own generation. For to Armstrong, the series was another case of poor against poorer: 'The standard of the cricket played by both countries in this series is below the average. While each side has its outstanding cricketers it must be said that both teams are weak, Australia being the weaker.' Successfully as he had bridged World War I as a cricketer, he remained a captive of the Golden Age as a critic.

In London, Armstrong's criticism of Bradman was seized on. 'One penetrating Australian critic has dubbed Bradman a cricket cocktail,' *Dispatch* sports editor J. J. Brebner reported with satisfaction. 'He would not have dared so to describe the idol of Australia before Larwood and his assistants got to work. How does Bradman stand with the Australian public today? As a good and punishing bat no doubt, but no superman.'

Armstrong's opinions of Jardine were also doubtless well-received: he felt the Englishman had 'fighting quality', was 'made of good stuff', and a 'great master of the game' who 'impressed me by his unswerving determination on methods even if I did not agree with those methods'. This view was echoed by Mailey in the *Dispatch*: 'A word of praise is due to Jardine's captaincy under conditions and circumstances which might have rattled a less courageous captain. He has welded the team into a solid combination whose mainspring is Larwood's bowling.' But Armstrong's relations to Bodyline in fact go back to his participation in its cultural antecedents. In debates that raged about the series, his name recurred frequently, usually in the context of English defences of Jardine's gambit.

For one, Armstrong was understood in England as the pioneer of leg theory. A common proposal after the tour was that Bodyline was merely the reinvention of a scheme of attack conceived by an Australian. In his foreword to Harris' *Jardine Justified*, Jardine himself did the accrediting: 'Briefly…leg-theory was…first practised by W. W. Armstrong in a three-day Test match in England, when he bowled it quite early on the second day of the match in order to avoid defeat.' The inference that Australians were merely protesting against their own stratagem, however, scarcely withstands inspection. If it comes to it, Armstrong himself borrowed leg theory from England's Len Braund, who had bowled it at Armstrong and his teammates in 1901–2. In any event, as Ray Robinson remarked, Bodyline was as different from traditional leg theory as an 'interconti-nental missile from a boy's paper dart'.

Armstrong is also invoked to this day, more melodramatically, as the Australian who originally baited Jardine. This pertains to Australia's drawn match against Oxford University in May 1921, when Jardine first met antipodean opposition, and was unfortunate enough to be stranded on 96 at its conclusion. A recent version of this story appears in Roland Perry's *Captain Australia*: 'Worse, when a young Oxford law student, Douglas Jardine, was 98 not out [sic] at the end of the second day's play, Armstrong refused to give him an extra over in order for him to reach a coveted century. Jardine saw it as a slight from the "colonial". It was not forgotten.'

This is nonsense: there is no evidence that Armstrong refused to bowl an extra over, or that Jardine interpreted it as a colonial slight, or that the Englishman later brooded on it. Firstly, it was only through the generosity of Armstrong, who agreed to continue the match at 4 p.m. on the last day after two and a half hours of rain, that Jardine made as many as he did: Oxford University's journal the *Isis* commented that this 'sporting action was greatly appreciated'. Secondly, Jardine did as much to cost himself the landmark as anyone: *The Times* reported that 'certainly more than the four runs by which he missed his century were thrown away' by the pusillanimous running of Oxford's batsmen. Most importantly, Jardine had no idea he was as close to his hundred as he was, as the Christ Church ground's scoreboard did not record batsmen's running tallies, and he declined to hit some inviting full tosses. Jardine's biographer Christopher Douglas noted:

> It would not have been the done thing for Jardine to have shouted to the scorers: 'How many have I got?' and it would hardly have been in his nature to do so. And he would, one feels certain, have been suspicious of big, tough Australians bowling full tosses and telling him to hit out for his hundred.

A third form of English self-exculpation after Bodyline, expressed in Harris' *Jardine Justified*, has somewhat more force:

> The [Australian Board of Control's] protest implied that blows and intimidation from a fast bowler are new in cricket. Have Australians no memories? In 1921, that famous pair of quick bowlers were touring England, Gregory and McDonald. Ernest Tyldesley was knocked senseless onto his wicket in a Test by a ball from Gregory and was laid up for three weeks…I cannot remember that the MCC spent good money on cables then.

This line of argument was so widespread after the series that it even found echo in Australia. Complaining of the 'boorish, bitter and insulting wording' of his countrymen's protests, Victorian parliamentarian Wilfrid Kent Hughes lectured: 'The English attitude in 1921 was very different. If a conference is held we must attend as fellow sinners.' And the idea took root in England that Jardine was a sort of English Armstrong, a Wellington to Armstrong's Napoleon. Neville Cardus voiced it fluently in 1934's *Good Days*:

> For my part, I admire Mr Jardine beyond words. I dislike his view of cricket. I believe the qualities of character he possesses would suit better a leader of armies. Nonetheless, I see in Jardine a personal force in a period which finds the game woefully short of personality. His influence on modern cricket has been sanitary. He has cleared away cant, to the Australians he has returned tit-for-tat. It is a pity his opponent is not Warwick Armstrong.

This reasoning gained perverse strength in November 1933 when

Marylebone supported the Australian Board of Control in condemning 'direct attack'. The impetus—English counties were concerned that Australia might not tour the following season if Bodyline's repetition was not ruled out—was interpreted by some as sop to wounded Australian sensibilities. Armstrong's old friend Percy Fender mourned forty years later:

> For the first time in my career, England had appointed a determined and resolute captain, a man cast in the toughest Australian mould, *a la* Armstrong if you like…and what happened? It all went wrong and was followed by the climb down when the counties thought the 1934 Australian visit was in jeopardy.

The thesis is debatable: it should be appreciated that neither Cardus nor Fender saw Bodyline implemented, and thus were spared its full ugliness. The parallel between McDonald–Gregory and Larwood is also inexact at best, as Frank Woolley pointed out:

> When the Bodyline campaign was at its height…I recall reading more than one reference to the tactics of Gregory and McDonald…I regretted very much that anyone should have taken it upon himself to complain publicly that these two bowlers had bowled 'at' me. I still regret that such complaints were made. If there was any necessity to complain, surely I was the only one entitled to make the complaint? I did not complain, I have never complained at what happened, for the sufficing reason that there was nothing to complain about. I am entirely unaware that either bowler bowled 'at' me. I am well aware that I was hit—quite painfully aware at the time—because of my own mistiming. That which made each hit sting more was the fact that in each case I was hit by a ball that ought to have been scored off.

What the debate does suggest, however, is a dissonance in English cricketing attitudes. Once there had been plangent pieties about 'fair play' and 'the game's the thing'. But having suffered under Armstrong's cosh, retaliation was ineradicably satisfying. Hence the ambivalence even of Jack Hobbs in his *Fight for the Ashes*, where he criticised Bodyline as 'not good for cricket in general', but confessed feeling that 'if Larwood and leg-theory had been Australian the crowds there would have laughed and applauded'. Perhaps Bodyline was Armstrong's final triumph at English expense: in many who had loathed him, there was now the incipient desire to imitate him.

Armstrong did not write regularly about cricket after Bodyline. On England's next visit to Australia, the *Evening News* was represented by cricket correspondent H. A. H. Carson. But that did not mean he was ever reconciled to modern cricket. He was vexed by the 1934 Ashes series, much of which he watched on a six-month business and pleasure trip, particularly the Australians' failure on a rain-affected pitch during the Lord's Test: to Armstrong, Bradman's reckless self-destruction confirmed Trumper's superiority. After the game, Fender, covering the series for the *Evening News*, found Armstrong holding court in a Lord's bar—cigar in mouth, drink in each hand—and asked him to compare the foremost batsmen of their generations:

> Do you really want to know, Percy? Let me put it this way—if we won the toss on a doubtful wicket we always batted anyway. If Vic did not like the look of it, he would 'shut up shop' and say: 'I think I better stay here till it gets better'. Do you want me to say anything more?

When Armstrong returned to Melbourne aboard the *Otranto* on 8 October, he denigrated Australia's achievement of regaining the Ashes in the *Herald:* 'English cricket is in a deplorable state at present. Australia, too, should look for new bowlers although we are fairly strong on the batting side.' These remarks infuriated London's *Daily Mail*:

> Warwick Armstrong, one of the least popular of Australian Test captains who has toured England, has even fewer admirers now. He enjoyed the English hospitality for months and immediately he reached home said that English cricket was in a deplorable condition. No 1934 Australian Test player would be guilty of such ill-mannered criticism.
>
> Armstrong has never been kind to English cricket. We have vivid memories of the bowlers Gregory and McDonald hurling down deliveries far more intimidating than any of Larwood's yet nobody was louder than Armstrong in condemning Larwood when he mowed down Australian wickets.

The *Mail* had Armstrong wrong: his allegiances were historic not national. They were, moreover, shared. English playwright Ben Travers recalled a day at Sydney when a Bradman cover drive caused an enthusiast to exclaim 'Trumper!' Travers wrote: 'He was pulled violently back into his seat and for the moment appeared in danger of being lynched.' Most of Armstrong's playing contemporaries were minded likewise, such as Monty Noble in his *Fight for the Ashes*:

Do not the household names of yesterday command greater response in the national mind than those of today? For instance, Spofforth, Murdoch, Blackham, Garrett, Massie, Giffen, Trott, Trumble, Gregory, Darling, Hill, Trumper, Armstrong, Macartney. I confess this is largely psychological. It is also hard fact.

The *Daily Express*'s William Pollock, in *So This Is Australia*, recalled similar conversations at the Melbourne Cricket Club with secretary Hugh Trumble, during 1936–37:

> He was scornful about much of the cricket we had seen on the tour, particularly of batting which allowed close-set fields to such bowlers as O'Reilly and Verity. But then, of course, he played in the days of W. G., Victor Trumper, Ranji, Clem Hill, Johnny Tyldesley, Jessop, Syd Gregory— and 'them were the days'.

Nostalgia is powerful, and often self-reinforcing. In April 1938, for example, Armstrong reunited in Sydney with his friendly rival of 1921, Lionel Tennyson: Third Baron Tennyson for the last decade, he was on a world cruise with his second wife. A photograph survives of their round at the Australian Golf Club, with Tennyson's characteristic dedication: 'To Warwick Armstrong, the finest captain Australia ever had, from Lionel Tennyson, the best captain England ever had, with all best wishes.'

In a way, it is sad that Armstrong should have succumbed to *laudator temporis acti*. Ironically, the interwar period now bulks at least as large in imagination as Armstrong's epoch, reflected in the title of Gerald Howat's history *Cricket's Second Golden Age*. Yet in another sense, Armstrong's stance is personally revealing. However great his strength as an individual—and none in cricket had gone his own way with firmer deliberation—he never surrendered his group identity. The team spirit of the XIs led by Joe Darling, Monty Noble and Clem Hill survived long after their dissolution.

Epilogue

'A Misleading Air
of Languor'

When the torpid Australian economy of the late 1920s lapsed into full-scale depression in the 1930s, cricketers were not spared. Both the Victorian Cricket Association and the New South Wales Cricket Association instigated funds to provide welfare for distressed cricketers, including many of Warwick Armstrong's contemporaries. Minutes of the Victorian body show that handouts were bestowed on, among others, the families of Jack Saunders, Barlow Carkeek, Jimmy Matthews and Hunter Hendry. Records of the New South Wales fund include a poignant 1931 interview with Herbie Collins, Armstrong's vice-captain and successor, only five years after his retirement: 'He has an invalid mother who has no hope of recovering. So short has he been of money that on occasions he has not been able to buy the necessary medicine, and more infrequently they have been short of food.'

For Armstrong, a lifetime's financial prudence, not to mention marriage into wealth, paid off. Quite detailed financial records of his affairs survive from this time in the form of ledgers tracking investments and loans. Armstrong was a judicious purchaser of shares from the mid-1920s, then more active in the early 1930s, mostly in blue-chip stocks with a little blue sky thrown in: at his death, he would hold shares in forty companies worth £42,000, earning annual dividends of about

£1400. His biggest holding was in BHP, which he began acquiring in January 1933, and in which his stake would eventually be worth £7348. He also banked on gold through Placer Development, which he started accumulating in August 1933, and where his investments would finally be valued at £3731. Some 'penny dreadfuls' were hidden away—Oriomo Explorations, Gold Mines of Papua, Coolgardie Brilliants—but Armstrong was no more speculator in stocks than in sport. By far his biggest individual holding was in government securities. He would eventually have more than £30,000 salted away in commonwealth inscribed stock, earning him about £1000 interest annually. The other practice in which both Warwick and Aileen Armstrong were involved in this time was money-lending: not uncommon in a period where banks rationed credit strictly. These activities fill their own ledger containing dozens of entries—too numerous, in fact, to trace to their origins. Most intriguing is a five-year £500 loan to 'W. M. Hughes' in September 1927. Was this Armstrong returning the compliments the prime minister had paid him at his testimonial? Rolled over once, it was repaid in June 1935.

Many sportsmen find it difficult to settle into ordinary life on retirement—after the freedom of the fields, the demands of earning a living seem paltry. Armstrong was not among them. He seems to have enjoyed the money, the travel, the companionship, particularly of Buchanan colleagues Norman Stuart and John Ruthven, White Horse representative Edward Box, and DCL director Peter Dewar. Dewar himself inaugurated an annual company golf trophy held at the Concord Links which, the *DCL Gazette* recorded, Armstrong coolly won with 'Homeric driving' in March 1932:

> Laid early at the outside figure of 40–1, he shortened suddenly to fives, and then, just before barrier time, or should we say 'tee-time', lengthened to twelves. The final drift was due to apparently authentic rumours concerning 'loss of form'. The information proved to have had reference merely to his increase of weight, which may also have accounted for his misleading air of languor.

Thursday afternoons at the bar of the Menzies with the Distillers Distributing Agency's travellers must have been quite a sight: like Armstrong, Box stood 190 centimetres, Ruthven 183 centimetres and 'Long Bill' Stuart 196 centimetres. Dewar himself, according to a former staff member, enjoyed a reputation as its most liberal tipper: 'The more improvident members of staff, of whom there were quite a few, provided they were strategically placed could always borrow money against his goings and comings.' Armstrong never became so carried away. Hunter Hendry, who sometimes dropped in at the Menzies to meet his former captain, recalled:

> All except Armstrong when it was their turn to shout put a £5 note on the counter and left the change there. Not so Armstrong; he pulled out a purse from his pocket and counted out the change. My best man Laurie Dugdale…always attended the cattle sales on Thursday and it was our amusement always to go there and watch this performance.

> Old habits died hard.

Armstrong's sporting celebrity never waned. When the Spanish tennis star Enrique Maier visited the Melbourne Cricket Ground in January 1935, while in town for the Australian Championships, it was Armstrong who entertained him on behalf of the committee. Maier was rather puzzled by cricket, and even more perplexed when Armstrong told him that the game drew attendances as great at 65,000. 'All I can say, Mr Armstrong,' he commented, 'is that they have never seen a bullfight.'

Nor did Armstrong's business fortunes recede. Promoted to general manager of James Buchanan's Australasian businesses in April 1935, he moved to Sydney with Aileen—according to his nephew Warwick Francis 'partly for business reasons and partly at his wife's request'. Aileen had always disliked Melbourne and, a month from his fifty-sixth birthday, Armstrong finally seems to have been ready to domiciliate. Their handsome two-storey brick house called 'Maidar' at 6 Darling Point Road in wealthy Edgecliff suggested a man made good, from the walnut pianola in the lounge to the new Dodge sedan in the garage.

It was not, however, to be a tranquil twilight. Both Armstrong and Aileen suffered increasingly from ill health, while their son Warwick Geoffrey had difficulty settling to a career after leaving St Ignatius' at intermediate level. He worked as a stockbroker then with an engineering firm and was invalided out of the army. There was also little personal contact between Armstrong and his family in Melbourne. On one occasion visiting Sydney, Armstrong's sisters Olivia and Amelia decided to call on Maidar: though no-one answered their knock, they sensed Aileen's eyes peeping through the drawn blinds.

Armstrong now found his generation dwindling. On one day, 14 August 1938, he had to provide suitable farewells to both Hugh Trumble and Jim Kelly. Four months later, he himself fell gravely ill with pneumonia and pleurisy, and was admitted to Darling Point's Travencore Private Hospital. One radio station even broadcast that he had died, and posterity began preparing judgments. An obituary compiled at the time by Charlie Macartney for the *Sydney Morning Herald*—dated 20 December 1938 and marked 'not used'—survives in that newspaper's files:

> Warwick Armstrong was manifestly unaffected by criticism whether favourable or adverse, and both on the cricket field and in private life he was extremely independent. A man of strong personality, he naturally aroused a good deal of opposition, but it never caused him to deviate from any course he had mapped out for himself, and even those who disagreed with his policy could not help but admire his inflexibility of purpose.

By now, in fact, some of Armstrong's more abrasive edges had worn away. When Hendry and Arthur Mailey visited, they found him mellower than in his playing days. 'Sorry I had that little tiff with you in London,' Armstrong suddenly told Mailey one day, recalling their disagreement over the fixtures on the 1921 tour. 'There is one thing that I must say—I always knew where you stood.' But there remained a disinclination to sentimentality. He added gruffly, 'I can't say the same about a couple of the other blokes.' Armstrong also never ceased to enjoy his resident nay-sayers' role. When Jack Fingleton of Sydney's *Sun* met him on a Sydney racecourse in January 1940, he found Armstrong at his most outspoken:

> He didn't think much of Bradman—many bowlers in his team would have clipped his wings. No, he didn't agree that Tate and O'Reilly were in world-class as bowlers. This, of course, was arrant nonsense—but I sensed that the 'Big Ship' hadn't been picking winners and was feeling somewhat out of sorts.
>
> When O'Reilly's name was mentioned, Armstrong reeled off a string of bowling names of the past with such spirited rapidity that one could almost imagine O'Reilly (W. J.) doing odd jobs for their souls in Valhalla and being glad of the privilege.
>
> 'He didn't turn a single ball against the Queenslanders. I was behind the wicket with glasses and I should know,' said Armstrong.
>
> 'But the Queenslanders…' I began to advance.
>
> Armstrong snorted and, when a twenty-two-stone man snorts, it's hard

to hold out against him. 'I could bowl the Queenslanders out even now,' he said.

I remembered that there was always a doubt whether Armstrong himself really turned the ball. His leg-breaks were reputed to be top spinners. 'Jack Hobbs once told me that you—' I began.

'Did you see Trumble bowl?' asked Armstrong.

'No.'

'Giffen?'

'No.'

'Howell?'

'No.'

'Noble?'

I felt, by this, like asking whether Armstrong himself had ever seen Bill the Conqueror, but he gave me no opening. Armstrong did not believe Bradman stood on a pedestal alone. Trumper, Duff, Syd Gregory (he did mention a fourth but I have forgotten him) were all as good as Bradman…

'No two cricketers in Australia today are up to Test standard,' was Armstrong's first criticism.

'It would seem, then,' I observed, mostly to myself, 'that the players of today are not as good as they were.'

'No,' said a meek little chap in the other corner who had not spoken before, 'they never were, my boy, and they never will be.'

I wrote what I thought was a human interest story of that friendly little discussion, but my editor, a timid soul, who knew nought of cricket, withdrew it in haste after the first edition. He thought Mr Armstrong might object to it! He didn't know Armstrong, of course.

Resisting opinion was one thing, time another. Six months later, after a long period suffering from endocarditis, Aileen died of a thrombosis on 17 July 1940; she was buried in South Head Cemetery by Armstrong's comrade Hanson Carter. Armstrong's own heart caused him increasing problems and, for really the first time in his life, he began shedding weight—massively. Having at his heaviest weighed almost 150 kilograms, he shrank back to just over 100 kilograms. The loss was so sudden and drastic, Hendry recalled, that Armstrong had to secure his trousers at the backside with a foot-long safety pin. When he retired from Buchanan's on 31 July 1946, staff presented him with a framed copy of a *Sydney Morning Herald* appreciation of his career by Neville Cardus, but 'Australia's Giant Cricketer' was by now a shadow of his former self. In a photograph of him meeting Walter Hammond's Englishmen at an NSWCA reception four months later, he is barely recognisable.

From his unruly life, Armstrong passed peacefully early on the morning of 13 July 1947 at Maidar. A requiem mass next day at St Joseph's was attended by Collins, Mailey, Hendry, Carter, Macartney, Bert Oldfield, Warren Bardsley, Tommy Andrews and Bill Whitty, who flew from Adelaide. He was buried alongside his wife in grave 125, section L, in the Catholic section of South Head Cemetery. Wreaths were sent by every state association, and even Syd Smith appeared, alongside the Board's Frank Cush and the NSWCA's Harold Heydon—perhaps like the mourners at Sam Goldwyn's funeral who turned up 'to make sure he was dead'. Certainly there were some unsympathetic commentaries: *Wisden's* editor Hubert Preston concluded an appreciative obituary with the remark that Armstrong's 'caustic Test criticisms created ill-feeling of a kind which should not be associated with cricket'. In the main, however, verdicts were kind, even grand. 'He was to Australian cricket what W. G. Grace was to this country,' averred London's *Sporting Life*. 'He was a giant of the game in every sense of the word, a great all-rounder as a bowler and batsman and unrivalled in his knowledge of the game.' Mythologising had already begun. Cardus's *Manchester Guardian* obituary cheerfully recalled Armstrong in his last Test, where he 'went into the deep field and read a newspaper between overs'.

Armstrong had died an extremely wealthy man, his estate worth £106,075—£90,546 in New South Wales and £15,529 in Victoria—composed mostly of investments. No other Australian captain had accumulated a fortune so great, and in real terms, if such comparisons are meaningful, few since.* Again the terms of an Armstrong will may contain some inferences: after distributing £1000 each to Muriel, Amelia and Tom (also bequeathed the cottage at Carrum), and £500 to Olivia and Lucia, the residual ended up with Armstrong's son, now twenty-seven and running an import-export agency in King's Cross, the secretary at which he married in September 1948. Armstrong's three unmarried sisters, finding Arra Glen increasingly difficult to maintain, felt they might have been remembered more generously.

Of Armstrong's kin, Tom might be felt to have fared next best. His

---

* For the purposes of comparison, Noble who died on 22 June 1940 left an estate valued at £3400, Darling who died on 2 January 1946 an estate worth £7000. Probably the biggest residual left by an Australian captain before Armstrong was by Hugh Massie, who died on 12 October 1938 worth £57,000, having been general manager of the Commercial Banking Company of Sydney.

wife died in April 1952, but he remarried and moved to Bairnsdale with the Wales bank, while both his sons raised families. To Olivia, Arden Armstrong proved a loving husband, and doting uncle to Joyce Taylor, an orphan they raised as their daughter. But Armstrong's three unmarried sisters experienced little good fortune, and Lucia became an increasingly irascible figure—something the family coyly ascribed to exposure to gas during her work as a theatre nurse. A tall, burly woman who wore size 11 boots, she would wander aimlessly in Caulfield Park in a huge trenchcoat, attracting the curiosity of children from the school at nearby St Aloysius. Joyce Taylor, a teacher there, recalls:

> One of the kiddies came up to me and said: 'Miss, that man carries a gun.' I said: 'I don't think she carries a gun.' The child said: 'But it's a he, Miss Taylor.' I didn't want them to know I was related so I said: 'Oh, is it? I thought it was a lady. Well, I don't think he'd be allowed to carry a gun'. Poor Auntie Toot.

When the sisters finally sold Arra Glen in April 1956, Lucia doggedly refused to leave, and was finally found by Arden Armstrong prowling Caulfield Park. Although she had a bedroom in their new house in Parkdale's Seventh Street, she insisted on sleeping on the verandah, and would often set off on long nocturnal treks, crossing roads regardless of weather and traffic. Even after being struck by a car in July 1972 while on one of these wanderings, huge, headstrong, obstinate Lucia outlived everyone, dying at the age of eighty-nine in January 1980. Given that she seems to have shared some aspects of her brother's character, there is something poignant about Lucia's lonely, unlucky, disappointed life. We might reflect that the personal qualities sometimes admired in sport are in other contexts socially rebarbative; perhaps, indeed, that is why we celebrate them. [*]

It is that character to which we continue to return in assessing Warwick Armstrong a century after his Test debut and eighty years after his

---

[*] Thomas Armstrong was the first of Armstrong's remaining siblings to die, in Bairnsdale on 15 April 1963, aged seventy-three. Amelia died on 18 March 1967 in Mordialloc at eighty, Muriel in Fitzroy on 19 September 1969 at eighty-five. Both had suffered strokes. Olivia, predeceased by her husband, died at eighty-eight in Toorak on 25 January 1971, a week after an operation for a carcinoma of the colon. Jack Armstrong's widow Leonie had already died on 24 August 1955.

chiefest triumph. His statistical stature bears comparison with almost any first-class cricketer of the twentieth century, but this is almost by the way. It is meaningless also to ask if he would have made runs and taken wickets today. In *Big Bill Tilden*, Frank Deford reminds us:

> An athlete, no less than a general or statesman, must be judged by what he accomplished in his time. That is the only appropriate standard…Johnny Weissmuller has had his best times lowered by adolescent girls. Are we to say then that Weissmuller at his peak was a lesser athletic presence than some fourteen-year-old girl? If we are…then it is also to say that kids in the Little League would strike out Babe Ruth, that Jack Dempsey would be knocked out in the Golden Gloves, and that Tracey Austin…would have beaten Big Bill Tilden in straight sets in the first round at Forest Hills in 1923. It is also to say that Napoleon was a failure as a general because he didn't know how to deploy air power and that Jefferson had an inconsiderable mind because he couldn't change a tire.

Deford goes on to argue that tennis's progress since Tilden's era is precisely an outcome of the scientific intelligence he applied to the game—something we blithely overlook in exercises like teams of the century and cricketers of all time. Each sporting generation is born into an accumulating inheritance of innovation and discovery. Was Bell not a great innovator because he invented merely the telephone, Marconi not an inspired engineer because he devised only the wireless? The telephone and wireless are today commonplace, yet we would be helpless without them. T. S. Eliot's remark about literature is no less true of sport: 'Someone said: "The dead writers are remote from us because we *know* so much more than they did."' Precisely, and they are that which we know.'

In assessing a sportsman's greatness, our questions should probably run more along the lines of how they found their game, and how they left it. And in this sense, Warwick Armstrong looms as large as he did physically. In an era when batsmen were assessed on technical and

---

Armstrong's son Warwick Geoffrey died on 8 June 1994. Tom's first son Warwick Francis Armstrong, an employee of the Reserve Bank, died on 15 June 1985. His widow Patricia *nee* McMahon still lives in Armstrong's cottage at Carrum, now considerably extended. Tom's second son John Arden Armstrong, a businessman and property developer, died on 28 January 1991. His first wife Patricia *nee* Allitt lives in Edithvale.

aesthetic bases, he espoused 'temperament temperament temperament'. During days in which it was said that 'the true bowler carries a flaming sword', he pecked at batsmen's patience. At the apogee of amateurism, he was as close to a professional as could be, and for some time unapologetically was one. As a captain, Armstrong was the first to cow opponents with two fast bowlers, the first to systematically dictate umpiring and playing conditions to his liking, the first even to speculate about gambling's impact on cricket—not that anyone listened. Representative of the period of player self-rule, he made himself almost a permanent opposition to the game's new governors, a state within a state—the many players afterwards who chafed at the board's yoke, even Sir Donald Bradman, followed in his huge footsteps. This was a vast bequest to subsequent generations; few could be advanced to rival it.

Warwick Armstrong's chief legacy, however, was in his uncompromising conduct. He was a winner at all costs—even to his reputation. This may partly explain his relative obscurity today. He does not conform to the unsullied idyll we imagine his era to have been. He was not a courtly Trumper or a punctilious Noble: he could be dictatorial, boorish, overbearing. We remain deeply ambivalent about aggression's place in cricket—not least because it nowadays often segues into outright cheating. Strangely, no-one could deny that the aggressive, the competitive, even the demonstrative, have their place in cricket: after all, it is the only game where it is incumbent on one side to call on the umpire to arbitrate by appealing. Yet 150 years of history bear down upon us about the game's immanent spirit—in fact, for many, this is one of the aspects of cricket that first enchanted them.

Often in invoking this spirit we hold modern mores up against an unspoiled past, a past as imagined as real, while there are sometimes more continuities than imagined. The Australian cricket way—stern, forthright, tenacious, sometimes grim, and occasionally involving conduct right at the edge of the Laws—draws on age-old traditions. Neville Cardus once proposed of Warwick Armstrong that Australian cricket was 'incarnate in him'; at least part of Warwick Armstrong became incarnate in Australian cricket.

Acknowledgments

When I began this book, I had visions of a lonely exercise. Hitherto, I had written mainly of cricketers within living memory, the pleasure being the people I met along the way. On this excursion, I suspected, the company might not be so congenial. This suspicion proved entirely unfounded.

My thanks should be settled first on members of the Armstrong family who were most generous with their time, co-operation and rec-ollections. I first met with the present bearer of the name Warwick Windridge Armstrong, my subject's grandson, and his mother Beryl. Later I was hospitably received by Joyce Taylor, who was raised by Warwick's sister Olivia, Patricia Armstrong, widow of Warwick's nephew Warwick Francis, and Patricia Armstrong, widow of Warwick's other nephew John Arden. All imparted important family lore, and entrusted valuable documentary and pictorial material to me. I hope I have gone part way to honouring their generosity.

Early in my researches, I visited Armstrong's birthplace of Kyneton, and was nearly killed by the kindnesses of David, Val and Helen Treloar. They placed before me the fruits of many years fossicking about the Armstrong family and its ancestors, and maintained regular contact over the next eighteen months. Also of invaluable assistance in genealogical research was Victor Batten, related by marriage to the O'Donnell family, and Wilma Henderson, a descendant of the Windridges. They gave freely of their work and advice.

Perusing a twenty-year-old Cricket Society newsletter, I discovered that my idea of an Armstrong book had been anticipated by the English cricket writer Lionel Brown, though for various reasons his book had never appeared. Lionel took some tracing, but could scarcely have been more obliging when located, volunteering chunks of his manuscript, and primary material that would otherwise have been unobtainable. After a year of enjoyable correspondence, it was a pleasure to meet him in England and thank him personally.

This was a book built on a mountain of documentary material, and as such dependent on the good offices of librarians and archivists. Chiefly important were the records of the Melbourne Cricket Club, which were accessed with the unfailing help and patience of Jean Johnson and Andrew Patterson of the Gallery of Sport, and Jennifer van Dam of the MCC Museum. Also vital were the minute books of the Victorian Cricket Association and the Australian Cricket Board; the co-operation here of Ken Jacobs, Peter Binns, Bob Parish and Brendan McClements demonstrates that attitudes in Australian cricket administration are today somewhat more enlightened than eighty or so years ago.

The Mitchell Library in Sydney contains a fascinating range of material relating to Armstrong's life and times; my thanks to Warwick Hirst for initiating me in their mysteries. Many enjoyable weeks were spent at the Victorian Public Records Office and New South Wales Archives, where it was a pleasure to meet someone so engaged by her task as Gail Davis. As she confided one evening on the train back into Sydney: 'They're always at us to wear coats so we don't get dust on us. I don't know why. I love dust.' I never had the good fortune to meet Aoife Martin of UDV Archives in the United Kingdom—our acquaintance is entirely through e-mail—yet here again was a willing helpmate.

If I single these people out, it is merely because they come to mind now. However unknowingly, this project was also abetted by obliging staff at the following institutions: the State Library of Victoria, the LaTrobe Library, the Baillieu Library, the City of Port Phillip Library Service Local History Section and the Victorian Supreme Court Prothonatory's Office (with special thanks to Joe Saltalamacchia) in Melbourne, the National Library of Australia, the Australian War Memorial and the Noel Butlin Archives Centre in Canberra, the Archives Office of Tasmania in Hobart, and the State Library of New South Wales and New South Wales Probate Office in Sydney.

The itinerant researcher on a modest budget lays his head wherever it's cheapest, but occasionally strikes it lucky. On my jaunts to Sydney, for example, I was able to doss with my friends Graem, Shirley and Heath Sims. For a fortnight in London, spent mostly at the British

Library Newspaper Collection, I was guest of the unfailingly tolerant Tanya Aldred, and also her parents Anthony and Cherry. With the Australian dollar worth two-thirds of diddly-squat, this important trip would not otherwise have been possible. As ever, I have cause to celebrate the kindness of my friend David Frith, whose priceless collection was lain at my disposal. Thanks also to those who took it upon themselves to show an Australian a good time: Simon Rae, Stephanie Bunbury, Stephen Fay, Tim de Lisle, Lawrence Booth, Graham Coster and Diran Adebayo. Kaz Cooke fitted me out for the journey with a superb pair of pyjamas.

Another group of people lent assistance in ways too complex to enumerate, though their help was in some cases no less valuable than the foregoing. I will list them here, democratically, in alphabetical order: Nabila Ahmed, Tony Bentley of Bickley Park Cricket Club, Cliff Butcher, Greg Campitelli of Christian Brothers College (St Kilda), Ronald Cardwell, Kevin Carroll of University Cricket Club, Stephanie Charlesworth, Colin Clowes of the New South Wales Cricket Association, Gabrielle Coyne, Peter Dalton of the Catholic Education Board, Phil Derriman, the late David Dobson, Ross Dundas, Ric Finlay, Suzy Freeman-Greene, Stephen Gibbs, Dr Jim Glaspole, Stephen Green of the Marylebone Cricket Club, Dr Bridget Griffen-Foley of Sydney University, Robert Grogan of South Melbourne Cricket Club, Susan Harcourt of Harcourt Legal Services, John Harms, Russell Holmesby, Col Hutchinson of the Australian Football League, Alfred James, James Kirby, Tony Korman of Monash Medical Centre, Tim Lane, Chip Le Grand, Father Peter McGrath of St Joseph's Catholic Church (Edgecliff), Dr Greg McKie, Dugald McKillop, Father Bob Maguire of St Peter's and St Paul's Catholic Church (South Melbourne), Angela Martinkus, Pat Mullins, Peter Murley QC, Barry Nicholls, Roger Page, Ross Peacock, Leo and Violet Ramsdale of St Mary's Catholic Church (Kyneton), Nick Richardson, Dr Brian Robinson (son of Ray), Pat Sanders of the Kyneton Historical Society, Jim Schembri, Malcolm Schmidtke, Peter Sharpham, Michael Shatin QC, Father Tony Spierings of St Aloysius Catholic Church (North Caulfield), Richard Sproull, Bill Kent Tickner of University Cricket Club, Greg Tootell (descendant of Charles), Charles and Robert Trumble (sons of Hugh), Wendy Tuohy, J. Neville Turner, postal services historian John Wanghorn, Marie Webster of St Joseph's Catholic Church (Malvern), Ronald Weir of the Department of

Economics and Related Studies at University of York, Bernard Whimpress of the South Australian Cricket Association, Ian Woodward. And my mum. And Trumper the cat.

For much of this project, Philippa Hawker and Amanda Smith showed a remarkable and apparently unappeasable interest in Warwick Armstrong—or at least faked it convincingly when I chose to witter on about him. I couldn't have asked for more perceptive or constructive readers when the manuscript was complete. Nor could I have had more solicitous publishers than Text Publishing, not only with this book but for the last eight years. Thanks, as ever, to Michael Heyward, Diana Gribble, Melanie Ostell, Donica Bettanin, Patty Brown, William Goodlad, Emily Booth, Emma Williams and the proofreading virtuoso George Thomas.

The last group to whom I extend thanks represents one of the most fruitful partnerships of my time writing about cricket: the staff, scholars and volunteers in the Melbourne Cricket Club Library. Chief librarian David Studham gave unreservedly of his time and know-how, as always, with his assistant Amanda Morris and David Allen. I was also the beneficiary of two important projects now in progress under its roof: a biographical dictionary of Australian first-class cricketers being edited by Ray Webster, Ken Williams, Rick Smith and Warwick Franks, and a history of the club by Alf Batchelder. It's been a privilege to work alongside them for the last two years, to enjoy their discoveries and share mine in a spirit of shared inquiry; Alf, in particular, was kind enough to peruse this book in manuscript, and engage me in conversations that must have sounded to others like an entirely foreign language.

The dedication of *The Big Ship*, meanwhile, is a small way of honouring a valued member of the South Yarra Cricket Club and a dear friend. Anthony Burnell died on 11 May 2001 in a car accident, aged thirty-one. His commitment and dedication made ours a better club; his integrity, humour and wisdom made ours better lives. We miss him very much.

Statistics

TEST RECORD (50 MATCHES)

BATTING/FIELDING

INNINGS	N/O	RUNS	HIGHEST	AVERAGE	100S	50S	CATCHES
84	10	2863	159*	38.68	6	8	44

BOWLING

BALLS	MAIDENS	RUNS	WICKETS	AVERAGE	5I	10M	BEST
8022	403	2923	87	33.59	3	–	6/35

Armstrong ranks twenty-sixth among Australian Test run-scorers. He made 1892 runs at 45.04 in Australia, 690 runs at 24.64 in England, and 281 runs at 70.25 in South Africa. He shared eleven partnerships of more than 100, the highest being the 194 he added for the fourth wicket with Charles Kellaway against England at Adelaide in January 1921. In making his highest Test score against South Africa at Johannesburg in October 1902, Armstrong became the second of nine Australians to carry his bat through a completed Test innings. His record from eleven Tests at the MCG was 918 runs at 61.20 and 20 wickets at 27.75.

Armstrong ranks thirty-fifth among Australian Test wicket-takers. He took 45 wickets at 36.20 in Australia, 40 wickets at 29.15 in England, and two wickets at 64.00 in South Africa. Forty-seven of his Test wickets were unassisted: 31 bowled, 12 lbw, four caught and bowled. Winning eight and drawing two of his ten Tests, he is the only Test captain to lead his country as often and remain undefeated. In those games, he made 616 runs at 56 and took 17 wickets at 24.47.

FIRST-CLASS RECORD (269 MATCHES)

BATTING/FIELDING

INNINGS	N/O	RUNS	HIGHEST	AVERAGE	100s	50s	CATCHES
406	61	16158	303★	46.83	45	57	274

BOWLING

BALLS	MAIDENS	RUNS	WICKETS	AVERAGE	5I	10M	BEST
43297	1999	16405	832	19.71	50	5	8/47

Armstrong is the sixteenth-highest Australian first-class run scorer. He made 9145 runs at 49.70 in Australia, 5641 runs at 40.58 in England, 1088 runs at 68.00 in New Zealand, and 284 runs at 47.33 in South Africa. Armstrong shared eleven partnerships of more than 200, including the highest Australian partnership for the sixth wicket (428 with M. A. Noble, Australians v Sussex, Hove 1902), the second highest for the seventh wicket (273★ with J. Darling, Australians v Gentlemen, Lord's 1905), and the third-highest for the ninth wicket (225 with E. A. C. Windsor, Australian XI v The Rest, Sydney 1907–8). He also shared the Victorian record partnership for the eighth wicket (215 with R. L. Park, v South Australia, Melbourne, 1919–20). At the MCG, he made 5103 runs at 54.28 and took 168 wickets at 21.60.

Armstrong is the seventh-greatest Australian first-class wicket-taker. Four-hundred and fifty-six of his wickets were unassisted: 281 bowled, 136 lbw and 39 caught and bowled. He scored 100 runs and took 10 wickets in a match twice and combined a century with a bag of five wickets in an innings on four occasions. He is one of ten Australians to have scored 10,000 first-class runs and taken 500 first-class wickets; among them he has the highest batting average and second-lowest bowling average. He won 46, lost 18 and drew 16 of his 80 matches as captain.

FIRST-GRADE CRICKET (164 MATCHES)

BATTING/FIELDING

INNINGS	N/O	RUNS	HIGHEST	AVERAGE	100s	50s	CATCHES
167	25	9395	438	66.16	29	37	107

BOWLING

WICKETS	RUNS	AVERAGE	5I	10M	BEST
467	6678	14.29	32	6	7/6

These totals encompass two matches for St Kilda, sixteen for South Melbourne and 146 for Melbourne played between 1895–96 and 1925–26. Neither Armstrong's batting average nor his highest score have been surpassed.

Appendix

Some of the more delightful tributes to Warwick Armstrong were in the form of verse. Here are two examples.

England's *Cricketer* published on 3 September 1921, a poem by E. C. Holt entitled 'To Armstrong', in the vein of Sir Owen Seaman (who is the 'OS' cited):

Master—for we who would not care to rate your
Abilities as higher than they are,
Avow you merit such a nomenclature—
To you, the bright Antipodean star,
Whose light is seen from Timbucktoo to Berwick,
We offer praise, Byronic and Homeric.

In you, good representative of Melbourne,
The game of cricket seems personified;
Upon your massive shoulders you have well borne
The hopes of your unconquerable side,
And, more than once, have laughed aloud for glee, as
You rescued it from burning like Aeneas.

Because your just and noble reputation
Extends from London right across the world,
Because you form a theme of conversation
Wherever sporting papers are unfurled,
Behold a fitting token of your prowess—
The fame of being eulogised by OS!

And so, in rhyme not quite devoid of reason,
We hope (and may our hoping not be in vain!)
That you have much enjoyed the present season,
Despite of raging drought or hurricane.
Good luck to you, my friend; and, oh I wonder
How long the Ashes will remain 'down under'!

Melbourne's *Truth* published the following acrostic in Armstrong's honour on 11 August 1921.

We saw Australia's giant
At early morn depart
Resplendent and defiant
With men who knew their art
Impatience for the tussle
Contracted every muscle
Knit stouter every heart.

Again we saw our lion
Resplendent as of yore
More dazzling than Orion
Strike hard on Britain's shore
The 'ashes' in his keeping
Remain, while England's weeping
On debacles galore
No leader e'er competing
Gained greater fame before.

Bibliography

COLLECTIONS

R. H. Campbell Papers (State Library of Victoria)

Statistician Campbell kept detailed handwritten records of first-class cricket and Australian Rules Football for forty years, encompassing Warwick Armstrong's career, and including many items of interest that escaped the press.

J. C. Davis Collection (Mitchell Library)

Editor of the *Referee*, John Davis, left a substantial archive of images covering all sports, cricketers being especially well-represented. There are also many boxes of books, scrapbooks and reference materials—some very rare—although the catalogue is unreliable and several items are in poor condition.

A. H. Gregory Collection (Mitchell Library)

A huge if idiosyncratic collection of scrapbooks assembled by 'Short Slip' of the *Sydney Mail* up to the First World War. Difficult to use for want of dates, but containing some information otherwise unobtainable.

Letters to Clem Hill (Frith Collection)

A thick bundle of letters and wires to Clem Hill during the 'Big Six' dispute of 1912, originally inherited by Wyndham Hill-Smith. Peter McAlister's infamous telegram is among them.

Hurry Papers (State Library of Victoria)

A large, mostly uncatalogued collection of cases handled by a group of Kyneton law firms, including some for which Warwick Armstrong's father John, uncle Henry and George Major worked during the 1880s.

Frank Laver Collection (Olympic Museum/Gallery of Sport)

A compendium of photographs and scrapbooks, with some correspondence, from Laver's career and travels. In excellent condition.

Syd Smith Papers (Mitchell Library)

Long-time Board of Control secretary Syd Smith Jnr kept extensive records of his administrative career, especially after World War I, including correspondence, scrapbooks and reports pertaining to Australia's 1921 tour of England. There is also a rich collection of photographs of the 1921 and 1926 Australian teams on tour.

OTHER PRIMARY SOURCES

Australian Board of Control for International Cricket

The Australian Cricket Board provided photocopied extracts of its minutes pertaining to Armstrong. Record-keeping in its early days does not seem to have been thorough, although it improves after World War I.

Melbourne Cricket Club

The minute books and their drafts are intact, as are the letter books of secretaries Ben Wardill, Sidney Tindall and Hugh Trumble, with the unfortunate exception of the period covering the club's 1906 dispute with the New South Wales Cricket Association. A goodly proportion of club nomination forms for Armstrong's period as pavilion clerk also survive.

New South Wales Archives

Syd Gregory's bankruptcy was the object of my search here, but there were also extensive deceased estate and foreign company records.

South Melbourne Cricket Club

Although many of its records were destroyed by fire, lifelong loyalist Hans Wilhelm created a sort of encyclopedia of the club and its players in twenty-five typewritten foolscap folders. It contains valuable statistics and some delightful esoterica, such as Armstrong's habit of marking his guard with a bail.

Tasmanian Archives Office

Provided shipping schedules and convict records for the Armstrong family's early years in Australia.

UDV Archives

Provided information about Peter Dawson Ltd and its sale, and extracts from the *DCL Gazette*, in-house periodical of the Distillers Company.

Victorian Cricket Association

The minute books of the committee are intact and very thorough, although those of the executive committee appear to be missing. There are also minutes of the VCA's fund for distressed cricketers.

Victorian Education Department

From records of 'registered' schools that have closed, provided information concerning University College.

Victorian Public Records Office

Of particular interest here were the company records, both for those entities with which Armstrong was associated, and for those which others were involved in: much of the information on Armstrong's best man, for instance, came from statutory filings by his company. There are also excellent records of the public service and bankruptcy rolls: the financial travails of Armstrong's grandfather are extensively documented.

BOOKS
BIOGRAPHIES/AUTOBIOGRAPHIES: CRICKET

Bradman, Sir Donald, *A Farewell to Cricket*, Hodder & Stoughton, London, 1950.

Brodribb, Gerald, *The Croucher: A Biography of Gilbert Jessop*, London Magazine Editions, London, 1974.

Cardus, Neville, *Autobiography*, Collins, London, 1947.

Cardwell, Ronald, *A Cameo from the Past: The Life and Times of H. S. T. L. Hendry*, The Cricket Publishing Company, Sydney, 1984.

Coldham, J. D., *Lord Harris*, Allen & Unwin, London, 1983.

Darling, D. K. ed., *Test Tussles on and off the Field*, self-published, Hobart, 1970.

Douglas, Christopher, *Douglas Jardine: Spartan Cricketer*, Allen & Unwin, London, 1984.

Down, Michael, *Archie: A Biography of A. C. MacLaren*, Allen & Unwin, London, 1981.

Ferguson, William, *Mr Cricket*, Sportsman's Book Club, London, 1960.

Fiddian, Marc, *A Life-Long Innings: The Story of Jack Ryder*, Pakenham Gazette, Melbourne, 1995.

Fingleton, Jack, *The Immortal Victor Trumper*, Collins, Sydney, 1978.

Foster, Frank, *Cricket Memories*, London Publishing Company, London, 1930.

Fry, Charles, *Life Worth Living*, Eyre & Spottiswoode, London, 1939.

Giffen, George, *With Bat and Ball*, Ward, Lock & Co, Melbourne, 1898.

Grace, Radcliffe, *Warwick Armstrong*, self-published, 1975.

Hammond, Walter, *Cricket My Destiny*, Stanley Paul, London, 1946.

Harris, Lord, *A Few Short Runs*, John Murray, London, 1921.

Hawke, Lord, *Recollections & Reminiscences*, Norgate, London, 1924.

Hendren, Patsy, *Big Cricket*, Hodder & Stoughton, London, 1934.

Hill, Les, *Eighty Not Out: The Story of W. J. (Bill) Whitty of Tantanoola*, self-published, Mt Gambier, 1974.

Hobbs, Jack, *My Cricket Memories*, Heinemann, London, 1924.

Hobbs, Jack, *Playing for England*, Gollancz, London, 1931.

Howat, Gerald, *Plum Warner*, Unwin Hyman, London, 1987.

Iredale, Frank, *Thirty-Three Years of Cricket*, Beatty, Richardson, Sydney, 1920.

Jessop, Gilbert, *A Cricketer's Log*, Hodder & Stoughton, London, 1922.

Larwood, Harold, *The Larwood Story*, Sportsman's Book Club, London, 1965.

Laver, Frank, *An Australian Cricketer on Tour*, Bell, London, 1905.

Lemmon, David, *Johnny Won't Hit Today: A Cricketing Biography of J. W. H. T. Douglas*, Allen & Unwin, London, 1983.

Lilley, Arthur, *Twenty-Four Years of Cricket*, Mills & Boon, London, 1912.

Macartney, Charles, *My Cricketing Days*, William Heinemann, London, 1930.

Mailey, Arthur, *10 for 66 and All That*, Phoenix House, London, 1958.

Mallett, Ashley, *Trumper: An Illustrated Biography*, Macmillan, Sydney, 1985.

J. Elliott Monfries, *Not Test Cricket*, Gillingham & Co Ltd, Adelaide, 1950.

Moyes, Johnnie, *Bradman*, Angus & Robertson, Sydney, 1948.

Murphy, Patrick, *'Tiger' Smith of Warwickshire and England*, Readers Union/Lutterworth Press, London, 1981.

Oldfield, Bert, *Behind the Wicket: My Cricket Reminiscences*, Hutchinson, London, 1938.

Parkin, Cecil, *Cricket Triumphs and Troubles*, C. Nicholls & Co Ltd, London, 1936.

Parkin, Cecil, *Parkin on Cricket*, Hodder & Stoughton, London, 1923.

Peebles, Ian, *Spinner's Yarn*, Collins, London, 1977.

Peebles, Ian, *Woolley—The Pride of Kent*, Hutchinson, London, 1969.

Reese, Daniel, *Was It All Cricket?*, Allen & Unwin, London, 1948.

Rosenwater, Irving, *Sir Donald Bradman*, Batson & Co, London, 1978.

Sewell, E. H. D., *The Log of a Sportsman*, T. Fisher Unwin, London, 1923.

Sharpham, Peter, *Trumper: The Definitive Biography*, Hodder & Stoughton, Sydney, 1986.

Sims, Arthur, *84 Not Out: The Story of Arthur Sims*, Hennel Locke, London, 1962.

Streeton, Richard, *P. G. H. Fender*, Faber & Faber, London, 1981.

Strudwick, Herbert, *Twenty-Five Years behind the Stumps*, Hutchinson, London, 1926.

Swanton, E. W., *Follow On*, Collins, London, 1977.

Tennyson, Lionel, *From Verse to Worse*, Cassell, London, 1933.

Tennyson, Lionel, *Sticky Wickets*, Christopher Johnson, London, 1950.

Thomson, A. A., *Pavilioned in Splendour*, Museum Press, London, 1956.

Travers, Ben, *94 Declared*, Elm Tree Books, London, 1981.

Trumble, Robert, *The Golden Age of Cricket*, self-published, Melbourne, 1968.

Warner, Pelham, *Long Innings*, Harrap, London, 1951.

Wilton, Iain, *C. B. Fry: An English Hero*, Richard Cohen Books, London, 1999.

Woolley, Frank, *King of Games*, Stanley Paul, London, 1936.

BIOGRAPHIES/AUTOBIOGRAPHIES: OTHER

Archer, Fred, *The Treasure House*, F. Archer, Armadale, 1974.

Archer, Fred, *Tell Me More: More of the Story of the Menzies Hotel*, F. Archer, Armadale, 1984.

Asquith, Cynthia, *Portrait of Barrie*, James Barrie, London, 1954.

Bolton, Geoffrey, *Edmund Barton*, Allen & Unwin, St Leonards, 2000.

Brennan, Niall, *John Wren: Gambler*, Hill of Content, Melbourne, 1971.

Buggy, Hugh, *The Real John Wren*, Angus & Robertson, North Ryde, 1986.

Christiansen, Arthur, *Headlines All My Life*, William Heinemann, London, 1961.

Deford, Frank, *Big Bill Tilden*, Victor Gollancz, London, 1977.

Evans, A. J., *The Escaping Club*, Bodley Head, London, 1921.

Glass, Margaret, *Thomas Bent: Bent by Name, Bent by Nature*, Melbourne University Press, Melbourne, 1993.

Godwin, John, *Battling Parer*, Rigby, Adelaide, 1968.

Hewitt, J. E., *The Black One*, Langate Publishing, South Yarra, 1984.

Jones, Ian, *Ned Kelly: A Short Life*, Lothian Books, Port Melbourne, 1996.

McMinn, W. G., *George Reid*, Melbourne University Press, Melbourne, 1989.

Melba, Dame Nellie, *Melodies and Memories*, Butterworth, London, 1925.

Parer, Raymond, *Flight and Adventures of Parer and McIntosh*, Stevens, Melbourne, 1921.

Roderick, Colin, *Henry Lawson: A Life*, Angus & Robertson, North Ryde, 1991.

Whyte, William, *William Morris Hughes: His Life and Times*, Angus & Robertson, Sydney, 1957.

HISTORY/LITERATURE: CRICKET

Bentley, Tony, *Bickley Park Cricket Club: 125 Years*, n.p., London, 1993.

Blunden, Edmund, *Cricket Country*, Collins, London, 1944.

Brodribb, Gerald, *Hit For Six*, Sportsman's Book Club, London, 1961.

Catton, J. A. H., *Wickets and Goals*, Chapman & Hall, London, 1926.

Coleman, Robert, *Seasons in the Sun: The Story of the Victorian Cricket Association*, Hargreen Publishing, Melbourne, 1993.

Cross Standing, Percy, *Cricket of Today and Yesterday*, Blackwood, Le Bas & Co, London, 1902.

Derriman, Phil, *True to the Blue*, Richard Smart Publishing, Sydney, 1985.

Dunstan, Keith, *The Paddock That Grew: The Story of the Melbourne Cricket Club*, Hutchinson, Melbourne, 1988.

Diehm, Ian, *From Green Hills to the Gabba*, Playright Publishing, Caringbah, 2000.

Fingleton, Jack, *Masters of Cricket*, William Heinemann, London, 1958.

Frith, David, *The Slow Men*, Horwitz Grahame, Sydney, 1984.

Frith, David, *The Golden Age of Cricket,* Lutterworth Press, London, 1978.

Gilligan, Arthur, *Sussex Cricket,* Chapman & Hall, London, 1933.

Gordon, Home, *Background of Cricket,* Arthur Barker, London, 1939.

Gutsche, Thelma, *Old Gold: The History of the Wanderer's Club*, Timmins, Cape Town, 1966.

Harte, Chris, *A History of Australian Cricket*, Andre Deutsch, London, 1993.

Harte, Chris, *The History of the South Australian Cricket Association*, Sports Marketing, Adelaide, 1990.

Howat, Gerald, *Cricket's Second Golden Age*, Hodder & Stoughton, London, 1989.

Luckin, Maurice, *The History of South African Cricket*, Hortor, Johannesburg, 1915.

Luckin, Maurice, *South African Cricket 1919–1927*, self-published, Johannesburg, 1928.

Morrah, Patrick, *The Golden Age of Cricket*, Eyre & Spottiswoode, London, 1967.

Moyes, Johnnie, *Australian Cricket: A History*, Angus & Robertson, Sydney, 1959.

Neely, Don and King, Richard, *Men in White*, Moa Publications, Auckland, 1986.

Noble, Monty, *The Game's the Thing*, Cassell, London, 1926.

Perry, Roland, *Captain Australia*, Random House, Sydney, 2000.

Plumptre, George, *The Golden Age of Cricket*, Queen Anne Press, London, 1990.

Pollard, Jack, *Australian Cricket: The Game and the Players*, Angus & Robertson, Sydney, 1988.

Reese, Thomas, *New Zealand Cricket 1841–1914*, Simpson & Williams, Christchurch, 1927.

Reese, Thomas, *New Zealand Cricket 1914–1933*, Whitcombe & Tombs, Auckland, 1936.

R. C. Robertson-Glasgow, *Crusoe on Cricket*, Pavilion Books, London, 1985.

Robinson, Ray, *On Top Down Under*, Collins, Sydney, 1975.

Ryder, Rowland, *Cricket Calling*, Faber & Faber, London, 1995.

Sandiford, Keith, *Cricket and the Victorians*, Scholar, Aldershot, 1994.

Sandiford, Keith and Stoddart, Brian eds, *The Imperial Game*, Manchester University Press, Manchester 1998.

Sewell, E. H. D, *Cricket under Fire*, Stanley Paul, London, 1941.

Sewell, E. H. D., *Well, Hit, Sir!*, Stanley Paul, London, 1947.

Sissons, Ric, *The Players: A Social History of the Professional Cricketer*, Pluto Press, Sydney, 1988.

Trevor, Philip, *The Problems of Cricket*, Sampson Low, London, 1907.

Trevor, Philip, *The Lighter Side of Cricket*, Methuen, London, 1901.

Warner, Pelham, *Lord's 1787–1945*, Pavilion, London, 1987.

Warner, Pelham ed., *Imperial Cricket*, London & Counties Press Association, London, 1912.

Williams, Jack, *Cricket and England: A Cultural and Social History of the Inter-War Years*, Frank Cass, London, 1999.

Wilson, Frederic, *Sporting Pie*, Chapman & Hall, London, 1922.

Wynne-Thomas, Peter, *A History of Cricket*, The Stationery Office, Norwich, 1997.

HISTORY: OTHER

Armstrong, H. J., *Random Reminiscences*, Kyneton Historical Society, Kyneton, 1994.

Backhouse, Sally, *Singapore,* Wren, Melbourne, 1972.

Batchelder, Alfred, *Playing the Greater Game: The Melbourne Cricket Club and Its Ground in World War I*, self-published, Melbourne, 1998.

Beamish, Jane, *A History of Singapore Architecture*, G. Brash, Singapore, 1985.

Campion, Edmund, *Australian Catholics*, Penguin, Ringwood, 1987.

Campion, Edmund, *Rockchoppers: Growing up Catholic in Australia*, Penguin, Ringwood, 1982.

Cashman, Richard, *Paradise of Sport: The Rise of Organised Sport in Australia*, Oxford University Press, Melbourne, 1995.

Cashman, Richard and McKernan, Michael, *Sport in History*, University of Queensland Press, Brisbane, 1979.

Cooper, John Butler, *The History of St Kilda*, Printers Proprietary, Melbourne, 1931.

Crotty, Martin, *Making the Australian Male: Middle-Class Masculinity 1870–1920*, Melbourne University Press, Melbourne, 2001.

Daley, Charles, *The History of South Melbourne*, Robertson & Mullens, Melbourne, 1940.

Davies, Donald, *Old Singapore*, D. Moore, Singapore, 1954.

Dixon, Robert, *The Catholics in Australia*, Australian Government Publishing Service, Canberra, 1996.

Dobbs, Brian, *Edwardians at Play: Sport 1890–1914*, Pelham, London, 1973.

Dorne, Nelly, *Down Under: A Year in Netherlands India, the Commonwealth, the Dominion*, n. p., Colombo, 1912.

Fabricius, Johan, *Java Revisited*, W. Heinemann, London, 1947.

History of Kyneton, Kyneton Guardian, Kyneton, 1935.

Inglis, Ken, *Sacred Places: War Memorials in the Australian Landscape*, Miegunyah Press, Melbourne, 1998.

Johnson, B. C. W., *A Brief History of Wrekin College,* n. p., 1964.

Jubilee History of the City of South Melbourne, Periodicals Publishing, Melbourne, 1905.

Kinglake, Edward, *The Australian at Home*, Leadenhall Press, London, 1892.

Laurence, L., *History of the South Melbourne Football Club*, n. p., Melbourne, 1963.

Lawson, Henry, *Autobiographical and Other Writings 1887–1922*, Angus & Robertson, Sydney, 1972.

Lechte, William, *Caulfield 1869–1935: Memories of the Past*, City of Caulfield, Melbourne 1992.

Lewis, Miles, *Melbourne: The City's History and Development*, City of Melbourne, Melbourne, 1995.

Macguire, Father R. J., *The Golden Jubilee Souvenir of St Joseph's Church, Age*, Melbourne, 1958.

Macintyre, Stuart, *The Oxford History of Australia, Volume 4, 1900–1941*, Oxford University Press, Melbourne, 1988.

McKernan, Michael, *The Australian People and the Great War*, Thomas Nelson, Melbourne, 1980.

McNally, Carole, *The Parish of St Aloysius, Caulfield: 1924–1999*, Carole McNally, North Caulfield, 1999.

Mandle, William, *Going It Alone: Australia's National Identity in the Twentieth Century*, Penguin, Ringwood, 1978.

Morris, James, *Farewell the Trumpets: An Imperial Retreat*, Faber & Faber, London, 1978.

Murray, Peter, *From Sand, Swamp and Heath: A History of Caulfield*, J. D. Burrows, Melbourne, 1980.

Murtagh, James, *Australia: The Catholic Chapter*, Polding Press, Melbourne, 1969.

Priestley, Susan, *South Melbourne: A History*, Melbourne University Press, Melbourne, 1995.

Solomon, Geulah, *Caulfield's Heritage*, City of Caulfield, Melbourne, 1989.

Souter, Gavin, *Acts of Parliament*, Melbourne University Press, Carlton, 1988.

Souter, Gavin, *Lion & Kangaroo: The Initiation of Australia*, Text Publishing, Melbourne, 2000.

Turner, Naomi, *Catholics in Australia: A Social History*, CollinsDove, North Blackburn, 1992.

Twopeny, Richard, *Town Life in Australia*, Elliot Stock, London, 1883.

Vamplew, Wray, *Pay up and Play the Game: Professional Sport in Britain 1875–1914*, Cambridge University Press, London, 1988.

Vamplew, Wray and Adair, Daryl, *Sport in Australian History*, Oxford University Press, Melbourne, 1997.

Willis, John, *Ceylon: A Handbook for the Resident and the Traveller*, Colombo Apothecaries Co., Peradeniya, 1907.

TOUR BOOKS

Brown, Lionel, *Victor Trumper and the 1902 Australians*, Secker & Warburg, London, 1981.

Cardus, Neville, *Good Days*, Jonathan Cape, London, 1934.

Cardwell, Ronald, *The AIF Cricket Team*, self-published, Balgowlah Heights, 1980.

Derriman, Phil, *Bodyline*, Collins, Sydney, 1984.

Fender, Percy, *Defending the Ashes*, Chapman & Hall, London, 1921.

Fender, Percy, *The Turn of the Wheel, MCC Team, Australia 1928–29*, Faber & Faber, London, 1929.

Fender, Percy, *Kissing the Rod: The Story of the Tests of 1934*, Chapman & Hall, London, 1934.

Fingleton, Jack, *Cricket Crisis*, Cassell, London, 1946.

Frith, David, *Stoddy's Mission*, Allen & Unwin, St Leonards, 1994.

Gibson, Alan, *Jackson's Year: The Test Matches of 1905*, Cassell, London, 1905.

Harris, Bruce, *Jardine Justified: The Truth about the Ashes*, Chapman & Hall, London, 1933.

Hobbs, Jack, *Recovering the 'Ashes'*, The Cricket Press, London, 1912.

Hobbs, Jack, *The Fight for the Ashes*, Harrap, London, 1933.

Le Quesne, Laurence, *The Bodyline Controversy*, Secker & Warburg, London, 1983.

Lynd, Robert, *The Sporting Life and Other Trifles*, Sportsmans Book Club, London, 1956.

McCleary, George, *Cricket with the Kangaroo*, Hollis & Carter, London, 1950.

Mailey, Arthur, *The Australian Fifteen for England*, McCubbin, London, 1921.

Mailey, Arthur, *And Then Came Larwood*, Lane, London, 1933.

Mahony, Peter, *Mary Ann's Australians*, Cricket Lore, London, 1993.

Mason, Ronald, *Warwick Armstrong's Australians*, Epworth Press, London, 1971.

Noble, Monty, *Those Ashes: The Australian Tour of 1926*, Cassell, London, 1927.

Noble, Monty, *The Fight for the Ashes 1928–29*, Harrap, London, 1929.

Pollock, William, *So This Is Australia*, Arthur Barker, London, 1937.

Ranjitsinhji, K. S., *With Stoddart's Team in Australia*, James Bowden, London, 1898.

Sharpham, Peter, *The 1899 Australians in England*, J. W. McKenzie, Ewell, 1997.

Smith, Rick, *Cricket Brawl: The 1912 Dispute*, Apple Books, Hobart, 1995.

Smith, Sydney, *With the Fifteenth Australians*, E. T. Kibblewhite, Sydney, 1921.

Trevor, Philip, *With the MCC in Australia 1907–8*, A. Rivers, London, 1908.

Trevor, Philip, *Cricket and Cricketers*, Chapman & Hall, London, 1921.

Warner, Pelham, *Cricket in Many Climes*, Heinemann, London, 1900.

Warner, Pelham, *Cricket across the Seas*, Longmans, London, 1903.

Warner, Pelham, *How We Recovered the Ashes*, Chapman & Hall, London, 1904.

Warner, Pelham, *England v Australia: The Record of a Memorable Tour*, Mills & Boon, London, 1912.

Wilmot, R. W. E., *Defending The Ashes*, Robertson & Mullens, Melbourne, 1933.

TEXTBOOKS

Armstrong, Warwick, *The Art of Cricket*, Methuen, London, 1922.

Barbour, Eric, *The Making of a Cricketer*, Sydney & Melbourne Publishing Company, Sydney, 1926.

Beldam, George and Fry, Charles, *Great Batsmen*, Macmillan, London, 1905.

Beldam, George and Fry, Charles, *Great Bowlers and Fielders*, Macmillan, London, 1906.

Knight, Albert, *The Complete Cricketer*, Methuen, London, 1906.

MacLaren, Archie, *Cricket Old and New: A Straight Talk to Young Cricketers*, Longmans, Green, London, 1924.

Wilkins, Brian, *Cricket: The Bowler's Art*, Kangaroo Press, Sydney, 1997.

PAMPHLETS CONCERNING 'BIG SIX' DISPUTE

Statement of the Citizens' Cricket Committee—March 1912.

Statement by the Victorian Cricket Association—27 March 1912.

The Cricket Dispute: A Reply to the VCA by Frank Laver—May 1912.

The Cricket Dispute: A Reply to Mr Frank Laver by Peter McAlister—29 June 1912.

Reply by the Melbourne Cricket Club to the Statement of the Victorian Cricket Association—August 1912.

The 1912 Australian XI in England: A Few Facts for Fair-Minded Sportsmen by E. E. Bean and H. R. Rush—7 September 1912.

REFERENCE: CRICKET

Boyle & Scott's Cricket Annual

Lillywhite's Cricketers' Almanack

Wisden Cricketers' Almanack

Bailey, Philip, Thorn, Philip and Wynne-Thomas, Peter, *Who's Who of Cricketers*, Hamlyn, London, 1993.

Webster, Ray, *First-Class Cricket in Australia 1850–51/1941–42*, self-published, Glen Waverley, 1991.

Williams, Ken, *W. W. Armstrong: His Record Innings-by-Innings*, Famous Cricketers series no. 10, Association of Cricket Statisticians, Nottingham, 1991.

REFERENCE: OTHER

Australian Dictionary of Biography

Encyclopedia Britannica

Who's Who in Australia

500 Victorians: Centenary Edition, M. G. Henderson, Melbourne, 1934.

Smith, James ed., *The Cyclopedia of Victoria,* The Cyclopedia Company, Melbourne, 1903–1905.

Rodgers, Stephen, *100 Years of AFL Players: Volume 1 1897–1936*, self-published, Mitcham, 1996.

MISCELLANEOUS

Beller, Anne Scott, *Fat and Thin: A Natural History of Obesity*, Farrar, Straus & Giroux, New York, 1977.

Boyce, Sir Rupert, *Mosquito or Man?*, John Murray, London, 1910.

Desowitz, Robert, *The Malaria Capers: More Tales of Parasites and People, Research and Reality*, W. W. Morton, New York, 1991.

Emmons, Frederick, *The Atlantic Liners 1925–1970*, David & Charles, Newton Abbot, 1972.

Emmons, Frederick, *American Passenger Ships 1873–1983*, University of Delaware Press, Newark, 1985.

Furphy, Joseph, *Such Is Life*, Angus & Robertson, Sydney, 1956.

Moss, Michael and Hume, John, *The Making of Scotch Whisky: A History of the Scotch Whisky Distilling Industry*, James & James, Edinburgh, 1981.

Pratt, Ambrose, *The Big Five*, Ward Lock, London, 1910.

Schwartz, Hillel, *Never Satisfied: A Cultural History of Diets, Fantasies and Fat*, Free Press, New York, 1986.

Spencer, Margaret, *Malaria: The Australian Experience 1843–1991*, Australian College of Tropical Medicine, Townsville, 1994.

Spielman, Andrew and D'Antonio, Michael, *Mosquito*, Hyperion, New York, 2001.

Spiller, Brian, *The Chameleon's Eye: James Buchanan 1884–1984*, James Buchanan & Co. Ltd, London and Glasgow, 1984.

Stearns, Peter, *Fat History*, New York University Press, 1997.

Weir, Ronald, *The History of the Distillers Company 1877–1939*, Oxford University Press, London, 1994.

Wilson, Ross, *Scotch: The Formative Years*, Constable & Co, London, 1970.

NEWSPAPERS

Asia

Malay Mail, Perak Pioneer and Malay Advertiser, Straits Budget, Straits Times, Times of Ceylon, Times of Malaya.

Australia

Age, Argus, Australian Cricketer, Australian Pastoralists' Review, Australian Statesman and Mining Standard, Australasian, Australasian Star, Bell's Life, Brisbane Courier, Bulletin, Caulfield and Elsternwick Leader, Corowa Free Press, Daily Telegraph (Sydney), *Daily Telegraph* (Launceston), *Herald, Kyneton Guardian, Kyneton Observer, Leader, Life, Malvern and Armadale Express, Melbourne Punch, Mercury, Referee, South Australian Register, Sporting and Dramatic News, Sun* (Sydney), *Sydney Mail, Sydney Morning Herald, Town and Country Journal, Truth* (Melbourne).

New Zealand

Auckland Star, Dominion, New Zealand Herald, Wellington Evening Post.

South Africa

Cape Argus, Cape Times, Natal Mercury, Rand Daily Mail.

United Kingdom

Bath Herald, Captain, C. B. Fry's Magazine, Cricket: A Weekly Record of the Game, Cricketer, Daily Express, Daily Graphic, Daily Mail, Daily Sketch, Daily Telegraph, Evening News, Evening Standard, Illustrated Sporting and Dramatic News, Isis, Leicester Mercury, Longman's Magazine, Manchester Evening News, Manchester Guardian, Morning Post, Observer, News Chronicle, Pall Mall Gazette, Penny Magazine, Punch, Siever's Monthly, Sporting Life, Sportsman, Star, Strand Magazine, Sunday Express, The Times, Town Topics, Truth (London), *Weekly Dispatch (Sunday Dispatch* after 1928), *Westminster Gazette, Winning Post, World, World of Cricket.*

Index